P9-BYF-544

Now Read This

Now Read This

A Guide to Mainstream Fiction, 1978–1998

Nancy Pearl

With assistance from
Martha Knappe and Chris Higashi

Foreword by Joyce G. Saricks
Literature and Audio Services Coordinator,
Downers Grove Public Library, and author, Readers'
Advisory Service in the Public Library

1999
Libraries Unlimited, Inc.
Englewood, Colorado

Libraries Unlimited, Inc.
P.O. Box 6633
Englewood, CO 80155-6633
1-800-237-6124
www.lu.com

Library of Congress Cataloging-in-Publication Data

Pearl, Nancy.
    Now read this : a guide to mainstream fiction, 1978-1998 / Nancy
Pearl, with the assistance of Martha Knappe and Chris Higashi ; foreword
by Joyce G. Saricks.
    xvii, 432 p., 19x26 cm.
    Annotated list of 1000 books categorized by setting, story,
characterization, or language.
    Includes bibliographical references and index.
    ISBN 1-56308-659-X
    1. Fiction--20th century Bibliography. 2. Fiction--20th century--
Stories, plots, etc.--Indexes. 3. Best books. I. Knappe, Martha.
II. Higashi, Chris. III. Title.
Z5916.P43 1999
[PN3503]
016.80883'04--dc21   99-015280
                                                                    CIP

Contents

Foreword

It is an honor to be asked to write a foreword for such an excellent readers' advisory resource. What is more, it is immensely satisfying to see one's ideas, the theory, put into practice—especially in such an elegant compilation! In *Now Read This* Nancy Pearl and her cadre of readers have made significant strides in exploring how readers respond to books and how readers' advisors assist readers. They have also created an excellent resource for practicing librarians, one that helps us—and patrons—see the possibilities, the range of books that might appeal to a reader.

This book offers a great deal to librarians and serious readers: an annotated list of a thousand acclaimed and award-winning novels, organized so we can really help those patrons who come in seeking, for example, "books with strong characters" or "poetic" books; suggestions of titles that lend themselves to book discussions; and, best of all, not just a list of similar authors, but also specific titles and the reason why a reader of one book might enjoy these others as well. Unfortunately, standard sources in the past have not been particularly helpful in guiding us to suggestions of other titles a reader might enjoy. The problem is, as Nancy Pearl points out in her introduction, that every reader "reads" a different version of every book. This volume takes that complication into account in its organization and in the descriptive nature of the "Now try" lists. Nancy Pearl's skill in creating such a resource will make our work at public service desks much easier.

Whether the type of fiction covered is to your taste or not, you will find much of value here. This is a book we will share with readers in our libraries, and one they will seek out on their own as they explore the wealth of reading suggestions.

Joyce G. Saricks

Acknowledgments

This book could not have been completed without the diligent assistance of intern extraordinaire, Stephanie Galvani. Her literary sleuthing and enthusiasm helped the process immeasurably. Many thanks also go to Dr. Peter Hiatt of the University of Washington Graduate School of Library and Information Science, whose encouragement and flexibility provided a wonderful learning opportunity for library school students interested in reading and evaluating literature. More than 40 students received graduate school credit for reading, discussing, and annotating books from the list of 1,000 titles. Contributors include Susan Anderson-Newman, Barbara Bayley, Christa Bindel, Amanda Cain, Barbara Diltz-Chandler, Ellen Fitzgerald, Kathleen Guenther, Christine Hagar, Kara Hannigan, C. Gaye Hinchcliff, J. Holder, Hioni Karamanos, Sarah Kielhack, Kathryn Kirkpatrick, Jan Lawrence, Darla Linville, Anna-Liisa Little, Edward Matuskey, Deirdre Mcdonough, Paula McMillen, Rayma Norton, Julia Parker, Bonnie Parks, Julia Paulsen, Christine Perkins, Paul Ruppel, Beata Rycharski, Renee Snyder, Patricia Stroschein, Ashland Thornton, Sarah Webb, Amy West, Heather Wilder, Mynique Williams, Megan Wood, Christiane Woten, and David Wright. Helene Smart helped with final proofreading.

Paul Feavel of the Seattle Public Library Development Office designed the databases used in *Now Read This* and answered untold numbers of questions with enormous patience and humor.

Finally, many thanks to Duncan Smith, who first suggested doing this book. This has been a lengthy, collaborative process involving many people. I hope that those whose names have been inadvertently omitted will forgive me.

Introduction

Recommending books is a tricky business. The nature of reading and human nature are such that no two people read exactly the same book. Each person brings to the reading of a novel a unique life history that determines how he or she will experience that book. Ask five members of a group about their reactions to the current book being discussed, and you might well get five different answers. One reader might be intrigued by the love story, another by the well-developed relationship between the main characters. A third might enjoy reading about the Southern setting. A fourth might appreciate the beautiful writing. And a fifth might say that the book was so outlandish he couldn't even read it.

So how do we go about deciding what books to recommend to our users? *Now Read This: A Guide to Mainstream Fiction, 1978–1998,* provides a method of understanding by what criteria a reader judges a novel and therefore makes it easier to recommend titles that fit those criteria.

It all begins with appeal characteristics. Joyce G. Saricks and Nancy Brown, in their book *Readers' Advisory Service in the Public Library* (2d ed., American Library Association, 1997) articulate a theory of why readers enjoy books that seem, at first glance, to be quite different from one another. Their theory involves the concept of "appeal characteristics," by which they mean "the elements in books that make patrons enjoy them." Saricks and Brown suggest that readers don't enjoy books simply because of specific plot details. A reader who loved Pat Conroy's *The Prince of Tides,* for example, and asks for another novel "just like it," is more likely to be looking for a novel that tells a good story, or has interesting, well-developed characters, rather than one in which a psychiatrist falls in love with her patient.

Each book in *Now Read This* was assigned a primary appeal characteristic. Some books could easily have been assigned two primary appeal characteristics. In those cases, we assigned a secondary characteristic as well. A good example of such a novel is Pat Conroy's *The Prince of Tides.* Although the primary appeal is language, character is a close second. (In fact, some readers argued that Conroy's novel appeals on all four of the appeal characteristics.)

In choosing the appeal characteristics for a particular book, we (a group of professional librarians, avid readers, and library school students) sought to identify the qualities of each book that both best describe its strengths and set it apart from other books. We arrived at the appeal characteristics for each book by asking the following question: When we imagine describing the book to an interested friend, what would we emphasize? Is it the setting, the rich description and establishment of a place or time? The story the book tells? The development of compelling characters? The writer's use of language? In some cases, a book's appeal characteristics were readily apparent, while in others, an often-spirited discussion was required before a consensus could be reached. Despite our care in assigning appeal characteristics, it is certainly true that these are, to a certain extent, subjective assessments. One person's character-driven novel might be viewed by another reader as emphasizing setting or plot. However, the appeal characteristics assigned to each title represent the best thinking of our contributors.

As we attempted to pin down the appeal characteristics of each book in *Now Read This,* we used the operative terms as follows:

1. In a book with **Setting** as an appeal characteristic, the setting is essential to understanding character, conflict, or theme. The novel is very much specific to its location, in place and/or time. In some novels the setting functions almost as another character. Two novels in which setting is a major appeal characteristics are E. Annie Proulx's *The Shipping News* and Bryce Courtenay's *The Power of One.*

   A reader who loved the physical descriptions of the small Newfoundland town where Proulx's novel takes place will also be moved by the meticulous descriptions Ivan Doig uses to bring his Montana setting alive in *Bucking the Sun* or the way that Graham Salisbury makes us part of the small Hawaiian village where *The Blue Skin of the Sea* is set.

   In addition, **Setting** can refer to the time period in which the book is set. Although Peter Hedges's *An Ocean in Iowa* could take place in almost any city, it is strongly tied to the late 1960s. Hedges brings the time period alive through use of specific references to television shows, toys, and food. The time period is also necessary to the novel's plot. Scotty Ocean's mother more than likely would not have deserted her family in the 1950s, and she would have done it with far greater ease in the 1980s. The choices women could make in the 1950s were much more circumscribed than those that were open to them during the subsequent decades. Hedges made this clear by setting the novel in the time period he did.

   Other novels in which **Setting** has a major impact on plot include Hanan al-Shaykh's *Women of Sand and Myrrh,* which describes the experiences of four women in a contemporary Middle Eastern country, and J. G. Ballard's *Empire of the Sun*, in which a young man comes of age during World War II.

2. In a book with **Story** as an appeal characteristic, the story dominates the novel; the reader is eager to turn the pages of the book to find out what happens; in describing the book readers talk mostly about the events of the novel. Two novels in which *Story* is a major appeal characteristic are Rita Kashner's *Bed Rest* and Bill Morrissey's *Edson.* The stories can be as dissimilar as the fantastic events involving the heroine of Rachel Ingalls's *Mrs. Caliban*, who falls in love with a sea monster, to Cynthia Kadohata's *The Floating World*, the realistic tale of 12-year-old Japanese American Olivia, who, along with her family, crosses the United States by car and encounters both racism and friendship. Novels with plot as the main appeal characteristic can be light reading (Jan Karon's *These High, Green Hills*) or heavy with foreboding (Molly Keane's *Queen Lear*).

3. In a book with **Characters** as an appeal characteristic, the characters are three-dimensional and seem to step off the page; in describing this novel we talk first about the people in them. Two novels in which characterization is the major appeal characteristic are Anne Tyler's *Dinner at the Homesick Restaurant* and Dan McCall's *Bluebird Canyon.* Characters can be adults (Abby Frucht's *Are You Mine*) or children (Esther Freud's *Hideous Kinky*). They can enjoy happy lives (Kaye Gibbons's *Charms for the Easy Life*) or difficult ones (Jim Grimsley's *My Drowning*). What sets these novels apart from those with *Story* as a primary characteristic is that we are interested in the people more than what happens to them.

4. Of course, language underlies all writing. Without language we would not have novels with three-dimensional characters, or a beautifully evoked setting, or a good story. In a book with **Language** as a major appeal characteristic, the quality of the writing is what makes the novel stand out; the author's use of language is evocative, unusual, thought provoking, or poetic. The writing style can be as distinctive as that used by Dorothy Allison in *Bastard Out of Carolina* (raw and gritty, with very little subtlety) or as subtle as that used by Michael Ondaatje in *The English Patient* (poetic and complex), yet it is impossible to describe either novel without referring to the author's use of language. Good writing cuts across story, setting, and characters. Novels with **Language** as an appeal characteristic make us look at the world in a different way. We can be inside the mind of an elderly man (Lars Gustafsson's *A Tiler's Afternoon*) or an adulterous woman (Renata Adler's *Pitch Dark*). We can experience the joys of falling in love (Alain de Botton's *On Love*) and the sights and sounds of the Nazis coming into a small Polish town (Anne Michaels's *Fugitive Pieces*). We can relive childhood (Seamus Deane's *Reading in the Dark*) and come to a better understanding of dealing with illness and approaching death (Harriet Doerr's *Stones for Ibarra*).

Sometimes, of course, it is the subject that draws a reader to a particular book. A planned trip to Turkey, for example, might lead someone to ask for suggestions for a good novel to read about that country, and it is helpful to be able to recommend Mary Lee Settle's *Celebration* or Rose Macaulay's *The Towers of Trebizond* as a place to start.

For the benefit of those readers, we have also assigned subject headings to each of the 1,000 novels included in *Now Read This*. Headings were chosen to reflect only the most obvious subjects of each novel, based on a thorough reading of the book. Thus, the subjects assigned to Paul Theroux's *Mosquito Coast* include "Eccentrics and Eccentricities," "Family Relationships," "Honduras," "Fathers and Sons," and "Central America" because we believe that those are the subjects readers readily associate with this novel.

The Selection Process

The vast majority of the titles chosen for *Now Read This* were published between 1980 and 1997. We included no books published before 1978 or after 1998. Our intention was to concentrate on mainstream fiction published in the last two decades of the twentieth century. By mainstream fiction we mean novels set in the twentieth century that realistically explore aspects of human experience: love, fear, despair, hatred, aging, and death, as well as the moral and ethical decisions and choices people make throughout a lifetime. Although elements of genre fiction are sometimes present in these novels, those elements are not the focus of the books. For example, the novels of Gabriel Garcia Marquez, Isabel Allende, Salman Rushdie, and Lawrence Thornton all make use of magic realism; events occur and people behave in ways that are not consistent with what we know about the physical world. Because these authors firmly ground their fiction in the real world, we would not include them in a fantasy collection. They make use of magic realism to further illuminate character, setting, or plot. The fantasy is a technique to help bring the novel to life, not the point of the novel.

Similarly, Frederick Busch's *Girls,* Frederick Reiken's *The Odd Sea,* and Jacquelyn Mitchard's *The Deep End of the Ocean* all involve the disappearance of a young person. Yet the focus of the novels is not on what happened or who caused the disappearance. Instead, the disappearance is used as a mechanism to explore how this cataclysmic event affected the other characters in the novel. Compare this to Joseph Harrington's Lieutenant Kerrigan mystery novel, *The Last Doorbell,* which has a similar plot. Harrington's focus is totally on unraveling the mystery of the child's disappearance. The mystery, and its solution, is the point of the novel.

Given these parameters, we began by including novels selected by the American Library Association's Notable Books Council from 1979 through 1997. We then added other award winners, including the Pulitzers, the National Book Awards, the National Book Critics Circle Awards, and the Booker Prize winners. Because our experience has shown us that our users frequently ask for a Booker Prize-winning novel, or the latest National Book Award winner, we have included these awards as part of the subject listings. A sampling from the lesser-known literary awards, including the IMPAC /Dublin Awards, the Guardian Prize, the Whitbread Awards, the Betty Trask Awards, and others, is included in the "Now try" section. In addition, all of the awards referenced are described in an appendix.

Finally, we chose additional novels published between 1978 and 1998 simply because we liked them so much we wanted to bring them to the attention of readers. One of our goals was to include as many midlist novels as possible, books that may not have received a great deal of publicity or critical attention when they were first published, but which we felt deserved a larger readership than they had so far received.

Genre novels—mysteries, science fiction, fantasy, romances, and westerns—were excluded from the database. There are many good readers' advisory tools that help librarians recommend titles within these genres, such as Diana Tixier Herald's *Genreflecting: A Guide to Reading Interests in Genre Fiction* (4th ed., Libraries Unlimited, 1995). Also excluded were collections of short stories and novels that take place before 1900. The exclusion of these types of books did not preclude referring to short story collections, or genre and historical novels, in the "Now try" section.

The Annotation Process

In addition to the author, a group of avid readers, professional librarians, and graduate students in the University of Washington Graduate School of Library and Information Science volunteered to read the books selected for inclusion. For over a year, groups of readers came together regularly to discuss the books they had read and annotated. It was at these meetings that the majority of the subject headings, appeal characteristics, and entries in the "Now try" section were decided upon.

How to Use This Book

The book is divided into four parts, corresponding to the four appeal characteristics, with each book listed under its primary appeal characteristic. Books as diverse in subject as Howard Norman's *The Bird Artist* and Sandra Benitez's *A Place Where the Sea Remembers* are linked by the fact that **Setting** is one of the major appeal characteristic for both books. Similarly, a beautiful use of **Language** links Lane Von Herzen's *The Unfastened Heart* and Paul Auster's *Leviathan.*

Each entry in *Now Read This* starts with the book's author, title, publisher and date of publication, and the number of pages in the book. Publisher and publication date were verified in the WLN/OCLC database and appear here as they do in the database. The date is the publication date, not the copyright date. ISBNs were not included because many of these books are no longer available in cloth editions and the paperback ISBN of a novel is different from the ISBN for the hardback edition. This is followed by a descriptive annotation, appeal characteristics, and subject headings. The annotation notes if the book is an Oprah Winfrey selection. In addition, novels that make good book club selections are marked with an icon. When a book is a translation, we note the original language and give the name of the translator in the annotation.

With regard to book club recommendations, we recognized that some books are enjoyable to read but don't lend themselves to a book discussion group. Books that are plot driven tend to offer less in the way of possibilities for a good discussion. Baxter Black's *Hey Cowboy, Wanna Get Lucky?* is great fun to read, but it doesn't have much to talk about besides its entertaining plot. Of course, some novels that are plot driven also have interesting characters, in which case they may be excellent choices for discussion purposes. One of the primary appeals of Rosellen Brown's *Before and After* is the story it tells, but it is also a good book to discuss. Why? Because **Characters** is the second appeal characteristic for this book and Brown's characters beg to have their motives understood: a wonderful basis for a book discussion.

In the section called "Now try," we make suggestions for further reading. This section broadens the scope of the book considerably, because a large percentage of the titles mentioned in this section do not themselves have main entries. Both fiction and nonfiction books are included in this section, as well as a few poems we felt would be of interest to the reader.

Following the four main sections are a title index, a subject index, and an author index. Authors and titles in those two indexes that have main entries in *Now Read This* are indicated with boldface type. When using the indexes, readers will notice that some titles are mentioned many times in the book. This is because those titles are so multidimensional that they can easily be linked to other books, either because of their subject or their appeal characteristics. One title that we found ourselves using again and again is Arundhati Roy's Booker Prize-winning first novel, *The God of Small Things*. There is so much in this novel—lovely writing, a beautifully described setting, a disastrous relationship between the main character and her brother, social unrest in India—that it naturally brought to mind interesting linkages with other titles.

Why This Book?

One of the joys of reading a novel is that it can lead to a seemingly unlimited number of other books. Novels, good novels in particular, stimulate and direct such wandering, such curiosity. It is this wandering—exploring the various paths and byways that come to mind as a novel is read—that makes reading fiction so exciting. The problem is that it is hard for people to know how to satisfy such curiosity, either for their own reading or to help another person choose books. All too often, unless the reader knows someone who can recommend another book, the curiosity and expansion of interests brought about by a good novel tend to peter out. A reference book is needed that facilitates the process of finding something else to read, that will easily guide readers from one book to another along the meandering and enlarging path of their own interests, encouraging the idiosyncratic and informal education that recreational reading can be.

Now Read This differs from other readers' advisory tools because of the use we make of appeal characteristics. These speak directly to why a person may like or dislike particular books. Because it is often not the subject of a novel that determines whether or not a reader enjoys the book, readers' advisory tools that are purely subject driven limit the possibility that readers will discover something else they will enjoy reading. It is the "feeling" a reader gets from a certain novel that is reflected in the appeal characteristics. For example, if I finished reading Michael Malone's *Handling Sin* and wanted another novel just like it, a subject search would lead me to a category (among others) of "humorous stories." Other books under this same category include Ellen Gilchrist's *The Age of Miracles* and Robert Asprin's *Another Fine Myth.* Yet neither of these novels bears the slightest resemblance to what appealed to me in *Handling Sin,* which was the exuberant writing and the hero haplessly chasing after his father. Asprin's novel is fantasy and Gilchrist's is a collection of short stories about a woman's experiences. *Now Read This* recommends John Kennedy Toole's *A Confederacy of Dunces,* Michael Chabon's *Wonder Boys*, and J. P. Donleavy's *The Ginger Man,* characterizing them all as fast-moving and humorous novels.

An illustration of the way one book can lead to another is included in Figure 1.

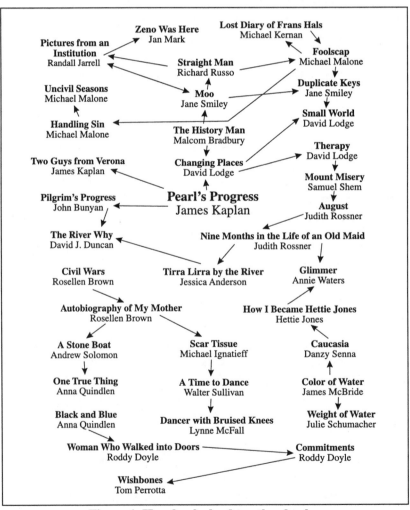

Figure 1. How books lead to other books.

As avid readers and experienced readers' advisors, we know that there is no guarantee that a recommended book will be just what's being looked for, even if the appeal characteristics seem to match. A person who enjoys good writing in a novel may find that after reading Dorothy Allison's *Bastard Out of Carolina,* Michael Ondaatje's *The English Patient* is just too slow and unbelievably romantic to be enjoyable. Similarly, someone who loves the gentle quirkiness of the characters that people Anne Tyler's novels may be totally put off by the hard-edged, more aggressive weirdness of the characters in Katherine Dunn's *Geek Love.*

However, appeal characteristics link novels that may on the surface appear to be completely dissimilar. Understanding novels in terms of their appeal is a new way of choosing fiction and may at first seem difficult to work out. Try a few novels that fall within the same appeal characteristic. Recommend them to your library users. Those of us who worked on *Now Read This* are hooked on this way of thinking about books. We'd love to hear your comments on the process, recommendations for other novels that fit together in unexpected ways, and suggestions for improving the process.

We hope that *Now Read This* serves multiple users: the individual looking for something to read; the reference librarian doing readers' advisory service; and book groups trying to select good titles for discussion. As you read through this book, prepare to jot down dozens of titles. And enjoy.

Chapter 1

Setting

Abraham, Pearl
The Romance Reader
Riverhead Books. 1995. 296 pp.

Rachel Benjamin, daughter of a Hasidic rabbi in upstate New York, escapes from her rigid upbringing through the romance novels she borrows from the library.

2d Appeal Story   Book Groups 📖

  Subjects   Coming-of-Age • First Novels • Jews and Judaism • New York

  Now try   Other books about Orthodox Jews and Jewish culture include Chaim Potok's *Davita's Harp*, Faye Kellerman's *The Ritual Bath* (and other mysteries about Rina Lazarus and Peter Decker, in which the two main characters are an Orthodox Jew and her non-Jewish husband); Naomi Ragen's *The Sacrifice of Tamar*, Allegra Goodman's *Kaaterskill Falls*, and Rebecca Goldstein's *The Mind-Body Problem*. *Now Molly Knows* by Merrill Joan Gerber, is another novel about the coming-of-age of a Jewish girl.

al-Shaykh, Hanan
Women of Sand and Myrrh
Anchor Books. 1992. 280 pp.

Four very different women find their lives circumscribed in the unnamed contemporary Middle Eastern country in which they live. Translated from the Arabic by Catherine Cobham.

2d Appeal Characters   Book Groups 📖

  Subjects   Arab Authors • Middle East • Muslims • Novels in Translation • Oppression of Women

  Now try   Diane Johnson's *Persian Nights* and Hilary Mantel's *Eight Months on Ghazzah Street* are both novels that look at the lives of Middle Eastern women from the perspective of, respectively, an American and a British couple. The novels of Henry James (*Washington Square*, for example) and Edith Wharton (*The Age of Innocence* and others) both explore the constrained lives of women in the late nineteenth and early twentieth centuries.

Alexander, Meena
Nampally Road
Mercury House. 1991. 107 pp.

After returning from England to Hyderabad, India, to teach literature at a local college, Mira Kannadical begins to question the value of her colonial education as she becomes involved in the growing civil unrest in the town.

Book Groups 📖

Subjects   Colonialism • Culture Clash • First Novels • India • Indian Authors

Now try   Alexander also wrote a memoir, *Fault Lines*, which explores the cultural differences that influenced her fiction writing. Anita Desai's *Clear Light of Day* and *Things Fall Apart* by Chinua Achebe both look seriously at the effects of British colonialism on third-world countries. The effects of American influences on third-world countries can also be appreciated in P. F. Kluge's *Biggest Elvis*.

Alvarez, Julia
In the Time of the Butterflies
Algonquin Books of Chapel Hill. 1994. 325 pp.

Patria, Minerva, Maria Theresa, and Dede struggle to be strong women, loving wives, dedicated mothers, and revolutionary compañeras during the oppressive Trujillo regime in the Dominican Republic.

2d Appeal   Characters
Book Groups 📖

Subjects   ALA Notable Books • Dominican Authors • Dominican Republic • Family Relationships • Political Fiction • Political Unrest • Sisters

Now try   Montserrat Fontes's *Dreams of the Centaur*, Lawrence Thornton's *Imagining Argentina*, and Omar Rivabella's *Requiem for a Woman's Soul* are all novels about life under a politically repressive government.

Amado, Jorge
Show Down
Bantam Books. 1988. 422 pp.

The story of Tocaia Grande, a rural outpost amidst the cacao plantations of Brazil, as it grew and died, then grew again through the grit and determination of its colorful and lusty settlers. Translated from the Portuguese by Gregory Rabassa and Jorge Amado.

2d Appeal   Characters

Subjects   Brazil • Brazilian Authors • Culture Clash • Novels in Translation • Poverty • Small-Town Life • South America • South American Authors

Now try   Amado is also the author of *Gabriela, Clove and Cinnamon*, *Tent of Miracles*, and *Shepherds of the Night*, all ALA Notable Books, as well as *Dona Flor and Her Two Husbands*. Lisa St. Aubin de Teran, in *The Keepers of the House*, describes a similar rural environment, this time in Venezuela. *Texaco*, by Patrick Chamoiseau, is also about the growth and development of a shanty town.

Anaya, Rudolfo
Alburquerque
University of New Mexico Press. 1992. 280 pp.

When ex-Golden Glove champion Abran Gonzalez receives a letter informing him that he is adopted and that his birth mother is white, he embarks on a search for his father and his own cultural identity in the mean, and politically charged, streets of Albuquerque.

2d Appeal   Story   Book Groups 📖

Subjects   Adoption • Cultural Identity • Culture Clash • Family Relationships • Mexican American Authors • Mexican Americans • New Mexico

Now try   Anaya's other books include ***Bless Me, Ultima, Tortuga***, and ***Chicano in China***. Another novel set in Albuquerque is ***The Lies That Bind*** by Judith Van Gieson. Manuel Ramos (***Blues for the Buffalo***, a mystery) also writes about Mexican Americans.

Auchincloss, Louis
The Book Class
Houghton Mifflin. 1984. 212 pp.

Christopher Gates, cynical homosexual son of a member of a ladies' book club, narrates this tale of upper-class women who struggle to find meaning within the strict confines of New York society in the first decade of the twentieth century.

2d Appeal   Characters

Subjects   1910s • Friendship • Gay Men • Upper Classes • Women's Friendships

Now try   Among Auchincloss's many other books of fiction are ***The Rector of Justin*** and ***Three Lives***. ***The Age of Innocence*** and ***The House of Mirth*** by Edith Wharton and ***The Wings of the Dove*** and ***Washington Square*** by Henry James are about the constrained lives of women. For a wonderfully humorous look at women's clubs, read Wharton's short story, "Xingu," which can be found in ***The Stories of Edith Wharton***. Helen Hooven Santmyer's ***... and Ladies of the Club*** is a sentimental story of a women's club over a period of many years.

Ballard, J. G.
Empire of the Sun
Simon and Schuster. 1984. 279 pp.

A boy becomes a man as a result of his horrific experiences during the Japanese invasion of China in World War II.

2d Appeal   Story   Book Groups 📖

Subjects   China • Coming-of-Age • World War II

Now try   Ballard is best known for his science fiction novels. His works include ***Running Wild*** and ***The Crystal World***, as well as collections of short stories. Other novels that relate the experiences of young men under difficult circumstances are Cormac McCarthy's ***All the Pretty Horses***, ***A Separate Peace*** by John Knowles, and Jim Anderson's ***Billarooby***. ***Empire of the Sun*** won Britain's James Tait Black Memorial Prize and the Guardian Fiction Prize.

Behr, Mark
The Smell of Apples
St. Martin's Press. 1995. 200 pp.

A young and naive Boer schoolboy's daily life reveals the pervasive humiliation and oppression of South African apartheid.

2d Appeal   Characters   Book Groups 📖

Subjects   Apartheid • Coming-of-Age • First Novels • Sexual Abuse • South Africa

Now try   Athol Fugard's play, "Master Harold and the Boys," also explores race relations in South Africa. Bryce Courtenay's *The Power of One* is a child's account of South African apartheid, but from a different viewpoint. Nadine Gordimer also writes about South Africa in *Occasion for Loving* and other novels. *The Smell of Apples* won the Betty Trask Award.

Benedict, Pinckney
Dogs of God
Doubleday. 1994. 354 pp.

The lives of Goody, a professional boxer, and Dwight, a tourist guide, become entangled with drug enforcement agents, marijuana growers, illegal immigrants, and gun runners in rural West Virginia.

2d Appeal   Language   Book Groups 📖

Subjects   Drugs and Drug Abuse • First Novels • Small-Town Life • West Virginia

Now try   The vividly described setting in *Dogs of God* is also found in Pinckney's collections of short stories, *The Wrecking Yard* and *Town Smokes*. The same gut-wrenching violence found in *Dogs of God* can be found in the early novels of Cormac McCarthy, such as *Blood Meridian* and *Suttree*.

Benitez, Sandra
A Place Where the Sea Remembers
Coffee House Press. 1993. 163 pp.

The wise healer Remedios links the bittersweet lives of the residents of a Mexican coastal village, from the sisters Chayo and Marta, who share a curse, to the lonely schoolteacher Rafael, who defies his mother to find love.

2d Appeal   Characters   Book Groups 📖

Subjects   First Novels • Magic Realism • Mexico • Rape • Sisters • Small-Town Life

Now try   Benitez's talent for describing characters and landscape is also found in her novel about three generations of Salvadoran women, *Bitter Grounds*. In *Like Water for Chocolate* by Laura Esquivel and Sandra Cisneros's *The House on Mango Street*, the authors explore the lives of Hispanics. *A Place Where the Sea Remembers* won the Minnesota Book Award.

Bhabra, H. S.
Gestures
Viking. 1986. 279 pp.

Now 85, diplomat Jeremy Burnham looks back on his tumultuous years as an assistant consul in Venice and how his relationships with two women and a man led to murder and a grave miscarriage of justice.

2d Appeal   Story   Book Groups 📖

Subjects   Elderly Men • First Novels • Indian Authors • Love Stories • Men's Friendships • Men's Lives • Murder • Venice, Italy

Now try   The issue of moral responsibility is also explored in Donna Tartt's *The Secret History*. Just as the events in Lawrence Durrell's *The Alexandria Quartet* are set in a city whose beauty and decadence parallel those of his characters, so Bhabra evokes Venice in *Gestures*. Another story set in a beautifully portrayed Venice is Thomas Mann's novella, *Death in Venice*. *Gestures* won the Betty Trask Award.

Bhattacharya, Keron
The Pearls of Coromandel St. Martin's Press. 1996. 254 pp.

As India moves toward independence from Britain, Indian civil servant John Sugden witnesses firsthand the growing animosity between Hindus and Muslims and faces expulsion from the Raj when he falls in love with Kamala, a Hindu woman whom Sugden invites to share his home.

2d Appeal   Story   Book Groups 📖

Subjects   Colonialism • First Novels • India • Indian Authors • Interracial Relationships • Love Stories

Now try   *Midnight's Children* by Salman Rushdie portrays the period following independence from the Indian perspective. Paul Scott's *The Jewel in the Crown* is also about the British in India during the final days of the Raj. *Freedom at Midnight* by Larry Collins and Dominique Lapierre is an excellent nonfiction account of events leading up to and following Britain's departure from India.

Boswell, Robert
American Owned Love A. A. Knopf. 1997. 323 pp.

In Persimmon, New Mexico, teenager Rudy Salazar's anger at his family's poverty threatens the lives of the Schaefer and Calzado families, whose destinies are linked by the love 14-year-old Enrique has for Rita Schaefer.

2d Appeal   Characters   Book Groups 📖

Subjects   Culture Clash • Juvenile Delinquents • Mothers and Daughters • New Mexico • Poverty • Teenage Boys • Teenage Girls • Teenagers

Now try   Boswell's other works of fiction include *Crooked Hearts* and *Dancing in the Movies*. Two other novels set in small towns in New Mexico are Antonya Nelson's *Nobody's Girl* and Rick Collignon's *Perdido*, which also explores the clash of Anglo and Spanish cultures.

Brown, Alan
Audrey Hepburn's Neck Pocket Books. 1996. 290 pp.

Growing up in a small Japanese village on the island of Hokkaido, Toshi daydreams about Audrey Hepburn and wonders why his beloved mother left him and his father.

2d Appeal   Story   Book Groups 📖

Subjects   Coming-of-Age • Culture Clash • First Novels • Japan • Korean-Japanese Relations • Mothers Deserting Their Families

Now try   The shocking story Toshi finally hears from his mother is similar to that told in Nora Okja Keller's *Comfort Woman*. The cultural differences between Japan and the United States are explored in *Salaryman* by Meg Pei and in Ruth Ozeki's *My Year of Meats*. Kyoko Mori's *One Bird* is another novel about a mother deserting her family and how it affects a child's life.

Camus, Albert
The First Man
Knopf. 1995. 325 pp.

At age 40, Jacques Cormery leaves France for Algeria to search for information about his father, who died in World War I when Jacques was an infant. Translated from the French by David Hapgood.

2d Appeal   Language

Subjects   ALA Notable Books • Algeria • Novels in Translation • Single Parents

Now try   This, Camus's last, unfinished novel, contains some of the same themes that can be found in his earlier books, such as *The Stranger*, *The Fall*, and *The Plague*. Thomas Givon's *Running Through the Tall Grass* is another novel set in Algeria.

Castedo, Elena
Paradise
Grove Weidenfeld. 1990. 328 pp.

Fleeing the ravages of the Spanish Civil War, 10-year-old Solita's mother moves the family to a country estate in Latin America, occupied by bored aristocrats, superstitious servants, quirky animals, and cunning children.

2d Appeal   Characters   Book Groups 📖

Subjects   Family Relationships • First Novels • Immigrants and Refugees • Spanish Civil War • Upper Classes

Now try   Isabel Allende's *The House of the Spirits* has a tone similar to Castedo's novel. Other novels about the Hispanic experience include *Bitter Grounds* by Sandra Benitez and *The Chin Kiss King* by Ana Veciana-Suarez.

Coelho, Paulo
By the River Piedra I Sat Down and Wept
Harper San Francisco. 1996. 210 pp.

The independent and practical Pilar tells how, while traveling through the French Pyrenees with a childhood friend, she discovers love as if for the first time. Translated from the Portuguese by Alan R. Clarke.

2d Appeal   Characters

Subjects   Brazilian Authors • France • Love Stories • Male/Female Relationships • Novels in Translation • Religion • South American Authors

Now try   Other books by Coelho include *The Diary of a Magus* and *The Alchemist*. *The Sparrow* by Mary Doria Russell is another novel concerned with issues of religious faith.

Connaughton, Shane
The Run of the Country
St. Martin's Press. 1992. 246 pp.

While grieving for his mother and struggling for independence from his domineering father, teenage Danny searches for solace by roaming the damp, desolate borderlands between the north and south of Ireland.

2d Appeal   Story   Book Groups 📖

   Subjects   Coming-of-Age • Family Relationships • Fathers and Sons • First Novels • Ireland • Irish Authors • Teenage Boys

   Now try   Roddy Doyle's ***Paddy Clarke Ha Ha Ha*** is another coming-of-age novel set in Ireland. ***Parrot in the Oven: Mi Vida*** by Victor Manning, winner of the National Book Award, tells the moving story of a Latino boy growing up in a dysfunctional family.

Courtenay, Bryce
The Power of One
Random House. 1989. 518 pp.

Growing up in a racially divided South Africa, Peekay, a young English boy, overcomes internal and external obstacles in his quest to become welterweight champion of the world.

2d Appeal   Story   Book Groups 📖

   Subjects   Apartheid • Boxing • Coming-of-Age • First Novels • South Africa • South African Authors

   Now try   Gus Lee's ***China Boy*** is also about a young man for whom learning to box is an important part of growing up in an often hostile environment. Life in South Africa from the point of view of a young Boer boy is the subject of Mark Behr's ***The Smell of Apples***.

Cowan, Andrew
Pig
Harcourt Brace & Co. 1996. 213 pp.

A 15-year-old boy fills the emptiness in his life after his grandmother's death, and his grandfather's increasingly swift decline, by taking care of their house and pet pig.

2d Appeal   Story

   Subjects   British Authors • Coming-of-Age • First Novels • Grandparents

   Now try   Cowan also wrote ***Common Ground***, which has as its central theme the decay of English society. ***A Day No Pigs Would Die*** by Robert Peck is a coming-of-age, young adult novel about a boy's devotion to a pig. And no list of books about pigs would be complete without E. B. White's ***Charlotte's Web***. ***Pig*** won the Betty Trask Award.

Darling, Diana
The Painted Alphabet
Graywolf Press. 1992. 208 pp.

On the lush island of Bali, the supernatural co-exists with tourism; characters both mythical and mundane experience the triumph of good over evil.

Book Groups 📖

Subjects   Bali • First Novels • Folktales • Good vs. Evil • Magic Realism

Now try   Darling's novel is based on a Balinese folktale. Vikram Chandra's *Red Earth and Pouring Rain* is also adapted from mythological tales.

Davenport, Kiana
Shark Dialogues
Atheneum. 1994. 492 pp.

The lives of four descendants who were born as a result of the improbable love affair between a nineteenth-century Yankee sailor and a runaway Tahitian princess encompass the history of Hawaii in all its beauty, pain, and contradictions.

2d Appeal   Story

Subjects   Cousins • Family Relationships • First Novels • Grandparents • Hawaii • Leprosy • Multigenerational Novels

Now try   *Miracle at Carville*, a memoir by Betty Martin, tells the story of the author's experiences with leprosy. Leprosy figures prominently in the plot of Gail Tsukiyama's *The Samurai's Garden*. Other books with a Hawaiian setting include *My Old Sweetheart* by Susanna Moore, *Hawaii* by James Michener, and *Comfort Woman* by Nora Okja Keller. Ann-Marie MacDonald's *Fall on Your Knees* and *Texaco* by Patrick Chamoiseau are both multigenerational novels.

Dawkins, Louisa
Natives and Strangers
Houghton Mifflin. 1985. 404 pp.

In 1950s Tanganyika, as the territory struggles for independence, Marietta Hamilton, granddaughter of British settlers, comes of age as she tries to balance her relationships with blacks and the demands of the white society in which she lives.

2d Appeal   Story

Subjects   1950s • Coming-of-Age • First Novels • Interracial Relationships • Love Stories • Mothers and Daughters • Race Relations • Tanganyika

Now try   Dawkins also wrote the novel *Chasing Shadows*. Although they are set in Europe rather than Africa, Olivia Manning's "The Balkan Trilogy" and "The Levant Trilogy" convey the same sense of everyday happenings played out against the background of world-changing events.

Desai, Anita
Clear Light of Day
Harper & Row. 1980. 183 pp.

During a visit to their decaying family mansion on the outskirts of Old Delhi, sisters Bim and Tara struggle to understand the forces that isolated their family and estranged their brother, Raja.

2d Appeal   Characters

Book Groups 📖

Subjects   ALA Notable Books • Brothers and Sisters • Delhi • Family Relationships • India • Indian Authors • Sisters

Now try Another of Desai's novels is *Fire on the Mountain*. Other novels that explore the complex dynamics of an Indian family are Arundhati Roy's *The God of Small Things* and Salman Rushdie's *The Moor's Last Sigh*.

Desai, Kieran
Hullabaloo in the Guava Orchard   Atlantic Monthly Press. 1998. 209 pp.

When Sampath Chawla, a hapless Indian postal clerk, runs away to a monkey-infested guava orchard, he finds himself acclaimed as the "Hermit of Shahkot" and inadvertently provides a wealth of economic opportunities for his ambitious family.

Subjects Bureaucracy • First Novels • Humorous Fiction • India • Small-Town Life

Now try Although critics have compared this book to Arundhati Roy's *The God of Small Things*, it is much closer in tone to the Malgudi novels by R. K. Narayan. Vikram Chandra's *Red Earth and Pouring Rain* is another Indian novel with monkeys playing an important part in the plot. Other novels featuring postal workers are Michael Palin's *Hemingway's Chair* and Antonio Skarmeta's *Burning Patience*.

Doig, Ivan
Bucking the Sun   Simon and Schuster. 1996. 412 pp.

When they lose their Montana farm to the planned Fort Peck Dam, the Duffs—father, mother, and three sons—all work on the project, which leads to love, marriage, and murder.

2d Appeal Story   Book Groups 📖

Subjects Adultery • Brothers • Family Relationships • Fathers and Sons • Montana • Murder

Now try With his many novels (including *Ride with Me*, *Mariah Montana*, *Dancing at the Rascal Fair*) and memoirs (*This House of Sky*, *Winter Brothers*), Doig has staked out the Northwest as his territory in much the same way that Mississippi is associated with Faulkner. Don and Ann Morehead's *A Short Season* has the same spare prose and sense of place as Doig's books. Craig Lesley's *Winterkill* offers another strong sense of the Northwest.

Donoso, Jose
A House in the Country   Knopf. 1984. 352 pp.

Games turn to nightmares during the summer holidays at the magnificent Chilean country estate of the Ventura family when the children—33 cousins ranging in age from 6 to 16—are left to themselves while their parents pursue their own pastimes. Translated from the Spanish by David Pritchard with Suzanne Jill Levine.

2d Appeal Language   Book Groups 📖

Subjects ALA Notable Books • Chile • Chilean Authors • Cousins • Family Relationships • Incest • Novels in Translation • South America • South American Authors • Upper Classes

Now try Donoso's other novels include *The Obscene Bird of Night* and *Coronation*. Other idyllic settings that turn violent can be found in Alex Garland's *The Beach* and William Golding's *The Lord of the Flies*.

Ehrlich, Gretel
Heart Mountain
Viking. 1988. 412 pp.

During World War II, the lives of Japanese Americans interned at the remote town of Heart Mountain, Wyoming, intersect with the townspeople.

2d Appeal   Story   Book Groups 📖

Subjects   Art and Artists • First Novels • Internment Camps • Japanese Americans • Love Stories • World War II • Wyoming

Now try   Ehrlich is known primarily for her nonfiction, including *The Solace of Open Spaces* and *A Match to the Heart*, her memoir of being struck by lightning and nearly dying. Monica Sone's 1952 memoir, *Nisei Daughter*, is about her family's life in Seattle and in the Minidoka internment camp. John Okada's novel, *No-No Boy*, is the story of a Japanese American who went to prison for refusing to be inducted into the U.S. Army during World War II. David Guterson's *Snow Falling on Cedars* is set in the Pacific Northwest during the same period.

Epstein, Leslie
King of the Jews
Coward, McCann & Geoghegan. 1979. 350 pp.

As a Jewish ghetto in Poland is being liquidated during World War II, the once-popular leader, I. C. Trumpelman, plays a morbid game with the Nazis to determine who will live and who will die.

2d Appeal   Characters   Book Groups 📖

Subjects   Holocaust • Jews and Judaism • Nazis • Poland • World War II

Now try   Other novels by Epstein include *Pandaemonium* and *Pinto and Sons*. Elie Wiesel's "Night Trilogy," made up of three books—*Night*, *Dawn*, and *The Accident*—includes descriptions of the author's World War II experiences as a victim of Nazi aggression. *Survival in Auschwitz* by Primo Levi is a gripping account of his experiences in Nazi death camps. Marisa Kantor Stark's *Bring Us the Old People* also describes life in Poland during World War II.

Fitzgerald, Penelope
The Bookshop
Houghton Mifflin. 1997. 123 pp.

Innocent widow Florence Green attempts to open a bookshop in an English seaside village and finds her enterprise thwarted by an upper-class snob and her toadying acolytes.

2d Appeal   Characters   Book Groups 📖

Subjects   Bookstores • British Authors • England • Small-Town Life • Upper Classes • Widows

Now try   Among Fitzgerald's other novels is *Gate of Angels*. Fitzgerald's writing style and understanding of class differences are similar to those found in Kazuo Ishiguro's *The Remains of the Day*. A lighter look at class differences in English life is found in E. F. Benson's *Mapp and Lucia* and other novels about the same characters.

Fontes, Montserrat
Dreams of the Centaur
W.W. Norton. 1996. 349 pp.

At the turn of the century, the Durcals, a Sonoran family, battle just to survive the brutal Porfirio Diaz regime and its attempts to wipe out the Yaquii Indian population.

2d Appeal   Story   Book Groups

Subjects   Coming-of-Age • Genocide • Mexican Authors • Mexico • Mothers and Sons • Political Fiction • Political Unrest • Yaquii Indians

Now try   The sequel to *Dreams of the Centaur* is *First Confession*. Julia Alvarez's *In the Time of the Butterflies* is about a totalitarian regime in the Dominican Republic and how a group of strong women struggle against it. Rudolfo Anaya's *Bless Me, Ultima*, is also set in Mexico and written in a style similar to Fontes's novel.

Galvin, James
The Meadow
H. Holt. 1992. 230 pp.

One hundred years in the life of a Colorado mountain meadow as viewed by the settlers, ranchers, and their descendants who were possessed by its beauty.

Subjects   Aging • ALA Notable Books • Colorado • Cowboys • First Novels • Friendship

Now try   Galvin is also a poet, whose many books include *Resurrection Update: Collected Poems 1975-1997*. Molly Gloss's *The Jump-Off Creek*, Glendon Swarthout's *The Homesman*, Craig Lesley's *Winterkill*, and Ivan Doig's *This House of Sky* all describe a sense of both isolation and community in the western United States. William Least-Heat Moon's *PrairyErth* is the history of one county in Kansas. *Plains Song, for Female Voices* by Wright Morris and John Thorndike's *The Potato Baron* are both novels in which landscape shapes character.

Ganesan, Indira
The Journey
Knopf. 1990. 171 pp.

Eighteen-year-old Renu learns that the world is not always fair and that fate is often unkind when she, her mother, and her younger sister travel from their Long Island, New York, home to an island off the coast of India to attend the funeral of Renu's cousin and best friend, Rajesh.

2d Appeal   Story   Book Groups

Subjects   First Novels • India • Indian Authors • Magic Realism • Sisters

Now try   Ganesan is also the author of *Inheritance*. Other novels focusing on contemporary Indian life include Indrani Aikath-Gyaltsen's *Daughters of the House*, Janette Turner Hospital's *The Ivory Swing*, and H. R. F. Keating's mysteries featuring Ganesh Ghote (*Inspector Ghote Breaks an Egg* and others). An entertaining novel set in nineteenth-century India is George MacDonald Fraser's *Flashman in the Great Game*.

Garland, Alex

The Beach
Riverhead Books. 1997. 371 pp.

After discovering a seemingly Edenic paradise on an island in a Thai national park, Richard soon finds that since civilized behavior tends to dissolve without external restraints, the utopia is hard to maintain.

2d Appeal   Story   Book Groups 📖

Subjects   British Authors • Coming-of-Age • Dystopia • First Novels • Thailand

Now try   The classic novel on this subject is William Golding's *Lord of the Flies*. Paul Theroux's *The Mosquito Coast* is another novel about an intended paradise gone wrong. Theodore Taylor's *The Cay* shows the less horrific side of life on a beach. Another view of survival on an idyllic beach is found in *I Was Amelia Earhart* by Jane Mendelsohn. *The Beach* won the Betty Trask Award.

Gillison, Samantha

The Undiscovered Country
Grove Press. 1998. 226 pp.

Biologist Peter Campbell and his wife June bring their young daughter Taylor to a small village in Papua New Guinea and are forced to try to understand themselves as well as the people and places they encounter there.

2d Appeal   Story   Book Groups 📖

Subjects   Family Relationships • Fathers and Daughters • First Novels • Husbands and Wives • Mothers and Daughters • Papua New Guinea • Science and Scientists

Now try   Other novels in which characters discover disturbing truths about themselves while living under difficult circumstances include Andrea Barrett's *The Voyage of the Narwhal*, Barbara Kingsolver's *The Poisonwood Bible*, and Audrey Schulman's *The Cage*. The lushness and potential evil of the setting of Gillison's novel resemble those of Joseph Conrad's *Heart of Darkness*.

Goodman, Allegra

Kaaterskill Falls
Dial Press. 1998. 324 pp.

In a small upstate New York town, summer home to a community of Orthodox Jews, model wife and mother Elizabeth Shulman opens a kosher food store with the elderly Rabbi's grudging approval, only to find herself in trouble with his son and successor.

2d Appeal   Characters

Subjects   Fathers and Sons • First Novels • Husbands and Wives • Jews and Judaism • New York • Small-Town Life

Now try   Goodman is also the author of *Total Immersion* and *The Family Markowitz*. A close-knit Jewish community is also described in Pearl Abraham's *The Romance Reader*.

Haviaras, Stratis

When the Tree Sings
Simon and Schuster. 1979. 219 pp.

A young boy comes of age during World War II while living in German-occupied Greece and consequently witnesses the ongoing destruction of his family, his village, and ultimately his way of life.

2d Appeal   Characters   Book Groups 📖

Subjects   ALA Notable Books • Coming-of-Age • First Novels • Greece • Greek Authors • World War II

Now try   Haviaras also wrote *The Heroic Age*. Two other novels about young people coming of age during wartime are *Casualties* by Lynne Reid Banks and Anne Michaels's *Fugitive Pieces*. (In fact, the characters in Michaels's novel live for a time in wartorn Greece.) Nicholas Gage's *Eleni*, a memoir of his mother, is set during Greece's civil war following World War II.

Hellenga, Robert

The Sixteen Pleasures
Soho. 1994. 327 pp.

When book conservator Margot Harrington goes to Florence to aid in restoring the treasures damaged in the flooding of the Arno in 1966, she is entrusted with a rare book that its owner, the abbess of a convent, hopes to sell without the bishop's knowledge.

2d Appeal   Story   Book Groups 📖

Subjects   Adultery • Erotica • First Novels • Florence • Italy • Research Novels

Now try   Hellenga is also the author of *The Fall of the Sparrow*. Another novel involving literary research is A. S. Byatt's *Possession*. Another novel set in Florence is Penelope Fitzgerald's *Innocence*.

Ikeda, Stewart David

What the Scarecrow Said
Regan Books. 1996. 445 pp.

After he is released from a Japanese internment camp near the end of World War II to create a working farm on widow Margaret Kelly's land in Massachusetts, William Fujita slowly begins to find in Margaret, her neighbor Livvie, and Livvie's young son Garvin a makeshift family to take the place of the one he lost.

2d Appeal   Characters   Book Groups 📖

Subjects   Farms and Farm Life • First Novels • Internment Camps • Japanese American Authors • Japanese Americans • Massachusetts • Racism • World War II

Now try   The sense of cold and isolation in the setting of Ikeda's novel is also evoked by the upstate New York setting of Frederick Busch's *Girls*. Kerri Sakamoto's *The Electrical Field* is another novel about the way lives were still affected years later by experiences in the Japanese internment camps during World War II.

Johnson, Joyce
In the Night Café
Dutton. 1989. 231 pp.

In 1960s Greenwich Village, Joanna tries to understand Tom, a free-spirited painter who, despite his remembered feelings of loneliness and dislocation after his father left the family, has abandoned his own two children.

2d Appeal   Story

Subjects   1960s • Adultery • Art and Artists • Beat Generation • Fathers and Sons • First Novels • Greenwich Village

Now try   Johnson also wrote *Minor Characters*, a memoir of her own life in the 1950s and 1960s, when she became friends with Jack Kerouac (*The Dharma Bums* and other novels) and other members of the Beat Generation. Mimi Albert's *Skirts* is set in the same time and place.

Johnston, Jennifer
The Old Jest
Doubleday. 1980. 203 pp.

In 1920, 18-year-old Nancy Gulliver befriends a mysterious stranger and unwittingly becomes involved in the bloody conflict between the English and the Irish.

2d Appeal   Characters   Book Groups 📖

Subjects   1920s • Fathers and Daughters • Ireland • Irish Authors • Orphans

Now try   Among Johnston's other books are *How Many Miles to Babylon?*, *Fool's Sanctuary*, and *Shadows on Our Skin*. Seamus Deane's *Reading in the Dark*, Patrick McCabe's *Breakfast on Pluto*, and Deirdre Madden's *One by One in the Darkness* are all about children growing up in families involved with Ireland's religious wars. *The Year of the French*, *Tenants of Time*, and *The End of the Hunt* make up Thomas Flanagan's "Irish Trilogy," which explores the history of Ireland from 1798 to the late twentieth century.

King, Thomas
Green Grass, Running Water
Houghton Mifflin. 1993. 360 pp.

Nothing in Blossom, Alberta, will ever be the same after Trickster Coyote decides to assist a motley group of Blackfeet men and women who are searching for the middle ground between their traditions and the modern world.

2d Appeal   Characters

Subjects   Alberta, Canada • American Indian Authors • American Indians • Blackfeet • Canada • Culture Clash • Humorous Fiction • Magic Realism

Now try   King's other books include *Medicine River*. He also edited *All My Relations: An Anthology of Contemporary Native Fiction*. Sherman Alexie's fiction and poetry (*Indian Killer* and *Summer of Black Widows*) also combine humor and sadness as the characters try to understand their lives both on and off the reservation. Another novel in which Coyote Trickster plays a part is Melinda Worth Popham's *Skywater*. E. Donald Two-Rivers's collection of stories, *Survivor's Medicine*, is also about contemporary Indian life.

Klein, Elizabeth
Reconciliations

Houghton Mifflin. 1982. 364 pp.

In an act that has repercussions for all the children and grandchildren of Naomi Silverstein, 18-year-old Gershom Lazarus walks away from his assimilated Jewish family during a Christmas dinner to escape his mother's possessiveness and explore his own religious beliefs.

2d Appeal   Story

Subjects   Cousins • Family Relationships • First Novels • Jews and Judaism • Male/Female Relationships • Teenage Boys

Now try   Zelda Popkin's *Dear Once*, Cynthia Freeman's *Always and Forever*, Michelle Herman's *Missing*, and Herbert Tarr's *A Woman of Spirit* present varied views of Jewish families. Other novels in which a young person becomes an observant Jew to the mystification of relatives are *Davita's Harp* by Chaim Potok and Allegra Goodman's *The Family Markowitz*.

Kluge, P. F.
Biggest Elvis
Viking. 1996. 341 pp.

A trio of Elvis impersonators working at Graceland, a rundown bar on a naval base in the Philippines, find their lives complicated and compromised when Biggest Elvis tries to better the lives of the prostitutes working there.

Subjects   Love Stories • Music and Musicians • Philippines • Presley, Elvis • Prostitutes and Prostitution

Now try   Kluge also wrote two works of nonfiction: *The Edge of Paradise: America in Micronesia* and *Alma Mater: A College Homecoming*. This novel—part mystery and part love story—is similar to the novels of Ross Thomas (*Chinaman's Chance* and *The Briarpatch*). *Stark Raving Elvis* by William McCranor Henderson is another novel about Elvis impersonators.

Kurtz, Don
South of the Big Four

Chronicle Books. 1995. 371 pp.

Thirty years old and still searching for meaning in his life, Arthur Conason returns to the family farm in Indiana and attempts to carve out a place for himself.

2d Appeal   Characters   Book Groups 📖

Subjects   Adultery • American Indians • Family Relationships • Farms and Farm Life • First Novels • Single Men

Now try   Both Jane Smiley's *A Thousand Acres* and Jane Hamilton's *A Map of the World* explore the pull of land and the farming life.

Madden, Deirdre
One by One in the Darkness
Faber and Faber. 1997. 181 pp.

Three sisters living in Northern Ireland, at a time when peace between Protestants and Catholics seems to be imminent, remember back to their childhood when violence among the Catholic and Protestant communities brought sorrow to their family.

Book Groups 📖

Subjects   Ireland • Irish Authors • Mothers and Daughters • Northern Ireland • Sisters • Violence

Now try   Madden's other books include ***Remembering Light and Stone*** and ***Birds of the Innocent Land***. Seamus Deane's ***Reading in the Dark*** is about violence in Northern Ireland seen through the eyes of a child. J. G. Farrell's novel of the early years of violence in Ireland is ***Troubles***, set at a resort hotel on the Irish coast in 1919.

Mallon, Thomas
Dewey Defeats Truman
Pantheon Books. 1997. 355 pp.

In 1948, citizens of presidential candidate Thomas Dewey's hometown are more concerned with their own lives than they are with the election and the outside world.

2d Appeal   Story

Subjects   1940s • Love Stories • Single Women • Small-Town Life • Triangles • Writers and Writing

Now try   Mallon's previous novels include ***Henry and Clara***, ***Arts and Sciences***, and ***Aurora 7***. He is also the author of ***Stolen Words***, a book about plagiarism, and ***A Book of One's Own***, about diaries and journals. Other novels that incorporate both real and fictional people are E. L. Doctorow's ***Ragtime***, and Mordecai Richler's ***Solomon Gursky Was Here***.

McGahan, Andrew
1988
St. Martin's Press. 1997. 314 pp.

Hoping for a chance to spend time in artistic pursuits, 20-somethings Gordon and Wayne head for a six-month job at a far-off-the-beaten-track weather station in Australia, only to find that Cape Don consists of a tumble-down shack, a host of crocodiles, an alcoholic park ranger, a dog named Kevin, and solitude enough to drive them mad.

2d Appeal   Characters

Subjects   Art and Artists • Australia • Australian Authors • Black Humor • Nihilism • Writers and Writing

Now try   ***1988*** is a prequel to McGahan's ***Praise***. Nick Hornby's ***High Fidelity*** is about another aimless 20-something, while Irvine Welsh's ***Trainspotting*** concerns a group of Generation X-ers with heroin problems.

McInerney, Jay
Brightness Falls

A. Knopf. 1992. 415 pp.

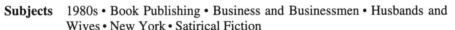

When Russell Calloway falls into disfavor at the publishing house where he works, he decides to put together a hostile takeover of the company, financing his initial payment by borrowing $50,000 from the credit card he received in the mail.

Subjects   1980s • Book Publishing • Business and Businessmen • Husbands and Wives • New York • Satirical Fiction

Now try   McInerney's first novel, ***Bright Lights, Big City*** propelled him to the forefront of young New York novelists. ***Brightness Falls*** is similar in tone and subject matter to Tom Wolfe's ***The Bonfire of the Vanities***. Readers familiar with the New York publishing industry will be able to recognize the characters and publishing houses thinly disguised here. The New York publishing world is described in Olivia Goldsmith's roman à clef, ***The Bestseller***, and in Rafael Yglesias's ***Hot Properties***.

McNamer, Deirdre
One Sweet Quarrel

HarperCollins Publishers. 1994. 280 pp.

In the early years of the twentieth century, Jerry Malone heads west from Minnesota to homestead in Montana, while his younger sister Daisy Lou tries her luck in New York as a singer, and his older brother Carlton makes his living as a less-than-honest, hard-drinking hustler.

2d Appeal   Characters

Subjects   Brothers and Sisters • Farms and Farm Life • Montana

Now try   McNamer's first novel, ***Rima in the Weeds***, is also set in Montana. Elizabeth Savage's novel, ***The Girls from the Five Great Valleys***, is about Montana in the 1940s and 1950s, overlapping in time with some of McNamer's novel. ***Buster Midnight's Café*** by Sandra Dallas is about hardscrabble times in Montana during the 1920s and 1930s.

Mekler, Eva
Sunrise Shows Late

Bridge Works Pub. Co. 1997. 272 pp.

Following World War II, Manya, a Jewish communist and veteran of the anti-Nazi underground during the war, flees the still rampant anti-semitism in her native Poland for a displaced persons camp in Germany; there she is forced to choose between the two very different men who fall in love with her.

2d Appeal   Story

Subjects   First Novels • Germany • Holocaust • Immigrants and Refugees • Israel • Jews and Judaism • Love Stories • Poland • World War II

Now try   Other novels about the founding of Israel include Leon Uris's ***Exodus*** and Meyer Levin's ***The Settlers***. Isaac Bashevas Singer's ***Meshugah*** is about Holocaust survivors in the 1950s.

Messud, Claire
When the World Was Steady
Granta Books. 1994. 270 pp.

Sisters Emmy and Virginia, with their very different outlooks on life, come to a tentative understanding of themselves and each other during emotion-laden trips to Bali (Emmy) and the Isle of Skye (Virginia).

2d Appeal   Characters

Subjects   Bali • British Authors • First Novels • Mothers and Daughters • Scotland • Sisters

Now try   Other pairs of sisters are found in Charles Dickinson's *The Widows' Adventures*, Janis Arnold's *Daughters of Memory*, and Lisa Grunwald's *New Year's Eve*.

Millhauser, Steven
Martin Dressler: The Tale of an American Dreamer
Crown. 1996. 294 pp.

As New York City rushes headlong to embrace the twentieth century, young entrepreneur Martin Dressler rises from bellhop to builder of dream palaces, only to lose himself in the process.

2d Appeal   Language   Book Groups 📖

Subjects   Architects and Architecture • Business and Businessmen • New York • Pulitzer Prize Winners • Rags-to-Riches Story

Now try   Among Millhauser's other works of fiction are *The Knife Thrower and Other Stories* and *Edwin Mullhouse: The Life and Death of an American Writer, 1943–1954*, which is a satirical look at biographies. The main characters in Penelope Lively's *City of the Mind* and Ayn Rand's *The Fountainhead* are architects.

Neihart, Ben
Hey, Joe
Simon & Schuster. 1996. 200 pp.

Ready for love, 16-year-old Joe Keith stumbles into big trouble in the back alleys of the French Quarter in New Orleans.

2d Appeal   Characters

Subjects   Coming-of-Age; First Novels; Gay Men; Gay Teenagers; New Orleans; Teenage Boys; Teenagers

Now try   Other novels about young men accepting their homosexuality include Jane Hamilton's *The Short History of a Prince*, Edmund White's *A Boy's Own Story*, and Shyam Selvadurai's *Funny Boy*. Other novels set in New Orleans include the mysteries by James Lee Burke (*Black Cherry Blues* and *Dixie City Jam*, among others), John Gregory Brown's novel *The Wrecked, Blessed Body of Shelton LaFleur*, and Harry Crews's *The Knockout Artist*.

Nordan, Lewis
Music of the Swamp
Algonquin Books of Chapel Hill. 1991. 191 pp.

In the Southern-fried heart of Arrow Catcher, Mississippi, adolescent Sugar Mecklin learns to deal with dead bodies popping up in unlikely places and with his parents' dying marriage, as well.

2d Appeal   Characters   Book Groups 📖

Subjects   ALA Notable Books • Alcoholics and Alcoholism • Coming-of-Age • Mississippi • Small-Town Life • Southern Authors • Teenage Boys • Teenagers

Now try   The Mississippi delta setting of Nordan's books is also the setting of *The River Is Home* and *Angel City* by Patrick D. Smith, Larry Brown's *Big Bad Love*, and William Faulkner's books (*As I Lay Dying*, *Absalom*, *Absalom!*, and others). Coming-of-age is the theme of Carson McCullers's *The Member of the Wedding* and William Faulkner's *The Reivers*. In William McPherson's *Testing the Current*, an adolescent boy observes the failure of his parents' marriage.

Norman, Howard

The Bird Artist

Farrar, Straus & Giroux. 1994. 289 pp.

Fabian Vas is known for three things in Witless Bay, Newfoundland: his moderate success as an artist, his longtime affair with the wild and irreverent Margaret, and the murder of a local lighthouse keeper.

2d Appeal   Language   Book Groups 📖

Subjects   Adultery • ALA Notable Books • Art and Artists • Birds • Canada • Love Stories • Male/Female Relationships • Mothers and Sons • Murder • Newfoundland, Canada • Small-Town Life

Now try   Both of Norman's other novels, *The Northern Lights* and *The Museum Guard*, display the same economy of writing as *The Bird Artist*. Another novel set in Newfoundland is E. Annie Proulx's *The Shipping News*. Other novelists who emphasize setting include Beryl Bainbridge in *The Birthday Boys*, Sandra Benitez in *A Place Where the Sea Remembers*, and Shena Mackay in *The Orchard on Fire*.

Payne, David

Ruin Creek

Doubleday. 1993. 373 pp.

The voices of 11-year-old Joey, his father Jimmy, and his mother May all describe how the dissolution of a family brings pain to everyone involved.

2d Appeal   Story

Subjects   Dysfunctional Families • Family Relationships • Southern Authors

Now try   Payne's first novel, *Early from the Dance*, was also set in the south. Fans of Pat Conroy's *The Prince of Tides* will see Conroy's influence on Payne's fiction. Lewis Nordan's *Music of the Swamp* is also about a family falling apart, told mainly from the perspective of the young son.

Popham, Melinda Worth

Skywater

Graywolf Press. 1990. 205 pp.

An aging husband and wife observe a band of coyotes who, faced with a diminishing water supply, set out across the Southwestern desert in search of the mythical source of all water.

2d Appeal   Story

Subjects   Aging • ALA Notable Books • Animals • Ecofiction • First Novels • Wildlife

Now try   The children's book, *Rabbit Hill*, by Robert Lawson is also about the relationships between man, animals, and the land they share. The classic novel told from an animal's point of view is *Watership Down* by Richard Adams. Other books about the desert Southwest include Edward

Abbey's *Desert Solitaire* and *Desert Images* and Richard Shelton's *Going Back to Bisbee*. Craig Childs's *Crossing Paths: Encounters with Animals in the Wild* has an interesting chapter on coyotes.

Proulx, E. Annie

The Shipping News
Scribner. 1993. 337 pp.

Awkward newspaperman Quoyle, his two daughters, and his aunt try to reclaim their lives in a small Newfoundland fishing town.

2d Appeal   Language   Book Groups 📖

Subjects   ALA Notable Books • Canada • Family Relationships • Journalists • Love Stories • National Book Award Winners • Newfoundland, Canada • Pulitzer Prize Winners • Small-Town Life

Now try   Proulx's other books include *Postcards* and *Accordion Crimes*. Other novels with a strong sense of place are Howard Norman's *The Bird Artist*, Shena Mackay's *The Orchard on Fire*, and *The Funeral Makers* and other "Mattagash" novels by Cathie Pelletier. *The Shipping News* shares its darkly comic vision and quirky characters with Lewis Nordan's novels *The Sharpshooter Blues* and *Wolf Whistle*. Another novel set in Newfoundland is Patrick Kavanagh's *Gaff Topsails*.

Quick, Barbara

Northern Edge
D.I. Fine. 1970. 217 pp.

When Tay MacElroy leaves her safe but boring position as an executive secretary and accepts a job in Fairbanks, Alaska, she encounters challenges that significantly change her life.

2d Appeal   Story

Subjects   Alaska • First Novels • Single Women • Women's Friendships

Now try   The mental and physical challenges Tay faces are similar to those faced by the main character in Audrey Schulman's *The Cage*. Jon Krakauer explores the difficulties of living in the wilderness in *Into the Wild*. Other novels set in Alaska include James Michener's *Alaska* and the mysteries of Dana Stabenow (*A Cold Day for Murder* and others) and John Straley (*The Woman Who Married a Bear* and others).

Rachlin, Nahid

Married to a Stranger
Dutton. 1983. 220 pp.

Minou longs for freedom from society's proscribed roles, but instead finds herself trapped in a loveless marriage with Javad, a revolutionary and adulterer.

2d Appeal   Characters   Book Groups 📖

Subjects   Adultery • Culture Clash • Iran • Irani Authors • Islamic Revolution • Marriage

Now try   Other works of fiction by Rachlin include *Foreigner* and *Veils*. Diane Johnson's *Persian Nights* and Susanne Parri's *Fortune Catcher* are also set in Iran.

Ricci, Nino

The Book of Saints
Knopf. 1991. 237 pp.

After his father emigrates to Canada, young Vittorio Innocente watches helplessly as the Italian village where the family lives silently condemns his mother, now pregnant by another man.

2d Appeal   Story   Book Groups ▢

   Subjects   Canada • Coming-of-Age • First Novels • Italian Authors • Italy • Mothers and Sons • Small-Town Life

   Now try   Ricci wrote a sequel to this novel entitled ***In a Glass House***. Another novel in which a child watches helplessly as her world falls apart is Sheila Bosworth's ***Almost Innocent***. ***The Book of Saints*** won a Governor General's Literary Award and the Betty Trask Award.

Richler, Mordecai

Solomon Gursky Was Here
Knopf. 1990. 413 pp.

Young author Moses Berger is obsessed with writing the history of the Gurskys, an important Jewish Canadian family whose members were seemingly present at every important event from the 1840s to the 1960s and were friends with all the important people.

2d Appeal   Characters

   Subjects   Canada • Canadian Authors • Humorous Fiction • Jews and Judaism • Multigenerational Novels • Writers and Writing

   Now try   Richler's other novels include ***Joshua Then and Now*** and ***The Apprenticeship of Duddy Kravitz***. Other obsessive personalities are found in Mark Helprin's ***Memoir from Antproof Case***, Jane Urquhart's ***The Underpainter***, and ***Martin Dressler: Tale of an American Dreamer*** by Steven Millhauser. Thomas Mallon's ***Dewey Defeats Truman*** also includes both real and fictitious characters.

Rivabella, Omar

Requiem for a Woman's Soul
Random House. 1986. 116 pp.

Latin American priest Father Antonio decides to denounce the human rights abuses of the ruling regime after he transcribes journal entries of a young woman describing her horrific ordeal of torture in a clandestine prison. Translated from the Spanish by Paul Riviera.

2d Appeal   Characters   Book Groups ▢

   Subjects   ALA Notable Books • Argentina • Argentinian Authors • Political Fiction • Political Prisoners • Torture

   Now try   Rivabella also wrote ***The Narrowing Circle***. Other novels that describe life under a politically repressive regime include Lawrence Thornton's ***Imagining Argentina***, Julia Alvarez's ***In the Time of the Butterflies***, Nawal Sa'dawi's ***Woman at Point Zero***, Herta Muller's ***The Land of Green Plums***, and Mitsuaki Iwago's ***In the Lion's Den***.

Salisbury, Graham
Blue Skin of the Sea
Delacorte. 1992. 215 pp.

As motherless Sonny Mendoza comes of age in a small Hawaiian village, he must deal not only with his father's emotional distance, but also with a primal terror of the ocean.

Subjects   Coming-of-Age • Fathers and Sons • First Novels • Hawaii • Single Parents

Now try   This novel is often considered a book for young adults, but it is thoroughly satisfying reading for adults as well. Like Julie Hecht's *Do the Windows Open?* and Allegra Goodman's *The Family Markowitz*, this is a series of interconnected short stories.

Savage, Thomas
The Corner of Rife and Pacific
Morrow. 1988. 226 pp.

In the early years of the twentieth century, the Metlen family of Grayling, Montana, confronts the vicissitudes of fate, from cruel neighbors to destructive weather, as well as a terrible war.

2d Appeal   Story

Subjects   Family Relationships • Fathers and Sons • Montana

Now try   Savage's other novels include *The Power of the Dog* and *Her Side of It*. Just as Savage evokes Montana in this novel, so does Willa Cather, in *My Antonia*, evoke Nebraska, and Loula Grace Erdman, in *The Edge of Time*, evoke Texas. Jonathan Raban's *Bad Land: An American Romance* is about the settling of eastern Montana during the same time period that Savage's novel covers.

Schulman, Audrey
The Cage
Algonquin Books of Chapel Hill. 1994. 228 pp.

When the cage Beryl is using to photograph bears in the Arctic fails to protect her, she has to rely on both her mental and physical strengths to survive.

2d Appeal   Story   Book Groups 📖

Subjects   ALA Notable Books • Arctic • First Novels • Photography and Photographers

Now try   Beryl Bainbridge's *The Birthday Boys*, Barbara Quick's *Northern Edge*, and *Antarctic Navigation* by Elizabeth Arthur are all books in which the protagonists need to find strength to survive in difficult situations. A nonfiction account of an adventure gone terribly wrong is Jon Krakauer's *Into Thin Air: A Personal Account of the Mt. Everest Disaster*.

Seth, Vikram
A Suitable Boy
HarperCollins Publishers. 1993. 1349 pp.

The clash between the old ways and the new is seen in the experiences of four families, played out against the backdrop of Indian life a decade after independence from Britain.

2d Appeal   Characters   Book Groups 📖

Subjects   1950s • Family Relationships • India • Male/Female Relationships

Now try   Seth also wrote *The Golden Gate: A Novel in Verse* and several books of poetry. Life in India after Independence is also expansively described in Paul Scott's "The Raj Quartet," made up of *The Jewel in the Crown*, *The Day of the Scorpion*, *The Towers of Silence*, and *A Division of the Spoils*, as well as his *Staying On*.

Shakespeare, Nicholas
The Vision of Elena Silves
Knopf. 1990. 249 pp.

Three old men sitting on a bench reveal the story of Elena and Gabriel, two lovers whose lives seem pre-determined by the politics and religion of Peru.

2d Appeal   Characters   Book Groups 📖

Subjects   British Authors • First Novels • Love Stories • Peru • South America

Now try   Shakespeare has received critical acclaim for his novel, *The Dancer Upstairs*, about a modern-day South American police officer who sets out to capture a terrorist. *Lovesick* by Angeles Mastretta is also about lovers during a revolution in a South American country. *The Vision of Elena Silves* won the Betty Trask Award.

Shalev, Meir
The Blue Mountain
Aaron Asher Books. 1991. 375 pp.

Now 38 years old, Ya'akov Mirkin recounts, through his relationship with the grandfather who raised him, the history of his family and the rest of the quirky inhabitants of a cooperative Israeli settlement in the Valley of Jezreel. Translated from the Hebrew by Hillel Halkin.

2d Appeal   Characters

Subjects   Eccentrics and Eccentricities • Family Relationships • Grandparents • Humorous Fiction • Israel • Israeli Authors • Novels in Translation • Small-Town Life

Now try   Another book by Shalev is *Esau*. Other novels that describe unconventional upbringings include Howard Frank Mosher's *Northern Borders* (which also has some quirky characters in its small town setting) and *Housekeeping* by Marilynne Robinson.

Sidhwa, Bapsi
Cracking India
Milkweed Editions. 1991. 289 pp.

The revolution following the partition of India and the creation of Pakistan in 1947 is seen through the eyes of four-year-old Lenny Sethi, the daughter of wealthy Parsee parents.

2d Appeal   Story   Book Groups 📖

Subjects   India • Indian Authors • Pakistan • Political Unrest

Now try   Among Sidhwa's other novels are *The Bride*, *The Crow Eaters*, and *An American Brat*. *Cracking India* was originally published under the title *Ice Candy Man*. Jessica Hagedorn's *Dogeaters* is about another country in turmoil (Philippines).

Silman, Roberta
Beginning the World Again   Viking. 1990. 414 pp.

Lily Fialka looks back more than four decades to her life in the early 1940s in Los Alamos, New Mexico, when her scientist husband was part of the Manhattan Project, working to build the atomic bomb.

Book Groups 📖

Subjects   1940s • Atomic Bomb • Family Relationships • Marriage • New Mexico • Science and Scientists

Now try   Silman also wrote the novel *Boundaries*. Joseph Kanon's mystery novel, *Los Alamos*, is set at exactly the same time, uses some of the same characters, and explores the same moral dilemma as Silman does in her novel. Ward Just's *The American Ambassador* is about a father and son who are at odds over their political beliefs.

Simecka, Martin M.
The Year of the Frog   Louisiana State University Press. 1993. 247 pp.

In the politically oppressive environment of 1980s Czechoslovakia, young intellectual Milan muddles through a succession of menial jobs and falls in love with Tania, an aristrocratic student, as he comes to an understanding of life, love, and death. Translated from the Czechoslovakian by Peter Petro.

Book Groups 📖

Subjects   1980s • Coming-of-Age • Communism • Czechoslovakia • Czechoslovakian Authors • First Novels • Novels in Translation • Political Fiction

Now try   Tibor Fischer's *Under the Frog*, set in Hungary, and Herta Muller's *The Land of Green Plums*, set in Romania, are both about life in Eastern Europe under politically repressive governments.

Skarmeta, Antonio
Burning Patience   Pantheon Books. 1987. 118 pp.

A young and lustful Chilean postman asks for the poet Pablo Neruda's assistance in securing the love of Beatriz, the beautiful daughter of an overbearing and overprotective tavern owner. Translated from the Spanish by Katherine Silver.

2d Appeal   Characters

Subjects   Chile • Chilean Authors • Humorous Fiction • Love Stories • Neruda, Pablo • Novels in Translation • Political Fiction • Small-Town Life

Now try   Skarmeta is a political novelist whose earlier novels dealt with Salvador Allende's Chile (*I Dreamt the Snow Was Burning*) and the Nicaraguan revolution (*The Insurrection*). Other political novels include Jorge Amado's *Pen, Sword, Camisole: A Fable to Kindle a Hope* and Madison Smartt Bell's *All Souls' Rising*.

Smiley, Jane
A Thousand Acres
Knopf. 1991. 371 pp.

A Midwestern family copes with long-buried memories of a father's abuse, disagreements among the three sisters and their husbands and lovers, cancer, and pollution of the land.

2d Appeal   Story   Book Groups 📖

Subjects   ALA Notable Books • Cancer • Farms and Farm Life • Fathers and Daughters • Iowa • National Book Critics Circle Award Winners • Pulitzer Prize Winners • Sexual Abuse • Sisters

Now try   Smiley is a versatile writer whose books range from *Moo*, a satire of academia, to *Duplicate Keys*, a mystery, to *The Age of Grief*, a collection of short stories and novellas. Jane Hamilton's *A Map of the World* is frequently compared to *A Thousand Acres*, due to their farm settings and heavy-duty plots. Richard Powers's *Gain* is also about a woman developing cancer probably caused by pollution.

St. Aubin de Teran, Lisa
The Long Way Home
Harper & Row. 1983. 183 pp.

The decline and fall through drought and dementia of the aristocratic Venezuelan Beltran clan is seen through the eyes of the young English wife of the last heir.

2d Appeal   Story   Book Groups 📖

Subjects   British Authors • Culture Clash • Family Relationships • First Novels • Male/Female Relationships • Marriage • South America • Venezuela

Now try   *The Long Way Home* was published in England under the title, *Keepers of the House*. St. Aubin de Teran also wrote a memoir, *The Hacienda*, as well as *The Slow Train to Milan*, *The Tiger*, and *Black Idol*, three novels. Other novels chronicling the decline and fall of a once-proud family include Carol Dawson's *Body of Knowledge* and Arundhati Roy's *The God of Small Things*. Jorge Amado's *Show Down* is another novel about rural South American politics.

Swift, Graham
Waterland
Poseidon Press. 1983. 309 pp.

History teacher Tom Crick, on the verge of a forced retirement, regales his students with a heartbreaking family tale of love and murder in England's Fen country, from Victorian times to the present.

2d Appeal   Language   Book Groups 📖

Subjects   ALA Notable Books • British Authors • Brothers and Sisters • England • Husbands and Wives • Incest • Murder

Now try   Among Swift's other books is *Out of This World*. Just as William Faulkner made Yoknapatawpha County come alive in his books (*Absalom, Absalom!* and *As I Lay Dying*, among others), so Swift brings to life the Fen country of England.

Thomas, Maria
Antonia Saw the Oryx First
Soho. 1987. 296 pp.

As the white colonialists leave a newly independent Tanzania, African-born and Harvard-trained Dr. Antonia Redmond remains behind with her African patient, Esther Moro, a prostitute and traditional healer.

2d Appeal   Characters   Book Groups 📖

Subjects   Africa • Doctors and Patients • East Africa • First Novels • Interracial Relationships • Love Stories • Prostitutes and Prostitution • Tanzania • Women's Friendships

Now try   Thomas wrote two collections of short stories: *Come to Africa and Save Your Marriage* and *African Visas: A Novella and Stories*. What Lawrence Durrell did for Egypt in *The Alexandria Quartet*, Thomas does for the end of British rule in Tanzania.

Thorndike, John
The Potato Baron
Villard Books. 1989. 285 pp.

Austin Pooler finds his world threatened when he is forced to choose between staying on his family's potato farm in Northern Maine or following his beloved wife to a new life elsewhere.

2d Appeal   Story

Subjects   Farms and Farm Life • Maine • Male/Female Relationships • Marriage

Now try   Other books by Thorndike include a novel, *Anna Delaney's Child*, and a memoir, *Another Way Home: A Single Father's Story*. *Dale Loves Sophie to Death* by Robb Forman Dew is another novel about a marriage in trouble. Other books that emphasize an attachment for the land are Douglas Unger's *Leaving the Land* and James Galvin's *The Meadow*.

Ty-Casper, Linda
DreamEden
University of Washington Press. 1996. 460 pp.

In the Philippines in the 1980s, attorney Benhur Vitaliano struggles to support his extended family as well as the revolutionary movement of Corazon Aquino, while his boyhood friend and employer, Osong Moscoso, exploits the corrupt and turbulent political climate to further his wealth and influence.

2d Appeal   Story

Subjects   1980s • Filipino Authors • Philippines • Political Fiction • Revolutionary Movements

Now try   Ty-Casper is one of the leading writers in the Philippines. Her other works of fiction include *Wings of Stone*, *Fortress in the Plaza*, and *A Three Cornered Sun: A Historical Novel*. Another book that deals with revolutionary movements is Jay Cantor's *The Death of Che Guevara*.

Vassanji, M. G.

The Book of Secrets

Picador USA. 1994. 337 pp.

When the 1913 diary of a British colonial administrator is unearthed in the walls of a dusty shop in 1980s Dar Es Salaam, retired school teacher Pius Fernandes attempts to unravel the mystery it represents.

2d Appeal Story

Subjects Africa • Colonialism • Culture Clash • East Africa • Research Novels • Tanzania • World War I

Now try Vassanji's other books of fiction include *The Gunny Sack, No New Land,* and *Uhuru Street.* The plot of Lee Langley's *Persistent Rumours* also involves a British colonial mystery, with tantalizingly few clues.

Watson, Larry

Montana 1948

Milkweed Editions. 1993. 175 pp.

Twelve-year-old David Hayden grows up very quickly when he learns that his war-hero uncle, the town's doctor, is about to be arrested by the town's sheriff, David's father.

2d Appeal Characters   Book Groups 📖

Subjects 1940s • ALA Notable Books • Brothers • Coming-of-Age • Family Relationships • Fathers and Sons • Montana • Sexual Abuse • Small-Town Life

Now try Watson also wrote *Justice,* which is a prequel to *Montana 1948,* as well as *White Crosses,* another tale set in Bentrock, Montana. Norman Maclean's *A River Runs Through It* is a lyrical account of shattering events affecting a group of Montanans. Jamie Harrison's mystery *The Edge of the Crazies* is also set in small-town Montana.

Wyndham, Francis

The Other Garden

Moyer Bell. 1987. 106 pp.

During World War II, Kay, an eccentric and unloved spinster, begins a relationship with the narrator, an adolescent boy.

Book Groups 📖

Subjects British Authors • Coming-of-Age • Eccentrics and Eccentricities • Family Relationships • First Novels • Older Women/Younger Men • Single Women • Small-Town Life • World War II

Now try Another set of dreadful parents in a terrible marriage can be found in Lawrence Naumoff's *The Night of the Weeping Women.* The tone of gentle nostalgia for a world long gone is similar to the tone of Muriel Spark's *A Far Cry from Kensington,* although Spark's tone is mixed with more than a touch of dryness and irony. *Tim* by Colleen McCullough is another novel about a middle-aged spinster who falls in love with a very young man. *The Other Garden* won the Whitbread Award.

Chapter 2

Story

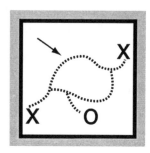

Abeel, Erica
Women Like Us
Ticknor & Fields. 1994. 396 pp.

Four friends, who meet during their undergraduate years at Sarah Lawrence College in the 1950s, live through marriage, careers, divorces, motherhood, successes, and failures.

Subjects 1950s • College Students • Middle-Aged Women • Women's Friendships

Now try Marilyn French (*The Women's Room*) and Erica Jong (*Fear of Flying*) have both written about the women who came of age in the late 1950s. Ruth Doan Mac-Dougall's *Wife and Mother* is another book about the life of a woman from her college years through a long marriage. Mary McCarthy's *The Group*, set in the 1930s, dissected the lives of a group of college friends. *Pretty Girls* by Garret Weyr also describes friendships among college-age women.

Abu-Jaber, Diana
Arabian Jazz
Harcourt Brace. 1993. 374 pp.

Now in their twenties, sisters Melvina and Jemorah Ramoud are still caught between two cultures: their Jordanian father's family heritage and the American way of their contemporaries.

2d Appeal Characters   Book Groups 📖

Subjects Acculturation • Arab Americans • Culture Clash • Family Relationships • First Novels • Immigrants and Refugees • Sisters

Now try Another novel about adjusting to life in the United States is Julia Alvarez's *How the Garcia Girls Lost Their Accents*. Eva Hoffman's *Lost in Translation: A Life in a New Language* is a memoir of her experiences moving from Europe to Canada after World War II.

Ackerman, Karl
The Patron Saint of Unmarried Women
St. Martin's Press. 1994. 246 pp.

Although they are unhappy together, Jack and Nina find they are even more miserable apart.

2d Appeal   Characters

Subjects   First Novels • Love Stories • Male/Female Relationships • Marriage

Now try   *A Marriage Made at Woodstock* by Cathie Pelletier is another look at the difficulties of maintaining relationships. Three movies also explore the joys and angst of modern romance: *Crossing Delancy*, *Say Anything*, and *Moonstruck.*

Akins, Ellen
Home Movie
Simon and Schuster. 1988. 302 pp.

After her father dies and her mother abandons her, 14-year-old Joey finds a surrogate father in local recluse Giffard, who, by showing her his home movies, motivates Joey to excavate the secrets of her own family history.

Subjects   Coming-of-Age • Death of a Parent • Family Relationships • First Novels • Mothers Deserting Their Families • Teenage Girls

Now try   Akins's other novels include *Little Woman*, *Public Life*, and *Hometown Brew*. Other novels about teenagers struggling to make sense of their world are Lowry Pei's *Family Resemblances* and Lorrie Moore's *Who Will Run the Frog Hospital?*

Albert, Mimi
Skirts
Baskerville Publishers. 1994. 259 pp.

In 1961, three friends explore the tricky and dangerous beat life in New York City.

Subjects   1960s • Beat Generation • New York • Women's Friendships

Now try   Albert is also the author of *The Second Story Man: A Novel*. Joyce Johnson's *Minor Characters* is a memoir about her experiences with Jack Kerouac and other members of the beat generation.

Alberts, Laurie
Tempting Fate
Houghton Mifflin. 1987. 342 pp.

Fleeing to Vladimir, Alaska, to escape her troubled past, 20-year-old Allie finds work as a deckhand on a commercial fishing boat, believing it will fill her life with meaning.

Subjects   Alaska • Coming-of-Age • First Novels • Male/Female Relationships • Tlingits

Now try   Alberts's other novels include *Goodnight Silky Sullivan* and *The Price of Land in Shelby*. Other novels with Tlingit Indians include *Death of an Alaskan Princess* by Bridget A. Smith, *The Great Alone* by Janet Dailey, and *The Woman Who Married a Bear* by John Straley.

Allende, Isabel
The Infinite Plan
HarperCollins Publishers. 1993. 382 pp.

Gregory Reeves goes from boy to man amid the conflicting philosophies of the Baha'i faith of his mother, his father's self-proclaimed plan, and the Catholicism of the barrio in which he grows up. Translated from the Spanish by Margaret Sayers Peden.

2d Appeal   Characters   Book Groups 📖

Subjects   Catholics and Catholicism • Chilean Authors • Coming-of-Age • Interracial Relationships • Magic Realism • South American Authors

Now try   Another book in which a family is divided by religion is David James Duncan's *The Brothers K*.

Amis, Martin
The Information
Harmony Books. 1995. 374 pp.

Writer Richard Tull descends into a spiral of failure and humiliation as he fumbles through a midlife crisis and lashes out at those whose success seems to mock him.

2d Appeal   Characters   Book Groups 📖

Subjects   Book Publishing • British Authors • Middle-Aged Men • Midlife Crisis • Writers and Writing

Now try   Amis's *The Rachel Papers* has a similar, horribly hapless hero. Other accounts of hilarious book tours are found in William Kotzwinkle's *The Bear Went Over the Mountain* and Michael Chabon's *Wonder Boys*. Tibor Fischer's *Under the Frog* shares some of the bleak humor of Amis's book.

Anderson, Jim
Billarooby
Ticknor & Fields. 1988. 321 pp.

Drought and a Japanese prisoner-of-war camp force a father and son to confront the bitter secrets of the past.

2d Appeal   Characters   Book Groups 📖

Subjects   Australian Authors • Family Secrets • Fathers and Sons • First Novels • Internment Camps • World War II

Now try   J. G. Ballard's *Empire of the Sun* is another story of a young boy living through the atrocities of World War II. Ella Leffland's *Rumors of Peace* is about the effects the war has on a young girl growing up in California during the 1940s. One of the main characters in Nevil Shute's *A Town Like Alice* is an Australian prisoner of war.

Ansa, Tina McElroy
Baby of the Family
Harcourt Brace Jovanovich. 1989. 265 pp.

African American Lena, the baby of the family, who was born with a caul, grapples with the complications it causes as she grows up.

2d Appeal   Characters

Subjects   1950s • African American Authors • African Americans • Coming-of-Age • Family Relationships • First Novels • Georgia

Now try   Ansa wrote a sequel to this novel called *The Hand I Fan With*. Her novel *Ugly Ways* is about three daughters preparing for their mother's funeral. Other novels about African Americans include Erika Ellis's *Good Fences*, Diane McKinney-Whetstone's *Tumbling*, and Omar Tyree's *Single Mom*.

Ansay, A. Manette
Vinegar Hill
Viking. 1994. 240 pp.

Ellen finds life unbearable for herself and her two children when her husband loses his job and the family moves in with her in-laws, a home dominated by James's father, a cruel and vindictive religious fanatic.

Book Groups 📖

Subjects   1970s • Domestic Violence • Family Relationships • First Novels • Religious Extremism • Small-Town Life

Now try   Roddy Doyle's *The Woman Who Walked Into Doors* and Susan Brownmiller's *Waverly Place* are other novels about abusive relationships. Janette Turner Hospital's *Oyster* is a chilling portrait of religious fanaticism in a small Australian outback town.

Appel, Allan
The Rabbi of Casino Boulevard
St. Martin's Press. 1986. 287 pp.

When he falls in love with a Japanese woman, Rabbi Arthur Bloom brings good luck to his congregation of gamblers, who spend most of their time at the Silver Dollar Casino next door to the synagogue.

Subjects   Humorous Fiction • Interracial Relationships • Jews and Judaism • Love Stories • Marriage

Now try   Appel also wrote *High Holiday Sutra: A Novel*. Other novels about rabbis include Herbert Tarr's *The Conversion of Chaplain Cohen*, Alan Cheuse's *Grandmother's Club*, *The Outsider* by Howard Fast, *God's Ear* by Rhoda Lerman, and *The Rabbi of Lud* by Stanley Elkin.

Appleman, Philip
Apes and Angels
Putnam. 1989. 269 pp.

In 1941, the looming world war irrevocably alters the lives of a varied group of Kenton, Indiana, residents, including high school junior Paul Anderson, the town's doctor Tom Roberts, biology teacher Elaine Edelman, and the Reverend Tucker.

2d Appeal   Characters

Subjects   1940s • Coming-of-Age • Indiana • Small-Town Life • Teenage Boys • World War II

Now try   Appleman also wrote *In the Twelfth Year of the War: A Novel* and several collections of poetry, including *Darwin's Ark* and *Let There Be Light*. *Rumors of Peace* by Ella Leffland and J. G. Ballard's *Empire of the Sun* are both coming-of-age novels set during the same time period.

Appleton, Janet
That Summer
Viking. 1989. 322 pp.

Naïve and sheltered 18-year-old Ann Merrill spends her last summer before college working in Boston at a used bookstore and experiencing first love amid the complications of friendship with an unstable housemate.

Subjects 1950s • Bookstores • Coming-of-Age • First Novels • Love Stories • Suicide • Teenage Girls

Now try *Greensleeves* by Eloise McGraw is a young adult novel about the first time a young woman lives on her own and falls in love. Other coming-of-age tales set in Boston include Kelly Dwyer's *The Tracks of Angels* and *The Very Rich Hours* by Jean McGarry.

Arnold, Janis
Excuse Me for Asking
Algonquin Books of Chapel Hill. 1994. 351 pp.

Although they seem to have nothing in common, their 20-year friendship allows Julia and Robin the opportunity to share their dreams and disappointments.

Subjects Family Relationships • Small-Town Life • Texas • Women's Friendships

Now try Arnold's first novel was *Daughters of Memory*. Like Arnold, Shelby Hearon frequently sets her novels, such as *The Second Dune*, in small Texas towns. Jill McCorkle's short story collection, *Crash Diet*, and Susan Kelly's *How Close We Come* are written in the same style as Arnold's novel.

Arthur, Elizabeth
Binding Spell
Doubleday. 1988. 372 pp.

When two Russian professors come to a small Indiana college, a local farmer fixates on the belief that they are part of a conspiracy of bankers to foreclose farms in the area.

Subjects Academia • Dogs • Humorous Fiction • Indiana • Love Stories • Magic • Small-Town Life

Now try Some of the best characters in this book are dogs. There is also a wonderful dog in Jon Cohen's *The Man in the Window*. The Russian professors' use of English is similar to the speech of the illegal alien in John Welter's *I Want to Buy a Vowel*.

Atlas, James
The Great Pretender
Penguin Books. 1986. 277 pp.

As he makes his way through the 1960s from his suburban Chicago high school to Harvard and on to graduate studies at Oxford, Ben Janis continues to lust after girls and the literary life.

2d Appeal Characters

Subjects 1960s • Chicago • Coming-of-Age • First Novels • Jews and Judaism • Oxford University • Writers and Writing

Now try   Atlas is also the author of a biography, ***Delmore Schwartz: The Life of an American Poet***. ***Dead Languages*** by David Shields is another autobiographical coming-of-age novel. Philip Roth's novels (***Portnoy's Complaint*** and others), echo the Jewish themes in Atlas's book. For much more about life in British academia, try the novels of Malcolm Bradbury (***The History Man***) and David Lodge (***Changing Places*** and others).

Auster, Paul
The Music of Chance   Viking. 1990. 217 pp.

When his long-absent father dies, Jim Nashe discovers the unexpected consequences of reckless adventuring and seemingly endless money.

2d Appeal   Language   Book Groups 📖

Subjects   Coming-of-Age • Gambling • Road Novels

Now try   Auster's other books include ***In the Country of Last Things***, ***Moon Palace***, and ***City of Glass***. ***The Music of Chance*** has hints of Tim O'Brien's ***In the Lake of the Woods*** and Sara Maitland's ***Ancestral Truths***, which both have mysteries that are never solved. Siri Hustvedt's ***The Blindfold*** is also about the difficulties of distinguishing between fact and fiction.

Babcock, Richard
Martha Calhoun   Random House. 1988. 310 pp.

With an unconventional mother and a brother who is a juvenile delinquent, 16-year-old Martha is already an outsider in Katydid, Illinois, even before she is arrested on a morals charge and sent to a foster home.

Subjects   1950s • Coming-of-Age • First Novels • Foster Children • Illinois • Juvenile Delinquents • Mothers and Daughters • Small-Town Life • Teenage Girls

Now try   Lowry Pei's ***Family Resemblances*** is another novel about an adolescent girl written by a male writer. Pamela Conrad's ***Pumpkin Moon*** and Tom McNeal's ***Goodnight, Nebraska*** are both about troubled adolescents.

Bache, Ellyn
Safe Passage   Crown. 1988. 234 pp.

In 1983, Percival Singer's parents and six brothers all wait anxiously to learn if he survived the bombing of the Marine headquarters in Beirut, Lebanon.

2d Appeal   Characters

Subjects   Brothers • Family Relationships • First Novels • Mothers and Sons

Now try   Bache also wrote ***The Activist's Daughter*** and ***The Value of Kindness: Stories***. ***Affliction*** by Russell Banks, Frederick Barthelme's ***Brothers***, David James Duncan's ***The Brothers K***, and ***The Paperboy*** by Pete Dexter are also about the complicated relationships between brothers.

Baker, Larry
The Flamingo Rising
Knopf. 1997. 309 pp.

The Flamingo Drive-In Theatre is the scene of Abraham Lee's drastic attempts to make peace between his own irascible father and their nearest neighbor, funeral home owner Turner Lee, who also happens to be the father of Grace, Abe's first and only love.

2d Appeal   Characters   Book Groups 📖

Subjects   Coming-of-Age • Family Relationships • Fathers and Sons • First Novels • Florida • Love Stories • Male/Female Relationships

Now try   John Irving's ***The World According to Garp*** and ***A Widow for One Year***, as well as his other novels, have the same mixture of humor and poignancy as Baker's novel. Another pair of lovers whose families are enemies can be found in Shakespeare's "Romeo and Juliet," although their fate is less happy than that of Baker's pair.

Baker, Sharlene
Finding Signs
Knopf. 1990. 241 pp.

Crisscrossing the United States on her way to meet her boyfriend Al, Brenda discovers that love isn't always where and what we expect it to be.

Subjects   1970s • First Novels • Hitchhiking • Love Stories • Road Novels

Now try   Cathryn Alpert's ***Rocket City*** and Simon Mawer's ***Mendel's Dwarf*** are both about the unpredictability of love.

Baldwin, William
The Hard to Catch Mercy
Algonquin Books of Chapel Hill. 1993. 451 pp.

In the winter of 1916, life changes forever for 14-year-old Willie T. Allson after his grandpa hires a legendary swamp man, the Hard to Catch Mercy, to rescue the family's milk cows from a South Carolina coastal marsh.

2d Appeal   Characters

Subjects   Coming-of-Age • Family Relationships • First Novels • Humorous Fiction • South Carolina • Southern Authors • World War I

Now try   Baldwin also wrote another humorous novel, ***The Fennel Family Papers***. ***The Hard to Catch Mercy*** combines the Southern charm of Olive Ann Burns's ***Cold Sassy Tree*** with the black humor of Lewis Nordan's novels (***Wolf Whistle*** and others) and the unrelenting menace of Robert McCammon's ***Boy's Life***.

Barnard, Josie
Poker Face
Virago. 1996. 174 pp.

Allie tries to hold the family together when her mother walks out of their remote Yorkshire house, abandoning elementary-school-age Allie, her distracted father, and her two younger siblings.

Subjects   British Authors • England • First Novels • Mothers Deserting Their Families • Single Parents • Small-Town Life

Now try   Allie's soldiering on through a difficult childhood is reminiscent of the struggle Frank McCourt describes in his memoir, *Angela's Ashes*, although their difficult childhoods are difficult in different ways. *Twopence to Cross the Mersey* by Helen Forrester is another novel of a childhood beset by poverty. *Poker Face* won the Betty Trask Award.

Bartolomeo, Christina
Cupid & Diana
Scribner. 1998. 222 pp.

Diana Campanella's vague dissatisfaction with her uptight lawyer boyfriend becomes intensified when she meets Harry, unhappily married and separated from his wife.

2d Appeal   Characters

Subjects   First Novels • Humorous Fiction • Love Stories • Male/Female Relationships • Sisters

Now try   Bartolomeo's novel is subtitled "A Novel About Finding the Right Man, the Right Career, and the Right Outfit." Two memoirs about women and clothes are Ilene Beckerman's *Love, Loss and What I Wore*, and Lois Gould's *Mommy Dressing*. Bartolomeo's writing style is similar to that of Cathleen Schine (*The Evolution of Jane* and others) and Caroline Preston (*Jackie by Josie*).

Bauer, Douglas
The Book of Famous Iowans
Henry Holt. 1997. 246 pp.

From his adult perspective, Will Vaughn looks back on his mother's scandalous love affair with Bobby Markum, the star of the local baseball team, and realizes that he has never successfully gotten over her desertion of the family.

2d Appeal   Characters   Book Groups 📖

Subjects   1940s • Adultery • Divorce • Family Relationships • Iowa • Marriage • Midlife Crisis • Mothers Deserting Their Families • Small-Town Life

Now try   Bauer's first novel was *Dexterity*, the story of a woman who leaves her husband. The restrained tone of this novel resembles *In the Deep Midwinter* by Robert Clark.

Bawden, Nina
Circles of Deceit
St. Martin's Press. 1987. 189 pp.

Deceptions, large and small, characterize the life of the unnamed narrator, a painter who makes a living copying great works of art, and the four women in his life: his mother, his aunt, and his first and second wives.

2d Appeal   Characters

Subjects   Adultery • Art and Artists • British Authors • Fathers and Sons • Male/Female Relationships

Now try   Among Bawden's many other novels are *Tortoise by Candlelight* and *Family Money*. The theme of this novel—that everyone practices deceptions—is similar to Margot Livesey's *Criminals*, in which she examines how lives are filled with criminal acts, great and small. Bawden's use of irony in a deceptively simple story is similar to Muriel Spark's *The Abbess of Crewe* and other works of fiction. The main character in Louis Buss's *The Luxury of Exile* produces fake antiques. Fay Weldon's *Life Force* is also about a group of women whose lives circle around one man.

Baxter, Charles
First Light
Viking. 1987. 286 pp.

As adults, Hugh (a car salesman) and his sister Dorsey (an astrophysicist) realize that their shared childhood both bound them together and created an unbridgeable chasm between them.

2d Appeal Characters

    Subjects Brothers and Sisters • Business and Businessmen • Dysfunctional Families • First Novels • Science and Scientists • Women Scientists

    Now try Baxter is also the author of ***Burning Down the House: Essays of Fiction***, as well as other novels, including ***Shadow Play***. Another novel that begins in the present and gradually uncovers the past is ***The Grass Dancer*** by Susan Power. Chet Raymo's ***The Dork of Cork*** features another character who, like Dorsey in ***First Light***, is fascinated with the sky.

Benedict, Helen
Bad Angel
Dutton. 1996. 293 pp.

Fifteen-year-old Dominican American Bianca Diaz; Theresa, her mother; and Robert, a young suitor, all struggle to survive in New York's roughest neighborhoods while trying to decide the fate of Bianca's unwanted baby.

2d Appeal Characters   Book Groups 📖

    Subjects Adoption • Dominican Americans • Ghetto Life • Mothers and Daughters • New York • Poverty • Single Parents • Teenage Pregnancy

    Now try Benedict's first novel was ***A World Like This***. Lois-Ann Yamanaka's ***Blu's Hanging*** is also about difficult decisions that a troubled teenager must make. In Avra Wing's ***Angie, I Says*** the main character has to decide what to do when she becomes pregnant and gives birth to a deformed child.

Bennett, James Gordon
My Father's Geisha
Delacorte Press. 1990. 165 pp.

Army brats Teddy and Cora are dragged unwillingly into the middle of their parents' disintegrating marriage when their war-hero father's infidelity becomes obvious.

2d Appeal Characters

    Subjects Adultery • Brothers and Sisters • Dysfunctional Families • Family Relationships • First Novels • Southern Authors

    Now try Teddy and Cora's relationship is similar to the relationship of the siblings in ***Dead Languages*** by David Shields and those found in Peter Hedges's ***An Ocean in Iowa***.

Bergen, David
A Year of Lesser
HarperCollins. 1996. 215 pp.

A year in the life of Lesser, a small Canadian town, as experienced by Johnny Fehr, his wife Charlene, and his pregnant mistress, Loraine.

2d Appeal Characters   Book Groups 📖

Subjects   Adultery • Canada • Canadian Authors • First Novels • Male/Female Relationships • Single Parents • Small-Town Life

Now try   Bergen has also published a collection of short stories, *Sitting Opposite My Brother*. Small-town life is also nicely evoked in Judy Troy's *West of Venus*, Jonis Agee's *South of Resurrection*, and Tom Drury's *The End of Vandalism*.

Berger, John
To the Wedding
Pantheon Books. 1995. 202 pp.

Events leading up to the marriage of Gino, an Italian peddler, and Ninon, his French sweetheart, are described by Tsobanakos, a blind vendor of religious tokens, and relived through the eyes of Ninon's parents, as they each travel from their homes in France and Bratislava to attend the wedding.

2d Appeal   Characters

Subjects   AIDS • British Authors • Italy • Love Stories • Marriage • Weddings • Women with AIDS

Now try   Louis Begley's *As Max Saw It* is another well-written novel about AIDS and intimate relationships. Rebecca Brown's *The Gifts of the Body* is about people with AIDS and the caretaker who visits them regularly.

Berger, Thomas
Meeting Evil
Little, Brown. 1992. 220 pp.

When suburban real estate agent and all-around-good-guy John Felton unwittingly comes to the aid of a homicidal sociopath, he finds himself swept up in a nightmarish crime spree that pits goodness against evil.

Subjects   Business and Businessmen • Crime • Good vs. Evil • Suburbia

Now try   Berger's other novels (including *The Houseguest*, *The Feud*, and *Neighbors*) are suspenseful accounts of moral dilemmas, as are the novels by Patricia Highsmith, including *Strangers on a Train* and *Ripley Under Ground* (and other Ripley novels). Iris Murdoch's novel, *A Fairly Honorable Defeat*, is also about good versus evil.

Bergland, Martha
A Farm Under a Lake
Graywolf Press. 1989. 199 pp.

While driving an Alzheimer's patient to her new home, nurse Janet Hawn also journeys through her own memories to save her husband from drowning in his lost dreams.

2d Appeal   Story
Book Groups 📖

Subjects   Alzheimer's Disease • Farms and Farm Life • First Novels • Marriage • Nurses

Now try   Two novels that share Bergland's lyrical writing style are Marilynne Robinson's *Housekeeping* and Harriet Doerr's *Stones for Ibarra*. Jane Smiley's *A Thousand Acres* and Jane Hamilton's *A Map of the World* are both set on Midwestern farms.

Bird, Sarah

Alamo House: Women Without Men, Men Without Brains

W.W. Norton. 1986. 317 pp.

At 27, Mary Jo finds a cheap rental and good friends among a collection of odd and talented women, as they humorously cope with communal living, boyfriends, girl-friends, meaningless jobs, school, and the outrageous behavior of the fraternity boys across the street.

Subjects   First Novels • Humorous Fiction • Southern Authors • Women's Friendships

Now try   Sarah Bird's other quirky novels include *The Boyfriend School*, *Virgin of the Rodeo*, *and The Mommy Club*. Fannie Flagg's *Fried Green To-matoes at the Whistle Stop Café* is another very funny novel set in the South.

Black, Baxter

Hey, Cowboy, Wanna Get Lucky?

Crown Publishers. 1994. 323 pp.

Complications abound when cowboy Cody falls in love and his pal Lick is an odds-on favorite to win at the National Finals Rodeo, but it takes a guardian angel named Pinto—who normally resides in a can of Copenhagen chewing tobacco—to make sure events proceed as the friends desire.

Subjects   Cowboys • First Novels • Humorous Fiction • Magic Realism • Men's Friendships • Rodeos

Now try   Black is a commentator on National Public Radio, a large-animal veteri-narian, and a poet. This novel does for the rodeo world what Dan Jenkins's *Semi-Tough* did for football. Another, less humorous portrait of rodeo life is found in Larry McMurtry's *Moving On*.

Blackaby, Mark

You'll Never Be Here Again

Gollancz. 1994. 331 pp.

Paul Richmond muses on the 10 years since his graduation from Oxford and the events—tragic and funny—that happened during the months he spent living in a posh flat in London with his friend David and David's various girlfriends.

Subjects   British Authors • Coming-of-Age • First Novels • Love Stories • Men's Friendships • Oxford University

Now try   Blackaby's description of a young man drifting through life brings to mind characters that Stephen McCauley has created in *The Object of My Affection*, *The Easy Way Out*, and *The Man of the House*. The mixture of poignancy and humor found in this novel can also be found in Jane Gardam's *Bilgewater* and *A Long Way from Verona*. *You'll Never Be Here Again* won the Betty Trask Award.

Blanchard, Stephen

Gagarin & I

Chatto & Windus. 1995. 249 pp.

Despite suffering from a rare disease, teenage Leonard's life is enlivened by his all-consuming interest in Yuri Gagarin's space flight and the eccentric lodgers in the boarding house run by his always-feuding mother and aunt.

Subjects   1960s • British Authors • First Novels • Illness • Teenage Boys

Now try   The hero of Chet Raymo's *The Dork of Cork* also finds his difficult life eased by studying the night sky.

Bohjalian, Chris
Water Witches
University Press of New England. 1995. 340 pp.

Environmentalists clash with developers during a long drought in Vermont, and attorney Scottie Winston is caught between the pro-development company his firm represents and his sister-in-law's ability to dowse for water, a gift his daughter seems to share.

2d Appeal   Characters   Book Groups 📖

   Subjects   Ecofiction • Family Relationships • Fathers and Daughters • Law and Lawyers • Vermont

   Now try   Bohjalian's novel, *Midwives*, also explores a moral dilemma, as does Jonathan Dee's *The Liberty Campaign*. Other novels about the resistance to land development include Thea Astley's *Vanishing Points*, Nat Brandt's *Land Kills*, amd Don Metz's *King of the Mountain*.

Bosworth, Sheila
Almost Innocent
Simon and Schuster. 1984. 268 pp.

As wealthy, manipulative Uncle Baby Brother wreaks havoc with the marriage of an aristocratic yet impoverished New Orleans couple, their helplessly mesmerized young daughter looks on.

2d Appeal   Characters   Book Groups 📖

   Subjects   Coming-of-Age • Dysfunctional Families • First Novels • Marriage • New Orleans • Southern Authors • Upper Classes

   Now try   Another of Bosworth's novels is *Slow Poison*. Rebecca Wells's *Divine Secrets of the Ya-Ya Sisterhood* and *Little Altars Everywhere* convey a sense of Southern life similar to that of Bosworth's. Another novel set in New Orleans is Nancy Lemann's *The Lives of the Saints*.

Bowen, John
The Girls: A Story of Village Life
H. Hamilton. 1986. 182 pp.

Two aging lesbians must cope with their lackluster business, impending motherhood, and a dead body in their septic tank.

2d Appeal   Characters

   Subjects   British Authors • Lesbians • Small-Town Life • Women's Friendships

   Now try   The eccentric characters and humor found in Bowen's novel are reminiscent of Anne Tyler's many novels, including *A Slipping-Down Life* and *Morgan's Passing*, although this is not a plot Tyler would use. Bowen's style of writing is similar to that of Mary Wesley in *Jumping the Queue*.

Bradley, John Ed
Tupelo Nights
Atlantic Monthly Press. 1988. 239 pp.

Coming home to Old Field, Louisiana, after graduating from college (where he starred on the football team), John Girlie tries to make peace with the long-ago disappearance of his father, his mother's inappropriate behavior, his best friend's dependence on alcohol and drugs, and his love for an older woman.

2d Appeal   Characters   Book Groups 📖

Subjects   Brothers • Dysfunctional Families • First Novels • Incest; Louisiana • Mothers and Sons • Older Women/Younger Men • Small-Town Life • Southern Authors

Now try   Bradley's other books include *The Best There Ever Was* and *Love and Obits*. Incest is the subject of Gina Berriault's novel, *The Son*. The decayed and decaying South described in Bradley's book is also the setting for Nancy Lemann's *The Lives of the Saints*.

Brainard, Cecilia Manguerra
When the Rainbow Goddess Wept
Dutton. 1994. 216 pp.

Nine-year-old Yvonne tells the story of her family's flight from their comfortable home to a guerrilla camp in the jungles of the Philippines when the Japanese invade her country during World War II.

Subjects   Coming-of-Age • First Novels • Japan • Philippines • World War II

Now try   Brainard mixes in Filipino myths and legends with her autobiographical narrative in much the same way that Maxine Hong Kingston does in *The Woman Warrior* and Heinz Insu Fenkl does in *Memories of My Ghost Brother*.

Breasted, Mary
Why Should You Doubt Me Now?
Farrar, Straus Giroux. 1993. 279 pp.

The announcement that the first woman vice president of the United States is coming to Ireland for a state visit sets off various events, including a demonstration by the Irish Unemployed Feminists and appearances by the Virgin Mary in places as diverse as a garage, a pub, and a Protestant's kitchen.

Subjects   Ireland • Irish Authors • Satirical Fiction

Now try   Breasted also wrote *I Shouldn't Be Telling You This*. John McGahern's *Collected Stories* offer other views of Irish life. There is another unusual occurrence in Nina Fitzpatrick's *The Loves of Faustyna*.

Bringle, Mary
True Confessions: The Novel
Donald I. Fine Books. 1996. 233 pp.

Grace Peacock's life, complicated by her ex-husbands, her creative writing students, and an overly attentive mother, is redeemed by her fantasy of someday being the heroine of a story in a romance magazine.

2d Appeal   Characters   Book Groups 📖

Subjects   Divorce • Humorous Fiction • Male/Female Relationships • Mothers and Daughters • New York • Writers and Writing

Now try   This wry and funny novel is similar in tone to Bringle's earlier book *Hacks at Lunch: A Novel of the Literary Life*. The heroine of Anita Brookner's *Hotel du Lac* is also an author of romance novels.

Brink, Andre
Imaginings of Sand   Harcourt Brace & Co. 1996. 352 pp.

After tending her dying grandmother and listening to her stories about the family's Boer heritage, expatriate Kristien Muller must decide whether or not she will stay on in South Africa.

Subjects   Apartheid • Grandparents • Magic Realism • South Africa • South African Authors

Now try   Brink fuses politics with family in his novel *A Dry White Season*. Another rebellious young South African woman can be found in Lynn Freed's *Home Ground*.

Brook, Rhidian
The Testimony of Taliesin Jones   Flamingo. 1997. 200 pp.

When his mother runs away with her hairdresser, 11-year-old Taliesin tries to focus instead on the existence of God, his proliferation of warts, and on establishing a street gang of healers.

Subjects   Coming-of-Age • Divorce • First Novels • Mothers Deserting Their Families • Small-Town Life • Welsh Authors

Now try   Eli Gottlieb's *The Boy Who Went Away*, John Nichols's *The Wizard of Loneliness*, and Seamus Deane's *Reading in the Dark* are other examples of children trying to understand the mysterious world of adulthood. Another child with an interest in religion is Charlotte in Patty Dann's *Mermaids*.

Brown, Rosellen
Before and After   Farrar, Straus Giroux. 1992. 354 pp.

The parents of a New Hampshire teenager who killed his girlfriend are forced to examine their own relationship as well as the moral principles they hold dear.

2d Appeal   Characters   Book Groups ▢

Subjects   ALA Notable Books • Death of a Child • Family Relationships • Murder • New Hampshire • Teenage Boys

Now try   Among Brown's other novels is *Tender Mercies*. Nadine Gordimer's *The House Gun* is another novel that explores how a family is affected when a child is accused of murder. The well-drawn family relationships found in *Before and After* can also be found in Sue Miller's *Inventing the Abbotts, and Other Stories* (as well as in her novels) and Chris Bohjalian's *Midwives*.

Buchan, James
A Parish of Rich Women   Hamilton. 1984. 185 pp.

Traveling between Europe and the Middle East, Arabist scholar Adam Murray compares the decadent London he experiences with his drink- and-drug-addicted friends to his life in war-torn Lebanon, where even the simplest acts of love and kindness are overwhelmed by the constant threat of death.

Subjects   1980s • Beirut, Lebanon • British Authors • First Novels • London • Men's Friendships • Writers and Writing

Now try   Buchan is also the author of ***High Latitudes*** (a novel) and ***Frozen Desire: The Meaning of Money***. John le Carre's ***Little Drummer Girl*** (which is also set in the Middle East) and John Banville's ***The Untouchable*** are both infused with the same sort of moral ambiguities found here. Buchan's novel won the Whitbread Prize for First Novels and the Betty Trask Award.

Bunkley, Anita
Wild Embers
Dutton. 1995. 386 pp.

Janelle, one of the first black registered nurses in the Army during World War II, experiences first hand the racial prejudice of the segregated South.

Subjects   African Americans • African American Authors • Interracial Relationships • Male/Female Relationships • Nurses • Race Relations • Racism • World War II

Now try   ***The Starlight Passage*** and ***Black Gold*** are other novels by Bunkley. Harper Lee's ***To Kill a Mockingbird*** is set around a highly charged racial incident in the South, as is Lewis Nordan's ***Wolf Whistle***. Another novel about an African American nurse is Steven Corbin's ***No Easy Place to Be***.

Burns, Olive Ann
Cold Sassy Tree
Ticknor & Fields. 1984. 391 pp.

Will Tweedy chronicles the scandal that occurs when his newly widowed grandfather elopes with the young shop assistant from his general store in a small town in Georgia in 1906.

2d Appeal   Characters

Subjects   Coming-of-Age • First Novels • Georgia • Older Men/Younger Women • Small-Town Life • Southern Authors • Widowers

Now try   William Faulkner's ***The Reivers***, Clyde Edgerton's ***Raney***, and Mark Childress's ***Crazy in Alabama*** all share with Burns an intensely evoked Southern setting. ***Leaving Cold Sassy***, left unfinished when Burns died, is about Will's life through World War I. In ***The Optimist's Daughter***, Eudora Welty describes the reactions of his family and friends when a retired judge marries a woman not only much younger than he but also clearly from a much lower social class. Michael Malone's ***Handling Sin*** is the very funny story of a grown man whose father escapes from a hospital and runs off in a yellow convertible with a young woman.

Burroway, Janet
Opening Nights
Atheneum. 1985. 305 pp.

During the rehearsals of her ex-husband's play—which comes to a comically tragic end—costume designer Shaara Soole becomes a reluctant ally of Boyd's new and much younger wife, Wendy.

2d Appeal   Characters

Subjects   Actors and Acting • Divorce • Marriage • Older Men/Younger Women • Remarriage • Theater • Women's Friendships

Now try   Burroway's *Raw Silk* is about a woman finding herself in the midst of a disintegrating marriage. Margaret Drabble (*The Garrick Year* and others) shares with Burroway an ability to fully evoke a woman's life. Michael Frayn's "Noises Off" is a very funny play about putting on a play.

Bushell, Agnes
Local Deities
Curbstone Press. 1990. 306 pp.

Two couples—Erika and Simon and Annie and Paul—face the turmoil of the 1960s in very different ways: Erika and Simon work within the existing political system to make it better while Annie and Paul go underground as a result of their radical activities.

Subjects   1960s • First Novels • Husbands and Wives • Political Fiction • Women's Friendships

Now try   The choices that the two women in this novel face are similar to those Marge Piercy's main character deals with in her novel, *Vida*.

Buss, Louis
The Luxury of Exile
J. Cape. 1997. 278 pp.

When Claude Wooldbridge, a more-than-slightly-crooked antiques dealer, discovers letters hinting at a scandal about the poet Byron, his hunt for the truth threatens his marriage, his career, and his relationships with friends.

Subjects   Adultery • British Authors • Business and Businessmen • Byron, George Gordon • First Novels • Incest • Marriage

Now try   Marguerite Duras's *The Lover* also describes the sexual relationship between a young woman and an older man. Another crooked antique dealer can be found in Nina Bawden's *Circles of Deceit*. *The Luxury of Exile* won the Betty Trask Award.

Buttenwieser, Paul
Free Association
Little, Brown. 1981. 239 pp.

Twenty-seven-year-old psychiatrist Roger Liebman finds that his own problems with life and love are the same as those he hears about from his patients.

Subjects   First Novels • Humorous Fiction • Love Stories • Male/Female Relationships • Psychiatrists, Psychoanalysts, Psychotherapists

Now try   Samuel Shem's novels, *Fine* and *Mount Misery*, are also about young psychiatrists, although *Mount Misery* is a much darker story than either of the others.

Cady, Jack
Inagehi
Broken Moon Press. 1994. 258 pp.

When Harriett Johnson returns home to North Carolina to unravel the mystery surrounding her father's murder seven years before, she rediscovers her American Indian heritage and ties to the Cherokee community.

Book Groups 📖

Subjects   American Indians; Cherokees; Culture Clash; Magic Realism; Murder; North Carolina

Now try Cady has also written fantasy and horror fiction, including *The Off-Seasons*. *Snow Falling on Cedars* by David Guterson is another book that is a murder mystery set within the framework of the clash of different cultures. For insights into contemporary American Indian culture, read Joseph Bruchac's *Aniyunwiya/Real Human Beings: An Anthology of Contemporary Prose*.

Campbell, Bebe Moore
Brothers and Sisters
Putnam's. 1994. 476 pp.

After the Los Angeles riots following the beating of Rodney King, two ambitious bankers, African American Esther and white Mallory learn, as their friendship develops, that surface differences are less important than shared values, hopes, and fears.

2d Appeal Characters   Book Groups 📖

Subjects 1990s • African American Authors • African Americans • Career Women • Interracial Relationships • Los Angeles • Race Relations • Racism • Women's Friendships

Now try Campbell's memoir, *Sweet Summer: Growing Up With and Without My Dad*, also reflects her interest in the subject of race relations. Her other novels include *Singing in the Comeback Choir* and *Your Blues Ain't Like Mine*. Ken Alder's *The White Bus* is another novel about friendships that cross racial boundaries.

Carkeet, David
The Error of Our Ways
Henry Holt. 1997. 320 pp.

Unemployed linguist Jeremy Cook and hotshot businessman Ben Hudnutt (the Nut King of St. Louis) find their lives increasingly entangled when Jeremy begins a research project using Hudnutt's youngest daughter as a subject and falls for Hudnutt's wife.

2d Appeal Characters

Subjects Adultery • Business and Businessmen • Humorous Fiction • Linguists • Marriage • Missouri • St. Louis, Missouri

Now try Carkeet's first two novels are *Double Negative* and *The Full Catastrophe*, both of which also feature Jeremy Cook. Jeremy Cook's character bears a resemblance to Hank Devereaux, Jr., the main character of Richard Russo's *Straight Man*. Like Mia in Marian Thurm's novel, *Walking Distance*, Molly, the child with whom Jeremy is working, nearly steals the novel from the adult characters.

Carpenter, William
A Keeper of Sheep
Milkweed Editions. 1994. 327 pp.

After Dartmouth freshman Penelope (Penguin) Solstice is expelled from college, she gets a job caring for a composer struggling to complete his last work while dying of AIDS.

2d Appeal Characters   Book Groups 📖

Subjects AIDS • Fathers and Daughters • First Novels • Gay Men • Music and Musicians

Now try Caring for AIDS patients is the subject of Rebecca Brown's *The Gifts of the Body*. Other novels that use different type styles for emphasis include Arundhati Roy's *The God of Small Things* and Wilton Barnhardt's *Emma Who Saved My Life*.

Chace, Susan
Intimacy
Random House. 1989. 161 pp.

Weaving a life from broken threads—warring Jewish and Catholic parents, alcoholism, faltering political idealism, adultery, divorce, an estranged son, mental illness, and domestic violence—Cecilia holds fast to her fragmented identity and struggles forward, gaining momentum as a survivor.

Subjects Adultery • Alcoholics and Alcoholism • Domestic Violence • Dysfunctional Families • Family Relationships • First Novels • Mental Illness • Women's Lives

Now try Chace also wrote the novel *You Will Learn to Love Me*. *She's Come Undone* by Wally Lamb is about a woman's struggle for identity amidst an untold number of adversities.

Chernoff, Maxine
Plain Grief
Summit Books. 1991. 222 pp.

While tracking down her runaway teenage daughter and niece in Los Angeles, Sarah recalls the history of her failing marriage, her relationship with her sister, her father's recent death, and her growing love for Jeremy, an American Indian.

Subjects Adultery • American Indians • Family Relationships • First Novels • Interracial Relationships • Mothers and Daughters • Runaways • Teenage Girls

Now try Chernoff's other books include *Bop*, a collection of stories, a novel, *American Heaven*, and several books of poetry, including *Leap Year Day: New and Selected Poems* and *A Vegetable Emergency*. Chernoff's talent for telling a good story is also found in Hilma Wolitzer's *In the Palomar Arms*.

Cleage, Pearl
What Looks Like Crazy on an Ordinary Day
Avon Books. 1997. 244 pp.

When Ava Johnson is diagnosed HIV positive, she returns home and begins to help her older sister Joyce teach the young black women in their small Michigan town survival skills in a dangerous world, all the while falling in love with Wild Eddie, a man with a background of violence. An Oprah selection.

2d Appeal Characters

Subjects African American Authors • African Americans • AIDS • First Novels • Love Stories • Male/Female Relationships • Sisters • Small-Town Life • Women with AIDS

Now try Cleage is best known as a playwright whose plays include "Blues for an Alabama Sky" and "Flying West." Although Toni Morrison's *Paradise* has a very different plot from Cleage's novel, they share a setting: an all-black town.

Cohen, Leah Hager

Heat Lightning
Avon Books. 1997. 326 pp.

Sisters Tilly and Mole have become inseparable during the nine years they have lived with their Aunt Hy following the mysterious drowning death of their parents, but now 11-year-old Mole finds her relationship with 12-year-old Tilly threatened by Tilly's growing independence and her involvement with a neighboring family.

2d Appeal   Characters   Book Groups 📖

Subjects   Coming-of-Age • First Novels • Orphans • Sisters • Teenage Girls

Now try   Cohen is also the author of *Train Go Sorry: Inside a Deaf World* and *Glass, Paper, Beans*. This novel is close in tone to Marilynne Robinson's *Housekeeping*. Other novels about sisters include Alice Hoffman's *Practical Magic*, Karin Cook's *What Girls Learn*, and Barbara Kingsolver's *Animal Dreams*.

Corey, Deborah Joy

Losing Eddie
Algonquin Books of Chapel Hill. 1993. 222 pp.

A rural New Brunswick family struggles after the death of their eldest child, while nine-year-old Laura watches and listens and comes to an understanding far beyond her years.

Subjects   Brothers and Sisters • Canada • Canadian Authors • Death of a Child • First Novels

Now try   Other novels that explore the effect a son's or daughter's death has on other family members include Anne Tyler's *The Tin Can Tree*, Luanne Rice's *Homefires*, Jane Hamilton's *The Short History of a Prince*, and Linda Gray Sexton's *Points of Light*.

Corman, Avery

The Old Neighborhood
Linden Press/Simon & Schuster. 1980. 219 pp.

With his marriage falling apart and his job uninspiring, successful advertising executive, middle-aged Steve Ross returns to his childhood neighborhood in the Bronx.

2d Appeal   Characters

Subjects   1970s • Bronx, New York • Business and Businessmen • Male/Female Relationships • Marriage • Middle-Aged Men • Midlife Crisis

Now try   Corman's other novels include *Kramer vs. Kramer* and *Oh, God!* Sloan Wilson's *The Man in the Grey Flannel Suit* is a far less upbeat account of a man's midlife crisis.

Coupland, Douglas

Microserfs
HarperCollins. 1995. 371 pp.

Dan Underwood and his housemates spend their days and nights as slaves to the software industry—breaking from work only occasionally to consume junk food and contemplate pop culture—but when they begin to search for some meaning in their lives, they enter unfamiliar emotional territory.

2d Appeal   Characters

Subjects   1990s • Family Relationships • Friendship • Generation X • Male/Female Relationships

Now try   Coupland's other books include *Life After God*, *Shampoo Planet*, *Generation X*, and *Girlfriend in a Coma*. Nick Hornby's *High Fidelity* and Andrew McGahan's *1988* are other books about life and love from a Generation X point of view. Julio Cortazar's *Hopscotch* is another novel about alienation and existential dilemmas.

Currey, Richard
Lost Highway
Houghton Mifflin Co. 1997. 258 pp.

In the years between World War II and the Vietnam era, banjo player Sapper Reeves and two friends try to make it in the country music business, only to question whether the sacrifice involved is worth the possible gain.

Subjects   Fathers and Sons • Marriage • Men's Friendships • Music and Musicians • Vietnam War

Now try   Currey is also the author of the novel *Fatal Light*. *Come and Go*, *Molly Snow* by Mary Ann Taylor-Hall, *Big Ballad Jamboree* by Donald Davidson, Laura Watts's *Carry Me Back*, and Bill Morrissey's *Edson* are all novels about country music and musicians. Singer Woody Guthrie's autobiography, *Bound for Glory*, gives another view of a musician's life.

Dallas, Sandra
Buster Midnight's Café
Random House. 1990. 277 pp.

Best friends Whippy Bird and Effa Commander reminisce about growing up in prohibition-era Butte, Montana, and recall their involvement with two famous people: the movie star, Marion Street, and her tragic lover, boxing champion Buster Midnight.

2d Appeal   Setting

Subjects   1920s • 1930s • Cafes and Restaurants • First Novels • Montana • Women's Friendships

Now try   Dallas is also the author of *The Persian Pickle Club*, a novel about a quilting group in 1930s Kansas. Two other novels set in Montana are *The Girls from the Five Great Valleys* by Elizabeth Savage and *Rima in the Weeds* by Dierdre McNamer. Fannie Flagg's *Fried Green Tomatoes at the Whistle Stop Café* is as amusing as Dallas's novel.

Davidson, Donald
The Big Ballad Jamboree
University Press of Mississippi. 1996. 295 pp.

Country balladeer Danny MacGregor and music scholar Cissy Timberlake attempt to reclaim their relationship, their families, and Appalachian culture from the negative influences of big business and greed.

Subjects   Academia • Appalachia • First Novels • Male/Female Relationships • Music and Musicians • Small-Town Life

Now try   This novel was written in the 1950s and left unfinished until it was found in Davidson's papers 28 years after his death. *Come and Go*, *Molly Snow* by Mary Ann Taylor-Hall, Lee Smith's *The Devil's Dream*, and *Lost Highway* by Richard Currey are also about music and musicians. *She Walks These Hills*, like many of the other mysteries by Sharyn McCrumb, takes place in a lovingly depicted Appalachia.

Davis, Thulani
1959
Grove Weidenfeld. 1992. 297 pp.

In 1959, desegregation finally arrives in a small Virginia town, and 12-year-old Willie Tarrant finds her world changed forever.

2d Appeal   Setting   Book Groups 📖

Subjects   1950s • African American Authors • African Americans • Civil Rights Movement • First Novels • Race Relations • Racism • Teenage Girls • Virginia

Now try   *Maker of Saints* is another novel by Davis. A powerful nonfiction account of integration from the point of view of a young adult can be found in Melba Patillo Beals's *Warriors Don't Cry*. Other novels written from the point of view of adolescent girls include Carson McCullers's *The Member of the Wedding* and Josephine Humphreys's *Dreams of Sleep*.

Dawson, Carol
Body of Knowledge
Algonquin Books. 1994. 471 pp.

The rise and fall of one Texas family centers around the life of Victoria Grace Ransom, a reclusive woman of gargantuan proportions.

2d Appeal   Characters   Book Groups 📖

Subjects   Family Relationships • Family Secrets • Multigenerational Novels • Overweight Women • Texas

Now try   Other books by Dawson include *The Waking Spell* and *Meeting the Minotaur*. An overweight woman is one of the main characters in Jon Cohen's *The Man in the Window*. Many of Shelby Hearon's novels are set in Texas, including *Armadillo in the Grass*. *Mason's Retreat* by Christopher Tilghman is another picture of the dissolution of a family.

Del Vecchio, John
The 13th Valley
Bantam Books. 1982. 606 pp.

For James Vincent "Cherry" Chelini, participation in the war in Vietnam means fear, struggle, and friendships he never expected.

2d Appeal   Characters

Subjects   ALA Notable Books • First Novels • Men's Friendships • Vietnam War

Now try   *The 13th Valley* is the first book in a trilogy, followed by *For the Sake of All Living Things*, which deals with the Khmer Rouge and Cambodia, and *Carry Me Home*, which looks at issues veterans faced when they returned to the United States and tried to adapt to civilian life. Other novels set in Vietnam include *The Things They Carried* and *Going After Cacciato*, both by Tim O'Brien, and portions of Stewart O'Nan's *The Names of the Dead*.

Dickinson, Charles
The Widows' Adventures
Morrow. 1989. 381 pp.

Two widowed sisters drive from Chicago to California: Helene, the driver, is a blind diabetic and Ina, the navigator, is overly fond of beer.

Subjects   Road Novels • Sisters • Widows

Now try   Dickinson also wrote *Waltz in Marathon*, *With or Without and Other Stories*, and *Crows*. Pagan Kennedy's *Spinsters* is another road novel about two sisters. Other books featuring unusual car trips are Doris Betts's *Heading West* and Anne Tyler's *Earthly Possessions*.

Dixon, Melvin
Trouble the Water
Fiction Collective Two. 1989. 243 pp.

Called back from a Vermont college teaching post to his rural North Carolina childhood home following the death of the grandmother who raised him, history professor Jordon Henry confronts his family's history and struggles with death, revenge, and smoldering relationships that refuse to stay buried in the past.

2d Appeal   Setting   Book Groups 📖

Subjects   African American Authors • African Americans • College Professors • Family Relationships • Fathers and Sons • First Novels • North Carolina

Now try   Dixon's *Vanishing Rooms* is a psychological mystery. Ernest Gaines's novel, *A Lesson Before Dying*, is also about a young man called back to his childhood home at the bidding of an elderly relative.

Dixon, Stephen
Interstate
H. Holt. 1995. 374 pp.

Eight different characters, each with his or her own perspective on the tragedy, recount the drive-by shooting of a child in the back seat of her father's car.

2d Appeal   Characters   Book Groups 📖

Subjects   Death of a Child • Fathers and Daughters • Murder • Violence

Now try   Dixon is also the author of *Frog*. Russell Banks's *The Sweet Hereafter* is told from the point of view of several characters. John Burnham Schwartz's *Reservation Road*, *Violence* by Richard Bausch, *Mr. Ives' Christmas* by Oscar Hijuelos, and *The Accidental Tourist* by Anne Tyler all relate the effects of random violence on various family members.

Dodd, Susan M.
No Earthly Notion
Viking. 1986. 215 pp.

Murana Bill lovingly cares for her younger brother after the death of their parents in an automobile accident but has to struggle to maintain a sense of her own self.

Subjects   Brothers and Sisters • Coming-of-Age • Death of a Parent • First Novels • Kentucky • Orphans • Single Women

Now try   Dodd's *Old Wives' Tales* and *Hell Bent Men and Their Cities* are both collections of stories. Her novels include *Mamaw* (about the mother of outlaw Jesse James) and *The Mourners Bench*. Another novel about an older sibling caring for a younger one is Catherine Cookson's *Our John Willie*.

Donnelly, Frances
Shake Down the Stars
St. Martin's Press. 1988. 505 pp.

World War II forever changes the lives of three very different young women from a village in Suffolk, England.

Subjects British Authors • England • First Novels • Small-Town Life • Women's Friendships • World War II

Now try Other similar romantic novels include include Maeve Binchy's ***Light a Penny Candle*** and Rosamund Pilcher's ***September***. Elizabeth Jane Howard's "The Cazelet Chronicle" includes four novels that cover much of the same period as Donnelly's book.

Dooling, Richard
White Man's Grave
Farrar, Straus and Giroux. 1994. 386 pp.

Boone Westfall goes to Sierra Leone to search for his best friend, a Peace Corps volunteer who has disappeared.

2d Appeal Setting   Book Groups 📖

Subjects Africa • Men's Friendships • Satirical Fiction • Sierra Leone • West Africa

Now try Dooling's other novels, including ***Critical Care*** and ***Brain Storm***, are also satirical novels. Christopher Hope's novel ***Darkest England*** is another satirical novel contrasting a civilized country to an uncivilized one.

Dundon, Susan
To My Ex-Husband
W. Morrow & Co. 1994. 255 pp.

The lingering finale to a marriage of 20 years is explored through the letters of Emily Moore to her estranged and finally ex-husband, dealing with money, their shared past, their children, and their attempts to reconcile.

Subjects Divorce • Epistolary Novels • First Novels • Marriage

Now try Other epistolary novels include Nick Bantock's ***Griffin and Sabine: An Extraordinary Correspondence***, Elizabeth Forsythe Hailey's ***A Woman of Independent Means***, and Elizabeth Berg's ***The Pull of the Moon***.

Ellis, Erika
Good Fences
Random House. 1997. 216 pp.

When African American attorney Tom Spader moves his family to Greenwich, Connecticut, in search of the American dream, he nearly loses his family and everything he's worked for in the process.

Book Groups 📖

Subjects African American Authors • African Americans • Family Secrets • First Novels • Law and Lawyers • Suburbia • Upper Classes

Now try Another upwardly mobile African American family is described in Omar Tyree's ***Single Mom***.

Ellison, Emily
First Light
W. Morrow. 1985. 252 pp.

Schoolteacher Marcy Betters returns to Georgia to look after her mother, a religious fundamentalist and keeper of secrets, hoping to discover the truth about her dead father and beloved uncle.

Subjects   Family Secrets • First Novels • Georgia • Mothers and Daughters • Religion • Religious Extremism; Southern Authors; Teachers

Now try   Gail Godwin's *A Mother and Two Daughters* and *The Odd Woman* are also about mothers and their grown daughters. Another novel with a mother who is a religious fundamentalist is David James Duncan's *The Brothers K*. Dennis Covington's *Salvation on Sand Mountain: Snake Handling and Redemption in Southern Appalachia* is a nonfiction exploration of religious fundamentalism.

Emecheta, Buchi
The Rape of Shavi
G. Braziller. 1985. 178 pp.

A group of Europeans escaping from what they believe to be a nuclear holocaust crash their plane near a desert tribe in Africa and change the Shavi people's way of life forever.

2d Appeal   Setting

Subjects   Africa • African Authors • Culture Clash

Now try   Emecheta's other novels include *The Bride Price*, *Double Yoke*, and *The Family*. European influences on African tribes (and vice versa) is also the subject of Chinua Achebe's *Things Fall Apart* and Nadine Gordimer's *July's People*.

Erhart, Margaret
Augusta Cotton
Zoland Books. 1992. 289 pp.

Suffering from lupus is not the only problem facing 12-year-old Helen Walsh, as Augusta Cotton discovers when she learns the truth about her best friend's family.

Book Groups 📖

Subjects   1960s • Coming-of-Age • Friendship • Lupus • Teenage Girls

Now try   Thulani Davis's *1959* is another view of the world as seen through the eyes of a 12-year-old child. Totally different in theme, but equally successful in getting inside the head of an adolescent girl, are Jane Gardam's *Bilgewater* and *A Long Way from Verona*. Brian Hall's *The Saskiad* also deals with a girl's feelings about her best friend's sexuality.

Esquivel, Laura
Like Water for Chocolate
Doubleday. 1992. 245 pp.

In turn-of-the-century Mexico, the youngest daughter of wicked Mama Elena is predestined to spend her life unmarried and can only communicate her love for Pedro (her sister's husband) through a culinary sorcery that wreaks havoc upon her entire family.

2d Appeal   Characters
Book Groups 📖

Subjects   Culinary Arts • Family Relationships • First Novels • Magic Realism • Mexican Authors • Mexico • Sisters

Now try   *Like Water for Chocolate* is subtitled "A Novel in Monthly Installments with Recipes, Romances, and Home Remedies." Isak Dinesen's short story, "Babette's Feast," John Lanchester's *The Debt to Pleasure*, Lucy Ellmann's *Sweet Desserts*, Chitra Banerjee Divakaruni's *Mistress of Spices*, and *The Priest Fainted* by Catherine Temma Davidson are filled with descriptions and discussions of food.

Estaver, Paul
His Third, Her Second
Soho Press. 1989. 245 pp.

When twice divorced, 50-year-old Henry marries Margo, a widow in her 30s, their life together revolves around blending Margo's three teenagers and Henry's young daughter into one family, concerns about Henry's health, and the ordinary give and take of a couple determined to make their marriage work.

2d Appeal   Characters

Subjects   Divorce • First Novels • Marriage • Stepfamilies

Now try   *Harry and Catherine* by Frederick Busch is another novel about people well out of their youth falling in love. The central male character in Carol Shields's *The Republic of Love* is also the veteran of several failed marriages.

Feldman, Ellen
Looking for Love
Little, Brown. 1990. 318 pp.

Forty-one-year-old Nora tries to balance her career as a magazine editor with a new boyfriend, a mother who is about to marry the wrong man, and a beautiful sister with a seemingly idyllic life.

Subjects   Career Women • Mothers and Daughters • Single Women • Sisters

Now try   Feldman is also the author of *God Bless the Child*, a novel about a mother searching for the son she gave up for adoption. Another book about mothers, daughters, and sisters is Gail Godwin's *A Mother and Two Daughters*. The wisecracking heroine of this novel is similar to Susan Isaac's eponymous heroine, Lily White. Other domestic novels include Hilma Wolitzer's *Tunnel of Love* and Rita Kashner's *Bed Rest*.

Fenkl, Heinz Insu
Memories of My Ghost Brother
Dutton. 1996. 271 pp.

As Insu, the son of an American soldier and a Korean woman, grows up in Inchon, Korea, prior to and during the Vietnam War, he and his mother are haunted by the knowledge that Insu's older brother was given up for adoption to an American family.

2d Appeal   Setting

Subjects   Adoption • Brothers • Coming-of-Age • First Novels • Korea • Korean Americans

Now try   The mixture of folktales and myths found in Fenkl's novel is similar to Maxine Hong Kingston's *The Woman Warrior*, Jerzy Kosinski's *The Painted Bird*, and Cecilia Brainard's *When the Rainbow Goddess Wept*.

Ferriss, Lucy
Against Gravity
Simon & Schuster. 1996. 303 pp.

Facing her parents' deteriorating marriage, the near death of her father, her own eating disorder, and the birth of her best friend's illegitimate baby, Gwyn (Stick) Stickney realizes that change is the only constant that life offers.

Subjects Coming-of-Age • Eating Disorders • Friendship • Single Parents • Teenage Girls • Teenage Pregnancy • Teenagers • Women's Friendships

Now try Ferriss's other novels include *Philip's Girl* and *The Gated River*. Lorrie Moore's *Who Will Run the Frog Hospital?* is another good picture of the friendship between two young women.

Findley, Timothy
Headhunter
HarperCollins. 1993. 440 pp.

When librarian Lilah Kemp accidentally releases Kurtz from page 92 of Conrad's *Heart of Darkness* into a Toronto of the near future, chaos and evil are brought forth.

2d Appeal Characters Book Groups 📖

Subjects Canada • Canadian Authors • Dystopia • Good vs. Evil • Librarians • Psychiatrists, Psychoanalysts, Psychotherapists • Psychological Fiction • Toronto

Now try Among Findley's other novels are *The Piano Man's Daughter* and *Famous Last Words*. Jonathan Franzen's *The Twenty-Seventh City* is also a psychological novel about good versus evil.

Finney, Ernest
The Lady with the Alligator Purse
Clark City Press. 1992. 228 pp.

Responsible Kay still looks out for her cousins Billy and Ann, just as she did when they were growing up as the children of sisters transplanted from Kansas to California, who brought their problems with them and passed them on to the next generation.

2d Appeal Characters

Subjects Brothers and Sisters • California • Cousins • Family Relationships • Single Women • Sisters

Now try Finney evokes wartime California in his novels, *Words of My Roaring* and *California Time*. His storytelling is similar to Chris Bohjalian's in *Midwives*.

Fitzpatrick, Nina
The Loves of Faustyna
Penguin Books. 1995. 216 pp.

In 1967 Poland, after a cloud in the shape of a human buttock appears over Krakow, Faustyna, a young psychology student, fearing that the end of the world is near, embarks on a series of love affairs and political adventures.

Subjects 1960s • Communism • Erotica • Humorous Fiction • Irish Authors • Magic Realism • Male/Female Relationships • Poland • Political Fiction • Satirical Fiction

Now try Fitzpatrick's first novel was *Fables of the Irish Intelligentsia*. She writes political satire in the grand style of Voltaire's *Candide*. There is another strange appearance in Mary Breasted's *Why Should You Doubt Me Now?*

Flanigan, Sara
Sudie
St. Martin's Press. 1986. 280 pp.

Ten-year-old Mary Agnes Clark tells the story of her best friend Sudie Harrigan's dangerous and secret friendship with Simpson, a black man hiding out in an all-white Georgia town in the 1940s.

Subjects   1940s • First Novels • Friendship • Georgia • Race Relations • Racism • Sexual Abuse • Small-Town Life • Southern Authors

Now try   Flanigan is also the author of *Alice: A Novel*. Both Harper Lee's *To Kill a Mockingbird* and Lillian Smith's *Strange Fruit* are about race relations in the south. Another young girl who befriends a possibly dangerous stranger can be found in John Welter's *I Want to Buy a Vowel*.

Flokos, Nicholas
Nike
Houghton Mifflin. 1998. 179 pp.

Photi Anthropotis, a humble fisherman from the Greek island of Samothrace, a glamorous American documentary filmmaker, and a museum guard at the Louvre all collaborate on a mission to bring the Winged Victory statue back home to Greece.

2d Appeal   Characters

Subjects   First Novels • Greece • Humorous Fiction • Male/Female Relationships

Now try   Another novel written in the unusual style of the first person plural is *The Virgin Suicides* by Jeffrey Eugenides.

Flook, Maria
Family Night
Pantheon Books. 1993. 291 pp.

Recently divorced Margaret, her stepbrother Cam (also recently divorced), and her boyfriend Tracy set out on an ill-tempered and sexually capricious quest to find Cam's biological father.

Subjects   Adoption • Brothers and Sisters • Divorce • First Novels • First Novels • Stepfamilies

Now try   Flook also wrote a memoir, *My Sister Life*. *Then She Found Me* by Elinor Lipman and Ellen Feldman's *God Bless the Child* are both about mothers who meet the children they gave up for adoption years before. Mona Simpson's *The Lost Father* is another novel about a young woman's search for her father.

Florey, Kitty Burns
Real Life
Morrow. 1986. 276 pp.

When Dorrie, a potter, becomes the guardian of her uncommunicative teenage nephew Hugo, her life changes radically.

Subjects   Art and Artists • Family Relationships • Orphans • Single Women • Teenage Boys • Teenagers

Now try   Florey's other novels include *The Garden Path*, *Duet*, and *Family Matters*. Like Florey, Jon Hassler in *Staggerford* and *North of Hope* tells a good story. Another aunt who takes over the rearing of teenagers can be found in Marilynne Robinson's *Housekeeping*.

Franzen, Jonathan
The Twenty-Seventh City
Farrar Straus Giroux. 1988. 517 pp.

The Probsts, an ordinary family in St. Louis, Missouri, are unwittingly involved in the clandestine attempt by Jammu, the mysterious, newly appointed Marxist-influenced police chief, to take over the city government by manipulating public opinion, buying up large blocks of real estate, and influencing ghetto residents to support her.

2d Appeal Language

Subjects Family Relationships • First Novels • Good vs. Evil • Missouri • Political Fiction • St. Louis

Now try Franzen is also the author of *Strong Motion*. Just as Franzen uses a slightly altered real city, St. Louis, as the backdrop for his novel, Peter Cameron uses the country of Andorra for his book of the same name. In Timothy Findley's *Headhunter* and Michael Malone's *Dingley Falls* a sense of menace pervades the plot, as both explore how innocent people are used for corrupt purposes. In 1996, *Granta Magazine* named Franzen one of the "20 Best Young American Novelists."

Free, Suzanne
The Blue Nature
St. Martin's Press. 1989. 418 pp.

As an adult, Maddie still struggles with the depression brought on by her beloved uncle's disappearance in the Alaskan wilderness when she was nine years old, and the death of her sister a few years later.

Subjects Alaska • First Novels • Mental Illness • Sisters • Wives of Clergymen

Now try Two nonfiction books set in Alaska are Jon Krakauer's *Into the Wild*, and Natalie Kusz's *Road Song*. *The Rector's Wife* by Joanna Trollope is another book about the life of a clergyman's wife.

Freeman, David
One of Us
Carroll & Graf Publishers. 1997. 278 pp.

Just prior to World War II, when Britain's colonial power is coming to an end, young James Peel arrives in Egypt to tutor 15-year-old Prince Farouk and becomes involved with the life of Vera Napier, the much younger wife of Sir Malcolm Cheyne, last British High Commissioner in Egypt.

2d Appeal Setting   Book Groups 📖

Subjects 1940s • Adultery • Colonialism • Egypt • Older Men/Younger Women

Now try Like Freeman, Beryl Bainbridge (in *Every Man for Himself* and *The Birthday Boys*) and Don DeLillo (in *Libra*) both write novels so convincing that, once read, it is impossible to look at history except through their eyes: What they have imagined becomes more real than what might have actually happened.

Freeman, Judith
The Chinchilla Farm
Norton. 1989. 308 pp.

After her husband of 17 years asks for a divorce, Verna Flake embarks on a trip of self-discovery from Utah to Mexico, by way of California.

Subjects   Divorce • First Novels • Middle-Aged Women • Mormons and Mormonism • Road Novels

Now try   Among Freeman's other books are *Body of Water* and *Set for Life*. Charles Dickinson's *The Widows' Adventures* and Pagan Kennedy's *Spinsters* are other road novels with women protagonists. Kathryn Lasky Knight's *The Widow of Oz* is about a middle-aged woman coping with changes in her life.

French, Marilyn
My Summer with George
Knopf. 1996. 243 pp.

Hermione Beldame, who writes romance novels for a living, patiently waits for romance to unfold in her own life, but George has other plans.

Subjects   Aging • Love Stories • Male/Female Relationships • Writers and Writing

Now try   French also wrote *The Women's Room*, one of the earliest novels about feminism. Another novel that explores developing relationships is Carol Shields's *The Republic of Love*. Other women intrigued by the possibility of romance as found in books and magazines can be found in Pearl Abraham's *The Romance Reader* and Mary Bringle's *True Confessions: The Novel*.

Furman, Laura
Tuxedo Park
Summit Books. 1986. 352 pp.

After Willard and Sadie's ill-matched marriage ends, Sadie raises their two daughters in the wealthy enclave of Tuxedo Park, Willard's boyhood home, where all three secretly believe that Willard will return home.

Subjects   1940s • Divorce • Marriage • Mothers and Daughters • Single Parents • Sisters • Upper Classes

Now try   Furman's earlier books, including *The Shadow Line* and her story collections, *Watch Time Fly* and *The Glass House*, are also about family relationships. The novels and short stories of Laurie Colwin (*Family Happiness* and others) are filled with characters who, despite their wealth, remain unhappy with their lives. Anne Tyler's *Searching for Caleb* is another novel about waiting for a missing family member to return.

Gardner, Mary
Boat People
W.W. Norton. 1995. 277 pp.

A variety of characters, including Dr. Nguyen, who only reluctantly acts as translator for his fellow Vietnamese refugees, the distraught and disturbed Hui Truong and her daughter Linh, and Trang, searching for the American father who abandoned her in Vietnam, experience all the difficulties of newcomers to the United States.

2d Appeal   Characters   Book Groups 📖

Subjects   Acculturation • Culture Clash • Immigrants and Refugees • Mental Illness • Texas • Vietnam War

Now try   Gardner's first novel, *Keeping Warm*, is about a widowed English teacher who runs away with the man of her dreams. Robert Olen Butler's *A Good Scent from a Strange Mountain* is a collection of short stories about Vietnamese refugees in Louisiana. *Comfort Woman* by Nora Okja Keller is another book in which terrible events lead to a woman's mental breakdown.

Gearino, G. D.
What the Deaf-Mute Heard
Simon & Schuster. 1996. 221 pp.

After being abandoned by his mother in a Georgia bus station, 10-year-old Sammy Ayers decides to pretend he is a deaf-mute, quietly and unobtrusively living out his life, only to gain widespread recognition when his secret is finally revealed.

Book Groups 📖

Subjects   Deafness • First Novels • Georgia • Mothers and Sons • Mothers Deserting Their Families • Southern Authors

Now try   Gearino is also the author of *Counting Coup: A Novel*, which explores many of the same themes found in *What the Deaf-Mute Heard*. Another novel about a deaf-mute boy is Catherine Cookson's *Our John Willie*. Two nonfiction books about living as a deaf person are Henry Kisor's *What's That Pig Outdoors? A Memoir of Deafness* and *Voyage to the Island* by Raija Niemienen.

Gernes, Sonia
The Way to St. Ives
Scribner. 1982. 266 pp.

The deaths of her overbearing mother and only brother cause 41-year-old Catholic spinster Rosie Deane to allow herself, at last, to blossom.

2d Appeal   Characters

Subjects   1960s • ALA Notable Books • Catholics and Catholicism • First Novels • Loneliness • Minnesota • Single Women • Small-Town Life

Now try   Gernes's other books include three collections of poetry, *Brief Lives*, *Women at Forty*, and *A Breeze Called the Freemantle Doctor: Poems/Tales*. Anne Michaels's *Fugitive Pieces* and James Galvin's *The Meadow* are both novels by writers who are also published poets. The effect an overbearing mother has on her adult children can be seen in Penelope Lively's *Passing On*.

Gilchrist, Ellen
The Anna Papers
Little, Brown. 1988. 277 pp.

When well-known writer Anna Hand discovers she has cancer and drowns herself in the Atlantic Ocean, her sister Helen, whose life as a wife and mother has always contrasted sharply with Anna's, discovers through reading her sister's papers that they have more in common than she ever thought possible.

2d Appeal   Characters

Subjects   Cancer • Sisters • Suicide • Writers and Writing

Now try   Gilchrist wrote other novels and short stories about the lives of various members of the Hand family, including *Drunk with Love*, *I Cannot Get You Close Enough*, and *Victory Over Japan*. Jennifer Egan's *The Invisible Circus* is also about the death of a sister and how it affects a younger sibling.

Gingher, Marianne
Bobby Rex's Greatest Hit
Atheneum. 1986. 308 pp.

In 1961, on the eve of her wedding, Pally Thompson discovers that Bobby Rex Moseley, country music star and native of her hometown of Orfax, North Carolina, has written a song that tells the world about about their torrid love affair, which never took place.

Subjects   First Novels • Love Stories • Music and Musicians • North Carolina • Small-Town Life • Southern Authors

Now try   Gingher also wrote *Teen Angel and Other Stories of Young Love*. *Come and Go*, *Molly Snow* by Mary Ann Taylor-Hall is also set around the world of country music. Set a decade earlier, *The Cheerleader*, by Ruth Doan MacDougall, describes the experiences of a teenage girl.

Goddard, Robert
In Pale Battalions
Poseidon Press. 1988. 296 pp.

An injured World War I lieutenant is drawn into the Hallows family's secrets and misdeeds, revolving around a beautiful widow and her daughter, a grieving father, and an American fortune hunter.

2d Appeal   Characters

Subjects   British Authors • Family Secrets • World War I

Now try   Other novels by Goddard include *Closed Circle*, *Hand in Glove*, and *Painting the Darkness*. Daphne DuMaurier's *Rebecca* and both John Fowles's *The French Lieutenant's Woman* and *The Magus* combine romance and suspense. Sebastien Japrisot (*A Very Long Engagement*), Patricia Anthony (*Flanders*), and Sebastian Faulks (*Birdsong*) all provide moving accounts of World War I. The main character in the mysteries by Charles Todd (*Wings of Fire* and *A Test of Wills*) is a shell-shocked World War I veteran.

Goethe, Ann
Midnight Lemonade
Delacorte Press. 1993. 277 pp.

Katherine seeks her own identity from the expectations of the past, the temptations of the present, and the struggle of the future, represented by her children, her lover, and herself.

Subjects   Coming-of-Age • Divorce • First Novels • Single Parents • Southern Authors

Now try   Fumiko Enchi's novel, *The Waiting Years*, presents the same situation as experienced by a woman in another culture. Florence King's autobiography, *Confessions of a Failed Southern Lady*, is a humorous account of the pressures put upon Southern women to conform, while Katherine Mosby's novel, *Private Altars*, offers a more serious view of the same subject.

Grant, Stephanie
The Passion of Alice
Houghton Mifflin Co. 1995. 260 pp.

Alice Forrester, a 25-year-old anorexic, encounters a varied group of people among the patients and staff at an clinic specializing in eating disorders, and finds a sense of identity along the way.

Book Groups 📖

Subjects	Coming-of-Age • Eating Disorders • First Novels • Psychiatric Hospitals
Now try	Other novels about anorexia are *My Sister's Bones* by Cathi Hanauer, Jillian Medoff's *Hunger Point*, and *Life-Size* by Jenefer Shute.

Greenberg, Joanne
Of Such Small Differences
Holt. 1988. 262 pp.

In his attempts to live a normal life despite being blind and deaf, John is both helped and hindered when he falls in love with Leda, the woman who interprets for him.

2d Appeal	Characters Book Groups 📖
Subjects	ALA Notable Books • Blindness • Deafness • Love Stories • Male/Female Relationships • Physical Disabilities
Now try	Greenberg's first novel, originally published under the pseudonym Hannah Green, was *I Never Promised You a Rose Garden*. Despite the fact that he lacks John's physical disabilities, Jeremy, the main character in Anne Tyler's *Celestial Navigation*, is also a solitary person whose life is changed when he falls in love. Another romance that doesn't seem to have a chance of succeeding can be found in Simon Mawer's *Mendel's Dwarf*.

Greene, Bob
All Summer Long
Doubleday. 1993. 387 pp.

Three men—best friends as boys—meet again at their twenty-fifth high school reunion and decide to spend the summer driving around the United States together.

Subjects	First Novels • Men's Friendships • Middle-Aged Men • Road Novels
Now try	Greene's other books include *Rebound: The Odyssey of Michael Jordan*, *The 50-Year Dash: The Feelings, Foibles and Fears of Being Half-a-Century Old*, and *Chevrolet Summers*, *Dairy Queen Nights*. Another book in which a man returns to his hometown—this time to defend his best friend on a murder charge—is Richard North Patterson's mystery, *Silent Witness*. Old friends travel together in Graham Swift's *Last Orders*.

Griffith, Patricia Browning
The World Around Midnight
Putnam's Sons. 1991. 254 pp.

The death of her father brings Dinah Reynolds back to Midnight, Texas, to take over as editor of the town's weekly paper, all the while coping with news of her husband's infidelity and the appearance in Midnight of her old boyfriend.

Subjects	Adultery • ALA Notable Books • First Novels • Humorous Fiction • Husbands and Wives • Journalists • Male/Female Relationships • Small-Town Life • Texas
Now try	Griffith also wrote *Supporting the Sky*, a novel about the tribulations of a divorced mother in Washington, D.C. Other novels set in contemporary Texas include Janis Arnold's *Daughters of Memory* and Larry McMurtry's *Duane's Depressed*.

Grimes, Martha
Hotel Paradise
Knopf. 1996. 347 pp.

Twelve-year-old Emma Graham, left to her own devices in the fading and remote resort community where she lives with her mother, tries to make sense of an old, unsolved murder and along the way sets memories and truths spinning wildly.

Subjects Coming-of-Age • Mothers and Daughters • Murder • Single Parents

Now try Martha Grimes (*The Old Silent* and *The Dirty Duck* among others) is best known as a mystery writer. Other novels in which the authors use a crime to propel the coming-of-age of a young person are Suzanne Berne's *A Crime in the Neighborhood*, Robert McCammon's *Boy's Life*, Stewart O'Nan's *Snow Angels*, and Harper Lee's *To Kill a Mockingbird*.

Grossman, Judith
Her Own Terms
Soho Press. 1988. 277 pp.

Irene leaves her working class family and home to attend Oxford University on a scholarship and finds that the men in her life try to turn her into the brilliant and beautiful woman they desire.

Subjects 1950s • Abortion • College Students • First Novels • Male/Female Relationships • Oxford University • Working Classes

Now try Other writers dealing acerbically with male/female relationships include Fay Weldon (*The Life and Loves of a She-Devil*) and, using a far gentler tone, Barbara Pym, especially in her novel, *No Fond Return of Love*.

Grumbach, Doris
The Magician's Girl
Macmillan. 1987. 200 pp.

Almost 40 years after they graduated from Barnard in the 1930s, Maud Noon and her two roommates are still trying to fulfill their childhood dreams.

Subjects 1930s • College Students • Women's Friendships • Writers and Writing

Now try Grumbach has also written a series of journals chronicling her life, including *Extra Innings: A Memoir* and *Fifty Days of Solitude*. *Letters Home* and *The Bell Jar* by Sylvia Plath are good books to read following *The Magician's Girl*, because the title of Grumbach's novel comes from a line of Sylvia Plath's, and Maud Noon is loosely based on Plath. The pain of growing up that Grumbach's characters suffer is also evoked in Margaret Atwood's *Lady Oracle*.

Grunwald, Lisa
New Year's Eve
Warner Books. 1997. 366 pp.

When estranged twin sisters Heather and Erica give birth to children just two weeks apart, they grow closer, until Heather's young son dies and she attempts to steal her niece Sarah's love from Erica.

Subjects Aging • Death of a Child • Family Relationships • Fathers and Daughters • Sisters • Twins

Now try This is Grunwald's third novel, following *The Theory of Everything* and *Summer*. Anne Rivers Siddons (*The Colony*) and Meg Wolitzer (*Sleepwalking*) both explore family dynamics in their novels.

Guest, Judith
Errands
Ballantine Books. 1997. 335 pp.

When her husband of 17 years dies of cancer, Annie gradually realizes that her three children desperately need her to stop grieving and bring the family back together.

Book Groups 📖

Subjects Cancer • Death of a Parent • Death of a Spouse • Family Relationships • Grief

Now try Guest's first novel, ***Ordinary People***, the story of a family destroyed by the death of a son, was an ALA Notable Book. The main characters in Abigail Stone's ***Recipes from the Dump*** and Beth Gutcheon's ***Domestic Pleasures*** are both divorced women doing their best to raise their families alone.

Gutcheon, Beth
Saying Grace
HarperCollins Publishers. 1995. 313 pp.

Rue Shaw, headmistress of a private school, finds her 17-year career in jeopardy when rumors arise that a fifth grader is being abused at home.

Subjects Career Women • Child Abuse • Male/Female Relationships • Private Schools

Now try Other novels by Gutcheon include ***The New Girls***, ***Still Missing***, and ***Five Fortunes***. Another novel dealing with an accusation of child abuse is Jane Hamilton's ***A Map of the World***.

Guterson, David
Snow Falling on Cedars
Harcourt Brace. 1994. 345 pp.

A middle-aged reporter covers the murder trial of a Japanese American fisherman, the husband of his first love.

2d Appeal Setting
Book Groups 📖

Subjects 1950s • First Novels • Interracial Relationships • Internment Camps • Japanese Americans • Journalists • Murder • Pacific Northwest • Racism

Now try Guterson is also the author of a collection of stories, ***The Country Ahead of Us***, ***The Country Behind***, and ***Family Matters: Why Homeschooling Makes Sense***. Jack Cady's ***Inagehi*** is also a novel combining a murder with the clash of cultures. Other writers have written about Japanese Americans in internment camps, including Gretel Ehrlich in her novel, ***Heart Mountain***. In 1996, *Granta Magazine* named Guterson one of the "20 Best Young American Novelists." ***Snow Falling on Cedars*** was also a PEN/Faulkner Award winner.

Haien, Jeannette
Matters of Chance
HarperCollins Publishers. 1997. 439 pp.

Joy and tragedy are both present in the life of Morgan Shurtliff, whose experiences include marriage to his beloved Maude, adopting and rearing twin girls, and combat duty in World War II.

Subjects Adoption • Infertility • Law and Lawyers • Marriage • Twins • World War II

Now try Haien also wrote ***The All of It***. Like Robert Clark's ***In the Deep Midwinter***, Haien believes that fiction can illuminate the moral complexities of life.

Hailey, Elizabeth Forsythe

Home Free
Delacorte Press. 1991. 293 pp.

After her husband of 25 years asks her for a divorce, Kate Hart takes a homeless family into her life and discovers that she's stronger than she ever would have believed.

Subjects   Adultery • Divorce • Homelessness • Marriage

Now try   Hailey's first novel was *A Woman of Independent Means*. Hilma Wolitzer's *Silver* is about a couple about to celebrate their silver anniversary when one of them decides that marriage is not fulfilling interpersonal needs.

Hamilton, Jane

A Map of the World
Doubleday. 1994. 390 pp.

Alice Goodwin's life turns upside down when the two-year-old daughter of her best friend drowns while in Alice's care and Alice is accused of sexual abuse by a student at the school where she works as a nurse.

2d Appeal   Characters   Book Groups 📖

Subjects   Adultery • Child Abuse • Death of a Child • Farms and Farm Life • Marriage • Sexual Abuse • Women in Prison • Women's Friendships

Now try   Hamilton also wrote *The Book of Ruth* and *The Short History of a Prince*. The plots of Beth Gutcheon's *Saying Grace*, Jessica Auerbach's *Catch Your Breath*, and Sue Miller's *The Good Mother* also involve accusations of child abuse.

Hanauer, Cathi

My Sister's Bones
Delacorte Press. 1996. 258 pp.

When the older sister she has always idolized comes home from college withdrawn and ill, 16-year-old Billie Weinstein is the only family member willing to acknowledge Cassie's anorexia.

Subjects   Coming-of-Age • Eating Disorders • First Novels • Sisters • Teenage Girls

Now try   *Eve's Apple* by Jonathan Rosen, *Hunger Point* by Jillian Medoff, and Rebecca Josephs's *Early Disorder* all deal with the subject of young women with anorexia nervosa.

Harris, MacDonald

Hemingway's Suitcase
Simon and Schuster. 1990. 288 pp.

Hack writer Nils-Frederik Glas refuses to tell his son Alan (his agent) or his best friend Wolf (a rare book dealer) whether a number of Hemingway-esque stories (five of them included in this novel) that have come into his possession are the real thing or fakes Glas has written himself.

Subjects   Hemingway, Ernest • Humorous Fiction • Writers and Writing

Now try   Other books by Harris include *Glad Rags*, *Herma*, *The Little People*, and *A Portrait of My Desire*. The plot of Harris's novel revolves around a true event: It is based on the fact that in 1922 a suitcase filled with Hemingway's writings was stolen from a railway station in Paris. Other novels that feature Ernest Hemingway as a character are Karl Alexander's *Papa & Fidel*, Allan Conan's *The Hemingway Sabbatical*, and Joe Haldeman's *The Hemingway Hoax*.

Hassler, Jon
Dear James
Ballantine Books. 1993. 438 pp.

Seventy-year-old Agatha McGee has always been Staggerford, Minnesota's most upstanding resident, but when rumors spread about Agatha's trips abroad and her relationship with Father James O'Hannon, an Irish priest, Agatha and her neighbors must find a new understanding of one another.

Subjects   Elderly Women • Male/Female Relationships • Ministers, Priests, Rabbis • Minnesota • Small-Town Life

Now try   This is Hassler's seventh in a series of novels about life in the fictional town of Staggerford; the first book in the series is *North of Hope*. Mitford, the setting for Jan Karon's *At Home in Mitford* and other novels, is a small town much like Staggerford. Elizabeth McCracken's *The Giant's House* has the same sort of intimate, though sometimes darker, view of small-town life.

Haynes, David
Live at Five
Milkweed Editions. 1996. 267 pp.

Brandon, an ambitious African American television news anchor, and Nita, a strong but struggling single mother, play out their schemes for a better life live on the five o'clock news.

2d Appeal   Characters

Subjects   African American Authors • African Americans • Male/Female Relationships • Race Relations • Single Parents

Now try   Haynes also wrote *Right by My Side* and *Somebody Else's Mama*. Terry McMillan (*Disappearing Acts* and others) offers another view of the relationships between African American men and women. Erika Ellis's *Good Fences* is another novel about an upwardly mobile African American family. In 1996, *Granta Magazine* named Haynes one of the "20 Best Young American Novelists."

Hearon, Shelby
Footprints
Knopf. 1996. 191 pp.

After the sudden death of their daughter, Nan and Douglas misinterpret each other's grieving process, opening a chasm in their marriage.

Book Groups 📖

Subjects   Death of a Child • Family Relationships • Marriage • Organ Transplants • Texas

Now try   Among Hearon's other novels are *Hannah's House*, *Life Estates*, and *Group Therapy*. In Frederick Busch's *Girls*, Fanny and Jack, parents of a dead child, are also unable to communicate their grief about the death of their daughter to one another. Other novels about the death of a child include Jonathan Burnham Schwartz's *Reservation Road*, Ian McEwan's *The Child in Time*, Judith Guest's *Ordinary People*, Martha Whitmore Hickman's *Such Good People*, and Anne Tyler's *The Accidental Tourist*.

Hemphill, Paul

King of the Road
Houghton Mifflin Co. 1989. 296 pp.

When English professor Sonny Hawkins learns that his 70-year-old retired, hard-living, hard-drinking truck driver father has been sent to Piney Woods, an alcohol rehabilitation center, he decides that he and his father should go on the road for one last trip.

Subjects   Alcoholics and Alcoholism • Alzheimer's Disease • College Professors • Elderly Men • Fathers and Sons • Road Novels

Now try   Hemphill's other books include *The Good Old Boys*, *The Sixkiller Chronicles*, and *The Nashville Sound*. Another novel about a difficult relationship between a father and son is Michael Malone's *Handling Sin*.

Hickman, Martha Whitmore

Such Good People
Warner Books. 1996. 323 pp.

The accidental death of their teenage daughter, Annie, forces Laura and Trace to re-evaluate their lives and their marriage.

Subjects   Death of a Child • First Novels • Marriage

Now try   Doris Betts's *Souls Raised from the Dead* and Shelby Hearon's *Footprints* are both about the death of a daughter. Memoirs about the death of a child include Isabel Allende's *Paula* and Doris Lund's *Eric*.

Hill, David

Sacred Dust
Delacorte Press. 1996. 388 pp.

Rose of Sharon's friendship with newcomer Lily gives her the courage to speak out against the violence local Klan members (including her husband) are perpetrating on the black citizens who live in Prince George County, Alabama.

2d Appeal   Setting   Book Groups 📖

Subjects   Abusive Relationships • Alabama • Coming-of-Age • First Novels • Race Relations • Southern Authors • Violence • Women's Friendships

Now try   Towns with secrets are also the settings for Shirley Jackson's *The Lottery*, Laura Hendrie's *Stygo*, and Rick Collignon's *Perdido*. Another character named Rose of Sharon can be found in John Steinbeck's *The Grapes of Wrath*.

Hill, Richard

Riding Solo with the Golden Horde
University of Georgia Press. 1994. 143 pp.

During the 1950s, Vic Messenger, alto sax player and high school senior, navigates uneasily between his middle-class life—with Juilliard as a goal—and his desire to play with local jazz musicians at clubs on Florida's Gulf Coast.

Subjects   1950s • Coming-of-Age • Florida • Jazz • Music and Musicians • Race Relations • Teenage Boys

Now try   *What Rough Beast* and *Shoot the Piper* are mysteries written by Hill. The main character in Hill's novel resembles the protagonist in Dorothy Baker's novel, *Young Man with a Horn*, which was loosely inspired by the music of Leon (Bix) Beiderbecke. Another teenager caught between conflicting goals is the main character in Enrico Brizzi's *Jack Frusciante Has Left the Band*.

Hobbet, Anastasia
Pleasure of Believing
Soho Press. 1997. 368 pp.

Rebecca Shea's all-consuming devotion to rehabilitating injured birds and anger at her neighboring Wyoming ranchers' use of poison to control predators of their livestock sets her at odds with both her politician husband, Glen, and the rest of the community.

Book Groups 📖

Subjects   Birds • Ecofiction • First Novels • Marriage • Wyoming

Now try   Chris Bohjalian's *Water Witches* pits environmentalists against developers in New England. Craig Childs's *Crossing Paths: Encounters with Animals in the Wild* has a fascinating chapter on coyotes.

Hood, Ann
Something Blue
Bantam Books. 1991. 215 pp.

Twentyish Katherine (who has left her fiancé at the altar), Julia (who lies about her background and cannot commit to a relationship), and Lucy (a gifted artist who is unhappy with her dancer boyfriend) all look for love and success in late 1980s Manhattan.

Subjects   1980s • Art and Artists • New York • Single Women • Women's Friendships

Now try   Hood's other novels include *Somewhere Off the Coast of Maine*, *Waiting to Vanish*, and *Three-Legged Horse*. Other good storytellers are the novelists Fern Kupfer (*Surviving the Seasons* and *No Regrets*) and Anita Shreve (*The Pilot's Wife* and *Where or When*).

Hood, Mary
Familiar Heat
Knopf. 1995. 451 pp.

Married at 20, Faye Rios's life is filled with disasters, including a womanizing husband, kidnapping, rape, and a car accident that leaves her an amnesiac.

Subjects   First Novels • Florida • Male/Female Relationships • Marriage • Rape • Small-Town Life

Now try   Hood also wrote *And Venus Is Blue: Stories*. Another novel filled with subplots is Ann-Marie MacDonald's *Fall on Your Knees*.

Huneven, Michelle
Round Rock
A.A. Knopf. 1997. 295 pp.

When Red Ray finally accepts the fact that he is an alcoholic, he opens Round Rock (the ranch he bought in a vain effort to save his marriage) as a treatment center for other addicts and involves himself in the lives of those who come to live there.

Book Groups 📖

Subjects   Alcoholics and Alcoholism • California • First Novels • Male/Female Relationships

Now try   David Foster Wallace also writes about a center for recovering addicts, Ennet House, in *Infinite Jest*. *Drinking: A Love Story*, a memoir by Caroline Knapp, offers insights into the seductiveness of alcohol.

Hyde, Elisabeth
Her Native Colors
Delacorte Press. 1986. 328 pp.

Returning home after six years away for the wedding of her best friend Molly, divorced mother Phoebe Martin questions the life choices both she and Molly have made.

Subjects   First Novels • Single Women • Vermont • Women's Friendships

Now try   Hyde also wrote *Monosook Valley*. Friendship is explored in Anne Bernays's *The School Book*, Zena Collier's *A Cooler Climate*, Joe Coomer's *Beachcombing for a Shipwrecked God*, and Margaret Drabble's *The Gates of Ivory*.

Ingalls, Rachel
Mrs. Caliban
Harvard Common Press. 1983. 125 pp.

A grieving housewife and a green sea monster who is hiding from the police develop a bizarrely matter-of-fact romance.

2d Appeal   Characters

Subjects   Death of a Child • Grief • Love Affairs • Love Stories • Magic Realism • Marriage

Now try   Ingalls's other books include *Binstead's Safari: A Novel*, *The Pearlkillers: Four Novellas*, and *The End of Tragedy: Four Novellas*. *Bear* by Marian Engel and Elizabeth McCracken's *The Giant's House* are other novels with unlikely romantic entanglements.

Isler, Alan
The Prince of West End Avenue
Bridge Works Pub. 1994. 246 pp.

As Otto Korner directs his fellow residents of the Emma Lazarus Retirement Home in a production of Hamlet, he recalls his life as a husband, father, and poet in Germany before World War II, his experiences in the concentration camps, and his life in America following the war.

Subjects   Actors and Acting • Concentration Camps • Elderly Men • First Novels • Hamlet • Holocaust • Men's Lives • New York • Retirement • World War II

Now try   Isler's other books include *The Bacon Fancier* and *Kraven Images*. *Bring Us the Old People* by Marisa Kantor Stark is also set in a retirement center. The stately narration of this novel brings to mind Mark Helprin's *Memoir from Antproof Case*.

Janowitz, Tama
The Male Cross-Dresser Support Group
Crown Publishers. 1992. 314 pp.

New Yorker Pamela Trowel is on a one-way trip to disaster, due to a boss who hates her, a slovenly apartment, a stowaway child, blood, guts, and plenty of sexual activity.

Subjects   Humorous Fiction • New York • Single Women • Transvestites

Now try   Janowitz's other books include *American Dad* and *A Cannibal in Manhattan*. Jay McInerney's *Bright Lights, Big City* is a harder edged novel about New York. There is also a cross-dressing character in Peter Lefcourt's *Abbreviating Ernie*. Transvestites play a major role in the life of Louis Ives, the protagonist of Jonathan Ames's *The Extra Man*.

Johnson, Nora
Perfect Together
Dutton. 1991. 262 pp.

Fran and Charlie's supposedly ideal life comes to an end when their maid becomes pregnant, and Charlie, who is identified as the father, insists on keeping the child.

Subjects   Adultery • Child Abuse • Marriage • Pregnancy

Now try   Johnson's first two novels are *The World of Henry Orient* and *A Step Beyond Innocence*. Other novels with an abundance of sub-plots include Mary Hood's *Familiar Heat* and Ruth Ozeki's *My Year of Meats*.

Jolley, Elizabeth
Foxybaby
Viking. 1985. 261 pp.

Spinster dramatist Alma Porch must deal with unexpected consequences when students at a Trinity College Better Body Through Arts seminar eagerly fling themselves into the dramatic possibilities of Alma's experimental play, Foxybaby.

Subjects   Academia • Actors and Acting • Australian Authors • Humorous Fiction • Single Women

Now try   Jolley's other novels include *Miss Peabody's Inheritance* and *Woman in a Lampshade*. T. Coraghessan Boyle's *The Road to Wellville* is another humorous novel on the joys of becoming healthy. Fay Weldon (*The Cloning of Joanna May* and *The Fat Woman's Joke*) shares Jolley's sharp tongue and skewed view of relationships. Penelope Lively's *Next to Nature, Art* is about an artist's retreat that goes awry.

Jones, Louis B.
Particles and Luck
Pantheon Books. 1993. 305 pp.

An unusual dispute causes an eccentric young professor to contemplate the role of physics and luck in his life.

Subjects   College Professors • Humorous Fiction • Law and Lawyers • Physics • Science and Scientists

Now try   Jones also wrote *Ordinary Money* and *California's Over*. Other novels incorporating physics in their plots are Jonathan Lethem's *As She Climbed Across the Table*, John Updike's *Toward the End of Time*, and Alan Lightman's *Einstein's Dreams*.

Judd, Alan
The Devil's Own Work
Knopf. 1994. 115 pp.

A younger writer makes his name by demolishing Old Man Tyrell, the reigning literary lion, only to take his place by inheriting the dark secret to Tyrell's phenomenal fame, at no small cost.

2d Appeal   Characters   Book Groups 📖

Subjects   Postmodern Fiction • Satirical Fiction • Writers and Writing

Now try   Judd's other books include *A Breed of Heroes*, *Short of Glory*, and *The Noonday Devil*. Henry James's *The Aspern Papers* is also an example of literary satire. Other books in which the Faust legend is explored include Oscar Wilde's *The Picture of Dorian Gray*, *Doctor Faustus* by Thomas Mann, Douglas Wallop's *The Year the Yankees Lost the Pennant*, and Michael Bulgakov's *The Master and Margarita*.

Kadohata, Cynthia

The Floating World

Viking. 1989. 196 pp.

Twelve-year-old Olivia, her parents, grandmother, and three younger brothers search for better times as they travel by car through the United States, encountering racism, friendship, and the magic in ordinary life.

2d Appeal   Characters   Book Groups 📖

> **Subjects**   1950s • Coming-of-Age • First Novels • Japanese American Authors • Japanese Americans • Racism • Road Novels
>
> **Now try**   Kadohata also wrote *In the Heart of the Valley of Love*. The dreamlike quality of Kadohata's prose is similar to that found in Kazuo Ishiguro's *An Artist of the Floating World*.

Kafka, Paul

Love Enter

Houghton Mifflin. 1993. 326 pp.

Remembering their idyllic and intense love affairs and friendships in Paris five years before, Dan uses his time between delivering babies to write to Bou, Margot, and Beck on the maternity ward's computer.

> **Subjects**   Computers • Epistolary Novels • France • Love Stories • Male/Female Relationships
>
> **Now try**   Kafka's other books include *Home Again*. Diane Johnson's *Le Divorce* is another novel about an American in France.

Karon, Jan

These High, Green Hills

Viking. 1996. 333 pp.

After years as Mitford's bachelor minister, Father Tim Kavanaugh is now enjoying married life and trying to plan for his future, but he still finds it hard to ignore the ups and downs in the lives of his parishioners.

2d Appeal   Setting

> **Subjects**   Marriage • Ministers, Priests, Rabbis • Small-Town Life
>
> **Now try**   This is the third book in the "Mitford Years" series, preceded by *At Home in Mitford* and *A Light in the Window*, and followed by *Out to Canaan*. Other novels about small-town life are Jon Hassler's *North of Hope*, which features the residents of Staggerford, Minnesota, Garrison Keillor's *Lake Wobegon Days* and other books set in Lake Wobegon, Minnesota, and Bailey White's *Quite a Year for Plums*.

Kashner, Rita

Bed Rest

Macmillan. 1981. 266 pp.

In her early 30s, housewife and mother Beth Clahr finds herself spending more and more time in bed as she struggles to deal with an unsatisfactory marriage, an unwanted pregnancy, and her desire for a singing career.

> **Subjects**   Cancer • First Novels • Husbands and Wives • Marriage • Music and Musicians • Pregnancy • Women's Friendships

> **Now try** Kashner's other novels include *To the Tenth Generation* and *Graceful Exit*. Depressed, neurotic women are to be found in many contemporary novels, including Sheila Ballantyne's *Norma Jean the Termite Queen*, Anne Roiphe's *Up the Sandbox*, Marge Piercy's *Woman on the Edge of Time*, Jean Rhys's *Wide Sargasso Sea*, and Sue Kaufman's *Diary of a Mad Housewife*.

Kaufman, Joan
Dogs, Dreams, and Men
Norton. 1988. 253 pp.

It is through her dog Emma (named for Flaubert's heroine) that Ann meets Rover's owner, a self-centered musician.

> **Subjects** Dogs • First Novels • Love Stories • Music and Musicians • New York • Single Women

> **Now try** Another novel with an interesting dog is Frederick Busch's *Girls*. Clifford Simak's *City* is a classic short story collection about a future earth in which the only beings left are dogs. *Lives of the Monster Dogs* by Kirstin Bakis is about a group of highly evolved dogs from somewhere in the solar system who come back to earth with definite plans in mind.

Kay, Terry
To Dance with the White Dog
Peachtree Publishers. 1990. 179 pp.

After the death of his beloved wife, elderly pecan farmer Sam Peek befriends a mysteriously elusive white dog.

> **Subjects** Death and Dying • Death of a Spouse • Dogs • Elderly Men • Farms and Farm Life • Southern Authors • Widowers

> **Now try** Kay's *Shadow Song* is another testament to the enduring power of love. Sandra Scofield's *A Chance to See Egypt* is also about a man coping with the death of his wife.

Keane, Molly
Queen Lear
Dutton. 1988. 232 pp.

In pre-World War II Northern Ireland, childish innocence plagues a daughter of the landed gentry as she copes with her mother's desertion of the family.

> **2d Appeal** Setting

> **Subjects** Coming-of-Age • Fathers and Daughters • Ireland • Mothers Deserting Their Families • Northern Ireland

> **Now try** Molly Keane presents a somewhat lighter, more humorous view of Irish aristocracy in her novel, *Good Behavior*. Annabel Davis-Goff's *The Dower House* is another look at the world of the Anglo-Irish later in the century.

Keegan, John
Clearwater Summer
Carroll & Graf Publishers. 1994. 317 pp.

Will Bradford and his friends, Taylor Clark and Wellesley Baker, abruptly leave their childhood behind when Wellesley's father is murdered and secrets about her family life are revealed.

> **Subjects** 1950s • Child Abuse • Coming-of-Age • First Novels • Love Stories • Murder • Pacific Northwest • Small-Town Life • Teenage Boys

Now try   Robert Cormier's *The Chocolate War* and John Knowles's *A Separate Peace* are other novels that describe how easily the innocence of childhood can come to a sudden end.

Keillor, Garrison
WLT: A Radio Romance
Viking. 1991. 401 pp.

The 1926 startup of a Minnesota radio station through its demise in the age of television is seen through the eyes of the station's owners, Ray and Roy Soderbjerg, and their eccentric employees.

Subjects   Brothers • Eccentrics and Eccentricities • First Novels • Humorous Fiction • Minnesota • Radio

Now try   Keillor's other books about Lake Wobegon include *Lake Wobegon Days* and *Wobegon Boy*. Other light and humorous novels about small-town life include Jon Hassler's *Dear James*, Fannie Flagg's *Fried Green Tomatoes at the Whistle-Stop Café*, Lorna Landvik's *Your Oasis on Flame Lake*, and *These High, Green Hills* by Jan Karon.

Keneally, Thomas
Schindler's List
Simon and Schuster. 1982. 400 pp.

Oskar Schindler, a German-Catholic industrialist and member of the Nazi party, attempts to save the lives of the 1,300 Jews who work in his kitchenware factory.

2d Appeal   Setting

Subjects   Australian Authors • Booker Prize Winners • Holocaust • Jews and Judaism • World War II

Now try   Among Keneally's many other books are *Bring Larks and Heroes*, *The Chant of Jimmie Blacksmith*, and *A River Town*, all of which are set in Australia. Lynne Alexander's *Safe Houses* presents, in Raoul Wallenberg, a flawed man who finds his humanity in helping others during World War II.

Keneally, Thomas
Woman of the Inner Sea
Nan A. Talese. 1993. 277 pp.

Thirty-something socialite Kate Gaffney-Kozinski attempts to heal her spirit by fleeing to the Australian outback, running from a disintegrating marriage and the loss of her children.

2d Appeal   Setting

Subjects   Australia • Australian Authors • Death of a Child • Grief • Husbands and Wives

Now try   Keneally also wrote *Confederates* and *Blood Red*, *Sister Rose*. Another novel about a young woman trying to heal her heart, mind, and body is *Celebration* by Mary Lee Settle.

Kennedy, Pagan
Spinsters

High Risk. 1995. 158 pp.

After their father dies, spinster sisters Frannie and Doris leave their small New Hampshire town and discover that life can still surprise and delight them.

Subjects   Coming-of-Age • Older Women/Younger Men • Road Novels • Single Women • Sisters

Now try   Among Kennedy's other books are *The Exes* and *Stripping, and Other Stories*. Other novels that deal with adults finally coming-of-age are Jessica Anderson's *Tirra Lirra by the River*, Constance Beresford-Howe's *A Population of One*, and Elizabeth Jolley's *Miss Peabody's Inheritance*. *The Widows' Adventures* by Charles Dickinson and *Turnip Blues* by Helen Campbell are both novels about two sisters who take a car trip together.

Kenney, Susan
In Another Country

Viking. 1984. 163 pp.

Sara, forever affected by the death of her father, copes with an insane mother, the illness that threatens to take her husband's life, and her own doubts and fears.

Subjects   ALA Notable Books • Death of a Parent • Family Relationships • Mental Illness

Now try   Sailing is the sequel to *In Another Country*. Connie May Fowler's *Before Women Had Wings*, in which two sisters have to learn how to deal with the death of their father and its effect on their mother, shares both subject and a similarity of voice with Kenney's novel.

Kercheval, Jesse Lee
The Museum of Happiness

Faber & Faber. 1993. 272 pp.

During the late 1920s, young widow Ginny Gillespie flees to Paris from Florida and finds herself faling in love with France and with Roland Keppi, a young man whose visions match her own.

Subjects   1920s • First Novels • France • Love Stories • Magic Realism

Now try   Kercheval also wrote *Space*, a memoir of growing up in Florida. Another tale of wounded souls attempting to heal themselves while falling in love is Mary Lee Settle's *Celebration*. Linda Ashour's *Speaking in Tongues* is also about Americans living in France.

Kincaid, Jamaica
Annie John

Farrar, Straus Giroux. 1985. 148 pp.

On the island of Antigua, precocious Annie John quietly rebels against her doting parents as she struggles to break the bonds of childhood.

2d Appeal   Language   Book Groups 📖

Subjects   ALA Notable Books • Antigua • Antiguan Authors • Coming-of-Age • Family Relationships • Fathers and Daughters • Mothers and Daughters

Now try   Kincaid also wrote *At the Bottom of the River*, a short-story collection reflecting memories of her Caribbean childhood and *My Brother*, a memoir. Edwidge Danticat's *Breath, Eyes, Memory*, Cecilia Manguerra Brainard's *When the Rainbow Goddess Wept*, and Janine Boissard's *Cecile* are all coming-of-age stories set outside the United States.

Kincaid, Nanci
Crossing Blood

Putnam. 1992. 285 pp.

In Tallahassee, Florida, during the early 1960s, adolescent Lucy becomes infatuated with irrepressible Skippy, the boy who lives right next door but is across the racial line.

Book Groups 📖

Subjects	1960s • Coming-of-Age • First Novels • Florida • Interracial Relationships • Race Relations • Southern Authors
Now try	Kincaid's other works of fiction include *Pretending the Bed Is a Raft: Stories* and *Balls: A Novel*. Albert French's *Holly*, Ann Fairbairn's *Five Smooth Stones*, and Helene Wiggin's *Dancing at the Victory Café* are all novels about interracial romances.

King, Tabitha
The Book of Reuben

Dutton. 1994. 354 pp.

As he approaches middle age, former Nodd's Ridge, Maine, high school basketball star Reuben Styles realizes that marriage and fatherhood, as well as having his own business, do not bring the satisfaction he covets.

Subjects	Business and Businessmen • Coming-of-Age • Family Relationships • Love Stories • Maine • Middle-Aged Men • Midlife Crisis • Small-Town Life
Now try	This is a prequel to both *Pearl* and *One on One*, which cover Reuben's life as a husband and father. King's other books about Nodd's Ridge are *The Caretaker* and *The Trap*. John Updike's Rabbit Angstrom (*Rabbit Is Rich* and others) and Richard Ford's Frank Bascombe (*Independence Day*) are other men who find their lives disappointing and unfulfilling.

Kinsella, W. P.
Shoeless Joe

Houghton Mifflin. 1982. 265 pp.

Iowa farmer Ray Kinsella constructs a baseball field in back of his house after hearing a voice say, If you build it, he will come …

Subjects	Baseball • Canadian Authors • First Novels • Iowa • Magic Realism • Marriage
Now try	Kinsella's other books include *The Iowa Baseball Confederacy*, *Dance Me Outside: More Tales from the Erminesken Reserve*, and *Box Socials*. Bernard Malamud's *The Natural* and Mark Harris's *Bang the Drum Slowly* are other novels about baseball. Shoeless Joe Jackson and the scandal of the 1919 World Series are described in the nonfiction book, *Eight Men Out: The Black Sox and the 1919 World Series*, by Eliot Asinof, and the novel, *Blue Ruin*, by Brendan Boyd.

Klass, Perri
Other Women's Children

Random House. 1990. 284 pp.

As Amelia tries to balance her role of pediatrician tending to other women's children with her role as wife and mother tending to her own son and husband, she faces inner conflict and uncertainty about her future.

Subjects   AIDS • Career Women • Doctors and Patients • Husbands and Wives • Mothers and Sons

Now try   Klass, a pediatrician herself, also wrote *Recombinations* and *Baby Doctor*. Janet Dawson's mystery *Nobody's Child* and Alice Hoffman's *At Risk* are both about children with AIDS.

Kline, Christina Baker

Sweet Water   HarperCollins Publishers. 1993. 292 pp.

Cassie Simon goes home to rural Tennessee to realize her dreams of becoming a sculptor and finds herself forced to face the tragedy that has ruled three generations of her family.

Book Groups 📖

Subjects   Art and Artists • Family Relationships • First Novels • Tennessee

Now try   Other novels set in Tennessee include Lisa Alther's *Kinflicks*, *A Summons to Memphis* by Peter Taylor, and *The Orchard Keeper* by Cormac McCarthy.

Koch, Christopher

Highways to War   Viking. 1995. 469 pp.

When combat photographer Michael Langford disappears, his oldest friend, Raymond, tries to puzzle out the reasons Langford chose to cross the border and risk his life in wartorn Cambodia.

2d Appeal   Setting   Book Groups 📖

Subjects   1970s • Australian Authors • Cambodia • Journalists • Men's Friendships • Photography and Photographers • Southeast Asia • Vietnam War

Now try   Koch is also the author of *The Year of Living Dangerously*, a novel about foreign journalists in Indonesia. *Highways to War* is a novel about the pull of Asia and the desire to penetrate its mysteries, a theme also present in Graham Greene's *The Quiet American*, a novel set prior to the Vietnam War. Marianne Wiggins's *Eveless Eden* is another novel about a war correspondent and a photojournalist. *Highways to War* won the Miles Franklin Award.

Kotzwinkle, William

The Bear Went Over the Mountain   Doubleday. 1996. 306 pp.

When a hungry bear finds a book manuscript hidden in a briefcase in the Maine woods, he transforms himself into author Hal Jam, gets the novel published, watches it become a best seller, and embarks on a whirlwind publicity tour.

Subjects   Bears • Humorous Fiction • Writers and Writing

Now try   Kotzwinkle's other books include *The Game of Thirty*, *The Fan Man*, and *Swimmer in the Secret Sea*, among many more. More descriptions of book tours can be found in Michael Chabon's *Wonder Boys* and Martin Amis's *The Information*. In Rafi Zabor's *The Bear Comes Home*, the eponymous hero becomes a jazz musician. Hal's experiences in the world are similar to those experienced by the main character in *Being There* by Jerzy Kosinski.

Kraft, Eric
Reservations Recommended
Crown Publishers. 1990. 277 pp.

Boston toy company executive Matthew Barber has little success trying to escape his daytime problems by assuming the pseudonym of B. W. Beath and writing restaurant reviews at night.

Subjects Business and Businessmen • Cafes and Restaurants • Culinary Arts • Humorous Fiction • Middle-Aged Men

Now try Kraft's other books include *Herb 'n' Lorna* (about a couple who design and make animated erotic jewelry) and a series of novels about the adventures of Peter Leroy, including *Little Follies*, *Where Do You Stop?* and *At Home with the Glynns*. Another novel with the same sort of humor as *Reservations Recommended* is Paul Rudnick's *I'll Take It*.

Kupfer, Fern
Surviving the Seasons
Delacorte Press. 1987. 327 pp.

Retirement in Florida gives Sarah and Jake Pearlman time to worry about their daughters, delight in their continuing sexual compatibility, and muse on their long and happy life together.

Subjects Death of a Spouse • Florida • Husbands and Wives • Marriage • Retirement

Now try Kupfer's other books include a memoir about her family's experiences with a brain-damaged child, *Before and After Zachariah: A Family Story About a Different Kind of Courage*, and a novel, *No Regrets*. Wallace Stegner's *Crossing to Safety* and Walter Sullivan's *A Time to Dance* are both about long marriages

Lanchester, John
The Debt to Pleasure
Holt. 1996. 251 pp.

Tarquin Winot, who is passionate about food, peels away the layers of his past and gradually reveals a history filled with sinister truths.

Subjects Black Humor • British Authors • Brothers • Culinary Arts • Family Relationships • First Novels • Murder

Now try Food plays a major role in Abigail Stone's *Recipes from the Dump*. Isak Dinesen's *Babette's Feast* and Laura Esquivel's *Like Water for Chocolate* both have food as their main focus. *The Debt to Pleasure* won both the Whitbread Award for First Novels and the Betty Trask Award.

Landvik, Lorna
Your Oasis on Flame Lake
Fawcett Columbine. 1997. 296 pp.

Friendship, tears, and laughter mark the relationship of two families in Flame Lake, Minnesota.

Subjects Adultery • Family Relationships • Minnesota • Small-Town Life • Women's Friendships

Now try   Landvik's first novel, also set in a small Minnesota town, is ***Patty Jane's House of Curl***, about a pair of wacky sisters. Although their novels couldn't be more different in tone and intent, both Landvik and T. Coraghessan Boyle (in ***The Tortilla Curtain***) use the technique of shifting viewpoints to broaden the scope of their books.

Lauber, Lynn
21 Sugar Street
Norton. 1993. 239 pp.

Repercussions from the interracial romance of Loretta Dardio and Luther Biggs are seen from the perspective of their families as well as the social worker who adopts their baby.

Book Groups 📖

Subjects   Adoption • Bi-racial Characters • Coming-of-Age • Interracial Relationships • Love Stories • Race Relations

Now try   This novel is a continuation of the story begun in Lauber's collection of short stories, ***White Girls***. ***Caucasia*** by Danzy Senna is an autobiographical novel about growing up with a black father and white mother.

Lefcourt, Peter
Abbreviating Ernie
Villard. 1997. 301 pp.

After her cross-dressing urologist husband has a fatal heart attack while they're having sex, Audrey, who is handcuffed to the stove, can think of only one way to escape Ernie's dead weight: by making good use of an electric carving knife.

Subjects   Death of a Spouse • Humorous Fiction • Law and Lawyers • Marriage • Murder

Now try   Lefcourt also wrote ***The Dreyfus Affair***, about a major league shortstop who announces that he is a homosexual, and ***Di and I***. Cross-dressing is also a theme in Tama Janowitz's ***The Male Cross-Dresser Support Group***.

Leimbach, Marti
Dying Young
Doubleday. 1990. 277 pp.

Hilary and Victor's love affair is complicated by the fact that he is dying of leukemia and Hilary is attracted to Gordon, a handsome and healthy young man.

Subjects   Death and Dying • First Novels • Leukemia • Male/Female Relationships • Triangles

Now try   Leimbach also wrote ***Sun Dial Street*** and ***Love and Houses***, a more humorous book whose plot includes both romance and real estate. Like Erich Segal's ***Love Story***, Leimbach's novel is a real tear-jerker. The main character in Marian Thurm's ***Walking Distance*** is also having an affair with a dying man.

Leland, Christopher
Letting Loose
Zoland Books. 1996. 340 pp.

Twenty-five years after he disappeared in Vietnam, Bobbo Starwick's body is returned to his hometown for burial, forcing three people to face their memories of the past: his old girlfriend, a fellow soldier who survived the war, and his gay half-brother Barry.

2d Appeal   Characters

Subjects   Brothers • Gay Men • Male/Female Relationships • Small-Town Life • Vietnam Veterans • Vietnam War

Now try Leland's other novels include *The Book of Marvels* and *Mrs. Randall. Dues: A Novel of War and After* by Michael H. Cooper and Richard Ford's *The Ultimate Good Luck* are both about the experiences of Vietnam veterans.

Lerman, Rhoda
Animal Acts
H. Holt. 1994. 263 pp.

Leaving with Moses, a trained gorilla, in tow, animal lover Linda Morris (sans both her wealthy husband and her mysterious lover) discovers in their Garden-of-Eden existence in Florida that she has more in common with Moses than with either man in her life.

Subjects Florida • Gorillas • Marriage • Midlife Crisis • Satirical Fiction

Now try Other novels by Lerman include *Eleanor* and *God's Ear*. Three other books in which the main female character becomes involved with an animal are *Bear* by Marian Engel, *After Roy* by Mary Tannen, and *Brazzaville Beach* by William Boyd.

Lethem, Jonathan
As She Climbed Across the Table
Doubleday. 1997. 212 pp.

When particle physicist Alice Coombs falls in love with Lack, who is, literally, a hole in the universe, it wreaks havoc on her relationship with Philip Engstrand, a university colleague.

2d Appeal Language   Book Groups 📖

Subjects Academia • Love Stories • Male/Female Relationships • Physics • Science and Scientists • Women Scientists

Now try Lethem's other novels include *Gun, with Occasional Music* and *Girl in Landscape*. Another penetrating look at academia can be found in John L'Heureux's *The Handmaid of Desire*. Physics also plays a role in Louis B. Jones's *Particles and Luck*.

Levenkron, Steven
The Luckiest Girl in the World
Scribner. 1997. 188 pp.

Katie Roskova responds to her mother's unreasonable expectations and her father's absence by turning her despair inward and mutilating herself with knives and scissors.

Subjects Dysfunctional Families • Emotional Disability • Mothers and Daughters • Psychiatrists, Psychoanalysts, Psychotherapists • Teenage Girls

Now try Other novels depicting sympathetic psychiatrists working with adolescents include Levenkron's first novel, *The Best Little Girl in the World*, about a teenager with anorexia, and *I Never Promised You a Rose Garden* by Joanne Greenberg.

Lindbergh, Reeve
The Names of the Mountains
Simon & Schuster. 1992. 237 pp.

Growing up under the intense public scrutiny that accompanied celebrity parents, and now a mother with her own family, Cressida struggles to reconcile public with private perceptions, sort out her extended family relationships, and cope with an aging mother.

2d Appeal Language   Book Groups 📖

Subjects Aging • Family Relationships • Mothers and Daughters

Now try Lindbergh, the daughter of Charles and Anne Morrow Lindbergh, is also the author of many books for children and *Under a Wing: A Memoir*. Wallace Stegner's *Crossing to Safety* is also about relationships and how they evolve over time. The later journals of May Sarton, such as *At Seventy*, discuss her own issues with aging.

List, Shelley
Forgiving
Dutton. 1982. 243 pp.

Naomi Lazarus Loeffler, a successful 35-year-old writer, wrestles with her own uncomfortable issue of repressed sexual abuse as she writes an article on child pornography.

Subjects Fathers and Daughters • Jews and Judaism • Sexual Abuse • Writers and Writing

Now try Among List's other novels are *Did You Love Daddy When I Was Born?* and *Nobody Makes Me Cry*. Richard Bausch's *Mr. Field's Daughter*, Joan Chase's *The Evening Wolves*, and Delia Ephron's *Hanging Up* all describe different types of relationships between a father and daughter.

Listfield, Emily
Acts of Love
Viking. 1994. 373 pp.

A family is torn and a town's allegiances are divided when Ted Waring shoots his estranged wife, and his troubled 13-year-old daughter Julia believes the shooting was deliberate.

Subjects Death of a Parent • Death of a Spouse • Family Relationships • Law and Lawyers • Murder • Sisters

Now try Listfield also wrote *The Last Good Night*. Both Rosellen Brown's *Before and After* and Larry Watson's *Montana 1948* explore how a crime committed by one member of the family affects everyone.

Lopez-Medina, Sylvia
Cantora
University of New Mexico Press. 1992. 306 pp.

Amparo listens to, explores, collects, and retells the story of the four generations of Mexican women who defied tradition to discover themselves and the inner strength that held the family together.

Book Groups 📖

Subjects First Novels • Love Stories • Mexican Americans • Multigenerational Novels

Now try *Mother Tongue* by Demetria Martinez also describes a passionate and forbidden love affair. Denise Chavez's *Face of an Angel* is another saga about a Latino family.

MacDonald, Ann-Marie
Fall on Your Knees

Simon & Schuster. 1996. 508 pp.

The sudden return of opera singer Kathleen Piper to her family's home on Cape Breton Island, Nova Scotia, provides the focal point for this multigenerational saga that encompasses race relations, incest, birth, death, marriage, and the insidiousness of family secrets.

Book Groups 📖

Subjects   Canadian Authors • Family Secrets • Fathers and Daughters • First Novels • Incest • Marriage • Multigenerational Novels • Nova Scotia

Now try   Other family sagas include Denise Chavez's *Face of an Angel*, Kate Atkinson's *Behind the Scenes at the Museum*, and Elizabeth Jane Howard's series, "The Cazelet Chronicle."

Mahoney, Tim
We're Not Here

Dell. 1988. 239 pp.

When the Americans abandoned Vietnam in 1975, Sergeant Bill Lemmen was forced to leave his longtime girlfriend Hoa and spends the next seven years searching San Francisco's expatriate Vietnamese community for some news of her.

Subjects   1970s • Interracial Relationships • Love Stories • San Francisco • Vietnam Veterans • Vietnam War

Now try   Mahoney's first novel was *Halloran's World War*, about a Vietnam veteran struggling to return to civilian life. Other novels about interracial relationships include Sunetra Gupta's *Memories of Rain, To a Native Shore* by Valerie Anand, *On Common Ground* by Deena Linett, and *Sweet Eyes* by Jonis Agee.

Manderino, John
Sam and His Brother Len

Academy Chicago Publishers. 1994. 234 pp.

Brothers Len and Sam learn that even though they've grown up with different interests and different dreams—Sam is the studious, moody one and Len is the jock who plans to marry his high school girlfriend—they can still love and support each other through difficult times.

Subjects   Brothers • Coming-of-Age • First Novels • Humorous Fiction

Now try   Manderino also wrote *The Man Who Once Played Catch with Nellie Fox: A Novel*. Another lighthearted look at brothers is *Big Babies* by Sherwood Kiraly.

Mapson, Jo-Ann
Shadow Ranch

HarperCollins Publishers. 1996. 375 pp.

Bop, nearing 80, searches for some way to console his granddaughter Lainie when her four-year-old son dies and to give some backbone to her brother Russell, who is living an aimless, guitar-playing existence.

2d Appeal   Characters

Book Groups 📖

Subjects   Brothers and Sisters • Death of a Child • Elderly Men • Family Relationships • Grandparents • Music and Musicians

Now try   Mapson always tells a good story, as seen in her other novels, including *Hank & Chloe*, *Blue Rodeo*, and *Loving Chloe*. The myriad of disasters that befall the characters in *Shadow Ranch* will bring to mind Mary Hood's *Familiar Heat*, Jane Smiley's *A Thousand Acres*, and *A Map of the World* by Jane Hamilton.

McCammon, Robert
Boy's Life
Pocket Books. 1991. 440 pp.

On a hot summer day in Zephyr, Alabama, 12-year-old Cory Jay Mackenson's life changes forever when he and his father witness the brutal murder of a stranger.

Subjects   Alabama • Coming-of-Age • Fathers and Sons • Magic Realism • Murder • Small-Town Life • Southern Authors • Violence

Now try   McCammon writes mainly horror/suspense novels but has moved toward Southern gothic with this book and *Gone South*, the tale of a Vietnam vet on the run from the police. Both Alice Hoffman's *Turtle Moon* and Lewis Nordan's *Music of the Swamp* are magical stories about interesting characters.

McCormick, Ann du Mais
Northern Exposure
St. Martin's Press. 1989. 234 pp.

Dianna sets out on a journey from San Francisco to Boston to reclaim her ex-husband (married for 10 years to her best friend) and discovers a new love, old talents, and the bonds of friendship.

Subjects   Art and Artists • Divorce • First Novels • Marriage • Road Novels • Women's Friendships

Now try   Alexandra Marshall's *Something Borrowed* is also has a reunion of a long-divorced couple, whereas Steve Tesich's *Karoo* is about a couple unable to finally end their marriage.

McCoy, Maureen
Walking After Midnight
Poseidon Press. 1985. 233 pp.

When Lottie Jay leaves her husband after a night of drinking, wrecks her car, and ends up at an alcohol rehabilitation center, she begins to make a new and sober life for herself among a varied group of friends, including her Lebanese landlady and her candy-selling son, a recovering alcoholic motorcyclist, a wheelchair-bound lesbian, and an adult education teacher who urges Lottie to get serious about her songwriting.

2d Appeal   Characters

Subjects   Alcoholics and Alcoholism • Car Accidents • First Novels • Lesbians • Music and Musicians • Presley, Elvis

Now try   McCoy also wrote *Divining Blood*, about a young woman returning home to Illinois to deal with the unresolved mysteries of her earlier life. Characters who worship Elvis Presley are found in Laura Kalpakian's *Graced Land* and P. F. Kluge's *Biggest Elvis*. Mark Childress's *Tender* is a fictional biography of Elvis Presley.

McFall, Lynne
Dancer with Bruised Knees
Chronicle Books. 1994. 215 pp.

Losing an eye in a barroom brawl leads 39-year-old photographer Sarah Blight to analyze the way she has lived her life with odd and dangerous people.

Book Groups

Subjects   Dysfunctional Families • Photography and Photographers • Single Women

Now try   Another novel by McFall is *The One True Story of the World*. Examples of other bleakly humorous lives are found in two memoirs, Geoffrey Wolff's *The Duke of Deception* and Laura Cunningham's *Living Arrangements*.

McMahon, Thomas
Loving Little Egypt
Viking. 1987. 273 pp.

Mourly Vold, a nearly blind genius, becomes involved in a scheme to connect blind people through a communications network and as a result is marked as a dangerous subversive by the U.S. government.

Subjects   1920s • ALA Notable Books • Humorous Fiction • Inventors and Inventions

Now try   McMahon's other novels include *McKay's Bees* and *Principles of American Nuclear Chemistry*. Both real and imagined characters can be found in E. L. Doctorow's *Ragtime* and T. Coraghesen Boyle's *The Road to Wellville*.

McManus, James
Going to the Sun
HarperCollins Publishers. 1996. 342 pp.

Now in her late 20s, Penny decides to bicycle from Chicago to Alaska, hoping it will help her make sense of her feelings about her diabetes, the trouble she's having finishing her doctoral dissertation, and her inability to forget the events—seven years before—that led to the death of her lover in an Alaskan hospital.

2d Appeal   Characters   Book Groups

Subjects   Alaska • Bicycling • College Students • Death and Dying • Diabetes • Road Novels

Now try   McManus's other works of fiction include *Out of the Blue* and *Chin Music*. Like Tim O'Brien's *In the Lake of the Woods*, the ending of this novel is left open to the interpretation of the reader. Other books about long-distance bicycle trips include Willie Weir's *Spokesongs: Bicycle Adventures on Three Continents* and *Miles from Nowhere: A Round the World Bicycle Adventure* by Barbara Savage. Andre Dominick's *Needles* is a memoir of his life as a diabetic.

McPhee, Martha
Bright Angel Time
Random House. 1997. 244 pp.

Kate, youngest of three sisters, watches as her mother falls in love with Anton, a New Age guru, con man, and abusive father.

2d Appeal   Characters   Book Groups 📖

Subjects   1960s • Coming-of-Age • Divorce • Family Relationships • First Novels • Hippies • Sisters

Now try   Ptolemy Tompkins's autobiography, ***Paradise Fever: Growing Up in the Shadow of the New Age***, is another view of the 1960s. Brian Hall's ***The Saskiad*** also shows the downside of the 1960s attitudes toward parenting. Tom Wolfe's ***The Electric Kool-Aid Acid Test*** is a drug-induced, upbeat view of the same period.

McVeigh, Alice
While the Music Lasts
Orion Books. 1994. 234 pp.

Life in the (fictional) Orchestra of London as seen through the eyes of several musicians, as well as the conductor, a member of the orchestra's board, and various friends and relations, includes love affairs, a misdirected love letter, and an unusual codicil to a will.

2d Appeal   Setting

Subjects   Adultery • British Authors • Love Affairs • Marriage • Music and Musicians

Now try   Janet Burroway's ***Opening Nights*** delves into the intertwined lives of people working on a theater project. Ngaio Marsh frequently sets her mysteries around the world of the theater, as seen in ***The Light Thickens***. Another mystery set around a drama production is Edmund Crispin's ***The Case of the Gilded Fly***, which gives readers (in addition to a good mystery) a backstage view of the friendships, love affairs, and feuds that develop among the cast and crew.

McWilliam, Candia
Debatable Land
Nan A. Talese. 1994. 284 pp.

As a ship, the Ardent Spirit, sails from Tahiti to New Zealand, the six people aboard the boat must learn to live not only with one another, but also with themselves and their pasts.

2d Appeal   Characters

Subjects   Boats and Boating • British Authors • Male/Female Relationships • Sailors and Sailing • Scottish Authors

Now try   McWilliam also wrote *A Little Stranger* and *A Case of Knives*. Other books centered around a storm at sea include Sebastian Junger's nonfiction account, ***The Perfect Storm***, and Robert Stone's ***Outerbridge Reach***. ***Debatable Land*** won the Guardian Fiction Prize.

Mendelsohn, Jane
I Was Amelia Earhart
A.A. Knopf. 1996. 146 pp.

During Amelia Earhart's final flight across the Pacific, the past (history) and present (fantasy) combine to offer the hope of survival and redemption.

2d Appeal   Language

Subjects   Earhart, Amelia • First Novels • Male/Female Relationships • Women Pilots

Now try Other novels that mythologize a real person include *The Birthday Boys* by Beryl Bainbridge, Walter Satterthwait's *Miss Lizzie*, and Gabriel Garcia Marquez's *The General in His Labyrinth*. Beryl Markham's autobiography, *West with the Night*, is a lyrical ode to the beauty of flight. Another novel about Amelia Earhart is *Hidden Latitudes* by Alison Anderson.

Mo, Timothy

Sour Sweet

Vintage Books. 1985. 279 pp.

When Chen immigrates to London, he expects difficulties understanding the customs and language of his new home, but he doesn't foresee how his ambitious wife and aging father will irrevocably link his life with the local Chinese mafia.

2d Appeal Characters

Subjects ALA Notable Books • Chinese British Authors • Culture Clash • Family Relationships • Immigrants and Refugees

Now try Mo's first novel was *The Monkey King*. *Sour Sweet* was shortlisted for the Booker Prize in 1982. Hanif Kureishi's *The Buddha of Suburbia* also explores the plight of immigrants coming to Britain from its former colonies.

Mooney, Ted

Easy Travel to Other Planets
Farrar, Straus Giroux. 1981. 278 pp.

Her mother Nona's terminal cancer, her friend Nikki's unexpected pregnancy, impending world war in Antarctica, and a 9 millimeter automatic pistol all influence 29-year-old Melissa's cataclysmic decision regarding a talking dolphin named Peter.

Subjects ALA Notable Books • Cancer • Dolphins • First Novels • Male/Female Relationships • Mothers and Daughters • Suicide • Twins • Women's Friendships

Now try Mooney's other books include *Traffic and Laughter* and *Singing into the Piano*. William Gibson (*Neuromancer* and others) and Don DeLillo (*White Noise* and others) both explore contemporary culture in their novels.

Moore, Lorrie

Who Will Run the Frog Hospital?
Knopf. 1994. 147 pp.

Approaching 40 and in Paris to try to save her marriage, Berie Carr recalls the summer of 1973 when she and her best friend, Sils, worked in an upstate New York storybook theme park and learned that not everything in life has a happy ending.

Subjects 1970s • Coming-of-Age • Friendship • Small-Town Life • Teenage Girls • Teenage Pregnancy

Now try Moore's other works of fiction include *Like Life: Stories*, *Anagrams: A Novel*, *Self-Help: Stories*, and *Birds of America*. Ruth Doan MacDougall's *The Cheerleader* is another good novel about teenage girls. Margaret Atwood writes vividly about the pangs of growing up in *Lady Oracle*, *Cat's Eye*, and *The Robber Bride*. In 1996, Moore was named by *Granta Magazine* as one of "20 Best Young American Novelists."

Morgan, Clay
Santiago and the Drinking Party
Viking. 1992. 274 pp.

After an abortive trip to South America at the age of 20, Daniel Cooper returns when he is 35 to the Amazonian village of Los Puentos-Caidos and involves himself in the lives of the villagers, particularly the local philosopher Santiago, his beautiful daughter Angelina, and the evil tourist guide, Hector Tanbueno.

Subjects   Coming-of-Age • Culture Clash • First Novels • Love Stories • Small-Town Life • South America

Now try   Another (much darker) tale of a restless Yankee trying to find himself along the Amazon can be read in Peter Matthiessen's *At Play in the Fields of the Lord*.

Morris, Bill
Motor City
A.A. Knopf. 1992. 337 pp.

General Motors executive Ted Mackey campaigns to move the 1954 Buick into prominence in the automobile industry.

Subjects   1950s • Automobiles • Business and Businessmen • First Novels

Now try   Morris also wrote *All Souls' Day*. Another novel looking at the unsatisfying life of a 1950s businessman is Sloan Wilson's *The Man in the Grey Flannel Suit*. Arthur Hailey's *Wheels* and Emma Lathen's mystery *Murder Makes the Wheels Go Round* offer other views of the Detroit automobile industry.

Morrissey, Bill
Edson
Knopf. 1996. 237 pp.

When ex-singer and songwriter Henry Corvine says good-bye to the country music business, he moves back to his hometown of Edson, New Hampshire, only to discover that the past is never quite gone.

Subjects   First Novels • Love Stories • Male/Female Relationships • Music and Musicians • New Hampshire • Small-Town Life

Now try   Morrissey is also a singer/songwriter whose albums include "Friend of Mine," "Night Train," and "You'll Never Get to Heaven." Richard Currey's *Lost Highway* is another novel about a country music singer whose plans to make it big never quite materialize. Small-town New Hampshire is also the setting for Ruth Doan MacDougall's *The Cost of Living*.

Morrissy, Mary
Mother of Pearl
Scribner. 1995. 281 pp.

The story of a stolen infant is told by the three women involved in the crime: Irene, whose longing for a child drives her life; Rita, the natural mother, whose guilt about her loss overwhelms her; and Mary, the child herself, who grows up haunted by her confusing memories.

Book Groups 📖

Subjects   First Novels • Irish Authors • Kidnapping • Mothers and Daughters

Now try   Kate Atkinson's *Behind the Scenes at the Museum* is also about a woman haunted by her shadowy past. Morrissy shares a similarity of style with William Trevor (*Fools of Fortune*, *The Silence in the Garden*, and others). Margot Livesey's *Criminals* has a group of characters who all commit crimes, both large and small, one of which involves stealing a baby.

Moskowitz, Bette Ann
Leaving Barney
Holt. 1988. 229 pp.

When Barney, her husband of 35 years, dies, Tessie gradually learns to live on her own, as she tries to decide what kind of future she wants for herself.

Subjects Bookstores • Death of a Spouse • First Novels • New York • Race Relations • Widows • Women's Friendships

Now try Tessie is very similar to the family matriarch in Allegra Goodman's *The Family Markowitz*.

Mukherjee, Bharati
The Holder of the World
Knopf. 1993. 285 pp.

Following leads that take her around the world, modern-day asset hunter Beigh Masters discovers the true story of Hannah Easton, a young Puritan woman who ended up in the seventeenth-century court of a Hindu rajah.

Book Groups 📖

Subjects India • Interracial Relationships • Mothers and Daughters • Research Novels

Now try Mukherjee has often focused on the issue of identity and culture in her writing. Her short story collection, *The Middleman and Other Stories*, won the National Book Critics Circle Award. Among her other novels are *Jasmine* and *Leave It to Me*. Bits and pieces of the plot of *The Holder of the World* connect interestingly with Nathaniel Hawthorne's *The Scarlet Letter*. Other novels in which a modern day researcher tries to reconstruct a story from the past include *Possession* by A. S. Byatt and *The Lost Diaries of Frans Hals* by Michael Kernan.

Murphy, Yannick
The Sea of Trees
Houghton Mifflin Co. 1997. 227 pp.

Ten-year-old Tian's experiences during and immediately after World War II begin with life in a Japanese prison camp with her French mother, a move to Tian's father's home in China, and a futile search for peace when mother and daughter move back to Vietnam, only to find themselves caught in the escalating violence between the French and the Vietnamese.

2d Appeal Setting
Book Groups 📖

Subjects China • Coming-of-Age • First Novels • Immigrants and Refugees • Indochina • Mothers and Daughters • Vietnam • World War II

Now try J. G. Ballard's *Empire of the Sun* is also about a child's experiences during World War II; both it and *The Sea of Trees* show the devastation war wreaks on everyone, even non-combatants.

Myerson, Julie
The Touch
Nan A. Talese. 1996. 308 pp.

When Donna, who is critically ill, her live-in lover Will, and her sister Gayle rescue an old man after he's been mugged, he informs them that he is a healer whose touch can cure Donna.

2d Appeal Characters
Book Groups 📖

Subjects   Illness • Male/Female Relationships • Sisters

Now try   Myerson's first novel was *Sleepwalking*. Tim O'Brien's *In the Lake of the Woods* and James McManus's *Going to the Sun* share with this novel an ending that is left open to the interpretation of the reader.

Narayan, Kirin
Love, Stars, and All That
Pocket Books. 1994. 311 pp.

Although a Hindu astrologer from her native India foresees that Gita Das will meet the right man in 1984, her experiences with men as a graduate student in California don't give her much hope.

Subjects   Academia • Astrology • College Students • Culture Clash • First Novels • Humorous Fiction • India • Interracial Relationships • Love Stories • Male/Female Relationships

Now try   Narayan also wrote *Mondays on the Dark Night*. Bharti Kirchner's *Shiva Dancing*, Bharati Mukherjee's *Jasmine*, and *Arranged Marriage* by Chitra Banerjee Divakaruni are also about the varied experiences of Indian women in the United States.

Nasrin, Taslima
Shame
Prometheus Books. 1997. 302 pp.

Although they are Hindus, the Dutta family have stayed in primarily Muslim Bangladesh, refusing to move to India as many of their Hindu friends have already done, but the events following the destruction of a Muslim mosque in Ayodhya, India, cause them to rethink their choice. Translated from the Bengali by Kankabati Datta.

2d Appeal   Setting

Subjects   Bangladesh • Hindus • India • Indian Authors • Muslims • Novels in Translation • Race Relations • Violence

Now try   Nasrin also wrote *The Game in Reverse: Poems*. Like novelist Salman Rushdie after he published *Satanic Verses*, Nasrin was placed under a sentence of death by Muslim fundamentalists. Another novel about Hindu-Muslim relationships in the twentieth century is *Train to Pakistan* by Khushwant Singh.

Naumoff, Lawrence
Silk Hope, NC
Harcourt Brace. 1994. 352 pp.

Two sisters, stable Natalie and flighty Frannie, inherit their family farmhouse and must reconcile what this home, passed through their mother's family, will mean to each of their lives.

Book Groups 📖

Subjects   Bequests • Family Relationships • North Carolina • Single Women • Sisters • Small-Town Life

Now try   Other books by Naumoff include *Rootie Kazootie* and *The Night of the Weeping Women*. *I'm Not Complaining* by Ruth Adam is another novel with a strong woman main character.

Nooteboom, Cees
The Following Story
Harcourt Brace. 1994. 115 pp.

A scholarly bachelor, Herman Mussert, goes to bed in his small Amsterdam apartment only to awaken and find himself in the Lisbon hotel room where 20 years earlier he had embarked on a love affair. Translated from the Dutch by Ina Rilke.

2d Appeal   Characters   Book Groups

Subjects   Amsterdam • Death and Dying • Dutch Authors • Elderly Men • Love Stories • Magic Realism • Novels in Translation • Single Men

Now try   Other novels by Nooteboom include ***The Knight Has Died*** and ***Rituals***. Like the Austrian writer Christoph Ransmayr in his novel, ***The Last World***, Nooteboom uses Ovid's ***Metamorphoses*** as a touchstone for this novel. Kazuo Ishiguro's novels, especially ***The Remains of the Day***, are also about the regrets people have as they reconsider their lives. *A **Tiler's Afternoon*** by Lars Gustafsson and ***Einstein's Dreams*** by Alan Lightman have themes similar to Nooteboom's novel.

Nunez, Sigrid
A Feather on the Breath of God
HarperCollins Publishers. 1995. 180 pp.

Normal adolescent problems are made more difficult for the unnamed narrator by the unhappy and uncommunicative marriage of her Chinese-Panamanian father and German mother.

Subjects   Culture Clash • Family Relationships • First Novels • Teenage Girls

Now try   Nunez also explores family relationships in her novel, ***Naked Sleeper***. She is also the author of ***Mitz: The Marmoset of Bloomsbury***, a novel about Virginia Woolf. Another novel about the difficulties of forging an identity in a world of different cultures is ***Memory Mambo*** by Achy Obejas, about an adolescent Cuban American trying to understand her family and herself.

O'Brien, Kevin
The Only Son
Kensington Books. 1997. 294 pp.

When Carl—single and childless—decides to kidnap a baby and raise him as his own—several lives are changed forever.

Book Groups

Subjects   Fathers and Sons • Husbands and Wives • Kidnapping • Loss of a Child • Oregon

Now try   O'Brien's first novel was ***Actors***. The loss of a child is senstively described in ***Losing Isaiah*** by Seth Margolis.

O'Connell, Sanjida
Theory of Mind
Black Swan. 1996. 254 pp.

While studying empathy in primates at a British zoo, Ph.D. candidate Sandra Roberts finds herself immersed in a society of bizarre humans as well: the beautiful but deadly Kim, who specializes in robotics; the seriously disturbed child, Paul, and his secret life in the zoo's back halls; and her own obsessive fiancé.

Book Groups

Subjects   British Authors • Child Abuse • First Novels • Male/Female Relationships • Science and Scientists • Women Scientists • Zoos

Now try   William Boyd's *Brazzaville Beach* and *After Roy* by Mary Tannen are other novels with a female protagonist involved in a study of primates. Peter Dickinson's *The Poison Oracle* is a mystery in which the only witness to a crime is a primate (and she is having some difficulty communicating what she knows). Russell Hoban's *Turtle Diary* is also about people meeting through their interest in animals. *Theory of Mind* won the Betty Trask Award.

O'Connor, Philip
Stealing Home
Knopf. 1979. 307 pp.

While his marriage dissolves around him, Benjamin Dunne finds himself caught up in the throes of another struggle when he volunteers to coach his son's little league baseball team.

Subjects   Baseball • Family Relationships • Fathers and Sons • First Novels • Marriage

Now try   O'Connor is also the author of a collection of stories, *Old Morals, Small Continents, Darker Times*, and the novels *Finding Brendan* and *Defending Civilization*. Baseball helps another man through a tragedy in Christopher Bohjalian's *Past the Bleachers*, when a father, after his son dies, agrees to coach what would have been the boy's little league baseball team.

Offutt, Chris
The Good Brother
Simon & Schuster. 1997. 317 pp.

Pressure to avenge his brother's murder drives Virgil Caudill from the only home he's ever known—the hill country of Kentucky—toward an alien landscape far more volatile than he realizes.

2d Appeal   Language   Book Groups 📖

Subjects   Brothers • Kentucky • Murder • Poverty • Small-Town Life • Southern Authors • Violence

Now try   Offutt also wrote *Kentucky Straight*, a collection of short stories, and *The Same River Twice*, a personal account of his wanderings before becoming a father. E. Annie Proulx's *Postcards* is also about a man who leaves home after a tragedy. Pete Dexter's *The Paperboy* and Russell Banks's *Affliction* are both about one brother trying to understand another. In 1996, *Granta Magazine* named Offutt one of the "20 Best Young American Novelists."

O'Hagan, Christine
Benediction at the Savoia
Harcourt Brace Jovanovich. 1992. 325 pp.

When Delia Mary Delaney becomes pregnant at 19 and marries Maurice, her long-time boyfriend, she finds herself enmeshed in a marriage not so different from her mother's and begins to acknowledge her desire for a different sort of life.

Book Groups 📖

Subjects   1950s • 1960s • Family Relationships • First Novels • Husbands and Wives • Irish Americans • Teenage Pregnancy

Now try   Other novels about Irish American families include James Carroll's *Mortal Friends*, Lester Goran's *Tales from the Irish Club*, and Michael Dorris's *Cloud Chamber*.

O'Nan, Stewart

The Names of the Dead

Doubleday. 1996. 399 pp.

Sixteen years after returning from his stint as a medic in Vietnam, Larry Markham is still haunted by memories of the past and troubled by the bleakness of his present life in a deteriorating marriage and in his dead-end job delivering snack cakes throughout New England.

2d Appeal Characters

Subjects Adultery • Fathers and Sons • Marriage • Mental Illness • Vietnam Memorial • Vietnam Veterans • Vietnam War

Now try Among O'Nan's other novels are *Speed Queen* and *A World Away*. Bobbie Ann Mason's *In Country* has a very moving scene set at the Vietnam Memorial in Washington, D.C. The protagonist of Bret Lott's *The Man Who Owned Vermont* is similar to O'Nan's main character. *Buffalo Afternoon* by Susan Fromberg Schaeffer and *Paco's Story* by Larry Heinemann are both about the difficulty Vietnam veterans faced after they returned home.

Osborn, Karen

Patchwork

Harcourt Brace Jovanovich. 1991. 309 pp.

Sisters Rose and Lily, along with Silvia, Rose's adopted daughter, take turns telling the stories of their family's births, deaths, joys, and griefs in a South Carolina mill town.

Subjects First Novels • Multigenerational Novels • Sisters • Small-Town Life • South Carolina • Southern Authors

Now try Osborn also wrote *Between Earth and Sky*, an epistolary novel set in pioneer times, and *Blood Lines*. Osborn's use of language and storytelling technique are reminiscent of the novels of Lee Smith, including *Oral History*, *Family Linen*, and *Black Mountain Breakdown*.

Owen, Howard

The Measured Man

HarperCollins Publishers. 1997. 259 pp.

Walker Fann's decision to support the building of a slavery museum in the small Southern town where he is the managing editor of his family's newspaper leads to several deaths, but also to a growing sense of his own values and strengths.

Subjects Death of a Spouse • Men's Friendships • Race Relations • Racism • Southern Authors

Now try Owen is also the author of *Answers to Lucky*, *Fat Lightning*, and *Littlejohn*. This story of a town divided over an important issue and a man forced to choose which side he is on is also the subject of Chris Bohjalian's *Water Witches* and David Guterson's *Snow Falling on Cedars*. Hamilton Basso's novel, *The View from Pompey's Head*, describes the South's quarrel with itself over race and caste.

Ozeki, Ruth
My Year of Meats
Viking. 1998. 366 pp.

Documentary filmmaker Jane Takagi-Little gets what she thinks will be a dream job: working on a series of television programs encouraging Japanese housewives to serve more meat to their families.

Subjects   Career Women • Domestic Violence • First Novels • Humorous Fiction • Japan • Japanese Americans • Male/Female Relationships • Single Women

Now try   Ozeki's use of multiple subplots is similar to the incident packed *A Thousand Acres* by Jane Smiley and *Familiar Heat* by Mary Hood. Ozeki's condemnation of the meat industry expresses an outrage similar to Upton Sinclair's muckraking novel, *The Jungle*.

Palin, Michael
Hemingway's Chair
St. Martin's Press. 1998. 280 pp.

After his quaint village postal office is privatized, Martin Sproale, a mild-mannered assistant postmaster who is obsessed with Ernest Hemingway, must decide whether he is going to fight for what he believes in.

Subjects   British Authors • First Novels • Hemingway, Ernest • Humorous Fiction • Small-Town Life

Now try   Michael Palin, of Monty Python fame, has written screenplays, nonfiction, and children's books. Another novel about a mild-mannered, but obsessed (with a woman), postal worker, is Antonio Skarmeta's *Burning Patience*. Other novels that depict a fictional version of Hemingway include Karl Alexander's *Papa and Fidel*, *I Killed Hemingway* by William Henderson, and *The Crook Factory* by Dan Simmons.

Pate, Alexs
Finding Makeba
Putnam. 1996. 244 pp.

When his daughter unexpectedly greets him at a book signing, author Ben Crestfield must explain to her—and himself—why he walked out on his family a decade before.

Subjects   African American Authors • African Americans • Fathers and Daughters • Fathers Deserting Their Families • First Novels • Writers and Writing

Now try   Pate's first novel was *Losing Absalom*, about an African American family struggling with the patriarch's inevitable death due to cancer. Benjamin Cheever's *The Partisan* is also about the child of a famous novelist.

Pelletier, Cathie
A Marriage Made at Woodstock
Crown Publishers. 1994. 276 pp.

After being married for 20 years, new-ager Chandra Stones decides to leave her husband Fred, an uptight accountant.

Subjects   Divorce • Husbands and Wives • Male/Female Relationships • Marriage

Now try   Karl Ackerman, writing about relationships between men and women in *The Patron Saint of Unmarried Women*, has the same combination of humor and pathos found in Pelletier's novel. *After Moondog* by Jane Shapiro is another novel about the end of a marriage.

Perrin, Ursula
Old Devotions
Dial Press. 1983. 264 pp.

After Isabel Schliemann returns to New York from a trip to Russia, she finds that her apartment and all of her belongings have been lost in a fire and, as a result, she reconnects with her college friend, Morgan Whiteside, and Morgan's affluent suburban New Jersey lifestyle.

Subjects   Adultery • Anti-Semitism • Death and Dying • Jews and Judaism • Suburbia • Women's Friendships

Now try   Among Perrin's other novels are *Heart Failure* and *The Looking-Glass Lover*. Elizabeth Berg's *Talk Before Sleep* and Iris Dart's *Beaches* are both novels about death and women's friendships. Rick Moody's *The Ice Storm* is also about adultery in the lives of wealthy suburbanites.

Picoult, Jodi
Mercy
G.P. Putnam's. 1996. 353 pp.

When Jamie McDonald confesses that he murdered his terminally ill wife, the news sets his cousin, Chief of Police Cameron McDonald, at odds with his own wife, Alice.

Book Groups 📖

Subjects   Adultery • Euthanasia • Husbands and Wives • Mercy Killing • Murder • Terminal Illness

Now try   Among Picoult's other books are *Picture Perfect*, *Songs of the Humpback Whale*, *The Pact*, and *Harvesting the Heart*. In Larry Watson's *Montana 1948*, a police chief has to deal with a crime committed by a member of his family. Anna Quindlen's *One True Thing* also deals with the morality of euthanasia.

Pierce, Constance
Hope Mills
Pushcart Press. 1997. 311 pp.

A year in the life of high school freshman Tollie, who is convinced her hometown should be renamed Hopeless Mills, since the mill itself is closing, her mother is incapacitated by grief over Tollie's dead brother, and Tollie herself is experiencing the traumas of growing up.

2d Appeal   Setting

Subjects   1950s • Coming-of-Age • Death of a Child • First Novels • Mothers and Daughters • Race Relations • Small-Town Life • Teenage Girls • Working Classes

Now try   Pierce's novel was the winner of Pushcart's 15th Annual Editors' Book Award. Her other books include a collection of stories, *When Things Get Back to Normal*, and a book of poetry, *Philippe at His Bath*. In *An Ocean in Iowa*, Peter Hedges conveys the sense of the late 1960s through everyday details about food, television programs, and movies; Pierce does the same for 1959. Ruth Doan MacDougall's *The Cheerleader* is about a young woman coming of age in a New Hampshire factory town during the 1950s.

Piercy, Marge
The Longings of Women
Fawcett Columbine. 1994. 455 pp.

As three women's lives take a turn for the worse, Leila, Mary, and Kathy each struggle to find a permanent physical and emotional home.

Subjects   Homelessness • Women's Friendships

Now try   Piercy, a poet as well as a novelist, frequently deals with societal issues in her novels, including protest against the Vietnam War in *Vida* and abortion in *Braided Lives*. Two books of Piercy's poetry, *Circle on the Water* and *What Are Big Girls Made Of?* were ALA Notable Books. Other novels that deal with the subject of homelessness include *Ironweed* by William Kennedy and *Ripley Bogle* by Robert McLiam Wilson.

Pinon, Nelida
Caetana's Sweet Song
Knopf. 1992. 401 pp.

Twenty years after her mysterious disappearance, performance artist Caetana returns home to call in old favors from cattle baron Polidoro (her tempestuous lover) and other friends to stage a final, triumphant performance. Translated from the Portuguese by Helen Lane.

2d Appeal   Setting

Subjects   Art and Artists • Brazilian Authors • Love Stories • Novels in Translation • South American Authors

Now try   Pinon's other novel, *The Republic of Dreams*, is also available in an English translation. Another novelist from Brazil is Clarice Lispector, whose books include *The Apple in the Dark* and *The Foreign Legion: Stories and Chronicles*. Gabriel Garcia Marquez's *Love in the Time of Cholera* is another epic love story.

Pope, Susan
Catching the Light
Viking. 1990. 226 pp.

Unmarried, pregnant, and disowned by the grandfather who raised her, Damaris Bishop discovers her own strengths with the help of four women: her grandmother, who defies her husband's disapproval to remain close to her granddaughter; Jose, the owner of a boarding house, who takes Damaris in; aged Winifred Cabot, who can identify with Damaris's plight; and independent Myra Bea, who offers a different sort of role model.

Subjects   Cape Cod • First Novels • Grandparents • Single Parents • Women's Friendships

Now try   Other novels about single mothers keeping their babies include Ann Patchett's *The Patron Saint of Liars* and Terri McFerrin Smith's *False Starts*.

Postman, Andrew
Now I Know Everything
Crown Publishers. 1995. 246 pp.

Andrew's job as advice columnist Vince, offering the women of America the male point of view in a well-known women's magazine, becomes problematical when he falls in love and is unable to distinguish what he believes from the opinions Vince expresses in his monthly column.

Subjects   First Novels • Humorous Fiction • Love Stories • New York • Writers and Writing

Now try   Both Nathanael West's *Miss Lonelyhearts* and *Dear Digby* by Carol Muske-Dukes are about advice columnists.

Power, Susan
The Grass Dancer
Putnam. 1994. 300 pp.

Like an archaeological dig, the lives of Sioux Indians on a North Dakota reservation are uncovered a layer at a time, moving backward to show how the past has influenced the present.

2d Appeal   Setting   Book Groups 📖

Subjects   ALA Notable Books • American Indian Authors • American Indians • Coming-of-Age • First Novels • Magic Realism • North Dakota • Sioux • South Dakota

Now try   Another novel in which the past is slowly uncovered is *First Light* by Charles Baxter.

Preston, Caroline
Jackie by Josie
Scribner. 1997. 314 pp.

Events in her own life are thrown into perspective when Josie Trask takes a job researching the life of Jacqueline Kennedy Onassis for a celebrity biography.

Subjects   First Novels • Marriage • Onassis, Jacqueline Kennedy • Writers and Writing

Now try   Rebecca Goldstein's *The Mind-Body Problem* and *Rameau's Niece* by Cathleen Schine are both about the difficulty women have being married to men considered to be much more intelligent than they themselves are. Josie's voice in this novel is similar to the voice of the main characters in Luanne Rice's *Crazy in Love* and Susan Trott's *Crane Spreads Wings: A Bigamist's Story*.

Preston, Douglas
Jennie
St. Martin's Press. 1994. 302 pp.

Anthropologist Hugo Archibald brings home Jennie, an orphan chimpanzee, to raise as part of his family, but problems arise when Jennie becomes an adolescent and realizes that she is different from the rest of the Archibalds.

Subjects   Chimpanzees • Family Relationships • First Novels

Now try   Preston also wrote *Relic*, *Reliquary*, and *Dinosaurs in the Attic: An Excursion into the American Museum of Natural History*, about his years working at the museum. The accounts of Jennie's life are so realistic that it's easy to mistake this novel for nonfiction. William Boyd's *Brazzaville Beach* and Mary Tannen's *After Roy* both deal with the strong bond between humans and animals.

Pym, Barbara
A Glass of Blessings
Dutton. 1980. 256 pp.

Wilmet Forsyth, bored to distraction with her marriage, involves herself with events at her church and her flirtation with the handsome and unattainable Piers Longridge.

2d Appeal   Characters

Subjects   ALA Notable Books • British Authors • Gay Men • Male/Female Relationships

Now try   Among Pym's other novels are *An Unsuitable Attachment*, *Excellent Women*, and *Jane and Prudence*. Pym's writing style is similar to that of Muriel Spark's *A Far Cry from Kensington*. Pym's novels, given her eye for the telling detail and her ability to evoke a particular time and place, have often been compared to Jane Austen's *Pride and Prejudice* and *Sense and Sensibility*.

Raymond, Linda
Rocking the Babies
Viking. 1994. 260 pp.

Two African American women, Martha Howard and Nettie Lee Johnson, become unlikely friends when they each volunteer to work feeding and rocking the babies in a neonatal care unit at a local hospital.

Subjects   African American Authors • African Americans • Elderly Women • First Novels • Single Parents • Women's Friendships

Now try   Another novel with two very dissimilar women who grow to become good friends is Agnes Rossi's *Split Skirt*.

Rice, Luanne
Crazy in Love
Viking. 1988. 307 pp.

Georgie's hopes that love for husband Nick and the rest of her family will keep them all safe from disaster are dashed when events threaten the stability of all those she cares deeply about.

Subjects   Family Relationships • Love Stories • Marriage • Mothers and Daughters

Now try   Among Rice's other novels are *Home Fires* and *Stone Heart*. Georgie's voice is similar to that of Josie in *Jackie by Josie* by Caroline Preston.

Rivera, Beatriz
Midnight Sandwiches at the Mariposa Express
Arte Publico Press. 1997. 182 pp.

Trish Izquierdo tries to rewrite the history of West Echevarria, in an attempt to give the small New Jersey town class and culture while simultaneously dealing with her teenage daughter and her divorced (though live-in) husband.

Subjects   Cafés and Restaurants • First Novels • Humorous Fiction • Male/Female Relationships • Mothers and Daughters • New Jersey • Small-Town Life • Women's Friendships

Now try   Rivera also wrote a collection of short stories, *African Passions and Other Stories*. *Bailey's Café* by Gloria Naylor, Karen Hubert Allison's *How I Gave My Heart to the Restaurant*, and Fannie Flagg's *Fried Green Tomatoes at the Whistle-Stop Café* are all set around restaurants. Another novel about an attempt to rewrite history is Jose Saramago's *The History of the Siege of Lisbon*.

Rivers, Caryl
Intimate Enemies
Dutton. 1987. 259 pp.

Jessie, a feminist anti-war radical, meets and surprisingly falls in love with Mark, a crippled Vietnam veteran now working as an army recruiter.

Subjects   1970s • First Novels • Love Stories • Vietnam Veterans

Now try   Among Rivers's other novels are *Virgins*, *Camelot*, and *Girls Forever Brave and True*. Marge Piercy's *Vida* is about a woman going underground as a result of her anti-war activities.

Robbins, Tom
Skinny Legs and All
Bantam Books. 1990. 422 pp.

While a Jew and an Arab jointly open a restaurant across from the United Nations building in New York, art, politics, and religion conflict and conflate as the century draws to a close; Jezebel puts on her make-up and Salome does The Dance of the Seven Veils, skinny legs and all.

2d Appeal   Characters

Subjects   Apocalyptic Fiction • Art and Artists • Belly Dancing • Cafes and Restaurants • Christianity • Goddess Worship • Humorous Fiction • Magic Realism • Male/Female Relationships • New York

Now try   Tom Robbins's other novels, *Jitterbug Perfume*, *Still Life with Woodpecker*, *Even Cowgirls Get the Blues*, and *Another Roadside Attraction*, are similar in style and tone. Francine Prose's *Hunters and Gatherers* is a satirical look at goddess worship. Ken Kesey's *Sailor Song* is another apocalyptic novel by a writer who shares some of Robbins's stylistic tics.

Rockcastle, Mary Francois
Rainy Lake
Graywolf Press. 1994. 278 pp.

Teenager Danny Fillian and her family spend idyllic summers during the 1960s at their house at Rainy Lake, but alcoholism and the Vietnam War tear the family apart.

Book Groups 📖

Subjects   1960s • Alcoholics and Alcoholism • Family Relationships • First Novels • Teenage Girls • Vietnam War

Now try   The extended family in Jane Hamilton's *The Short History of a Prince* has the same love for their summer home as the Fillians do. *The Brothers K* by David James Duncan is another book about the effect of the Vietnam War on a particular family.

Rodriguez, Jr., Abraham
Spidertown
Hyperion. 1993. 323 pp.

Miguel, a 16-year-old crack dealer in the South Bronx, battles with his sense of loyalty to friends and his mentor, the kingpin drug dealer Spider, and fears for his life in his efforts to break away from his criminal world.

2d Appeal   Setting   Book Groups 📖

Subjects   Coming-of-Age • Drugs and Drug Abuse • Ghetto Life • New York • Teenage Boys • Violence

Now try   Rodriguez also wrote *The Boy Without a Flag: Tales of the South Bronx*, short stories that introduce the world of Miguel and Spider. Piri Thomas's *Down These Mean Streets* is a memoir of growing up in Spanish Harlem. Richard Price's *Clockers* also explores inner-city ghetto life and how drugs and crime have affected the lives of those who live there.

Roiphe, Anne
Lovingkindness
Summit Books. 1987. 279 pp.

When 22-year-old Andrea resurfaces after a disappearance of five months, her mother Annie goes to Yavneh, Israel, in an attempt to convince Andrea to return home, only to discover that Andrea needs rescuing from a disaster Annie could never have foreseen.

Book Groups 📖

Subjects Israel • Jews and Judaism • Mothers and Daughters • Religious Extremism

Now try Among Roiphe's other novels is an absorbing multigenerational saga, *The Pursuit of Happiness*. John le Carre's *Little Drummer Girl* is also about religious extremism in the Middle East. The novels of Chaim Potok, such as *The Chosen*, *My Name Is Asher Lev*, and *The Promise*, are about Jews living religious lives in a secular, American society.

Rossi, Agnes
Split Skirt
Random House. 1994. 223 pp.

When 20-something Rita is sent to prison for drunk driving and possession of cocaine, she meets 50-ish Mrs. Tyler, who, despite her wealth, has at last been arrested after a lifetime of shoplifting; in the three days the two very different women spend together in a jail cell, each comes to understand herself better.

Subjects Drugs and Drug Abuse • First Novels • Shoplifting • Women in Prison • Women's Friendships

Now try Rossi's other books include two collections of short stories, *Athletes and Artists: Stories* and *The Quick: A Novella & Stories*. Linda Raymond's *Rocking the Babies* is another novel about a friendship between very different women.

Rossner, Judith
August
Houghton Mifflin. 1983. 376 pp.

As psychoanalyst Lulu Shinefeld helps her new patient, Barnard College freshman Dawn Henley, explore her painful childhood, Lulu's own life—past and present—is brought into focus as well.

Subjects College Students • Doctors and Patients • Mothers and Daughters • New York • Psychiatrists; Psychoanalysts; Psychotherapists

Now try Rossner's many novels vary in subject, from *Attachments*, to *Nine Months in the Life of an Old Maid*, to her most famous, *Looking for Mr. Goodbar*. Other books with psychoanalysts or psychiatrists as a major character are *Every Woman Loves a Russian Poet* by Elizabeth Dunkel, Daniel Menaker's *The Treatment*, Penelope Mortimer's *The Pumpkin Eater*, and Amanda Cross's mystery, *In the Last Analysis*, in which a young woman is murdered on her analyst's couch.

Ryman, Geoff
Was
Knopf. 1992. 371 pp.

Dorothy Gael, Judy Garland, and a young actor dying of AIDS all seek the meaning of home in this dark homage to *The Wizard of Oz*.

Book Groups 📖

Subjects AIDS • Family Relationships • Friendship • Gay Men • Sexual Abuse

Now try   Ryman also writes science fiction, including ***Unconquered Countries: Four Novellas***. Stephen Dobyns's ***The Wrestler's Cruel Study*** uses fictional characters from other books as characters in his own novel. ***Shoeless Joe*** by W.P. Kinsella mixes real people and fictional characters to explore the theme of loss and longing.

Saiter, Susan Sullivan
Cheerleaders Can't Afford to Be Nice
D.I. Fine. 1990. 313 pp.

Crosby Rawson escaped her troubled family for the prospect of an ordinary life in California, but her mentally ill brother's disappearance from a New York homeless shelter forces her to confront all she left behind in her determination to achieve middle-class respectability.

Book Groups 📖

Subjects   Brothers and Sisters • Dysfunctional Families • Family Relationships • First Novels • Homelessness • Mental Illness

Now try   Saiter is also the author of the novel ***Moira's Way***. Wally Lamb's ***She's Come Undone*** is the story of a woman trying to create a life for herself after an emotionally devastating childhood. Living with a mentally ill brother is the subject of Elizabeth Swados's ***The Four of Us: The Story of a Family***.

Salzman, Mark
The Soloist
Random House. 1994. 284 pp.

At 34, former child prodigy Renne Sundheimer is faced with two events that will alter his life: He is chosen to serve on the jury considering the murder of a Zen master, and he agrees to teach nine-year-old Kyung-hee, another brilliant child cellist.

2d Appeal   Characters   Book Groups 📖

Subjects   Gifted Children • Korean Americans • Murder • Music and Musicians

Now try   Salzman's memoirs, ***Lost in Place*** and ***Iron and Silk***, and his novel, ***The Laughing Sutra***, reflect some of the same themes found in ***The Soloist***. Bernice Rubens's ***Madame Sousatzka*** is another novel about a music teacher. Erik Fosnes Hansen's ***Psalm at Journey's End*** imagines the lives of the musicians who played on the *Titanic* as it sank. ***Rookery Blues*** by Jon Hassler is about a group of men who play jazz together.

Sams, Ferrol
Run with the Horsemen
Peachtree Publishers. 1982. 422 pp.

On a Georgia farm during the Great Depression, Porter Osborne, Jr. faces his greatest challenge: coming to terms with a father he both loves and despises.

Subjects   Coming-of-Age • Farms and Farm Life • Fathers and Sons • First Novels • Georgia • Racism • Southern Authors

Now try   There are two sequels to this novel: ***The Whisper of the River*** and ***When All the World Was Young***. Sams himself trained as a physician, and, like his hero Porter Osborne, grew up in rural Georgia between the wars. Sams writes in the grand, gentle Southern tradition of Kaye Gibbons (***Ellen Foster***, ***Sights Unseen***, and others) and Olive Ann Burns (***Cold Sassy Tree***.) Sams frequently deals with the same themes as Lewis Nordan (***Music of the Swamp*** and others), but he handles them with a far lighter touch.

Savage, Elizabeth
Toward the End
Little, Brown. 1980. 237 pp.

A diverse group of summer residents on an island in Maine decide to spend the winter there and find themselves coping with two disastrous storms.

Subjects   Adultery • Divorce • Friendship • Maine • Male/Female Relationships

Now try   This Maine novel is based on events that occurred during the Great Blizzard of 1978. Two other novels by Elizabeth Savage that share the somewhat unusual writing style of *Toward the End* are *The Girls from the Five Great Valleys* and *The Last Night at the Ritz*. Another novel set in Maine is Elisabeth Ogilvie's *An Answer in the Tide*.

Savage, Georgia
The House Tibet
Graywolf Press. 1991. 345 pp.

After 13-year-old Vicky is raped by her straitlaced father, she and her younger brother leave Adelaide for Queensland, where they meet up with a group of other runaways who lead them to an eccentric named Xam and a ramshackle house called Tibet.

Book Groups 📖

Subjects   Australia • Australian Authors • Brothers and Sisters • Child Abuse • Incest • Rape • Runaways • Sexual Abuse • Teenagers

Now try   Another chilling novel of sexual abuse is Susan Palwick's *Flying in Place*. Thomas Keneally's protagonist in *Woman of the Inner Sea* is also on the run from painful events in her life.

Schine, Cathleen
The Love Letter
Houghton Mifflin Co. 1995. 257 pp.

After receiving an anonymous love letter, 40-ish bookstore owner Helen MacFarquhar finds herself falling for Johnny, her 20-year-old summer employee, whom she suspects of sending the letter.

2d Appeal   Characters

Subjects   Bookstores • Humorous Fiction • Love Affairs • Older Women/Younger Men

Now try   Among Schine's other novels are *Rameau's Niece*, *To the Birdhouse*, *The Evolution of Jane*, and *Alice in Bed*. Other contemporary comedies of manners are Muriel Spark's *A Far Cry from Kensington* and Barbara Pym's *No Fond Return of Love*. Other interesting bookstores appear in Christopher Morley's *The Haunted Bookshop* and the mysteries by Joan Hess (*Closely Akin to Murder* and others) and Carolyn Hart (*The Christie Caper* and others).

See, Carolyn
Golden Days
McGraw-Hill. 1987. 196 pp.

Gem specialist Edie Langley returns to her childhood home in Southern California and meets Lorna Villanelle, an old friend turned television evangelist, shortly before the onset of a nuclear explosion.

2d Appeal   Setting

Subjects   Apocalyptic Fiction • Nuclear War • Southern California • Women's Friendships

Now try See is also the author of *Rhine Maidens* and *Making History*. Other apocalyptic novels include Nevil Shute's *On the Beach*, Russell Hoban's *Riddley Walker*, Meg Files's *Meridian 144*, Jean Hegland's *Into the Forest*, and David Brin's *The Postman*. See's portrait of Southern California as a land of strange and quirky people is similar to Alison Lurie's vision of Los Angeles in *The Nowhere City*.

Shapiro, Dani

Fugitive Blue
N.A. Talese. 1993. 246 pp.

When artist Georgia Hirsch walks out on her family, her daughter Joanna is comforted by the friendship she develops with Billy Overmyer, a relationship that will bring both happiness and tragedy throughout Joanna's life.

2d Appeal Characters

Subjects Actors and Acting • Art and Artists • Dysfunctional Families • Gay Men • Mothers and Daughters • Mothers Deserting Their Families

Now try Shapiro's first novel was *Playing with Fire*. She is also the author of *Slow Motion: A True Story*, a memoir about her family. Another novel with a similarly selfish and self-referential mother is Rebecca Stowe's *The Shadow of Desire*. Maureen Brady's *Give Me Your Good Ear* also deals with mother/daughter relationships.

Sharp, Paula

Crows Over a Wheatfield
Hyperion. 1996. 403 pp.

Attorney Melanie Klonecki, herself the abused daughter of a criminal defense lawyer, befriends Mildred Steck, an abused woman who sets up an underground railroad for women and children to escape domestic violence when the legal system fails them.

Book Groups 📖

Subjects Abusive Relationships • Child Abuse • Domestic Violence • Family Relationships • Fathers and Daughters • Fathers and Sons • Law and Lawyers • Women's Friendships

Now try The author, like her character, is a criminal defense lawyer, and a major theme of all of her novels, including *Lost in Jersey City* and *The Woman Who Was Not All There*, is the self-empowerment of women. Roddy Doyle's *The Woman Who Walked into Doors* and Susan Brownmiller's *Waverly Place* are both painful novels about domestic abuse. Another woman who becomes involved in an underground railroad to help people achieve better lives is the main character in Gayl Jones's *Mosquito*.

Shea, Suzanne Strempek

Selling the Lite of Heaven
Pocket Books. 1994. 275 pp.

When the unnamed narrator is jilted by her fiancé (who decided he wanted to become a priest), she puts an ad in the local paper to sell her 2.75-carat diamond engagement ring, The Lite of Heaven.

2d Appeal Characters

Subjects First Novels • Humorous Fiction • Male/Female Relationships • Polish Americans • Single Women

Now try   Shea also wrote *Hoopi, Shoopi Donna*. The closed-in life of the narrator and her family is similar to those described in Anna Quindlen's *Object Lessons* and Alice McDermott's *At Weddings and Wakes*.

Sheldon, Dyan
My Life as a Whale
Villard Books. 1992. 258 pp.

Michael, one of the seemingly few remaining single, heterosexual men in Manhattan, finds creative ways to avoid the clutches of women pursuing a marriage partner.

2d Appeal   Characters

Subjects   Humorous Fiction • Male/Female Relationships • New York • Single Men

Now try   Sheldon is also the author of several children's books. The confusion of a young Manhattan man not knowing exactly what—or who—he wants in life can also be found in Michael Kernan's *The Lost Diaries of Frans Hals*, Jonathan Ames's *The Extra Man*, and Jay McInerney's *Bright Lights, Big City*.

Shem, Samuel
Mount Misery
Fawcett Columbine. 1997. 436 pp.

As Dr. Roy Basch rotates through training at one of the finest psychiatric hospitals in the country, he finds to his shock and dismay that the cure for mental illness is often worse than the disease itself.

2d Appeal   Setting

Subjects   Doctors and Patients • Mental Illness • Psychiatrists, Psychoanalysts, Psychotherapists • Satirical Fiction

Now try   Samuel Shem is the pseudonym of a Boston area psychiatrist. His earlier novel, *Fine*, is also about a psychiatrist in training, although it is much less intense and disturbing than this novel. Paul Buttenwieser's *Free Association* is another story of a psychiatrist in training. Two novels that offer a patient's view of therapy are Sylvia Plath's *The Bell Jar* and *I Never Promised You a Rose Garden* by Joanne Greenberg.

Shigekuni, Julie
A Bridge Between Us
Anchor Books. 1995. 253 pp.

Four generations of Japanese American women who share a large home in San Francisco tell their life stories in alternating chapters, slowly revealing the family secrets.

Book Groups 📖

Subjects   Family Secrets • First Novels • Japanese Americans • Mothers and Daughters • Multigenerational Novels • San Francisco

Now try   *The Joy Luck Club* by Amy Tan is also about mothers and daughters and family secrets.

Shreve, Anita
The Weight of Water
Little, Brown. 1997. 246 pp.

Sent by her magazine editor to New England to photograph a crime scene on Smutty Nose Island, Jean watches her life spiral out of control as she immerses herself in the emotional drama of the 100-year-old crime.

Book Groups 📖

Subjects   Adultery • Death of a Child • New England • Photography and Photographers • Unsolved Crimes

Now try   Shreve's other books include ***The Pilot's Wife***, ***Eden Close***, and ***Resistance***. Other family dramas that are set in New England are Christopher Tilghman's ***Mason's Retreat***, Ann Beattie's ***My Life, Starring Dara Falcon***, Kathryn Davis's ***Labrador***, and Ernest Hebert's ***The Dogs of March***.

Shreve, Susan Richards
The Visiting Physician
N.A. Talese. 1996. 288 pp.

Two cases of children gone missing from Meridian, Ohio, are linked by Helen Fielding, a young pediatric resident who comes to town to treat a medical crisis.

Subjects   Career Women • Doctors and Patients • Loss of a Child • Ohio • Single Women • Small-Town Life

Now try   Shreve's other books include ***Daughters of the New World*** and ***The Train Home***. Other novels about the disappearance of children are Malcolm Macdonald's ***For I Have Sinned*** and Beth Gutcheon's ***Still Missing***.

Shriver, Lionel
Double Fault
Doubleday. 1997. 317 pp.

Willy Novinsky finds her marriage to Eric Oberdorfer increasingly threatened by her feelings of jealousy as Eric's success in professional tennis eclipses her own.

Subjects   Career Women • Male/Female Relationships • Marriage • Tennis

Now try   Shriver also wrote a novel called ***The Bleeding Heart***. Anne Lamott's ***Crooked Little Heart*** is another novel about the pressures a young woman puts on herself to succeed on the tennis court. Tennis champions Martina Navratilova (***The Total Zone***, ***Breaking Point***, and ***Killer Instinct***) and Ilie Nastase (***Break Point*** and ***The Net***) both wrote novels about tennis and the men and women who play it.

Shute, Jenefer
Life-Size
Houghton Mifflin. 1992. 231 pp.

Hospitalized for anorexia, graduate student Josie chronicles her obsession with food and her ambivalent feelings about trying to overcome her eating disorder.

Subjects   Eating Disorders • First Novels • Psychiatric Hospitals

Now try   Shute is also the author of ***Sex Crimes***. Margaret Atwood's ***The Edible Woman***, Cathi Hanauer's ***My Sister's Bones***, and Jillian Medoff's ***Hunger Point*** are also about young women and anorexia.

Sinclair, April
Coffee Will Make You Black
Hyperion. 1994. 239 pp.

Smart and feisty, Jean "Stevie" Stevenson tackles growing up black, losing her virginity, and making it through high school on Chicago's south side in the late 1960s.

Book Groups 📖

Subjects   1960s • African American Authors • African Americans • Chicago • Coming-of-Age • First Novels • Teenage Girls

Now try   Sinclair also wrote *Ain't Gonna Be the Same Fool Twice: A Novel*. Other books narrated by a young woman include Thulani Davis's *1959* and Lorrie Moore's *Who Will Run the Frog Hospital?*

Skibell, Joseph
A Blessing On the Moon
Algonquin Book of Chapel Hill. 1997. 256 pp.

Instead of resting peacefully in his grave after he and the rest of the Jews in his small Polish village are shot by the Nazis, Chaim Skibelski experiences strange and wondrous events.

2d Appeal   Setting

Subjects   First Novels • Holocaust • Magic Realism • Poland • World War II

Now try   Peter Beagle's novel, *A Fine and Private Place*, is about a man who withdraws from the world to live in a mausoleum, where he converses with birds and ghosts of the dead. In Edgar Lee Masters's *Spoon River Anthology*, a group of deceased members of the community recount their lives in poems. Thornton Wilder's classic play, "Our Town," is also about the dead looking back at their lives. *Growing Through the Ugly* by Diego Vazquez, Jr. is another haunting novel about life after death.

Smith, Mary Burnett
Miss Ophelia
Wm. Morrow. 1997. 277 pp.

In the summer of 1948, in segregated Mason County, Virginia, 11-year-old Isabel (Belly) Anderson learns about the mysteries of love when she is sent to help her Aunt Rachel and Uncle Avery and witnesses the secret love between her uncle and Miss Ophelia, the next door neighbor who is teaching Belly to play the piano.

Subjects   1940s • Adultery • African American Authors • African Americans • First Novels • Male/Female Relationships • Race Relations • Virginia

Now try   *An Ocean in Iowa* by Peter Hedges, Ardashir Vakil's *Beach Boy*, and William McPherson's *Testing the Current* are all about children trying to make sense of the world around them.

Smith, Mary-Ann Tirone
Masters of Illusion: A Novel of the Connecticut Circus Fire
Warner Books. 1994. 210 pp.

Ten-year-old Charlie was present at the 1944 Barnum & Bailey circus when a fire broke out in the tent, killing more than 150 people and injuring thousands; he grows up to marry Margie Potter, the youngest survivor, who has no memories of the event that killed her mother and left her back badly scarred.

Subjects   1940s • Circuses • Fires • Male/Female Relationships

Now try   Smith is also the author of *The Book of Phoebe*, *Lament for a Silver-Eyed Woman*, and *The Port of Missing Men*. Circuses play a part in the plots of John Irving's *A Son of the Circus* and Tom Hollis's *Honky Tonk Logic*.

Smith, Terri McFerrin
False Starts
Knopf. 1988. 171 pp.

Through one abortion and the birth of a daughter three years later, Mara's relationship with the father, Mac, seemingly goes nowhere.

Subjects   Abortion • First Novels • Male/Female Relationships • Montana • Single Parents • Single Women

Now try   Diane Schoemperlen's *In the Language of Love* is told in short, impressionistic chapters like Smith's *False Starts*. Margaret Drabble's *The Millstone* and *Catching the Light* by Susan Pope both deal with unwed mothers who decide to keep their children.

Spanier, Muriel
Staying Afloat
Random House. 1985. 314 pp.

Sylvie Weyman, consumed by grief after the death of her daughter, awakens to her own needs when she takes a job as household manager to a young professional couple living in Manhattan.

Subjects   Death of a Child • First Novels • Grief • New York • Widows

Now try   Many of Hilma Wolitzer's novels, including *Hearts* and *In the Palomar Arms*, are sympathetic portraits of older women discovering (or rediscovering) love and a zest for life. Both Bette Ann Moskowitz's *Leaving Barney* and Stanley Elkin's *Mrs. Ted Bliss* tell the story of a widow trying to figure out what she wants to do with the rest of her life.

Stark, Marisa Kantor
Bring Us the Old People
Coffee House Press. 1998. 218 pp.

Now living in a nursing home, Maime recalls growing up in a shtetl and the terrible choice she was forced to make when the Nazis took over her Polish town.

Subjects   Elderly Women • First Novels • Holocaust • Jews and Judaism • Poland • Retirement • Women's Lives • World War II

Now try   Another character forced to make a terrible choice during World War II is Sophie, in William Styron's *Sophie's Choice*. Maime's voice and sensibility are similar to that of Ruth Hubble, the main character in *White Rabbit* by Kate Phillips.

Stegner, Lynn
Undertow
Baskerville Publishers. 1993. 367 pp.

When Anne, a marine biologist working in the San Juan Islands in Washington State, discovers she is pregnant by her married lover, she is forced to face her own childhood of neglect and sexual abuse.

Book Groups 📖

Subjects   Adultery • Child Abuse • First Novels • Male/Female Relationships • Science and Scientists • Sexual Abuse • Women Scientists

Now try   Stegner also wrote *Fata Morgana*. The protagonist of Julie Schumacher's novel, *The Body Is Water*, is another pregnant woman looking back on her unhappy childhood.

Stuart, Sarah Payne
The Year Roger Wasn't Well
HarperCollins. 1994. 224 pp.

When Lizzie meets Roger, she thinks she's finally met the perfect guy—until they've been married a year and Roger walks out on her and their marriage.

Subjects   1970s • Humorous Fiction • Love Stories • Male/Female Relationships • Marriage

Now try   Lizzie Reade, the main character in *The Year Roger Wasn't Well*, also appears in *Men and Trouble*. *Raney* by Clyde Edgerton is another very funny novel about the first years of a marriage. Cathie Pelletier's *A Marriage Made at Woodstock* also deals with the end of a marriage.

Szczypiorski, Andrzej
The Beautiful Mrs. Seidenman
Grove Weidenfeld. 1990. 204 pp.

The humanity shown by a random group of people leads them to save a small Polish child and a Jewish widow from death at the hands of the Nazis. Translated from the Polish by Klara Glowczewska.

2d Appeal   Characters

Subjects   Coming-of-Age • Holocaust • Novels in Translation • Poland • Polish Authors • World War II

Now try   Szczypiorski also wrote *A Mask for Arras* and *The Shadow Catcher*. Ida Fink's *The Journey* is another novel about the kindness of strangers during World War II. Oskar Schindler, the subject of Thomas Keneally's novel *Schindler's List*, is the best known of "the righteous Gentiles," those men and women who risked their own lives to save Jews during the Holocaust.

Tamaro, Susanna
Follow Your Heart
Delta Trade Paperbacks. 1996. 204 pp.

An elderly woman, nearing death, reflects on her life, the mistakes made and the secrets kept, in a series of long letters to her estranged granddaughter in America. Translated from the Italian by John Cullen.

Subjects   Elderly Women • Epistolary Novels • Family Relationships • Family Secrets • Grandparents • Italian Authors • Male/Female Relationships • Mothers and Daughters • Novels in Translation • Women's Lives

Now try   This is Tamaro's first novel to be translated into English. It won the Premio Donna di Roma award. Mark Helprin's *Memoir from Antproof Case* is also the story of someone looking back on a life filled with mistakes and secrets.

Tan, Amy
The Kitchen God's Wife
Putnam. 1991. 415 pp.

Many years after she left China to live in California, Winnie Louie finally recounts for her daughter Pearl the details of her life in China in the 1930s and 1940s.

2d Appeal   Language   Book Groups 📖

Subjects   ALA Notable Books • China • Chinese Americans • Culture Clash • Family Relationships • Family Secrets • Mothers and Daughters • World War II

Now try   Tan is also the author of *The Hundred Secret Senses*. Other books about Chinese families who have moved to America include Fae Myenne Ng's novel, *Bone*, and Lisa See's story of her family, *On Gold Mountain*.

Tartt, Donna
The Secret History
Knopf. 1992. 523 pp.

Fatally influenced by their classics professor's belief that they must fully experience the world of the senses as expressed in a Dionysian rite, six college students find themselves complicit in two deaths.

2d Appeal   Characters   Book Groups 📖

Subjects   Academia • College Students • First Novels • Friendship • Male/Female Relationships • Murder

Now try   Iris Murdoch's *The Good Apprentice* is another study of guilt and redemption.

Tevis, Walter
The Queen's Gambit
Random House. 1983. 243 pp.

After she's orphaned at the age of eight, the next 12 years of Beth Harmon's life are shaped by her genius at the game of chess.

Subjects   Chess • Coming-of-Age • Drugs and Drug Abuse • Obsessive Love • Orphans

Now try   Tevis's novel *The Hustler* is another look at an obsessive love, not for a person, but for a game. A chess prodigy is a subject of one of the stories in Amy Tan's *The Joy Luck Club*. Fred Waitzkin's *Searching for Bobby Fischer: The Father of a Prodigy Observes the World of Chess* complements *The Queen's Gambit*.

Thayer, Nancy
Belonging
St. Martin's Press. 1995. 341 pp.

After a harrowing car accident, television celebrity Joanna Jones decides to give up her fast-paced New York lifestyle, high profile job, and married lover and move to Nantucket, where, through some painful experiences, she learns what true belonging is all about.

Subjects   Adultery • Cape Cod • Car Accidents • Career Women • Death of a Child • Male/Female Relationships • Single Parents • Women's Friendships

Now try   Thayer's novel *Three Women at the Water's Edge* is about women making changes and taking charge of their lives. Anne Rivers Siddons's *Up Island* also describes how a woman finds peace and self-acceptance while living on Cape Cod.

Thon, Melanie Rae
Iona Moon
Poseidon Press. 1993. 315 pp.

Iona Moon, a girl from the wrong side of the tracks, struggles to find love and escape from her past in Kila Flats, Idaho.

2d Appeal   Characters   Book Groups 📖

Subjects   Coming-of-Age • Idaho • Small-Town Life

Now try   Thon also wrote *Meteors in August: A Novel* and *Girls in the Grass: Stories*. Potato farming is part of the life of Kila Flats, and it is also the subject of John Thorndike's novel, *The Potato Baron*. In 1996, *Granta Magazine* named Thon one of the "20 Best Young American Novelists."

Toppel, Lori
Three Children
Summit Books. 1992. 207 pp.

Siblings Clarissa, Cora, and Michael take turns relating the story of their family's life in Puerto Rico and their move to the United States amid the wreckage of their parents' relationship.

Subjects   Adultery • Brothers and Sisters • Family Relationships • Family Secrets • First Novels • Puerto Rico

Now try   The relationship between Julia and her children in this novel is similar to the relationships between parents and children in Susanna Moore's *My Old Sweetheart* and *The Tribes of Palos Verdes* by Joy Nicholson. In Lan Cao's *The Monkey Bridge*, Mai Nguyen leaves Vietnam, moves to the United States, and unearths secrets about her family's past.

Tsukiyama, Gail
The Samurai's Garden
St. Martin's Press. 1995. 211 pp.

As Japan invades China, Stephen, a Chinese student, recuperates from tuberculosis in a Japanese beach village where he befriends Matsu, an aging gardener, and Sachi, whose leprosy led to her ostracism from the village.

Book Groups 📖

Subjects   First Novels • Friendship • Japan • Leprosy • Male/Female Relationships • Small-Town Life

Now try   Tsukiyama also wrote *Women of the Silk* and *Night of Many Dreams*. Kiana Davenport's novel, *Shark Dialogues*, also describes how lepers were feared by others in their communities.

Vandenburgh, Jane
Failure to Zigzag
North Point Press. 1989. 329 pp.

Sixteen-year-old Charlotte's desire for a normal family is thwarted by her mother Katrinka, an alcoholic mental patient who works as a ventriloquist in a second-rate circus; a grandfather whose days as a successful banker are well behind him; a grandmother who wants Charlotte to be everything Katrinka isn't; and her father, killed in the war, whom she never knew.

Subjects   1960s • Alcoholics and Alcoholism • Circuses • Dysfunctional Families • First Novels • Grandparents • Mental Illness • Mothers and Daughters

Now try   Kaye Starbird's *The Lion in the Lei Shop* is also about a young woman whose father is killed in World War II and how that event shapes her life. *Drinking: A Love Story* by Caroline Knapp and Pete Hamill's *A Drinking Life: A Memoir* are both moving descriptions of the seductive qualities of alchohol.

Vea, Alfredo
La Maravilla
Dutton. 1993. 305 pp.

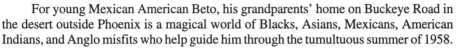

For young Mexican American Beto, his grandparents' home on Buckeye Road in the desert outside Phoenix is a magical world of Blacks, Asians, Mexicans, American Indians, and Anglo misfits who help guide him through the tumultuous summer of 1958.

2d Appeal   Setting   Book Groups 📖

Subjects   1950s • Arizona • Family Relationships • Interracial Relationships • Mexican Americans • Small-Town Life

Now try   Vea is also the author of ***Silver Cloud Café***. Other writers who explore the lives of Mexican Americans include Rudolfo Anaya (***Tortuga***, ***The Silence of the Ilano: Short Stories***, and others), Rick Collignon (***The Journal of Antonio Montoya*** and ***Perdido***), and Sandra Cisneros (***The House on Mango Street***, ***Woman Hollering Creek***, and others).

Villasenor, Victor
Macho!
Arte Publico Press. 1991. 236 pp.

On a dangerous trip north from his Mexican home to work as an illegal alien following the harvest in California, 17-year-old Roberto Garcia learns about love, loyalty, and death.

Subjects   Chavez, Cesar • Coming-of-Age • First Novels • Labor Unions • Mexican Authors • Mexico • Teenage Boys • Teenagers

Now try   Villasenor's other books include ***Wild Steps of Heaven*** and ***Rain of Gold*** (both nonfiction). Much of Cormac McCarthy's ***All the Pretty Horses*** takes place in Mexico and also explores young men coming of age under difficult conditions. T. Coraghessan Boyle's novel ***The Tortilla Curtain*** describes the life of illegal Mexican immigrants in California.

Vogan, Sara
Blueprints
Bantam. 1990. 278 pp.

When Emery Lanier returns home (after an absence of more than a decade), she finds herself drawn back into her parents' world of alcohol-influenced self-delusion and she is forced to re-evaluate both the past and the present.

Book Groups 📖

Subjects   Aging • Alcoholics and Alcoholism • Brothers and Sisters • Death of a Child • Dysfunctional Families • Family Relationships • Mothers and Daughters

Now try   Vogan's other books include ***In Shelly's Leg***, ***Scenes from the Homefront***, and ***Loss of Flight***. Her stories of family relationships are similar to the novels of Josephine Humphreys (***The Fireman's Fair***, ***Rich in Love***, and others).

Volk, Toni
Maybe in Missoula
Soho. 1994. 280 pp.

Annie leaves her comfortable but boring marriage to Morton and reconnects with her first love—Morton's younger brother Paul.

Subjects   Brothers • Male/Female Relationships • Montana • Mothers and Sons • Single Parents • Triangles

Now try   Volk also wrote *Montana Women*. A triangular relationship involving two family members and an outsider is the subject of Anne Tyler's *The Clock Winder*, David Long's *The Falling Boy*, and Laurie Colwin's *Shine On, Bright and Dangerous Object*.

Vonnegut, Kurt
Jailbird
Delacorte Press. 1979. 246 pp.

After being released from prison for the minor crimes he committed in the Watergate scandal, Walter F. Starbuck regains a position of wealth and status because of his unlikely run-in with the reclusive but powerful Mrs. Jack Graham, the majority stockholder in the RAMJAC Corp.

Subjects   Business and Businessmen • Good vs. Evil • Political Fiction

Now try   Vonnegut's other books include *God Bless You, Mr. Rosewater* and *The Sirens of Titan*. Although they are totally different in tone from *Jailbird*, Ayn Rand's *Atlas Shrugged* and *The Fountainhead* both look at relationships against a background of corporate America.

Warlick, Ashley
The Distance from the Heart of Things
Houghton Mifflin. 1996. 256 pp.

When Mavis Black returns home to South Carolina after graduating from college to take over the accounting duties for the family vineyard, she realizes how different she is from the family she loves.

2d Appeal   Setting

Subjects   Adultery • Death of a Child • Family Relationships • First Novels • Grandparents • South Carolina • Southern Authors • Vineyards

Now try   There's a crotchety grandfather in Warlick's novel: stubborn Punk Black. Other well-drawn grandfathers are found in Jo-Ann Mapson's *Shadow Ranch* and Beverly Coyle's *In Troubled Waters*. The plots of both Bill Barich's *Carson Valley: A Novel* and Peter Gadol's *The Long Rain* revolve around vineyards.

Warloe, Constance
The Legend of Olivia Cosmos Montevideo
Atlantic Monthly Press. 1994. 316 pp.

After her only child is killed in the Vietnam War, Roberta Masters decides to leave her unsatisfactory marriage in Virginia and embark on a search to understand the meaning of life.

Subjects   Adultery • Death of a Child • First Novels • Marriage • Mothers and Sons • Older Men/Younger Women • Vietnam War

Now try   Jacquelyn Mitchard's *The Deep End of the Ocean* and Ellyn Bache's *Safe Passage* both explore a mother's response to a son's disappearance and possible death.

Webster, Susan
Small Tales of a Town
St. Martin's Press. 1988. 184 pp.

The happenings of a small Australian outback town—the feuds, joys, sorrows, and friendships—are seen through the eyes of a newspaper reporter who has come from Melbourne to write for the Weekly Advertiser.

2d Appeal   Characters

Subjects   Australia • Australian Authors • First Novels • Journalists • Small-Town Life • Writers and Writing

Now try   Although the subject matter and writing style are totally different, Janette Turner Hospital's *Oyster* is also set in a small, lonely town in Australia. The Australian outback is the setting of Nevil Shute's *A Town Like Alice* and Thomas Keneally's *Woman of the Inner Sea*. Patricia Browning Griffith's *The World Around Midnight* is also about a small-town newspaper.

Weiss, Daniel Evan
The Roaches Have No King
High Risk Books. 1994. 249 pp.

When Ira Fishblatt's tidy new girlfriend moves into his apartment, he has the kitchen remodeled for her, thereby starving a long-established colony of cockroaches, whose plans to eliminate Ruth eventually end in a gruesome revenge on Ira.

Subjects   Cockroaches • Drugs and Drug Abuse • Male/Female Relationships

Now try   Weiss's other books include *Hell on Wheels*, *The Swine's Wedding*, and *The Great Divide*. Donald Harington's *The Cockroaches of Stay More* is another contemporary novel about cockroaches. The classic novel about a cockroach is Franz Kafka's *Metamorphosis*. *Doctor Rat* by William Kotzwinkle also has a cynical animal narrator (a rat) with a grim view of people and their activities.

Welch, James
The Indian Lawyer
Norton. 1990. 349 pp.

Sylvester Yellow Calf leaves the Blackfoot Indian Reservation to attend Stanford Law School and then joins a prominent Montana law firm on his way to a political career, but finds his plans derailed by a convict desperate for parole.

2d Appeal   Characters

Subjects   American Indian Authors • American Indians • Blackfeet • Law and Lawyers • Montana

Now try   Welch's other books, *Fools Crow* and *Winter in the Blood*, both are concerned with the attempt of American Indians to become integrated into white society. One of the earliest novels about American Indians is Oliver LaFarge's *Laughing Boy*, which won the 1930 Pulitzer Prize. Sherman Alexie, author of poetry, short stories, and screenplays, as well as the novel, *Reservation Blues*, is one of the younger American Indian writers who greatly admires Welch's writings.

Weller, Anthony
The Garden of the Peacocks
Marlowe & Co. 1996. 290 pp.

While the world still mourns the tragic death of a famed Cuban sculptor, the truth is that he has retreated to a tropical paradise to create one last, magnificent work of art, but his daughter Esther may have inadvertently revealed her father's secret Bahamian sanctuary to her latest lover.

Subjects   Art and Artists • Fathers and Daughters • First Novels • Midlife Crisis • Mothers Deserting Their Families • Suicide

Now try   Weller's other books include *The Polish Lover* and *Days and Nights on the Grand Trunk Road*. John Fowles's *The Magus* also includes a central mystery, islands, a controlling egomaniac, and love affairs.

West, Dorothy
The Wedding
Doubleday. 1995. 240 pp.

Despite the misgivings of her upper-class parents, African American Shelby Coles is determined to marry a white jazz musician, and her decision reflects the choices made by six generations of family members, whose lives spanned the period of Reconstruction to the 1950s.

2d Appeal   Setting   Book Groups 📖

Subjects   1950s • African American Authors • African Americans • Interracial Relationships • Martha's Vineyard, Massachusetts • Music and Musicians • Upper Classes • Weddings

Now try   West's other books include *The Richer, the Poorer: Stories, Sketches, and Reminiscences* and *The Living Is Easy*. West's use of language resembles that of Eudora Welty (*Delta Wedding* and others).

West, Michael Lee
American Pie
HarperCollins. 1996. 324 pp.

When Jo-Nell McBride's car—with her in it—is demolished by a train, her hospital stay forces Jo-Nell's two older sisters, Eleanor and Freddie, and her grandmother, Minerva Ray, to reassess their pasts and rethink their futures.

Subjects   Car Accidents • Family Relationships • Grandparents • Male/Female Relationships • Sisters • Southern Authors • Tennessee

Now try   West also wrote *Crazy Ladies* and *She Flew the Coop*. The unbreakable bond between sisters is also the theme of David Long's *The Falling Boy*.

Weyr, Garret
Pretty Girls
Crown. 1988. 232 pp.

Very tall, very intelligent, and very ill at ease, college sophomores Caroline, Alexandra, and Penelope are not typical pretty girls, but as they struggle through a critical semester, pretty girls are what they long to be.

Subjects   College Students • Coming-of-Age • First Novels • Male/Female Relationships • Southern Authors • Women's Friendships

Now try   Other books about the friendships of college-age women include Erica Abeel's *Women Like Us* and Mary McCarthy's *The Group*.

Wilcox, James
Polite Sex
HarperCollins Publishers. 1991. 279 pp.

When Emily and Clara arrive in New York in 1971 from their small Louisiana hometown, they discover that they have to compromise their dreams of love and success.

Subjects   1970s • Humorous Fiction • New York • Southern Authors • Women's Friendships

Now try   Among Wilcox's other humorous novels are *Miss Undine's Living Room*, *Sort of Rich*, *North Gladiola*, and *Modern Baptists*. The changing nature of women's friendships is explored in Margaret Atwood's *The Robber Bride*.

Winegardner, Mark
The Veracruz Blues
Viking. 1996. 251 pp.

Fact blurs into fiction as sportswriter Frank Bullinger recalls Jorge Pasquel's post-war attempt to build an integrated Mexican Baseball League by luring the States' best baseball players south.

Subjects   1940s • Baseball • First Novels • Interracial Relationships • Mexico • Writers and writing

Now try   Winegardner's other books are *We Are What We Ate; 24 Memories of Food* and *The 26th Man: One Minor League Pitcher's Pursuit of a Dream*. Other baseball novels include Bernard Malamud's *The Natural* and Mark Harris's *Bang the Drum Slowly*.

Witt, Lana
Slow Dancing on Dinosaur Bones
Scribner. 1996. 416 pp.

Lives and loves and coal-mining companies collide in small-town Pick, Kentucky, as Tom Jett drifts into town from California and meets auto mechanic Gilman Lee, his helper Ten-Fifteen (born with his arms sticking out like the hands of a clock), Gilman's old flame Rosalee Wilson (on the run from a troublesome boyfriend), and Gemma Collet, the object of Gilman's undying lust.

2d Appeal   Setting

Subjects   First Novels • Kentucky • Male/Female Relationships • Small-Town Life • Southern Authors

Now try   Other novelists have lovingly depicted small-town Kentucky, including Harriette Arnow (*The Dollmaker*), Wendell Berry (*A Place on Earth* and *Fidelity: Five Stories*, among others) and Bobbie Ann Mason (*In Country* and *Feather Crowns*). Witt's novel is similar in tone to the novels of Cathie Pelletier's *The Funeral Makers* and her other novels set in Mattagash, Maine.

Wolitzer, Hilma
Silver
Farrar, Straus and Giroux. 1988. 324 pp.

Howard Flax's heart attack on the eve of his 25th wedding anniversary complicates his wife's plans to leave him.

Subjects   Adultery • Marriage

Now try   This is a sequel to *In the Flesh*. Among Hilma Wolitzer's other books are *Tunnel of Love* and *In the Palomar Arms*. A. B. Yehoshua's *Five Seasons* also describes the effect of the death of a spouse after a long marriage.

Wolitzer, Meg

Friends for Life
Crown Publishers. 1994. 213 pp.

As they approach the age of 30, three professional women who have been inseparable since the 5th grade face choices that threaten their friendship.

Subjects   1980s • 1990s • Career Women • Women's Friendships

Now try   Wolitzer also wrote *This Is Your Life* and *Hidden Pictures*. Alice Adams's *Families and Survivors* also explores the ups and downs of her character's friendships.

Yalom, Irving

Lying on the Couch
Basic Books. 1996. 369 pp.

Dr. Ernest Lash becomes the target of revenge by Carol, the wife of one of his patients, even as she creates havoc in the life of Lash's supervising analyst.

Subjects   California • Doctors and Patients • Male/Female Relationships • Psychiatrists, Psychoanalysts, Psychotherapists

Now try   Other books by Yalom include *When Nietzche Wept, Every Day Gets a Little Closer: A Twice-Told Therapy*, and *Love's Executioner and Other Tales of Psychotherapy*. Other novels about therapy include Steven Schwartz's *Therapy*, Rafael Yglesias's *Dr. Neruda's Cure for Evil*, and Daniel Menaker's *The Treatment*.

Yamaguchi, Yoji

Face of a Stranger
HarperCollins. 1995. 202 pp.

In a California town early in the twentieth century, Kikue and Shino, two Japanese women who believed they were coming to America for arranged marriages and were instead sold into lives of prostitution, hatch a plot to revenge themselves on the man they both thought they were going to marry.

Subjects   California • First Novels • Japan • Japanese Americans • Male/Female Relationships • Prostitutes and Prostitution

Now try   Yamaguchi's writings also appeared in *Charlie Chan Is Dead: An Anthology of Contemporary Asian-American Literature*. A more serious look at the plight of picture brides is found in Yoshiko Uchida's novel, *Picture Bride*.

Zabor, Rafi

The Bear Comes Home
Norton. 1997. 480 pp.

When a saxophone-playing, mystically inclined bear gets his big break as a jazz artist, all sorts of things begin to happen in his life: a recording contract, fame, and love.

2d Appeal   Language

Subjects   Bears • First Novels • Humorous Fiction • Jazz • Magic Realism • Music and Musicians

Now try   Another tongue-in-cheek novel about the development of an artist is Steven Millhauser's *Edwin Mullhouse: The Life and Death of an American Writer, 1943–1954*. Dorothy Baker's *Young Man with a Horn* is a novel about a jazz musician. A bear is the main character in William Kotzwinkle's *The Bear Went Over the Mountain*. *The Bear Comes Home* won a PEN/Faulkner Award.

Zigman, Laura

Animal Husbandry

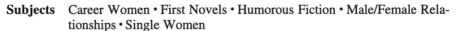

Dial Press. 1998. 304 pp.

Late night television producer Jane Goodall (not the scientist), after finding herself suddenly jilted by the man of her dreams, undertakes a study of male mating behavior and develops the Old Cow-New Cow Theory.

Subjects   Career Women • First Novels • Humorous Fiction • Male/Female Relationships • Single Women

Now try   Christina Bartolomeo's *Cupid & Diana* and Susan Trott's *Crane Spreads Wings: A Bigamist's Story* are other humorous novels about the interaction between men and women.

Chapter 3

Characters

Adams, Alice
Superior Women
Knopf. 1984. 367 pp.

In 1943, five very different young women meet at Radcliffe College and find that their lives remain intertwined over the next four decades.

Subjects 1940s • 1950s • 1960s • 1970s • 1980s • College Students • Male/Female Relationships • Women's Friendships

Now try Adams's early novel, ***Families and Survivors***, is also about friendship between young women. ***Beautiful Girl*** and ***To See You Again*** are two collections of Adams's short stories. Mary McCarthy's novel, ***The Group***, set a bit earlier than ***Superior Women***, has a similar plot.

Adebayo, Diran
Some Kind of Black
Virago. 1996. 238 pp.

Coming of age as a black man in London, Nigerian Dele struggles without the support of his best friend, his sister Dapo, who suffers from sickle cell anemia.

2d Appeal Story   Book Groups 📖

Subjects African Authors • Brothers and Sisters • Child Abuse • Coming-of-Age • First Novels • Illness • Immigrants and Refugees • Nigerian Authors

Now try ***The Buddha of Suburbia*** by Hanif Kureishi is also about the difficulties of living in England as an immigrant. ***Some Kind of Black*** won the Betty Trask Award.

Agee, Jonis

Sweet Eyes
Crown Publishers. 1991. 405 pp.

A year in the life of Honey Parrish, of Divinity, Iowa, as she tries to make a better life for herself than her parents had.

2d Appeal   Setting
Book Groups 📖

Subjects   First Novels • Interracial Relationships • Iowa • Love Stories • Middle-Aged Women • Racism • Single Women • Small-Town Life

Now try   *The Way Men Act* by Elinor Lipman and Tim Mahoney's *We're Not Here* are both about interracial relationships. Judy Troy's *West of Venus* and Tom Drury's *The End of Vandalism*, as well as Agee's novel, *South of Resurrection*, are about life in a small town in middle America.

Alexander, Lynne

Safe Houses
Atheneum. 1985. 261 pp.

In post-World War II Brooklyn, Gerda, a hardened prostitute who claims to have been the mistress of both Adolf Eichmann and Raoul Wallenberg, and Jack, a former pastry chef for the Nazis and a prisoner of the Russians, both retreat into their safe houses: for Gerda, an ego-serving agoraphobia, and for Jack, amnesia and madness.

2d Appeal   Language
Book Groups 📖

Subjects   Culinary Arts • First Novels • Holocaust • Mental Illness • Prostitutes and Prostitution • World War II

Now try   Another poetic, painful view of Holocaust survivors can be found in Anne Michaels's *Fugitive Pieces*. Steven Bloom's *No New Jokes* is about World War II veterans trying to find meaning in their lives when they return to their families and jobs in Brooklyn after the war.

Alexie, Sherman

Reservation Blues
Atlantic Monthly Press. 1995. 306 pp.

Legendary blues guitarist Robert Johnson's path crosses with Thomas Builds-the-Fire on the Spokane Reservation, leaving Thomas with a possessed guitar that leads to a series of adventures on and off the reservation for the members of a newly formed band, Coyote Springs.

2d Appeal   Setting
Book Groups 📖

Subjects   American Indian Authors • American Indians • First Novels • Magic Realism • Music and Musicians

Now try   Alexie was inspired by the writing of James Welch, author of *Fools Crow* and other novels. Alexie's other books include a collection of interconnected short stories, *The Lone Ranger and Tonto Fistfight in Heaven*, *Indian Killer*, and *The Business of Fancydancing: Stories and Poems*. Louise Erdrich (*Love Medicine*) and the late Michael Dorris (*A Yellow Raft in Blue Water*) wrote novels about American Indian life on the "rez," as do novelists Thomas King (*Green Grass, Running Water*) and Susan Power (*Grass Dancer*). Another dead man turns up unexpectedly in the lives of characters in W. P. Kinsella's Shoeless Joe. In 1996, *Granta Magazine* named Alexie one of the "20 Best Young American Novelists."

Alpert, Cathryn
Rocket City
MacMurray & Beck. 1995. 348 pp.

Marilee Levitay's plans to marry her high school sweetheart change when she picks up a seductively intelligent dwarf while driving through New Mexico's back country.

| **2d Appeal** | Story | Book Groups 📖 |

Subjects   Dwarfs • First Novels • Male/Female Relationships • New Mexico • Road Novels

Now try   The energy in this novel can also be found in Pam Houston's short story collection, ***Cowboys Are My Weakness***, Tom Robbins's ***Even Cowgirls Get the Blues***, Katherine Dunn's ***Geek Love***, and Larry McMurtry's ***Moving On*** and ***All My Friends Are Going to Be Strangers***. Another good novel about a dwarf is Simon Mawer's ***Mendel's Dwarf***. ***Finding Signs*** by Sharlene Baker also explores the unexpected ways love can appear in a person's life.

Alther, Lisa
Original Sins
Knopf. 1981. 592 pp.

Set against the events and changing lifestyles of the 1950s through the 1970s, five friends come of age in Newland, Tennessee.

| **2d Appeal** | Story | Book Groups 📖 |

Subjects   1950s • 1960s • 1970s • Coming-of-Age • Family Relationships • Friendship • Southern Authors • Tennessee

Now try   Alther's other books include the novel, ***Kinflicks***. Alther's characters share some of the same experiences as do the women in Mimi Albert's ***Skirts***. ***Civil Wars*** by Rosellen Brown is a good picture of a white family's involvement in the Civil Rights movement. Marilyn French's novel, ***The Women's Room***, echoes some of Alther's sentiments about the early days of the feminist movement.

Alvarez, Julia
How the Garcia Girls Lost Their Accents
Algonquin Books of Chapel Hill. 1991. 290 pp.

Uprooted from their family home in the Dominican Republic, the four Garcia sisters arrive in New York City in 1960 to find a life far different from the genteel existence of maids, manicures, and extended family they left behind.

| **2d Appeal** | Language | Book Groups 📖 |

Subjects   Acculturation • ALA Notable Books • Dominican Authors • Family Relationships • First Novels • New York • Sisters

Now try   Alvarez has also published books of poetry, including ***The Other Side***, ***Homecoming***, and ***The Housekeeping Book***. Eva Hoffman's memoir about adjusting to life in a different culture is ***Lost in Translation: A Life in a New Language***. Lore Segal's novel, ***Her First American***, is a fictional account of the same process. Maxine Chernoff's ***American Heaven*** is about a recent Polish immigrant who works as a nurse/companion to an aging jazz musician. Yolanda, one of the characters in this novel, is the main character in Alvarez's ***Yo!***

Alvarez, Julia
Yo!
Algonquin Books of Chapel Hill. 1997. 309 pp.

Yolanda Garcia's life is seen through the eyes of the friends, lovers, and family members who know her best.

2d Appeal Story

Subjects ALA Notable Books • Dominican Authors • Family Relationships • Sisters

Now try Yolanda Garcia also appears in Alvarez's *How the Garcia Girls Lost Their Accents*. The different ways a person's life can be interpreted is the subject of Carol Shields's *Swann*. Other books about Hispanic families include *The House on Mango Street* by Sandra Cisneros, *Bless Me, Ultima* by Rudolfo Anaya, and *Rain of Gold* by Victor Villasenor.

Ames, Jonathan
The Extra Man
Scribner. 1998. 333 pp.

After being caught trying on a bra belonging to a fellow teacher, 26-year-old Louis Ives moves to Manhattan and embarks on a diligent campaign to understand his sexual identity.

2d Appeal Setting

Subjects Humorous Fiction • Men's Friendships • New York • Sexual Identity • Single Men • Transvestites

Now try Ames's first novel is *I Pass Like Night*. The main character in Mark O'Donnell's *Let Nothing You Dismay* has a lot in common with Louis Ives. Transvestites also play a role in Tama Janowitz's *The Male Cross-Dresser Support Group*.

Amis, Kingsley
The Old Devils
Summit Books. 1987. 294 pp.

After 30 years away, the return home to Wales of famous writer Alun Weaver and his still-beautiful wife Rhiannon causes consternation among their old (in both senses of the word) friends, as they remember and relive the tangled relationships of the past.

2d Appeal Language

Subjects Booker Prize Winners • British Authors • Elderly Men • Elderly Women • Friendship • Male/Female Relationships • Satirical Fiction • Wales • Writers and Writing

Now try Graham Swift's *Ever After* and Wallace Stegner's *Crossing to Safety* are both about complicated friendships over a period of years.

Anderson, Jessica
Tirra Lirra by the River
Macmillan. 1978. 141 pp.

Returning to her childhood home in a small Australian town, elderly Nora Porteus recalls her unhappy marriage, her escape to Sydney, a botched operation, and the many years she spent in London.

2d Appeal Language   Book Groups 📖

Subjects Aging • Australia • Australian Authors • Coming-of-Age • Elderly Women • Women's Friendships

Now try   Anderson's other novels include ***The Only Daughter*** and ***An Ordinary Lunacy***. ***A Time to Dance*** by Walter Sullivan and Kate Phillips's ***White Rabbit*** both describe old age from the point of view of an elderly person. ***Mrs. Palfrey at the Claremont*** by Elizabeth Taylor and Doris Lessing's ***The Diaries of Jane Somers*** are both moving novels about elderly women. James Laughlin's book of poetry, ***The Country Road***, includes many poems about aging. Other books about women coming-of-age late in life include Pagan Kennedy's ***Spinsters*** and Stanley Elkin's ***Mrs. Ted Bliss***. ***Tirra Lirra by the River*** won the Miles Franklin Award.

Anderson-Dargatz, Gail
The Cure for Death by Lightning Houghton Mifflin. 1996. 294 pp.

Family life in remote British Columbia during World War II is seen through the eyes of 15-year-old Beth Weeks, as she and her best friend, American Indian Nora, learn to survive the daily trials of living as they strive for independence and their place in the world.

2d Appeal   Setting Book Groups 📖

Subjects   American Indians • British Columbia, Canada • Canadian Authors • Coming-of-Age • Farms and Farm Life • First Novels • Friendship • Teenage Girls • Teenagers • World War II

Now try   Anderson-Dargatz is also the author of ***The Miss Hereford Stories***, which revolve around the life of a young boy in a fictitious Canadian town. Ella Leffland's ***Rumors of Peace*** is also about the coming-of-age of a young girl during World War II.

Astley, Thea
Reaching Tin River Putnam. 1990. 223 pp.

Belle's life is defined by three men: the American father—a musician—whom she never knew; Seb, her partner in a loveless marriage; and Gaden Lockyer, the subject of Belle's research, a pioneer Australian whose love for his country mirrors Belle's own.

2d Appeal   Story Book Groups 📖

Subjects   Australia • Australian Authors • Coming-of-Age • Family Relationships • Male/Female Relationships • Research Novels

Now try   Astley's others novels include ***Coda*** and ***Beachmasters***. Another book about growing up in Australia is ***My Brilliant Career*** by Miles Franklin.

Atkinson, Kate
Behind the Scenes at the Museum St. Martin's Press. 1996. 332 pp.

The secrets of four generations of a Yorkshire, England, family are slowly uncovered by Ruby Lennox, who along the way also discovers the truth about her own life.

2d Appeal   Language Book Groups 📖

Subjects   ALA Notable Books • British Authors • Family Relationships • Family Secrets • First Novels • Humorous Fiction • Multigenerational Novels

Now try Atkinson also wrote *Human Croquet*. Secrets being slowly uncovered is the main theme of Arundhati Roy's *The God of Small Things*. The family relationships in Atkinson's book are reminiscent of those found in Tim Winton's *Cloudstreet*. *Behind the Scenes at the Museum* won a Whitbread Award.

Atwood, Margaret
Cat's Eye
Doubleday. 1988. 446 pp.

The ambiguous nature of friendship is revealed as Elaine Risley, a Canadian artist, returns home to Toronto and finds she cannot forget (or forgive) her childhood friend, Cordelia.

2d Appeal Language   Book Groups 📖

Subjects ALA Notable Books • Art and Artists • Canadian Authors • Toronto • Women's Friendships

Now try *Lady Oracle* and *The Robber Bride* are other Atwood novels about childhood friendships and the terrible ways girls often treat one another. The fine quality of Atwood's writing is similar to Dennis McFarland's style in *The Music Room* and Diane Schoemperlen's in *In the Language of Love*. Sandra Birdsell's *The Chrome Suite* is another example of an intense and interior novel set in Canada.

Atwood, Margaret
Life Before Man
Jonathan Cape. 1979. 317 pp.

As Elizabeth and Nate's marriage finally ends, and Lesje and William's long-term relationship stagnates, all four look for emotional satisfaction elsewhere.

2d Appeal Language   Book Groups 📖

Subjects ALA Notable Books • Canadian Authors • Dysfunctional Families • Male/Female Relationships

Now try Atwood's novel *The Edible Woman* also deals with a woman trying to understand her relationships with the public world and her private self. Alice Munro, in her short story collections (*Open Secrets, The Moons of Jupiter*, and others) and her novel, *The Lives of Girls and Women*, describes the lives of seemingly ordinary women.

Ba, Mariama
So Long a Letter
Heinemann. 1981. 90 pp.

A Senegalese woman reflects on her life, her marriage, and her place in society, all of which were radically changed by her husband's decision to take a second wife after 25 years of marriage. Translated from the French by Modupe Bode-Thomas.

2d Appeal Language

Subjects African Authors • First Novels • First Novels • Male/Female Relationships • Polygamy • Senegal • Senegalese Authors

Now try Ba also wrote *Scarlet Song*, which was translated into English in 1986. Both books concern women struggling against an opresive society. Alice Walker's *Possessing the Secret of Joy* is another book about an African woman's struggle for independence in the modern world. In Nayantara Sahgal's *Rich Like Us*, a similar situation is described from the point of view of the second wife.

Bainbridge, Beryl
The Birthday Boys
Carroll & Graf. 1994. 189 pp.

Five members of the doomed 1912 Scott expedition to the Antarctic recount, at first with naive optimism and then poignant despair, their progressively disastrous trek to the ends of the earth.

2d Appeal   Setting   Book Groups 📖

Subjects   ALA Notable Books • Antarctica • Death and Dying • Men's Friendships

Now try   Bainbridge's other novels include *An Awfully Big Adventure* and *Master Georgie*. *The Cage* by Audrey Schulman and *Antarctic Navigation* by Elizabeth Arthur are two novels in which the female heroines risk their lives in search of adventure. Just as the Antarctic is a character in Bainbridge's novel, the settings of E. Annie Proulx's *The Shipping News* and Howard Norman's *The Bird Artist* are characters in those novels. Other loosely fictionalized characters are found in Jane Mendelsohn's *I Was Amelia Earhart*, Tomas Eloy Martinez's *Santa Evita*, Jay Cantor's *The Death of Che Guevara*, Judith Farr's *I Never Came to You in White*, and Don DeLillo's *Libra*. Another bone-chilling account of an Antarctic expedition gone wrong (albeit with a happier ending) is *Endurance: Shackleton's Incredible Voyage* by Alfred Lansing.

Ballantyne, Sheila
Imaginary Crimes
Viking Press. 1982. 265 pp.

Even as an adult, Sonya Weiler's unhappy childhood, caused by her father's get-rich-quick con games and her mother's early death from cancer, continues to haunt her.

2d Appeal   Language   Book Groups 📖

Subjects   1950s • ALA Notable Books • Coming-of-Age • Death of a Parent • Dysfunctional Families • Fathers and Daughters

Now try   Ballantyne also wrote *Life on Earth: Stories* and *Norma Jean the Termite Queen*. Another difficult childfood is described in Dorothy Allison's *Bastard Out of Carolina*. Two good books about growing up with a Christian Scientist parent are Barbara Wilson's *Blue Windows* and *The Unseen Shore* by Thomas Simmons.

Banks, Lynne Reid
Casualties
St. Martin's Press. 1987. 243 pp.

Writer Sue McClusky gains perspective on her own unhappy marriage when she visits an old friend, Mariolain, and her husband Niels, and discovers that the roots of their troubled marriage lie in the horrors they endured as children in Holland during World War II.

2d Appeal   Story   Book Groups 📖

Subjects   British Authors • Holland • Husbands and Wives • Male/Female Relationships • Marriage • Women's Friendships • World War II

Now try   Banks is also the author of many children's books, including *The Indian in the Cupboard;* her novels for adults include *The L-Shaped Room*. Other novels about troubled marriages with their roots in traumatic experiences during World War II are Marisa Kantor Stark's *Bring Us the Old People* and Anne Michaels's *Fugitive Pieces*.

Banks, Russell
Continental Drift
Harper & Row. 1985. 366 pp.

Tired of his dead-end life and hoping to make a new start for himself, Bob Dubois moves his family from New Hampshire to Florida, only to find his problems multiplied and his old foibles still dogging his heels.

2d Appeal   Story   Book Groups 📖

Subjects   ALA Notable Books • Drugs and Drug Abuse • Florida • Immigrants and Refugees • Male/Female Relationships • Middle-Aged Men • Midlife Crisis

Now try   Banks is also the author of *Cloudsplitter*, a novel about radical abolitionist John Brown. Other families that leave their homes only to find themselves unable to extricate themselves from their old lives can be found in John Steinbeck's *The Grapes of Wrath*, Samantha Gillison's *The Undiscovered Country*, and Paul Theroux's *The Mosquito Coast*.

Banks, Russell
Rule of the Bone
HarperCollins Publishers. 1995. 390 pp.

Fourteen-year-old Chapman, nicknamed Bone, negotiates his way through adolescence in the 1990s with the help of an unusual group of friends: I-Man, Froggy, and Russ.

2d Appeal   Story   Book Groups 📖

Subjects   Coming-of-Age • Drugs and Drug Abuse • Dysfunctional Families • Friendship • Jamaica • Juvenile Delinquents • Rastafarians • Sexual Abuse • Teenage Boys

Now try   Among Banks's works of fiction are *The Book of Jamaica, Continental Drift*, and *Affliction*. Other books about troubled adolescent boys include Tobias Wolff's memoir, *This Boy's Life*, and J. D. Salinger's *The Catcher in the Rye*. The gritty style of this novel is similar to Richard Ford's writing in *Clockers*.

Barfoot, Joan
Duet for Three
Beaufort Books. 1985. 252 pp.

As 80-year-old Aggie and her 59-year-old daughter June await a visit from June's daughter, each struggles with the indignities of aging, the need for independence, and a desire to be loved.

2d Appeal   Language   Book Groups 📖

Subjects   ALA Notable Books • Elderly Women • Family Relationships • Mothers and Daughters • Widows

Now try   *Abra* is another novel by Barfoot. Doris Lessing's *The Diaries of Jane Somers* also concerns the indignities of aging. *Charms for the Easy Life* by Kaye Gibbons is a more lighthearted look at the relationship of three generations of women.

Barnhardt, Wilton
Emma Who Saved My Life
St. Martin's Press. 1989. 470 pp.

In the 1970s, a wide-eyed midwestern student (and wannabe actor) struggles to become successful in the New York theater world with the help of Emma, an outspoken poet.

2d Appeal   Story

Subjects   1970s • Actors and Acting • Friendship • Male/Female Relationships • New York

Now try   Barnhardt's other novels include *Gospel* and *Show World*. Stephen McCauley's *The Object of My Affection* is a more concise story about friendships in New York. Other novels written with a creative use of type styles, such as lots of italics, many parenthetical phrases, and CAPITALIZATION for EMPHASIS are William Carpenter's *A Keeper of Sheep*, *A Widow for One Year* by John Irving, and Arundhati Roy's *The God of Small Things*.

Barrett, Andrea
The Forms of Water

Pocket Books. 1993. 292 pp.

By leaving half the family land to his grown niece Wiloma and half to her brother Henry, ex-monk Brendan hopes the two can overcome the disabling turmoil caused by the early deaths of their parents, an event that has continued to haunt them throughout their lives.

2d Appeal   Language   Book Groups 📖

Subjects   Bequests • Brothers and Sisters • Death of a Parent • Ecofiction • Family Relationships

Now try   Barrett also wrote *Ship Fever*, which won the National Book Award, as well as *Lucid Stars*, *The Voyage of the Narwhal*, and *Secret Harmonies*. *Saint Maybe* by Anne Tyler is also about a family trying to heal its wounds.

Barthelme, Donald
Paradise

Putnam. 1986. 208 pp.

Fifty-three-year-old Simon, an architect on a self-imposed sabbatical from work, finds his life changed—and yet not so different—when three temporarily homeless, beautiful young women move in with him.

2d Appeal   Language

Subjects   Adultery • Architects and Architecture • Fathers and Daughters • Male/Female Relationships • New York • Older Men/Younger Women • Postmodern Fiction

Now try   Among Barthelme's other books are *The Dead Father*, *Come Back, Dr. Caligari*, and *Overnight to Many Distant Cities*. Ann Beattie's collections of stories (*Secrets and Surprises: Short Stories* and others) share Barthelme's characteristic elliptical prose. In a style similar to that of Barthelme, novelists William Gass (*The Tunnel*) and John Barth (*The Floating Opera*) explore the world with a strong sense of irony.

Barthelme, Frederick
Second Marriage

Simon and Schuster. 1984. 217 pp.

During a separation from Theo, his second troubled wife, dissatisfied Henry moves desolately between Theo and her precocious daughter Rachel, and Mariana, his beautiful, sharp-tongued mistress.

Subjects   Adultery • First Novels • Male/Female Relationships • Marriage • Mothers and Daughters

Now try   Barthelme's other books include the novels *Bob the Gambler*, *Brothers*, and several collections of short stories. Other troubled marriages are described in Rick Moody's novel, *The Ice Storm*, Mary Karr's memoir *The Liars' Club*, and Gustave Flaubert's classic novel, *Madame Bovary*.

Bausch, Richard
Mr. Field's Daughter
Linden Press. 1989. 347 pp.

James Field's only daughter, Annie, disappoints him when she elopes with ne'er-do-well Cole Gilbertson, only to return home with a child and a broken marriage five years later.

2d Appeal   Story

Subjects   ALA Notable Books • Fathers and Daughters • Older Men/Younger Women • Single Parents

Now try   Among Bausch's other works of fiction are *Rebel Powers* and *Violence*. Richard Russo in *Mohawk* and *The Risk Pool* also writes about men who are less than successful. Russell Banks's *Continental Drift* is about a man trying to be in control of his own life.

Beattie, Ann
Falling in Place
Random House. 1980. 342 pp.

In the suburbs of Connecticut in the early 1980s, a family disintegrates under the weight of boredom and discontent.

2d Appeal   Language   Book Groups 📖

Subjects   1980s • Dysfunctional Families • Marriage • Suburbia

Now try   Beattie's short story collections include *Park City, Secrets and Surprises*, and *The Burning House*, among others. Beattie's novels include *Picturing Will* and *Chilly Scenes of Winter*. Rick Moody's *The Ice Storm* is also about families bored and discontented with their lives and the tragedies that occur.

Bell, Betty Louise
Faces in the Moon
University of Oklahoma Press. 1994. 193 pp.

As she struggles to separate the legacy of an abusive and poverty-stricken childhood from her adult self, Lucie retells the history of three generations of Cherokee women.

Book Groups 📖

Subjects   Alcoholics and Alcoholism • American Indian Authors • American Indians • Cherokees • Child Abuse • First Novels • Mothers and Daughters • Multigenerational Novels • Poverty • Sisters

Now try   Other novels that deal with hardships, humble beginnings, and beating the odds are Henry Roth's *Call It Sleep* and Dorothy Allison's *Cavedweller*. Louise Erdrich's *Love Medicine* also looks at the lives of several generations of an American Indian family.

Bell, Christine
The Perez Family
W.W. Norton. 1990. 256 pp.

In Miami, after the Marielito boat lift, former political prisoner Juan Raul Perez finds himself with two families: a long-suffering wife and daughter who have waited 20 years for him, and an artificial family consisting of a vivacious wife, a loony father, and a petty criminal son, all acquired to make it easier to emigrate to the United States.

Book Groups 📖

Subjects   ALA Notable Books • Bigamists and Bigamy • Cuba • Culture Clash • Immigrants and Refugees • Marriage • Miami, Florida

Now try Bell's other books include *The Seven Year Atomic Make-Over Guide: And Other Stories* and *Saint. The Death of Che Guevara* by Jay Cantor is a remarkable novel about Castro's closest friend during the Cuban revolution. Both *Dreaming in Cuban* and *The Aguero Sisters* by Cristina Garcia are about families divided by the Cuban Revolution. Life in Castro's prisons is graphically described in *Against All Hope: The Prison Memoirs of Armando Valladares*.

Bell, Madison Smartt
Ten Indians
Pantheon Books. 1996. 272 pp.

Child therapist Mike Devlin and his daughter open a martial arts studio in inner-city Baltimore, where they come face to face with the vast differences between their world and the world of the children who come to use the studio.

Book Groups 📖

Subjects Baltimore, Maryland • Drugs and Drug Abuse • Fathers and Daughters • Interracial Relationships • Martial Arts • Psychiatrists, Psychoanalysts, Psychotherapists • Racism • Teenage Boys • Violence

Now try Bell's other works of fiction include *All Souls' Rising*, *Straight Cut*, and *Zero db and Other Stories*. Jonathan Kozol's *Savage Inequalities* demonstrates how schools serving white, middle- and upper-class children and those serving the ghettos are radically different. Racism is explored in Beverly Coyle's *In Troubled Waters*. In 1996, *Granta Magazine* named Bell one of the "20 Best Young American Novelists."

Bell, Madison Smartt
The Year of Silence
Ticknor & Fields. 1987. 194 pp.

Marian's suicide is seen through the effects it has on a variety of people: her lover Weber, her cousin and best friend Gwen, a dwarf named Jocko, and other characters whose lives intersected hers.

2d Appeal Story

Subjects Abortion • Dwarfs • Male/Female Relationships • Music and Musicians • Suicide • Women's Friendships

Now try Bell's other books include *Soldier's Joy* and *Barking Man and Other Stories*. Larkin, one of the characters in this novel, is in New York to search for his missing brother Clarence, who was the main character in Bell's earlier novel, *Waiting for the End of the World*. Other novels about the friends and family a suicide leaves behind include *The Suicide's Wife* by David Madden and *The Bubble Reputation* by Cathie Pelletier. In 1996, *Granta Magazine* named Bell one of the "20 Best Young American Novelists."

Bellow, Saul
The Dean's December
Harper & Row. 1982. 312 pp.

Academic dean and former journalist Albert Corde falls victim to a bureaucratic entanglement in Bucharest, Rumania, and becomes increasingly unpopular in his hometown of Chicago because of his involvement in a racially charged murder trial.

2d Appeal Language

Book Groups 📖

Subjects	Academia • Chicago • Journalists • Race Relations • Romania • Violence • Writers and Writing
Now try	Saul Bellow's other novels include *Herzog* and *Humboldt's Gift*. *Eveless Eden* by Marianne Wiggins, the story of a journalist covering Romania and other political hotspots, includes a scathing indictment of that country's political and social corruption. *The Dean's December* shares with the novels of John le Carre (*Tinker, Tailor, Soldier, Spy* and others) some lengthy cryptic dialogues and Cold War intrigue.

Benedict, Elizabeth
Slow Dancing
Knopf. 1985. 276 pp.

Cynical about the world and her life in particular, young attorney Lexi encounters a man who quietly challenges her perspectives and pushes her to make changes by asking questions and being willing to change his life for her.

Subjects	1980s • First Novels • Law and Lawyers • Love Stories • Male/Female Relationships • Marriage
Now try	Benedict also wrote *The Beginner's Book of Dreams* and *Safe Conduct*. Other books about yuppies in the 1980s include Ann Hood's *Somewhere Off the Coast of Maine*.

Beresford-Howe, Constance
The Marriage Bed
St. Martin's Press. 1981. 232 pp.

Married right after graduating from college because she was pregnant, Anne Graham, now expecting her third child in three years, suddenly finds herself alone with her unhappy childhood memories after her husband leaves her for another woman.

2d Appeal	Story
Subjects	1970s • Adultery • Canadian Authors • Male/Female Relationships • Marriage
Now try	Beresford-Howe's *The Voices of Eve* and *A Population of One* make up a loose trilogy with the *The Marriage Bed*, by looking at three women of different ages and distinct stages in their lives. In Ruth Doan MacDougall's *Wife and Mother*, also set in the 1970s, the main character, a college student, also gets married because she's pregnant and finds that it is not the best basis for a relationship.

Berg, Elizabeth
Talk Before Sleep
Random House. 1994. 210 pp.

When Ruth Thomas is diagnosed with rapidly metastasizing breast cancer, her best friend Ann Stanley shares doctor's visits, funeral plans, and long talks about men, children, sex, the past, and the future.

2d Appeal	Language	Book Groups 📖
Subjects	Cancer • Death and Dying • Grief • Women's Friendships	
Now try	Berg's other novels include *Durable Goods* and *Range of Motion*. Other novels dealing with cancer include Gail Godwin's *The Good Husband*, Anna Quindlen's *One True Thing*, Larry McMurtry's *Terms of Endearment*, Alexandra Marshall's *Gus in Bronze*, and Abby Frucht's *Life Before Death*.	

Billington, Rachel
Loving Attitudes

Morrow. 1988. 250 pp.

Mary Tempest thinks she has settled comfortably into middle age, marriage, and motherhood, but a shocking visit from a long-lost daughter from a love affair 20 years before leaves her desperate to reclaim passions of the past.

2d Appeal Story

Subjects British Authors • Male/Female Relationships • Mothers and Daughters

Now try Billington's other novels include *The Garish Day, A Painted Devil*, and *Theo and Matilda*. Two other novels in which parents and their long-lost children reconnect are Elinor Lipman's *Then She Found Me* and Joshua Henkin's *Swimming Across the Hudson*.

Bills, Greg
Consider This Home

Simon & Schuster. 1994. 318 pp.

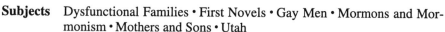

When Kath heeds her father's pleas and returns to her dysfunctional Utah Mormon family to help out in a crisis, she realizes she must come to terms with the ultra-religious husband she abandoned, the confining bounds of her religion, and the father of her son, if she wants to have a satisfying life.

Subjects Dysfunctional Families • First Novels • Gay Men • Mormons and Mormonism • Mothers and Sons • Utah

Now try Bills also wrote *Fearful Symmetry*. Another picture of a dysfunctional Mormon family can be found in Diane Johnson's *Loving Hands at Home*. Terry Tempest Williams's *Refuge: An Unnatural History of Family and Place* is a memoir of the author's close and loving Mormon family.

Binding, Tim
In the Kingdom of Air

W.W. Norton. 1994. 374 pp.

Obsessed with his sexual prowess, middle-aged Giles, a divorced weather forecaster, relives in a series of flashbacks the events of his unhappy childhood and their lasting effects on his life.

Book Groups 📖

Subjects British Authors • Coming-of-Age • Dysfunctional Families • First Novels • Middle-Aged Men • Sex and Sexuality • Small-Town Life

Now try Binding also wrote *A Perfect Execution*, a novel rich in metaphors. Other middle-aged men having trouble coping with their lives can be found in David Lodge's *Therapy* and Richard Russo's *Straight Man*. *The Information*, by Martin Amis and David Gates's *Preston Falls* also feature less-than-likable male protagonists.

Birdsell, Sandra
The Chrome Suite
McLelland & Stewart. 1992. 364 pp.

On a trip from Toronto to Winnipeg with her lover Piotr, scriptwriter Amy Barber looks back over the years since the summer of her childhood when her older sister's death was followed by the breakup of her family, the loss of a friend, and a search for both love and self.

2d Appeal   Story

Subjects   Canada • Canadian Authors • Child Abuse • Coming-of-Age • Death of a Child • Family Relationships • Small-Town Life

Now try   Birdsell also wrote *Agassiz: A Novel in Stories* and *The Two-Headed Calf*. This claustrophobic, interior novel shares a sense of the difficulties of childhood with the works of other Canadian writers, including Diane Schoemperlen (*In the Language of Love*) and Margaret Atwood (*Cat's Eye* and others).

Bloom, Amy
Love Invents Us
Random House. 1999. 205 pp.

As she moves from adolescence to middle age, desire and love become confused in Elizabeth Taube's life, first as she becomes the target of an older man's desire and then as she falls in love with a black basketball player.

2d Appeal   Language   Book Groups 📖

Subjects   1960s • First Novels • Interracial Relationships • Older Men/Younger Women • Single Parents

Now try   Bloom's collection of short stories, *Come to Me*, was a finalist for the National Book Award. Her short stories have appeared in many magazines, including *The New Yorker* and *Story*; they were included in the 1991 and 1992 editions of *Best American Short Stories*, as well as in the *O. Henry Prize Story Collection* in 1994. Vladimir Nabokov's *Lolita* is the classic novel about an older man's desire for a young girl. Other novels about interracial romances are Lynn Lauber's *21 Sugar Street* and Nanci Kincaid's *Crossing Blood*.

Bloom, Steven
No New Jokes
Norton. 1997. 187 pp.

Left with shrapnel in his head as a result of a wound suffered during World War II, Izzy meets regularly with a group of friends in a Brooklyn luncheonette, where the jokes they tell to one another are an attempt to forget both the past and their fears for the future.

2d Appeal   Setting

Subjects   1940s • Brooklyn, New York • First Novels • Jews and Judaism • Men's Friendships • Single Men • World War II

Now try   Steve Katz's *Florry of Washington Heights* also looks at New York life just before the breakout of the Korean War.

Boswell, Robert
Mystery Ride
Knopf. 1993. 333 pp.

The lives of a variety of characters, including a divorced couple and a teenager and her stepfather, demonstrate the intricacies of love, family dynamics, and friendship.

2d Appeal Story

Subjects Adultery • Divorce • Family Relationships • Fathers and Daughters • Stepfamilies • Teenage Girls

Now try John Thorndike's *The Potato Baron* also conveys the strong sense of pride and ownership men and women feel for the land.

Boyd, Blanche McCrary
Terminal Velocity
Alfred A. Knopf. 1997. 255 pp.

Ellen Burns's journey from happily married heterosexual to a name change (Rain), life in a radical lesbian commune, drugs and drink, electroshock therapy, involvement in sexual politics, and the women's liberation movement is prompted by her immediate attraction to Artemis, an artist with a trust fund.

2d Appeal Story

Subjects 1970s • Humorous Fiction • Lesbians • Women's Friendships

Now try Ellen (Rain) is also the main character in Boyd's earlier novel, *The Revolution of Little Girls*. Boyd's very funny presentation of the rhetoric of women's issues in the 1970s is reminiscent of Francine Prose's satirical *Hunters and Gatherers*.

Boyd, William
Brazzaville Beach
W. Morrow. 1990. 316 pp.

British ecologist Hope Clearwater flees a tragic marriage for Africa and the opportunity to study chimpanzee behavior with a famous scientist.

2d Appeal Setting   Book Groups 📖

Subjects Africa • British Authors • Chimpanzees • Congo • Marriage

Now try Boyd's sardonic writing style is showcased in *The Destiny of Nathalie X and Other Stories*, as well as his novels, *A Good Man in Africa* and *Armadillo*. Mary Tannen's *After Roy*, Peter Hoeg's *The Woman and the Ape*, and Marian Engel's *Bear* all describe a young woman's attachment to animals. Douglas Preston's *Jennie* is about a chimpanzee raised by a normal American family. Maria Thomas's *Come to Africa and Save Your Marriage*, Norman Rush's *Mating*, and Richard Dooling's *White Man's Grave* are very different types of novels that have in common their African setting. *Brazzaville Beach* won the James Tait Black Award.

Boyle, T. Coraghessan
East Is East
Viking. 1990. 364 pp.

Able-bodied seaman Hiro Tanaka jumps ship off the coast of Georgia and lands in the middle of floundering writer Ruth Dershowitz's life.

Book Groups 📖

Subjects   ALA Notable Books • Culture Clash • Georgia • Japanese Americans • Male/Female Relationships • Racism • Sailors and Sailing • Writers and Writing

Now try   Other books by Boyle include *World's End, Budding Prospects*, and *Water Music*. Pete Dexter's *Paris Trout* deals with racism in Georgia, as well.

Bracewell, Michael
Divine Concepts of Physical Beauty
Knopf. 1990. 261 pp.

Two self-absorbed men in London's swinging art scene experience the pangs of love when one falls in love with a fashion model and another is jilted by his male lover.

2d Appeal   Setting
Book Groups 📖

Subjects   Art and Artists • British Authors • Gay Men • London • Male/Female Relationships • Obsessive Love

Now try   Bracewell's other books include *Saint Rachel* and *The Conclave*. Toni Morrison's *Tar Baby* is also about a fashion model, beauty, desire, and love. The New York art world is the background for David Lipsky's *The Art Fair* and Fernanda Eberstadt's *When the Sons of Heaven Meet the Daughters of the Earth*.

Bradbury, Malcolm
Rates of Exchange
Knopf. 1983. 309 pp.

Professor of Linguistics Angus Petworth goes on a speaking tour to an imaginary Iron Curtain country and discovers a world of political intrigues, misunderstandings, and romance with a magical realist novelist.

2d Appeal   Language

Subjects   Academia • British Authors • College Professors • Humorous Fiction • Love Stories

Now try   Bradbury's other books include the novel *Doctor Criminale*, as well as works of nonfiction, including *The Modern American Novel*. David Carkeet's main character in *Double Negative* and *The Error of Our Ways* is a linguist. David Lodge's *Nice Work* and *Paradise News* are both satirical novels. Jan Morris's *Last Letters from Hav* is about an imaginary country, as is Peter Cameron's *Andorra* (although he borrowed the name of a real place).

Brady, Maureen
Give Me Your Good Ear
Spinsters Ink. 1979. 141 pp.

Almost 30, unmarried, and trapped in a miserable relationship, Francie Kelly realizes that in order to find healing and strength in her relationship with her mother, she must confront her lingering memories of the family violence that culminated in the death of her father.

Book Groups 📖

Subjects   Alcoholics and Alcoholism • Child Abuse • Dysfunctional Families • Mothers and Daughters • Single Women

Now try   Other novels exploring the relationship between mothers and their grown daughters include Rebecca Stowe's *The Shadow of Desire*, Anna Quindlen's *One True Thing*, and Dani Shapiro's *Fugitive Blue*.

Brizzi, Enrico
Jack Frusciante Has Left the Band
Grove Press. 1997. 175 pp.

Alex and Aidi fall in love, despite the fact that she has only five months left in Italy before she goes abroad to study for a year and he is trying to decide just who he wants to be, the model student and obedient son or pal to delinquents, druggies, drinkers, and oddballs. Translated from the Italian by Stash Luczkiw.

2d Appeal   Story

Subjects   Coming-of-Age • First Novels • Italian Authors • Italy • Love Stories • Music and Musicians • Novels in Translation • Teenage Boys

Now try   This novel could be considered an Italian *The Catcher in the Rye*, J. D. Salinger's classic novel about adolescence. An amusing look at love and rock and roll is Tom Perrotta's *The Wishbones*. The exhilaration of first love is also found in Patty Dann's *Mermaids* and Ruth Doan MacDougall's *The Cheerleader*.

Brown, John Gregory
Decorations in a Ruined Cemetery
Houghton Mifflin. 1994. 244 pp.

The collapse of a causeway bridge in New Orleans is the catalyst for many secrets to be revealed about Thomas Eagen's family, as seen from the viewpoint of his 12-year-old daughter Meredith; Murphy Warrington, an elderly black man who worked for Eagen's father; and Eagen's second wife, Catherine.

2d Appeal   Story   Book Groups 📖

Subjects   Family Relationships • Family Secrets • Fathers and Daughters • First Novels • Race Relations • Southern Authors

Now try   Brown also wrote *The Wrecked, Blessed Body of Shelton Lafleur*. Pat Conroy's *The Prince of Tides* is also the story of tangled family relationships in the contemporary South. Another Southern novelist who deals with the issue of race relations is Beverly Coyle in *In Troubled Waters*. Long-hidden family secrets are revealed in Hamilton Basso's *The View from Pompey's Head* and Fannie Flagg's *Welcome to the World, Baby Girl!*

Brown, Rebecca
The Gifts of the Body
HarperCollins. 1994. 165 pp.

An unnamed home care worker assists various people through the years, weeks, and moments of individuals dying of AIDS and finds among them the lonely, the angry, and the compassionate.

Book Groups 📖

Subjects   AIDS • Death and Dying • Gay Men

Now try   Brown also wrote *The Children's Crusade* and *The Terrible Girls*. Iris Murdoch's *Bruno's Dream* is about the last days of a man's life and his feelings as he approaches death. The narrator of *Plays Well with Others* by Allan Gurganus watches with horror as his friends die of AIDS. *The Gifts of the Body* won the Boston Book Review/Fisk Fiction Prize.

Brown, Rita Mae

Southern Discomfort
Harper & Row. 1982. 249 pp.

Beautiful Southern blueblood Hortensia Barastre falls unexpectedly into a scandalous (and passionate) relationship with a young African American prizefighter, while fun-loving prostitutes Banana Mae and Blue Rhonda taunt the abstain-from-everything Reverend Linton Ray.

2d Appeal   Story

   Subjects   Humorous Fiction • Interracial Relationships • Male/Female Relationships • Prostitutes and Prostitution • Race Relations • Southern Authors

   Now try   *Murder, She Meowed* is one of Brown's mysteries featuring a cat. Olive Ann Burns's *Cold Sassy Tree* is another story of a scandalous relationship. In a totally different tone, but with the same theme of falling in love with the wrong person, is Dianne Highbridge's *A Much Younger Man*. Stephen Dobyns's *The Wrestler's Cruel Study* is another novel filled with wacky characters.

Brown, Rosellen

Civil Wars
Knopf. 1984. 419 pp.

Living in Mississippi after their years in the Civil Rights movement, Jessie and Teddy Carll not only must come to terms with their faltering marriage, but also with the uncomfortable task of raising their suddenly orphaned niece and nephew, whose parents' views differ sharply from those of the Carlls.

2d Appeal   Setting   Book Groups 📖

   Subjects   1960s • ALA Notable Books • Civil Rights Movement • Family Relationships • Interracial Relationships • Marriage • Mississippi • Orphans

   Now try   Another of Brown's novels with well-drawn, three-dimensional characters is *Autobiography of My Mother*, which was also an ALA Notable Book. Lisa Alther's *Original Sins*, and *Meridian*, a novel by Alice Walker, both deal with the struggle for civil rights.

Busch, Frederick

Girls
Harmony Books. 1997. 279 pp.

Jack and Fanny, unable to share the grief each feels over the death of their infant daughter, find their marriage increasingly shaky as Jack devotes his time and energy to locating a missing 14-year-old girl.

2d Appeal   Setting   Book Groups 📖

   Subjects   Adultery • Death of a Child • Grief • Male/Female Relationships • Marriage

   Now try   This novel was based on Busch's short story, "Ralph the Duck," which appears in two of his collections, *Absent Friends* and *The Children in the Woods*. "Ralph the Duck" was also selected for inclusion in *Best American Short Stories 1989*. One of the strengths of this novel is the way Busch has used the setting—upstate New York in the dead of winter—as though it were another character. Rick Moody's *The Ice Storm* is another novel in which the starkness of a winter landscape mirrors the stark loneliness of the characters. Another novel that begins at the end of the story is Toni Morrison's *Paradise*.

Busch, Frederick
Harry and Catherine
Knopf. 1990. 290 pp.

Meeting after more than a decade spent apart, on-again off-again lovers Harry and Catherine, now in their 40s, find themselves drawn to each other despite complicating situations involving Harry's job and Catherine's new boyfriend.

2d Appeal   Story   Book Groups 📖

Subjects   Love Stories • Male/Female Relationships • Single Parents • Triangles

Now try   Busch is also the author of *War Babies* and *Closing Arguments*. Jo-Ann Mapson's *Hank and Chloe* is another novel about a love affair between people who are over 40. Like Catherine in Busch's novel, Jim Harrison's *Dalva* is a strong woman who must make difficult decisions in her life. Other novels exploring triangular relationships are Julian Barnes's *Talking It Over*, *Jadis*, by Ken Chowder, and *The End of Vandalism* by Tom Drury.

Busia, Akosua
The Seasons of Beento Blackbird
Little, Brown. 1996. 367 pp.

Under the pen name of Beento Blackbird, Solomon Wilberforce is a successful author of books for children, but when his father dies and disrupts space, time, and Solomon's carefully constructed life, Solomon is forced to examine the words he and Beento have created.

Book Groups 📖

Subjects   African American Authors • African Americans • Fathers and Sons • First Novels • Male/Female Relationships • Writers and Writing

Now try   Other novels about authors of children's books include *Zod Wallop* by William Browning Spencer and *The Land of Laughs* by Jonathan Carroll.

Butler, Robert Olen
They Whisper
H. Holt. 1994. 333 pp.

Ira Holloway, a 35-year-old Vietnam veteran, analyzes his history of sexual experiences, relationships, and feelings.

2d Appeal   Language   Book Groups 📖

Subjects   Male/Female Relationships • Sex and Sexuality • Vietnam Veterans • Vietnam War

Now try   Butler won the Pulitzer Prize in 1993 for his collection of short stories, *A Good Scent from a Strange Mountain*. Other intensely written novels dealing with sexuality include Kathryn Harrison's *Exposure*, Josephine Hart's *Damage*, Hanan al Shaykh's *The Story of Zahra*, Nicholson Baker's *Vox*, Marguerite Duras's *The Lover*, and Choderlos de LaClos's *Les Liaisons Dangereuses*.

Cameron, Peter
The Weekend
Farrar, Straus Giroux. 1994. 241 pp.

On the first anniversary of his brother Tony's death from AIDS, wealthy John and his wife Marian host a weekend get-together for Tony's old lover Lyle, who unexpectedly brings along his new friend Robert.

2d Appeal   Setting   Book Groups 📖

Subjects   AIDS • Brothers • Family Relationships • Friendship • Gay Men • Upper Classes

Now try   Cameron's earlier novel, *Leap Year*, is a bit less intense than *The Weekend*. E. M. Forster in *Maurice* and *Howards End* shows a similar compassion for his characters. F. Scott Fitzgerald's *The Great Gatsby* also eloquently portrays a life of privilege and inherited wealth.

Canin, Ethan
Blue River
Houghton Mifflin. 1991. 222 pp.

Edward attempts to reconcile his childhood memories of growing up with the adult reality of having grown apart from his older brother Lawrence.

Subjects   Brothers • Coming-of-Age • Family Relationships • First Novels

Now try   In 1996, *Granta Magazine* named Canin one of the "20 Best Young American Novelists." His other books include a collection of novellas, *The Palace Thief*, *Emperor of the Air*, a book of short stories, and *For Kings and Planets*, another novel. Brothers growing apart as they mature is also part of David James Duncan's *The Brothers K*.

Canty, Kevin
Into the Great Wide Open
Nan A. Talese. 1996. 244 pp.

Seventeen-year-old Kevin, who watches as his father drinks himself to distraction and his mother languishes in a mental hospital, finds comfort in his love for Junie Williamson, his troubled high school classmate.

2d Appeal   Story

Subjects   Dysfunctional Families • First Novels • Love Stories • Teenage Boys • Teenage Girls • Teenage Love • Teenagers

Now try   The teenage characters in Scott Spencer's *Endless Love* and Alice McDermott's *That Night* both share with Canty's characters a certain desperation about their love for one another.

Cao, Lan
The Monkey Bridge
Viking. 1997. 260 pp.

Not until she reads her mother's secret journal and discovers the long-hidden secrets of her family's past in South Vietnam does teenage Mai Nguyen understand why her mother is having such a difficult time adjusting to a new life in suburban Washington, D.C., in 1978.

Book Groups 📖

Subjects   Family Secrets • First Novels • Immigrants and Refugees • Mothers and Daughters • South Vietnam • Vietnam War • Vietnamese Authors • Washington, D.C.

Now try The importance of understanding a family's past is also the theme of Alan Brown's ***Audrey Hepburn's Neck***, Seamus Deane's ***Reading in the Dark***, and Nora Okja Keller's ***Comfort Woman***. Cao mixes myths and legends into her narrative in much the same way Maxine Hong Kingston did in ***The Woman Warrior***. Robert Olen Butler's short story collection, ***A Good Scent from a Strange Mountain***, is about Vietnamese immigrants in Louisiana; Mary Gardner's ***Boat People*** is about the immigrant experience in Texas.

Carey, Jacqueline
The Other Family
Random House. 1996. 207 pp.

For four summers, beginning in 1968 when she is 14, Joan Toolan and her younger brother Hugh puzzle out the mysteries of love and marriage as they visit their divorced, pseudo-hippie mother and their glamorous, wealthy aunt and uncle, the Eberlanders.

2d Appeal Setting   Book Groups 📖

Subjects 1960s • Brothers and Sisters • Divorce • Family Relationships • Mothers Deserting Their Families

Now try ***Little Miss Strange*** by Joanna Rose, ***Bright Angel Time*** by Martha McPhee, and ***The Saskiad*** by Brian Hall are all about the downside of the 1960s generation, and how the behavior and beliefs of hippie parents affected the lives of their children. Elizabeth Berg's ***The Pull of the Moon*** and Anne Tyler's ***Ladder of Years*** both describe a mother's feelings as she abandons her family to find herself.

Carey, Peter
Bliss
Harper & Row. 1981. 296 pp.

Following a near-death experience, Harry Joy realizes that the world he inhabits is Hell, and so begins a strange, eventful journey away from his career in advertising and his scheming family, towards Heaven.

2d Appeal Language   Book Groups 📖

Subjects Australian Authors • Business and Businessmen • Near-Death Experiences • Satirical Fiction

Now try Carey is also the author of the Booker Prize-winning novel ***Oscar and Lucinda***, which was made into a movie. John Irving's ***The World According to Garp*** and Jerzy Kosinski's ***Being There*** share Carey's blend of cynicism and fantastic situations. ***Bliss*** won the Miles Franklin Award.

Carillo, Charles
Shepherd Avenue
Atlantic Monthly Press. 1986. 299 pp.

When his mother dies and his grief-stricken father abandons him, 10-year-old Joey is sent to his father's parents, Connie and Angelo, where he becomes friends with his baseball-playing Uncle Vic and tomboy Mel, and meets other residents of the boisterous Italian American community in Brooklyn.

2d Appeal   Story

Subjects   ALA Notable Books • Baseball • Brooklyn, New York • Coming-of-Age • First Novels • Italian Americans

Now try   Carillo also wrote *My Ride With Gus*, a surreal tour of Brooklyn, New York. A young man's devotion to baseball can also be found in David James Duncan's *The Brothers K* and Nancy Willard's *Things Invisible to See*.

Carter, Angela
Wise Children
Farrar, Straus Giroux. 1992. 234 pp.

Septuagenarian Dora Chance looks back over a lifetime in vaudeville with her twin Nora and their always-futile attempts to get their famous father to acknowledge them.

2d Appeal   Language   Book Groups 📖

Subjects   Elderly Women • Family Relationships • Fathers and Daughters • Humorous Fiction • Twins • Vaudeville

Now try   This particular novel by Carter shares some of the same themes that can be found in her earlier book, *Nights at the Circus*. Jeanette Winterson's *Oranges Are Not the Only Fruit* shares both a wry sensibility and a depiction of a quirky family with Carter's book. Fay Weldon (who has a nastier tongue than Carter) and Muriel Spark both share with Carter the ability to create memorable characters in their novels, as can be seen in Weldon's *Lives and Loves of a She-Devil* and Spark's *The Girls of Slender Means*. Joanna Trollope's *The Men and the Girls* displays a gentler, but still pointed, humor.

Castillo, Ana
So Far from God
W.W. Norton. 1993. 251 pp.

As four Chicana girls grow up in New Mexico, each discovers and comes to understand her own unique, magical gift.

2d Appeal   Language   Book Groups 📖

Subjects   Catholics and Catholicism • First Novels • Magic Realism • Mothers and Daughters • New Mexico

Now try   Castillo also wrote *Loverboys, Massacre of the Dreamers: Essays on Xicanisma*, and *Mixquiahuala Letters*. Rudolfo Anaya uses magic realism in his tale of Chicano society, *Bless Me, Ultima*. The books of Sandra Cisneros, another Chicana writer, include a novel, *The House on Mango Street*, and *Loose Woman*, a collection of poetry. Clarice Lispector's short tale of a girl in Brazil, *Hour of the Star*, offers a slightly different approach to magic realism.

Cates, David
Hunger in America
Simon & Schuster. 1992. 202 pp.

One night, during the trickle down economics era in America in the 1980s, Jack Dempsey Cliff, a lonely cabdriver, and other sad, hopeful, and disconnected people in Kodiak, Alaska, search for an end to their physical and emotional hunger.

2d Appeal   Setting   Book Groups 📖

Subjects   1980s • Alaska • Boxing • Fathers and Sons • First Novels • Male/Female Relationships • Poverty

Now try   Carson McCullers's *The Heart Is a Lonely Hunter* and John Steinbeck's *Of Mice and Men* both describe a diverse group of people searching for love and contentment. *Outside Passage: A Memoir of an Alaskan Childhood* by Julia Scully is also about being poor in Alaska.

Cela, Camilo Jose
Mazurka for Two Dead Men
New Directions Pub. Corp. 1992. 312 pp.

The intertwined lives of a rural community in civil war-torn Spain are described by multiple narrators. Translated from the Spanish by Patricia Haugaard.

2d Appeal   Setting   Book Groups 📖

Subjects   Aging • Family Relationships • Small-Town Life • Spain • Spanish Authors • Spanish Civil War

Now try   Leslie Marmon Silko's *Almanac of the Dead* is also told through the voices of multiple narrators. Other novels set in the period of the Spanish Civil War include *The Disinherited* by Michel Del Castillo, Ernest Hemingway's *For Whom the Bell Tolls*, Jose Maria Gironella's *One Million Dead*, and *Man's Hope* by Andre Malraux. Two nonfiction accounts of the Spanish Civil War are George Orwell's *Homage to Catalonia* and Gerald Brennan's *Spanish Labyrinth*.

Chabon, Michael
Wonder Boys
Villard Books. 1995. 368 pp.

Former wonder boy Grady Tripp—a young writer whose first books catapulted him to fame in the literary world—loses his only copy of *Wonder Boys*, the novel he's been working on for seven years, which he hopes will salvage his fading reputation.

2d Appeal   Language

Subjects   Humorous Fiction • Men's Friendships • Writers and Writing

Now try   Chabon's first novel was *The Mysteries of Pittsburgh*. Michael Malone's novel *Straight Man* is about a former wonder boy who never lived up to his early promise. Another book about the process of writing fiction is John L'Heureux's *The Handmaid of Desire*. *Wonder Boys* echoes some of the themes of Philip Roth's *The Ghost Writer*. John Irving shares Chabon's ability to write slapstick episodes in the middle of a serious novel, as can be found in Irving's *A Widow for One Year*. Other novels that have very funny accounts of book tours are Scott Spencer's *Men in Black*, Martin Amis's *The Information*, and William Kotzwinkle's *The Bear Went Over the Mountain*.

Chai, May-Lee
My Lucky Face
Soho Press. 1997. 257 pp.

Lin Jun appears to have it all—a handsome husband, a respectable career, and good connections—but the changing climate in modern China and her friendship with a young American teacher have her questioning her choices and struggling to find her independence.

Subject   China • Chinese American Authors • First Novels • Friendship • Male/Female Relationships

Now try   Two novels by Anchee Min, *Katherine* and *Red Azalea*, are excellent accounts of China's Cultural Revolution, as is Jung Chang's memoir, *Wild Swans*. Other novels in which women characters struggle to find their place in their culture include Alice Walker's *Possessing the Secret of Joy* and Amy Tan's *The Kitchen God's Wife*.

Chandra, Vikram
Red Earth and Pouring Rain
Little, Brown and Co. 1995. 542 pp.

Parasher, mortally wounded while in a monkey's body, tells the stories of his past lives to save himself in the present.

Subjects   India • Indian Authors • Indian Mythology • Magic Realism • Postmodern Fiction

Now try   Chandra is also the author of *Love and Longing in Bombay*. *His Monkey Wife*, a novel by John Collier, is a delightful fantasy. *The Painted Alphabet* by Diana Darling is a novel based on Balinese folktales.

Chappell, Fred
I Am One of You Forever
Louisiana State University Press. 1985. 184 pp.

As Jess grows up as an only child in the Carolina mountains, his life is enhanced by his partners in adventure—his father and the hired hand—and periodic visits by his bizarre uncles.

Subjects   Coming-of-Age • Eccentrics and Eccentricities • Humorous Fiction • Magic Realism • North Carolina • Southern Authors

Now try   Chappell is the author of several books of poetry, as well as other novels, including *Farewell, I'm Bound to Leave You* and *Pete & Shirley: The Great Tar Heel Novel*. Clyde Edgerton's *Floatplane Notebooks* and *In Memory of Junior* are two other laugh-out-loud novels set in the southern United States. Alice Hoffman's *Second Nature* has an element of magic in an otherwise realistic novel. Franz Lidz's *Unstrung Heroes* is a memoir of his life with four very strange uncles.

Chase, Joan
During the Reign of the Queen of Persia
Harper & Row. 1983. 215 pp.

Tough matriarch Gram, dubbed the Queen of Persia by a son-in-law, presides over the lives of her daughters and granddaughters in rural Ohio.

2d Appeal   Story   Book Groups 📖

Subjects   1950s • ALA Notable Books • Dysfunctional Families • Family Relationships • First Novels • Grandparents • Ohio • Sisters • Teenage Girls

Now try   Chase also wrote *The Evening Wolves* and *Bonneville Blue*. Other novels about three generations of women are Kaye Gibbons's *Charms for the Easy Life* and Joan Barfoot's *Duet for Three*.

Chatwin, Bruce
On the Black Hill   Viking Press. 1983. 248 pp.

Twin brothers Lewis and Benjamin Jones, born in a Welsh border town in 1900, struggle for more than 80 years to reconcile their subconsciously joined identities with their need to be separate individuals.

2d Appeal   Setting   Book Groups 📖

Subjects   ALA Notable Books • Brothers • Elderly Men • First Novels • Twins • Wales

Now try   Beautiful evocations of country life can be found in Thomas Hardy's *Tess of the D'Urbervilles* and Ronald Blythe's *Akenfield*. Chatwin's works of nonfiction include *Anatomy of Restlessness: Selected Writings* and *The Songlines*. Chatwin's novel, *Utz*, is about a man imprisoned by his belongings, much like the obsession the twin brothers in *On the Black Hill* have about their farm. *On the Black Hill* won the James Tait Black Memorial Prize and the Whitbread Prize for First Novels.

Chavez, Denise
Face of an Angel   Farrar, Straus and Giroux. 1994. 467 pp.

Soveida Dosamantes tells the story of her 30 years as a waitress at a border restaurant, her two unhappy marriages that left her once a widow and once divorced, and especially her Mexican American family, past and present: the lovers, wastrels, storytellers, and drinkers.

Book Groups 📖

Subjects   First Novels • Male/Female Relationships • Mexican Americans • Multigenerational Novels • New Mexico

Now try   Chavez is the author of *The Last of the Menu Girls*, a collection of short stories. Rick Collignon's *Perdido* and *The Journal of Antonio Montoya*, Rudolfo Anaya's *Rio Grande Fall*, and Antonya Nelson's *Nobody's Girl* are all set in New Mexico.

Cheek, Mavis
Dog Days   Simon & Schuster. 1990. 223 pp.

Newly divorced after 11 years of marriage, Pat feels attracted to Roland, a married man, especially after he gets her out of a tricky situation involving her dog Brian and a rabbit named Bulstrode.

2d Appeal   Language

Subjects   British Authors • Divorce • Dogs • Humorous Fiction • Love Stories • Male/Female Relationships • Single Parents • Veterinarians

Now try   Cheek's satirical writing style can also be found in her other novels, *Parlor Games* and *Pause Between Acts*. A similar satirical tone can be found in the novels of Fay Weldon, as seen in *The Shrapnel Academy* and *Splitting*. A dog plays an important role in Anne Tyler's *The Accidental Tourist*.

Childress, Mark
Crazy in Alabama
Putnam. 1993. 383 pp.

During the summer of 1965, 12-year-old Peejoe's Aunt Lucille murders her husband with an electric carving knife and takes off for Hollywood (with his severed head in a tupperware container) while Peejoe becomes involved in the local conflict over integrating the town's swimming pool.

2d Appeal   Story

Subjects   Alabama • Eccentrics and Eccentricities • Humorous Fiction • Murder • Orphans • Race Relations • Racism • Road Novels • Southern Authors

Now try   Childress also wrote a wonderful novel about Elvis Presley called *Tender*. In Peter Lefcourt's *Abbreviating Ernie*, an electric carving knife plays an important role (though it is used on another part of the body). Fannie Flagg's novels, including *Daisy Fay and the Miracle Man* and *Coming Attractions*, and the series of novels by Cathie Pelletier set in Mattagash, Maine (including *The Weight of Winter* and *Beaming Sonny Home*), are also filled with Childress's form of wacky humor.

Chin, Frank
Donald Duk
Coffee House Press. 1991. 173 pp.

During the Chinese New Year celebration in San Francisco, 12-year-old Donald Duk learns some valuable lessons about his cultural heritage from his dance instructor, his Uncle Donald of the Cantonese Opera, his father's model airplanes, and a series of dreams about the building of the railroad by Chinese laborers.

2d Appeal   Setting   Book Groups 📖

Subjects   Chinese American Authors • Chinese Americans • Coming-of-Age • San Francisco

Now try   Another novel with a Chinese American hero is Gus Lee's *China Boy*. Karen Joy Fowler's *Sarah Canary* is about a woman who stumbles into a group of Chinese laborers working to build a railroad in Washington Territory in the late nineteenth century. Shawn Wong's *Homebase* deals with many of the same issues as *Donald Duk*.

Chowder, Ken
Jadis
Harper & Row. 1985. 231 pp.

Shakespeare lover and toyshop owner Egg Lambert must choose between his wife Jadis (who left Egg for her ice-dancing teacher and has since returned) and Tory, Egg's exotic mistress.

2d Appeal   Story

Subjects   Adultery • Marriage • Triangles

Now try   Chowder's earlier novels include *Blackbird Days* and *Delicate Geometry*. Frederick Busch's *Harry and Catherine* tells the story of two men in love with the same woman.

Choy, Wayson
The Jade Peony
Picador USA. 1997. 238 pp.

Jook-Liang, Jung-Sum, and Sek-Lung, three children of an immigrant Chinese family living in Vancouver, Canada, in the 1940s, are torn between the ways of Old China that their parents expect and their desire to be true Canadians.

2d Appeal Story   Book Groups 📖

Subjects ALA Notable Books • Boxing • Brothers and Sisters • Canadian Authors • Chinese Canadians • Family Relationships • First Novels • Immigrants and Refugees • Vancouver, Canada • World War II

Now try A nonfiction book about Chinese Canadians is Denise Chong's *The Concubine's Children*. Like Jung-Sum in this novel, the main character in Gus Lee's *China Boy* gains acceptance and self-respect by learning to box, as does the young man in Bryce Courtenay's *The Power of One* (although Courtenay's novel is set in South Africa).

Chute, Carolyn
The Beans of Egypt, Maine
Ticknor & Fields. 1985. 215 pp.

Earlene Pomerleau all too soon becomes entrapped in the world of her in-laws, the Beans, which is full of poverty and despair.

2d Appeal Language   Book Groups 📖

Subjects ALA Notable Books • Family Relationships • First Novels • Maine • Poverty

Now try There are two sequels to this novel: *Letourneau's Used Auto Parts* and *Merry Men*. *Bastard Out of Carolina* by Dorothy Allison is about growing up in poverty in the southern United States.

Ciresi, Rita
Blue Italian
Ecco Press. 1996. 287 pp.

The marriage between Italian Roman Catholic Rosa Salvatore and New York Jew Gary Fisher is changed forever by Gary's prostate cancer.

2d Appeal Story

Subjects Cancer • Death of a Spouse • First Novels • Illness • Love Stories • Marriage

Now try Ciresi is also the author of *Pink Slip*. Susan Dworkin's *Stolen Goods* is also about a young couple whose hopes for a happy marriage are not fulfilled. Erich Segal's *Love Story* has the opposite situation: a healthy man and a dying woman. *Mail* by Mameve Medwed is a more lighthearted look at the relationship between a working-class man and an upper-class woman. Francine Prose's *Household Saints* is about an Italian Americans family.

Cobbold, Marika
Guppies for Tea
St. Martin's Press. 1993. 286 pp.

Amelia Lindsay just floats along, waiting for her real life to begin, until her beloved grandmother needs her help in escaping from a nursing home so she can return to the old family home for Christmas.

2d Appeal   Language   Book Groups 📖

Subjects   Aging • British Authors • Elderly Women • First Novels • Grandparents • Male/Female Relationships • Mothers and Daughters

Now try   This novel won England's Sunday Express Book of the Year award. Cobbold's writing style is similar to Jane Gardam's (*God on the Rocks*, *Faith Fox*, and others). Clyde Edgerton's novel *Walking Across Egypt* is about an elderly woman and a young man helping each other.

Cohen, Jon
The Man in the Window
Warner Books. 1992. 245 pp.

Louis Malone has not left his parents' house since he was horribly scarred in a fire when he was 16, but his father's death catapults Louis, now 35, back into the real world.

2d Appeal   Language   Book Groups 📖

Subjects   Disfigurement • Love Stories • Male/Female Relationships • Nurses

Now try   Jon Cohen also wrote *Max Lakeman and the Beautiful Stranger*. The unlikely relationship between Louis and Iris Shula is similar in its unexpectedness to the love story described by Chet Raymo in *The Dork of Cork*. There are other good dog characters in *Binding Spell* by Elizabeth Arthur and Frederick Busch's *Girls*. *Face*, by Cecile Pineda, is also about a character's physical disabilities.

Collignon, Rick
Perdido
MacMurray & Beck. 1997. 221 pp.

Consumed by his desire to discover the secrets surrounding a death that occurred more than 20 years before in the dusty New Mexico town where he lives, Will Sawyer stirs up memories the townspeople would rather forget.

2d Appeal   Language   Book Groups 📖

Subjects   Culture Clash • Interracial Relationships • Love Stories • New Mexico • Race Relations • Small-Town Life

Now try   Collignon's first novel was *The Journal of Antonio Montoya*. Collignon's technique of dropping us into the middle of the story—we don't know Will's background or whether his relationship with his girlfriend will endure—is like a photograph of a particular time and place. A small town in New Mexico is also the setting for Robert Boswell's *American Owned Love* and Antonya Nelson's *Nobody's Girl*. There is another town with a secret in David Hill's *Sacred Dust*.

Colwin, Laurie

Family Happiness
Knopf. 1982. 271 pp.

Polly Solo-Miller Demarest's happy marriage co-exists somewhat uneasily with her ongoing love affair with a painter.

2d Appeal   Setting

Subjects   Adultery • Art and Artists • Jews and Judaism • Marriage • Upper Classes

Now try   Colwin's short stories, particularly those in *The Lone Pilgrim*, showcase her unique writing style. Her first novel, ***Shine On, Bright and Dangerous Object***, deals with themes she uses throughout her writing career. Lane Von Herzen's ***The Unfastened Heart*** is close to Colwin in terms of style. Another wife who tries to understand how she can have a love affair while still loving her husband is found in Marian Thurm's ***Walking Distance***.

Constantini, Humberto

The Long Night of Francisco Sanctis
Harper & Row. 1985. 184 pp.

When Francisco Sanctis receives a message from an old friend that two men will be taken by government agents, his revolutionary past intrudes upon his comfortable present, forcing him to re-evaluate all that he believes and what he would actually risk for those beliefs. Translated from the Spanish by Norman Thomas di Giovanni.

2d Appeal   Setting   Book Groups 📖

Subjects   ALA Notable Books • Argentina • Argentinian Authors • Moral/Ethical Dilemmas • Novels in Translation • Political Fiction • Political Unrest • South American Authors

Now try   Other books in which characters are faced with a moral dilemma include Jonathan Dee's ***The Liberty Campaign*** and Frederick Durenmatt's ***The Visit***. Another novel set in Argentina during the same time period is Lawrence Thornton's ***Imagining Argentina***.

Cook, Karin

What Girls Learn
Pantheon Books. 1997. 304 pp.

Twelve-year-old Tilden longs to keep things as they once were for herself, her mother, and her younger sister, while living through a move North with a new stepfather, the changes of adolescence, and her mother's struggle with breast cancer.

Book Groups 📖

Subjects   Cancer • Coming-of-Age • Death and Dying • Death of a Parent • Illness • Mothers and Daughters • Sisters • Teenage Girls

Now try   ***Rumors of Peace*** by Ella Leffland is another novel told in a strong female adolescent's voice, although the catastrophe Leffland's character faces has to do with World War II rather than the illness of a parent. ***One True Thing*** by Anna Quindlen is about a daughter's relationship with her dying mother. ***Dharma Girl*** by Chelsea Cain is a memoir of a young woman coming to terms with her mother's cancer.

Cook-Lynn, Elizabeth
From the River's Edge
Arcade Pub. 1991. 147 pp.

When Dakotah Indian John Tatekeya's cattle are stolen, he is forced to enter the white man's courts, where he eventually must search not only for justice for the theft of his own property, but for a way to reconcile the unavenged thefts of his people's culture and honor.

Book Groups 📖

Subjects   American Indian Authors • American Indians • Dakotas • First Novels

Now try   Cook-Lynn also published a collection of stories called *The Power of Horses and Other Stories*. Tony Hillerman's *Sacred Clowns* and *The Thief of Time* and other mysteries all depict the inroads white culture has made into tribal life, and how those changes affect the lives of American Indians. In *Reservation Blues, Indian Killer*, and *The Business of Fancydancing*, as well as his other fiction and poetry, Sherman Alexie writes about the relationship between American Indians and white culture.

Coomer, Joe
The Loop
Faber and Faber. 1992. 201 pp.

Thirty-year-old Lyman's life takes a detour from normalcy (his job as a courtesy patrolman on the loop highway surrounding Fort Worth and his endless series of practical college courses) when a parrot enters his life, along with Fiona, a librarian.

2d Appeal   Story

Subjects   Birds • Librarians • Loneliness • Love Stories • Parrots • Single Men

Now try   Coomer's other books include *The Decatur Road: A Novel of the Appalachian Hill Country*, *Kentucky Love*, and *Sailing in a Spoonful of Water*. Lyman's lonely life is reminiscent of the main characters in Chet Raymo's *The Dork of Cork* and Jon Cohen's *The Man in the Window*. Fiona resembles the librarian-heroine of Elizabeth McCracken's *The Giant's House*.

Cooper, Douglas
Amnesia
Hyperion. 1994. 227 pp.

The stories told and retold by the characters, including a librarian, a mentally ill young woman, and Izzy Barlow, the narrator, intersect, diverge, contradict, embellish, and ultimately lay bare each life.

Subjects   Canadian Authors • Dysfunctional Families • First Novels • Librarians • Magic Realism • Mental Illness • Obsessive Love

Now try   The relationship between Izzy and Katie evokes the relationship between the lovers in Scott Spencer's *Endless Love*.

Covington, Vicki
The Last Hotel for Women
Simon & Schuster. 1996. 300 pp.

In 1961, in the heart of Birmingham, Alabama, a family-run hotel becomes the meeting place for freedom riders, reporters, and townspeople, all struggling with issues of civil rights.

2d Appeal   Setting
Book Groups 📖

Subjects   1960s • Alabama • Civil Rights Movement • Family Relationships • Race Relations • Racism • Southern Authors

Now try Among Covington's other books are the novels *Night Ride Home* and *Gathering Home*. Eudora Welty's *The Optimist's Daughter* has a similar languid, southern tone. Tom Spanbauer's novel, *Faraway Places*, although set in Idaho, also portrays a family caught up in a time of change.

Coyle, Beverly

In Troubled Waters

Ticknor & Fields. 1993. 324 pp.

When Lois returns to her father's Florida home with her husband Paul, who is in the early stages of Alzheimer's disease, the extended family must deal with painful memories and the present reality of racial prejudice.

2d Appeal Story   Book Groups 📖

Subjects ALA Notable Books • Alzheimer's Disease • Child Abuse • Family Relationships • Florida • Grandparents • Racism • Southern Authors

Now try Coyle's first novel was *The Kneeling Bus*. Another book about a family member suffering from Alzheimer's disease is Michael Ignatieff's *Scar Tissue*.

Dangarembgo, Tsitsi

Nervous Conditions

Seal Press. 1989. 204 pp.

In Zimbabwe in the 1970s, Tambu awakens to a life of possibilities beyond the restricting expectations of her family and the culture in which she lives.

2d Appeal Setting   Book Groups 📖

Subjects 1970s • Africa • African Authors • Coming-of-Age • Family Relationships • First Novels • Gender Roles • Zimbabwe • Zimbabwean Authors

Now try Other novels that depict the struggles of women to break free of the constricted life that is expected of them include Mildred Walker's *Winter Wheat*, Zora Neale Hurston's *Their Eyes Were Watching God*, and *My Brilliant Career* by Miles Franklin.

Dann, Patty

Mermaids

Ticknor & Fields. 1986. 147 pp.

After non-stop travels around the country with her flighty and promiscuous mother and beloved younger sister, 14-year-old Charlotte is ready to settle down for awhile in the small Massachusetts town where she has fallen in love with the caretaker of the convent next door.

Subjects First Novels • Massachusetts • Mothers and Daughters • Single Parents • Sisters • Teenage Girls

Now try Dann also wrote *The Baby Boat: A Memoir of Adoption*. Other novels in which the first person narrative voice is remarkably distinctive include *Do the Windows Open?* by Julie Hecht, *Karoo* by Steve Tesich, and Jane Gardam's *Bilgewater*. Esther Freud's *Hideous Kinky* is about another girl whose mother cannot stay long in one place.

Davis-Gardner, Angela
Forms of Shelter
Ticknor & Fields. 1991. 276 pp.

Beryl has never gotten over the loss of her father when she was a child; now, as a middle-aged single mother, she remembers what it was like growing up with an emotionally distant mother, an abusive stepfather, and a deeply troubled brother.

Book Groups 📖

Subjects   Abusive Relationships • Brothers and Sisters • Dysfunctional Families • Fathers and Daughters • Mothers and Daughters • Rape • Single Parents • Southern Authors

Now try   Davis-Gardner also wrote *Felice*, about a young woman sent to a convent school after she is orphaned. Dorothy Allison's *Bastard Out of Carolina* is another novel about a woman whose childhood of abuse and poverty scarred her for life.

Dee, Jonathan
The Liberty Campaign
Doubleday. 1993. 272 pp.

Advertising executive Gene Trowbridge finds his comfortable life at risk after he discovers his friend and neighbor is about to be deported for war crimes he may or may not have committed.

Book Groups 📖

Subjects   Business and Businessmen • Good vs. Evil • Men's Friendships • Moral/Ethical Dilemmas

Now try   Dee also wrote *The Lover of History*. Thomas Berger's *Meeting Evil* is another exploration of the presence of evil in our lives. Characters in Chris Bohjalian's *Water Witches*, Ward Just's *Echo House*, and Humberto Constantini's *The Long Night of Francisco Sanctis* all face moral dilemmas in their lives.

Desai, Anita
Baumgartner's Bombay
A.A. Knopf. 1989. 229 pp.

In the final days of his life, Baumgartner remembers the circumstances beyond his control that caused him to leave his native Germany for India, and how it was that he came to settle in Bombay.

Subjects   ALA Notable Books • Bombay • Culture Clash • India • Indian Authors • Internment Camps • World War II

Now try   Among Desai's other books are *In Custody* and *Where Shall We Go This Summer?* Desai's daughter, Kieran Desai, is the author of *Hullabaloo in the Guava Orchard*. As described in *Baumgartner's Bombay*, the British set up internment camps for Indian enemies of the government. Both Joy Kogawa's *Obasan* and David Guterson's *Snow Falling on Cedars* explore the issue of interning perceived enemies during times of war.

Dew, Robb Forman
Dale Loves Sophie to Death
Farrar, Straus Giroux. 1981. 217 pp.

After eight summers spent at her parents' home in the small Ohio town where she grew up, Dinah Howells finally feels comfortable with her adult self, as a daughter, mother of three, and wife.

Book Groups 📖

Subjects   Adultery • Family Relationships • First Novels • Marriage • Ohio • Small-Town Life

Now try   *Fortunate Lives* is the sequel to this novel. Dew also wrote *The Family Heart: A Memoir of When Our Son Came Out*, a nonfiction account of how she and her family reacted when their oldest son told them that he was homosexual. Carol Shields's *Happenstance* also tells the story of a marriage from the point of view of both the husband and wife. Rosellen Brown's *Autobiography of My Mother* (as well as her other novels) shares with Dew an attention to the details of her characters' lives.

Doane, Michael
The Surprise of Burning
Knopf. 1988. 251 pp.

While traveling to most of the late-twentieth-century hot spots to photograph incidents of violence and death, Hunter Page searches for information about his mother, a jazz singing drug addict, who died giving birth to him.

2d Appeal   Language   Book Groups 📖

Subjects   Music and Musicians • Orphans • Photography and Photographers • Vietnam War • World War II

Now try   Doane's first novel was *The Legends of Jesse Dark*. The lyricism of Doane's language brings to mind the writing of Marianne Wiggins in *Eveless Eden*.

Dobyns, Stephen
The Wrestler's Cruel Study
W.W. Norton. 1993. 426 pp.

Everybody's hero, Marduk the Magnificent, must follow a convoluted trail, strewn with fellow wrestlers, reincarnated fairy tale characters, and comic book thugs, in order to save his kidnapped fiancée, the pure and perfect Rose White.

2d Appeal   Language

Subjects   Comic Book Characters • Humorous Fiction • Magic Realism • Men's Friendships • Wrestling

Now try   Dobyns is a poet as well as the author of a series of mysteries set in Saratoga Springs, New York, starring Charlie Bradshaw (*Saratoga Backtalk, Saratoga Bestiary*, and others). John Irving's *The World According to Garp* and Joseph Heller's *Catch 22* have the same surreal qualities as Dobyns's book.

Donnelly, Nisa
The Love Songs of Phoenix Bay
St. Martin's Press. 1994. 301 pp.

Searching for a place to call home after a devastating break up with her boyfriend, Phoenix Bay comes to San Francisco to stay with her oldest friend Rennie, who is coping with increasing debilitation from AIDS, and Cecelie, reluctantly returned from Peru; together the three friends create the sense of family they all need.

2d Appeal   Setting   Book Groups 📖

Subjects   AIDS • Dysfunctional Families • Gay Men • Lesbians • Mental Illness • San Francisco • Women's Friendships

Now try   Donnelly is also the author of *Bar Stories: A Novel After All*. Making a family out of a group of friends is the theme of Armistead Maupin's *Tales of the City* and its sequels.

Dorris, Michael
A Yellow Raft in Blue Water
H. Holt. 1987. 343 pp.

Three generations of American Indian women—the mixed-blood teenager Rayona, the dying party girl Christine, and the embittered, TV-obsessed Ida—are isolated from one another by secrets not shared and misunderstandings never cleared up.

2d Appeal   Language   Book Groups 📖

Subjects   ALA Notable Books • American Indian Authors • American Indians • Family Secrets • First Novels • Montana • Mothers and Daughters • Multigenerational Novels

Now try   Rayona is also a character in Dorris's novel *Cloud Chamber*. Louise Erdrich's *Tracks*, Craig Lesley's *Winterkill*, Susan Power's *The Grass Dancer*, Albertine Strong's *Deluge*, and Thomas King's *Green Grass, Running Water* are other novels about American Indian life in contemporary times. Both *Deluge* and *The Grass Dancer* use the technique of uncovering the past in an effort to understand the present.

Douglas, Ellen
Can't Quit You, Baby
Atheneum. 1988. 256 pp.

Cornelia, a white middle-class wife and mother, and her black employee, Tweet, live through the personal and societal upheavals of 1960s and 1970s Mississippi together, discovering in the process that they have more in common than either is comfortable admitting.

2d Appeal   Story   Book Groups 📖

Subjects   1960s • 1970s • Interracial Relationships • Marriage • Mississippi • Race Relations • Southern Authors • Women's Friendships

Now try   Douglas also wrote *Truth: Four Stories I Am Finally Old Enough to Tell*. In *Can't Quit You, Baby*, Douglas shows readers how the storyteller (the novelist) shapes the story that is told. Similarly, John L'Heureux in *The Handmaid of Desire* and Philip Roth in *My Life as a Man* use their novels to explore the process of novelists at work. The voices in this novel, black and white, sing the blues, just as the voices in Toni Morrison's *Jazz* sing, although to a different beat. Another friendship between a white woman and her black employee is described in Diane Johnson's *The Shadow Knows*.

Dove, Rita
Through the Ivory Gate
Pantheon Books. 1992. 278 pp.

A single, unconventional African American woman—puppeteer, intellectual, cellist—struggles to unravel the secrets of her childhood while defining herself, the qualities of love, and her art.

2d Appeal   Language   Book Groups 📖

Subjects   African American Authors • African Americans • Family Relationships • First Novels • Music and Musicians • Single Women

Now try   Dove, a playwright and a poet, won the 1987 Pulitzer Prize for Poetry for *Thomas and Beulah*. Her other books of poetry include *Ten Poems, The Only Dark Spot in the Sky*, and *Museum*. Omar Tyree's *Single Mom* is another novel about an African American woman trying to overcome the effects of a ghetto childhood.

Doyle, Roddy
Paddy Clarke Ha Ha Ha

Viking. 1993. 282 pp.

A spirited glimpse into the life of a pre-adolescent Irish boy, his friends and family, and his everyday adventures growing up.

2d Appeal Language

Subjects Booker Prize Winners • Coming-of-Age • Ireland • Irish Authors • Working Classes

Now try Sue Townsend's ***The Adrian Mole Diaries*** also deals humorously with the pangs of a young man growing up, as does Ardashir Vakil's ***Beach Boy***.

Doyle, Roddy
The Woman Who Walked into Doors

Viking. 1996. 226 pp.

Thirty-nine-year-old housewife Paula Spencer suffers through almost constant domestic violence while wrestling with her twin demons of alcoholism and a continuing physical attraction to her abuser, her husband Charlo.

2d Appeal Language   Book Groups 📖

Subjects Abusive Relationships • ALA Notable Books • Alcoholics and Alcoholism • Domestic Violence • Husbands and Wives • Ireland • Irish Authors

Now try Doyle's other novels include ***The Commitments, The Snapper***, and ***The Van***. ***The Woman Who Walked into Doors*** is Doyle's only novel told in a woman's voice. Other novels of domestic abuse include Susan Brownmiller's ***Waverly Place*** and ***Picture Perfect*** by Jodi Picoult.

Drabble, Margaret
The Middle Ground

Knopf. 1980. 277 pp.

What now? asks Kate Armstrong, a 40-something British journalist who has combined a spectacular career with child rearing, marriage, a long affair, and the ups and downs of her eccentric friends, as a midlife crisis causes her to look within herself for answers.

2d Appeal Language

Subjects ALA Notable Books • British Authors • Career Women • Journalists • Marriage • Middle-Aged Women • Midlife Crisis • Women's Friendships

Now try Drabble's early novels include ***The Garrick Year*** and ***The Millstone***. The books written by Drabble's sister, A. S. Byatt (***The Virgin in the Garden, Angels and Insects***, and others), also have strong and intelligent female characters.

Drury, Tom
The End of Vandalism

Houghton Mifflin. 1994. 321 pp.

Life in Grouse County, Iowa, is seen mainly through the eyes of Sheriff Dan Norman, his wife Louise, and Louise's ex-husband Tiny, a plumber and a thief.

2d Appeal Language

Subjects Abandoned Babies • ALA Notable Books • First Novels • Iowa • Marriage • Small-Town Life • Triangles

Now try   Drury is also the author of *The Black Brook*. Frederick Busch's *Harry and Catherine* is another novel about two men in love with the same woman. Peter Hedges's *An Ocean in Iowa* is also set in Iowa. Another novel in which an abandoned baby is important to the plot is Margot Livesey's *Criminals*. In 1996, *Granta Magazine* named Drury one of the "20 Best Young American Novelists."

Duffy, Bruce
Last Comes the Egg   Simon & Schuster. 1997. 359 pp.

Twenty-seven years after his mother died, Frank Dougherty remembers himself at age 12, when the shock of her death created a wedge between Frank and his father and sent Frank into a tailspin, culminating in the theft of a car and a week-long adventure with two friends, one black and one white.

2d Appeal   Language   Book Groups 📖

Subjects   1960s • Coming-of-Age • Death of a Parent • Fathers and Sons • Juvenile Delinquents • Mothers and Sons • Racism • Teenage Boys

Now try   Other novels with a strong narrative voice include J. D. Salinger's *The Catcher in the Rye*, Mark Twain's *Huckleberry Finn*, Julie Hecht's *Do the Windows Open?* and Steve Tesich's *Karoo*.

Dufresne, John
Love Warps the Mind a Little   Norton. 1997. 315 pp.

In the 1990s, LaFayette Proulx juggles the ironies of his life: his questionable writing career, the occasional intrusions into his life by his fictional creations, his failing marriage, and a promising new relationship with a woman who is dying.

2d Appeal   Language   Book Groups 📖

Subjects   1990s • Cancer • Death and Dying • Family Relationships • Male/Female Relationships • Writers and Writing

Now try   Dufresne's other works of fiction include *Louisiana Power and Light: A Novel* and *The Way Water Enters Stone: Stories*. Men struggling with life's ironies are the main characters in Carol Shields's *Larry's Party*, Frederick Reuss's *Horace Afoot*, and *Nobody's Fool* by Richard Russo.

Duncan, David James
The Brothers K   Doubleday. 1992. 645 pp.

The Chance family is united by its love of baseball and nearly destroyed by Mrs. Chance's fanatical devotion to the Seventh Day Adventist Church.

2d Appeal   Story   Book Groups 📖

Subjects   1960s • 1970s • ALA Notable Books • Baseball • Brothers • Brothers and Sisters • Family Relationships • Religion • Religious Extremism • Vietnam War

Now try   Duncan also wrote *The River Why* and *River Teeth: Stories and Writing*. Baseball plays a central role in Nancy Willard's *Things Invisible to See*. Other novels in which plot, characters, and writing all come together beautifully to fashion a novel that the reader hates to finish are Michael Malone's *Dingley Falls* and Pat Conroy's *The Prince of Tides*. Ken Kesey's novel, *Sometimes a Great Notion*, also gives a good sense of life in the Northwest.

Duncker, Patricia
Hallucinating Foucault

Ecco Press. 1996. 175 pp.

An English major at Cambridge studying the works of (fictional) novelist Paul Michel travels to France to search out the elusive, possibly insane, writer.

2d Appeal   Language

Subjects   College Students • First Novels • Gay Men • Obsessive Love • Research Novels • Writers and Writing

Now try   *Possession* by A. S. Byatt is also about a student researching the life of a writer. The sparse beauty of Duncker's prose can be found in Larry Watson's *Montana 1948*, although the books are otherwise totally unalike. *Pinball* by Jerzy Kosinski is also about a search for a reclusive artist (a rock star).

Dunmore, Helen
A Spell of Winter

Viking. 1995. 313 pp.

As the world around them collapses into war, siblings Catherine and Rob, abandoned by their parents, turn to each other for love and then must suffer the emotional consequences.

2d Appeal   Language   Book Groups 📖

Subjects   British Authors • Brothers and Sisters • Incest • World War I

Now try   Dunmore also wrote *Talking to the Dead* and *Your Blue-Eyed Boy*. Other novels that describe (overly) close relationships between brothers and sisters include Arundhati Roy's *The God of Small Things*, Katherine Dunn's *Geek Love*, and John Irving's *The Hotel New Hampshire*. *A Spell of Winter* won Britain's Orange Prize.

Dunn, Katherine
Geek Love

Knopf. 1989. 347 pp.

Olympia Binewski, an albino hunchback dwarf, looks back over her life peforming with her brothers and sisters, who were all bred by their loving parents to be members of a traveling carnival freak show.

2d Appeal   Story   Book Groups 📖

Subjects   Black Humor • Brothers and Sisters • Dwarfs • Family Relationships • First Novels

Now try   The combination of black humor and ultra-quirky characters found in *Geek Love* is also found in the novels of John Irving (*The Hotel New Hampshire* and others), Lewis Nordan (*Sharpshooter Blues* and others), and Carolyn Chute (*The Beans of Egypt, Maine*). *Nights at the Circus* by Angela Carter and *The Giant's House* by Elizabeth McCracken are both novels about people considered to be freaks. Simon Mawer's *Mendel's Dwarf* and Chet Raymo's *The Dork of Cork* both have a dwarf as a main character.

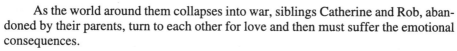

Duong, Thu Hong
Novel Without a Name
W. Morrow. 1995. 292 pp.

Quan, a North Vietnamese soldier, experiences the devastation of his people and country during more than a decade of war in the jungles of Vietnam. Translated from the Vietnamese by Phan Huy Duong and Nina McPherson.

2d Appeal   Setting

Subjects   North Vietnam • Novels in Translation • Vietnam War • Vietnamese Authors

Now try   Duong's novel was banned in Vietnam. His first novel, *Paradise of the Blind*, is about a family divided by Communism. Other novels that created a backlash against their authors include Salman Rushdie's *The Satanic Verses* and Arundhati Roy's *The God of Small Things*.

Dworkin, Susan
The Book of Candy
Four Walls Eight Windows. 1996. 359 pp.

Candy, a self-described Jewish American Princess, finds her life changed after she discovers her husband's infidelities and hears the prophecy of a rabbi-cum-nightclub comic.

2d Appeal   Story

Subjects   Adultery • Humorous Fiction • Jews and Judaism

Now try   Dworkin's first novel, *Stolen Goods*, also has a cast of interesting, three-dimensional characters. Dworkin's humor resembles that of author Susan Isaacs (*Lily White, Compromising Positions*, and other novels) and Elinor Lipman (*Isabel's Bed* and other novels).

Eberstadt, Fernanda
Isaac and His Devils
Knopf. 1991. 337 pp.

As young genius Isaac Hooker moves towards adulthood, he must come to terms with the conflicting visions of his overbearing, cab-driving mother and his passive, defeated-by-life schoolteacher father.

2d Appeal   Language   Book Groups 📖

Subjects   Coming-of-Age • Family Relationships • Fathers and Sons • Gifted Children • Mothers and Sons • New Hampshire • Older Women/Younger Men

Now try   Eberstadt used Isaac again as a character in her novel, *When the Sons of Heaven Meet the Daughters of the Earth*. Isaac is somewhat reminiscent of Ignatius Reilly in John Kennedy Toole's *A Confederacy of Dunces*.

Edgarian, Carol
Rise the Euphrates
Random House. 1994. 370 pp.

Seta Loon tells the story of four generations of Armenian American women whose lives are shaped by the terrible events of 1915, when Seta's grandmother saw her own mother murdered by the Turks.

2d Appeal   Story

Subjects   Armenia • Culture Clash • Family Relationships • First Novels • Genocide • Mothers and Daughters • Murder

Now try   Susan Dworkin's *Stolen Goods* is about an Armenian family whose lives are less obviously affected by the past.

Edgell, Zee
Beka Lamb
Heinemann. 1982. 171 pp.

Beka Lamb, a young Belizean girl, finds a focus and determination in the face of political turmoil in her country, her own personal tragedies, and the hopes and expectations that have been laid upon her.

2d Appeal Setting   Book Groups 📖

Subjects Belize • Coming-of-Age • Family Relationships • First Novels • Friendship • Teenage Pregnancy

Now try Dorothy Allison's *Bastard Out of Carolina* is about a young girl struggling against her environment and the judgments and expectations of others. Joyce Carol Oates's *Foxfire: Confessions of a Girl Gang* explores how friendship and the bond of sisterhood are a strengthening and liberating experience for young women.

Edgerton, Clyde
Walking Across Egypt
Algonquin Books of Chapel Hill. 1987. 216 pp.

Seventy-eight-year-old widow Mattie Rigsbee finds her own life rejuvenated when she is faced with the challenge of helping Wesley, a juvenile delinquent in need of a grandmother's love, home-cooking, and stability.

2d Appeal Story

Subjects Elderly Women • Juvenile Delinquents • North Carolina • Southern Authors

Now try Clyde Edgerton's first novel, *Raney*, is the warm and humorous story of how a young couple adjusts to being married. *Once Upon a Time On the Banks* and other novels of Cathie Pelletier display a similar sort of humor.

Egan, Jennifer
The Invisible Circus
N.A. Talese. 1995. 338 pp.

Following a trail of old postcards, 18-year-old Phoebe O'Connor travels to Europe and retraces her older sister Faith's footsteps, hoping to understand both Faith's tragic death and the turmoil of the 1960s that provided its context.

2d Appeal Story

Subjects 1960s • Family Relationships • First Novels • Sisters

Now try Egan also wrote *Emerald City*, a collection of short stories. Another book set in the same period with a similar descriptive style is *Little Miss Strange* by Joanna Rose, which recounts a young girl's unorthodox, and often dark, upbringing in the late 1960s. Ellen Gilchrist's *The Anna Papers* is also about the effects of a sister's death on her sibling. Maria Flook's memoir *My Sister Life: The Story of My Sister's Disappearance* is a wrenching account of Flook's sister and the life she led during the 1960s.

Elkin, Stanley
George Mills
Dutton. 1982. 508 pp.

Living under the cloud of a centuries-old family curse, George Mills finds that his daily life is complicated, and enriched, by history.

2d Appeal   Language

Subjects   Magic Realism • Male/Female Relationships • Men's Lives • National Book Critics Circle Award Winners • Working Classes

Now try   Among Elkin's other novels are *The Living End* and *The Franchiser*. Elkin's use of wordplays and passing literary references is similar to the style of Salman Rushdie in *Midnight's Children* and *The Satanic Verses*.

Ellmann, Lucy
Sweet Desserts
Viking. 1989. 145 pp.

The destructive relationship between sisters Franny and Suzy also dominates other aspects of their lives.

Subjects   British Authors • Culinary Arts • Eating Disorders • Family Relationships • First Novels • Sisters

Now try   Ellmann is also the author of *Man or Mango? A Lament*. In Laura Esquivel's *Like Water for Chocolate*, the relationships among siblings, food, and sexuality are all intermingled. *Sweet Desserts* won England's Guardian Prize for best first novel.

Engel, Monroe
Statutes of Limitations
Knopf. 1988. 215 pp.

Ben Morrison, a retired bookstore owner, is both actor and audience in a drama that moves between the present and the anti-war protests of the 1960s.

Subjects   1960s • Fathers and Daughters • Men's Friendships • Vietnam War

Now try   Marge Piercy's *Vida* also focuses on the anti-war movement of the 1960s.

Erdrich, Louise
The Beet Queen
Holt. 1986. 338 pp.

On a frosty morning in 1932, newly orphaned Karl and Mary Adare arrive at the North Dakota home of their Aunt Fritzie and embark on lives filled with love, tragedy, and interesting people.

2d Appeal   Language   Book Groups 📖

Subjects   ALA Notable Books • American Indian Authors • American Indians • Brothers and Sisters • Family Relationships • North Dakota • Orphans

Now try   Some of the same characters in *The Beet Queen* appeared first in *Love Medicine*. Other novels by Erdrich include *The Antelope Wife* and *Tracks*.

Erdrich, Louise
Love Medicine
Holt Rinehart and Winston. 1984. 275 pp.

On a North Dakota Indian reservation, the lives of three American Indians and their families intertwine through marriage and friendship.

2d Appeal   Language   Book Groups 📖

Subjects   ALA Notable Books • Alcoholics and Alcoholism • American Indian Authors • American Indians • Culture Clash • Dysfunctional Families • First Novels • National Book Critics Circle Award Winners • North Dakota • Poverty • Triangles

Now try   Erdrich wrote three sequels to *Love Medicine* and published a new and expanded edition of this novel in 1989. Michael Dorris's *A Yellow Raft in Blue Water* has a similar theme as *Love Medicine*. Larry Woiwode's *Beyond the Bedroom Wall* is also set in North Dakota. *Faces in the Moon* by Betty Louise Bell also describes several generations of an American Indian family.

Erdrich, Louise

Tracks
Henry Holt. 1988. 226 pp.

Two members of a North Dakota Indian tribe relate their years of struggle to adapt to the changes around them, to relate to the outside world, and to survive in the face of both internal and external threats.

2d Appeal   Language

Subjects   ALA Notable Books • American Indian Authors • American Indians • Male/Female Relationships • North Dakota

Now try   *Tracks* is the earliest in a cycle of novels that includes *Love Medicine* and *The Beet Queen*. Susan Power's *The Grass Dancer* and Thomas King's *Green Grass, Running Water* are also about contemporary American Indian life.

Espinosa, Maria

Longing
Cayuse. 1986. 298 pp.

In the 1960s, Rosa, a dependent and insecure young American woman living in Paris, struggles against her unhealthy marriage to an abusive, self-destructive Chilean.

Subjects   1960s • Abusive Relationships • Alcoholics and Alcoholism • Dysfunctional Families • Family Relationships • First Novels • France • Marriage

Now try   Other novels about women remaining in abusive relationships are Susan Brownmiller's *Waverly Place* and Roddy Doyle's *The Woman Who Walked into Doors*. Lisa St. Aubin de Teran's memoir, *The Hacienda*, is about her difficult marriage to an abusive man.

Evans, Elizabeth

The Blue Hour
Algonquin Books of Chapel Hill. 1994. 347 pp.

Penny Powell looks back on the events of 1959, when, at age 10, she and her parents and sister moved to Meander, Illinois, where her father's poor business judgment and her mother's unhappiness led to disaster.

2d Appeal   Setting   Book Groups 📖

Subjects   1950s • Family Relationships • First Novels • Illinois • Sisters • Small-Town Life

Now try   *That Night* by Alice McDermott provides the same very real sense of what living in the 1950s was like. *1959* by Thulani Davis tells a very different story of events that took place in the life of her main character in that year.

Fakinou, Eugenia
The Seventh Garment
Serpent's Tail. 1991. 127 pp.

Three generations of Greek women voice their personal triumphs and sorrows, as well as the roles they played in contemporary Greek history. Translated from the Greek by Ed Emery.

2d Appeal Setting   Book Groups 📖

Subjects Greece • Greek Authors • Magic Realism • Multigenerational Novels • Novels in Translation • Women's Lives • World War II

Now try Mystery fans will also want to read Emma Lathen's *When in Greece*, featuring banker John Putnam Thatcher. *The Priest Fainted* by Catherine Temma Davidson is about three generations of a family of Greeks and Greek Americans and is set primarily in Greece.

Fielding, Helen
Bridget Jones's Diary
Viking. 1998. 271 pp.

Thirty-something Bridget, stuck in a dull job in London and suffering from post-holiday distress syndrome, determines to lose weight, stop smoking, develop "inner poise," and find the perfect husband.

2d Appeal Story

Subjects British Authors • First Novels • Humorous Fiction • Male/Female Relationships • Single Women

Now try Sue Townsend's *The Adrian Mole Diaries* is another novel written in diary form.

Flagg, Fannie
Fried Green Tomatoes at the Whistle-Stop Café
Random House. 1987. 403 pp.

Evelyn Couch finds her life rejuvenated as she listens to Mrs. Threadgoode, a nursing home resident, relate the story of the tomboy Idgie and her friend Ruth, who, back in the 1930s, ran The Whistle Stop Café outside Birmingham, Alabama.

2d Appeal Setting

Subjects 1930s • Alabama • Cafes and Restaurants • Humorous Fiction • Small-Town Life • Southern Authors • Women's Friendships

Now try Fannie Flagg also wrote *Coming Attractions, Daisy Fay and the Miracle Man*, and *Welcome to the World, Baby Girl!* Authors Garrison Keillor (*Lake Wobegon Days*) and Lorna Landvik (*Patty Jane's House of Curl*) share Flagg's sense of humor. Other novels set around cafés include Gloria Naylor's *Bailey's Café*, Sandra Dallas's *Buster Midnight's Café*, and Beatriz Rivera's *Midnight Sandwiches at the Mariposa Express*.

Ford, Elaine
Ivory Bright
Viking. 1986. 229 pp.

Reality sets in after eccentric 31-year-old Ivory Bright succeeds in snagging middle-aged life insurance executive Ray Bartlett and then discovers how little they have in common and how difficult it is to sustain love.

Subjects Business and Businessmen • Eccentrics and Eccentricities • Love Stories • Marriage • Older Men/Younger Women • Working Classes

Now try   Ford's other novels include *Missed Connections*, *Monkey Bay*, and *Life Designs*. The character Ivory Bright is very much like Muriel, the dog walker in Anne Tyler's *The Accidental Tourist*. Francine Prose's *Household Saints* also portrays working-class families.

Fowler, Karen Joy
The Sweetheart Season
H. Holt. 1996. 352 pp.

A young woman tells the story of her mother's life in Magrit, Minnesota, after World War II, as a member of the Sweetwheat Sweethearts, an all-girls baseball team formed by the owner of the town's cereal mill to help the girls find husbands.

2d Appeal   Setting

Subjects   1940s • Baseball • Minnesota • Mothers and Daughters • Small-Town Life

Now try   Fowler's first novel, *Sarah Canary*, about a mysterious woman who appears in a railroad camp in Washington Territory in the 1880s, is also filled with artfully depicted characters. The main character of *The Sweetheart Season* tells readers that this is a story told by two liars. Another book that challenges the reader to discover whether or not the narrator is truthful is Ann Patchett's *The Patron Saint of Liars*.

Freed, Lynn
Home Ground
Summit Books. 1986. 273 pp.

In a small South African town, Ruth Frank, youngest daughter in a self-absorbed theatrical family, longs to flee from the hypocrisy of her home life as well as the ominous tensions brought about by apartheid.

2d Appeal   Setting

Subjects   Apartheid • Family Relationships • First Novels • Jews and Judaism • South Africa

Now try   Freed also wrote *The Bungalow*, a sequel to *Home Ground*, and *The Mirror*, a novel about an immigrant woman in South Africa after World War I. J. M. Coetzee's *Life & Times of Michael K* offers a different perspective on apartheid. Andre Brink's *Imaginings of Sand* is another novel about a rebellious young South African woman.

Freud, Esther
Hideous Kinky
Harcourt Brace Jovanovich. 1992. 186 pp.

The five-year-old narrator describes her months-long stay in Morocco with her adventure-seeking mother, her bossy older sister, and the assorted Europeans and Moroccans whom she meets.

2d Appeal   Setting

Subjects   British Authors • First Novels • Morocco • Mothers and Daughters • Sisters

Now try   Freud also wrote *Summer at Gaglow*. Other books that look at the world through the eyes of a child include Harper Lee's *To Kill a Mockingbird* and Nicholson Baker's *The Everlasting Story of Nory*. Patty Dann's *Mermaids* is another novel about a daughter whose mother can't settle down in one place.

Frucht, Abby
Are You Mine?
Grove Press. 1993. 293 pp.

Douglas and Cara's happy marriage is threatened by an unwanted pregnancy and Cara's desire to have an abortion.

Book Groups 📖

Subjects   Abortion • Husbands and Wives • Marriage • Pregnancy

Now try   Frucht has a talent for creating engaging and sympathetic characters, as can be seen in her short story collection, *Fruit of the Month*, and her other novels, *Snap*, *Licorice*, and *Life Before Death*. Another picture of a generally happy marriage is described in Carol Shields's *Happenstance*. Other books whose plots turn on a woman's decision whether to have an abortion are Walter Kirn's *She Needed Me* and Thomas Keneally's *Passenger*.

Fuentes, Carlos
The Old Gringo
Farrar, Straus Giroux. 1985. 199 pp.

Ambrose Bierce, who has come to Mexico to die, becomes a father figure to an American governess and her doomed lover, a young general in Pancho Villa's army. Translated from the Spanish by Margaret Sayers Peden.

2d Appeal   Language

Book Groups 📖

Subjects   Culture Clash • Death and Dying • Love Affairs • Mexican Authors • Mexico • Novels in Translation

Now try   Fuentes's other books include *The Death of Artemio Cruz* and *Constancia and Other Stories for Virgins*. Other examples of novels in which the author uses a real person as the protagonist include Thomas Keneally's *Schindler's List* and James Hamilton Patterson's *Gerontius*.

Gadol, Peter
The Mystery Roast
Crown Publishers. 1993. 306 pp.

In a moment of weakness during a bad time in his 20s, Eric Auden steals a 4,500-year-old miniature statue of the Goddess of Desire and finds it unexpectedly brings him friendship, love, and money—everything that's been lacking in his life.

2d Appeal   Story

Subjects   Art and Artists • Gay Men • Love Stories • Men's Friendships • New York

Now try   Gadol's other novels include *Closer to the Sun* and *The Long Rain*. Stephen McCauley's characters in *The Easy Way Out* and Mark O'Donnell's in *Getting Over Homer* have a lot in common with Gadol's characters in *Mystery Roast*. Another book in which coffee plays a central role is Mark Helprin's *Memoir from Antproof Case*.

Gale, Patrick
Kansas in August
E.P. Dutton. 1988. 140 pp.

Hilary's failure to make a living as an actor parallels his failure in his relationship with his sometime lover Rufus, who falls in love with Hilary's sister, Henry.

Book Groups 📖

Subjects   Actors and Acting • British Authors • Brothers and Sisters • Gay Men • Triangles

Now try Gale also wrote *The Aerodynamics of Pork* and *Ease*. Gale's style and the intertwining lives of his characters are reminiscent of Armistead Maupin's *Tales of the City*.

Gardam, Jane
The Queen of the Tambourine

St. Martin's Press. 1995. 226 pp.

In a series of increasingly personal letters to Joan, a former neighbor who has apparently decamped to Bangladesh, Eliza Peabody writes about her life as an abandoned wife, with no children and no career, in an upper-class section of London.

2d Appeal Story   Book Groups 📖

Subjects British Authors • Deserted Wives • Epistolary Novels • Upper Classes • Women's Friendships • Women's Lives

Now try Gardam is also the author of *Bilgewater* and *A Long Way from Verona*, two charming novels with adolescent narrators. Hilary Mantel's novels, including *A Change of Climate*, *Eight Months on Ghazzah Street*, and *An Experiment in Love* are, like Gardam's novels, funny and poignant. *The Queen of the Tambourine* won the Whitbread Award.

Gates, David
Jernigan

Knopf. 1991. 237 pp.

Approaching 40, Jernigan's life spins out of control at an alarming rate, as he mourns the violent deaths of his wife and his father, tries to understand his teenage son Danny, and becomes involved in a destructive relationship while trying to blur his despair with alcohol.

2d Appeal Language   Book Groups 📖

Subjects Alcoholics and Alcoholism • Death of a Spouse • Fathers and Sons • First Novels • Male/Female Relationships

Now try Gates's second novel is *Preston Falls*. Richard Yates's *Revolutionary Road* is also an examination of a despairing life. Other novels whose characters struggle with an addiction to alcohol are Frederick Exley's *A Fan's Notes*, John O'Hara's *Appointment in Samarra*, and Emile Zola's *The Drunkard*.

Gee, Maurice
Meg

St. Martin's Press. 1981. 251 pp.

Spanning two world wars in New Zealand, the 12 Plumb children experience passion, success, and defeat, all the while relying on their sentimental sister, Meg, for caretaking and peacemaking.

Subjects Brothers and Sisters • Family Relationships • New Zealand • New Zealand Authors

Now try Gee's other books include *The Champion* and *The Fire-Raiser*. The novels of Maurice Shadbolt (*Season of the Jew* and *Monday's Warriors*) also explore life in New Zealand. The complexity of family relationships is the subject of *Tamarind Men* by Anita Rau Badami and Martha Bergland's *Idle Curiosity*.

Gibbons, Kaye
Charms for the Easy Life
Putnam. 1993. 254 pp.

From the turn of the century through World War II, three generations of women survive the deaths of spouses, divorce, and hard times with indomitable spirit and resiliency.

2d Appeal   Story   Book Groups 📖

Subjects   Coming-of-Age • Grandparents • Mothers and Daughters • Multigenerational Novels • Southern Authors

Now try   Gibbons's novels (***Ellen Foster, A Cure for Dreams, Sights Unseen***, and others) showcase strong women and their lives. Other books with strong women characters include Lois McMaster Bujold's science fiction novel ***Barrayar***, ***Dalva*** by Jim Harrison, and ***Harry and Catherine*** by Frederick Busch. The often difficult relationship between mothers and daughters is the subject of Gail Godwin's ***A Mother and Two Daughters***. Jill McCorkle's ***Tending to Virginia*** is another novel about intergenerational relationships.

Godwin, Gail
The Good Husband
Ballantine Books. 1994. 468 pp.

Now in her 60s and dying of ovarian cancer, English professor Magda Danvers and her husband befriend another couple, whose marriage is also beset by adversities.

2d Appeal   Language   Book Groups 📖

Subjects   Cancer • Death and Dying • Death of a Spouse • Friendship • Marriage

Now try   Other novels by Godwin include ***The Odd Woman, A Mother and Two Daughters, Evensong, Father Melancholy's Daughter***, and ***Violet Clay***. ***Crossing to Safety*** by Wallace Stegner is another book in which illness affects the relationship of two couples. Doris Betts in ***Souls Raised from the Dead*** handles the death of a character with the same deep compassion as Godwin does.

Gold, Herbert
A Girl of Forty
D.I. Fine. 1986. 254 pp.

Suki Read, a girl of 40, and her on-again, off-again lover, Frank Curtis, find their relationship dangerously threatened by Suki's son, Peter.

2d Appeal   Language

Subjects   1980s • Male/Female Relationships • Mothers and Sons • San Francisco

Now try   Among Gold's other novels are ***She Took My Arm as if She Loved Me*** and ***Dreaming: A Novel***. Gold has also written nonfiction, including ***Best Nightmare on Earth: A Life in Haiti*** and ***A Walk on the West Side: California on the Brink***. San Francisco is the setting for Armistead Maupin's ***Tales of the City*** and Vikram Seth's novel in verse, ***The Golden Gate***. Another example of an on-again, off-again relationship is explored in Frederick Busch's ***Harry and Catherine***.

Gold, Ivan
Sams in a Dry Season
Houghton Mifflin. 1990. 244 pp.

During Jason Sams's weekend trip from Boston to New York and back again, he looks back on his life as a serious drinker and less-than-successful novelist.

2d Appeal   Language   Book Groups 📖

Subjects   Alcoholics and Alcoholism • Husbands and Wives • Writers and Writing

Now try   Gold's first novel, *Sick Friends*, is also about Jason Sams. Other novels dealing with alcoholism include Anne Lamott's *Rosie* and Malcolm Lowry's *Under the Volcano*. *Drinking: A Love Story* by Caroline Knapp is a memoir of her days as an alcoholic.

Golding, William
The Paper Men
Farrar, Straus, Giroux. 1984. 191 pp.

With a failed marriage, a failing writing career, and a growing dependence on alcohol, middle-aged author Wilfred Barclay develops a wanderlust to soothe his fears of growing old and becomes involved in an academic game of cat-and-mouse when he's asked to be the subject of a biography written by a colleague.

Subjects   Academia • Alcoholics and Alcoholism • British Authors • Male/Female Relationships • Middle-Aged Men • Writers and Writing

Now try   Other books by Golding include *Lord of the Flies* and *Darkness Visible*. The plot of Brian Morton's *Starting Out in the Evening* also involves the writing of a biography of a famous man.

Goldstein, Rebecca
The Mind-Body Problem
Random House. 1983. 275 pp.

A philosophy graduate student who is majoring in seduction and minoring in parties meets and marries an eccentric mathematical genius.

2d Appeal   Language   Book Groups 📖

Subjects   Academia • Adultery • College Students • First Novels • Jews and Judaism • Marriage • Philosophical Novels

Now try   Other books by Goldstein include *Strange Attractors* and *Mazel*. Another novel that weaves philosophy into its plot is *Disturbances in the Field* by Lynne Sharon Schwartz. The heroine of Pearl Abraham's *The Romance Reader* is also an Orthodox Jew. Another woman who struggles with marriage to an eccentric mathematical genius is found in William Boyd's *Brazzaville Beach*.

Gordon, Mary
Men and Angels
Random House. 1985. 239 pp.

Anne Foster's life as an art historian, a mother, and a wife seems peaceful and happy until Laura, a young woman with strong and unusual religious convictions, enters her life.

2d Appeal   Language   Book Groups 📖

Subjects   ALA Notable Books • Art and Artists • Male/Female Relationships • Mothers and Daughters • Religious Extremism • Women's Lives

Now try   Among Gordon's other books are *Final Payments*, *The Company of Women*, and *Spending*. She is also the author of *The Shadow Man*, a memoir about her father. Both Kim Barnes's memoir, *In the Wilderness: Coming of Age in Unknown Country* and Barbara Kingsolver's novel, *The Poisonwood Bible*, describe the effects of religious fanaticism on a family.

Gordon, Mary
The Other Side
Viking. 1989. 386 pp.

Stories of the MacNamara family covering two countries and five generations are recalled by cousins Dan and Camilla and their grandparents Vincent and Ellen, when Vincent leaves the nursing home where he lives to be at the bedside of his dying wife.

Book Groups 📖

Subjects   ALA Notable Books • Cousins • Family Relationships • Irish Americans • Multi-generational Novels

Now try   All of Gordon's fiction explores family relationships and the compromises life forces her characters to make. *Temporary Shelter*, a collection of stories, was an ALA Notable Book. Both Alice McDermott in *At Weddings and Wakes* and Michael Stephens in *The Brooklyn Book of the Dead* write about Irish American families. The action of *The Other Side* takes place during one day, as does James Joyce's *Ulysses*.

Gottlieb, Eli
The Boy Who Went Away
St. Martin's Press. 1997. 208 pp.

A young boy uses espionage to cope with his overly optimistic mother, his autistic/schizophrenic brother, and his silent, alcoholic father.

Book Groups 📖

Subjects   1960s • Autism • Brothers • Dysfunctional Families • Family Relationships • First Novels • Mental Illness

Now try   This is similar to—but much more intense than—Louise Fitzhugh's classic children's book, *Harriet the Spy*. One of the earliest novels about schizophrenia is Joanne Greenberg's *I Never Promised You a Rose Garden*. A good mystery in which the main character is schizophrenic is George Dawes Green's *The Caveman's Valentine*. Three nonfiction accounts of schizophrenia are Lori Schiller's *The Quiet Room: A Journey Out of the Torment of Madness*, Sylvia Nasar's *A Beautiful Mind*, and Jay Neugeboren's *Imagining Robert: My Brother, Madness, and Survival*.

Gowdy, Barbara
Mister Sandman
Steerforth Press. 1996. 268 pp.

A somewhat quirky middle-class family copes with raising the oldest daughter's illegitimate child, a strange, silent girl with remarkable musical talent, who becomes the repository for the family's secrets and deceptions.

2d Appeal   Characters Story
Book Groups 📖

Subjects   Canadian Authors • Eccentrics and Eccentricities • Family Relationships • Family Secrets • Gay Men • Lesbians • Music and Musicians

Now try   Gowdy also wrote *Through the Green Valley*. *Even Cowgirls Get the Blues* by Tom Robbins also centers around a character who can be termed a freak. Tim Winton's *Cloudstreet* portrays relationships in a family filled with quirky characters.

Grau, Shirley Ann

Roadwalkers
Knopf. 1994. 292 pp.

Mary Woods, an African American orphaned during the Depression, tells the story of her wanderings as a child; her grown daughter, Nanda, also reflects on Mary's life.

Book Groups 📖

Subjects   1930s • African Americans • Family Relationships • Mothers and Daughters • Orphans • Southern Authors

Now try   Grau won the Pulitzer Prize for her 1964 novel, *The Keepers of the House*. Although she is white, Grau's novels explore the South through the black experience. Ellen Douglas's *Can't Quit You, Baby* is about the friendship of a white woman and her black maid.

Greene, Harlan

What the Dead Remember
Dutton. 1991. 180 pp.

A young man struggles to accept his emerging homosexuality and to find his place in the world.

Subjects   AIDS • Coming-of-Age • Gay Men • Gay Teenagers

Now try   Greene also wrote *Why We Never Danced the Charleston*. Brian Bouldrey's *The Genius of Desire*, Bernard Cooper's *A Year of Rhymes*, Shyam Selvadurai's *Funny Boy*, and Jane Hamilton's *The Short History of a Prince* are all coming-of-age stories about young, gay men.

Grimsley, Jim

My Drowning
Algonquin Books of Chapel Hill. 1997. 258 pp.

Ellen Tote's triumphant survival of the abuse, neglect, and poverty of her North Carolina childhood is undermined by two recurrent dreams.

2d Appeal   Language
Book Groups 📖

Subjects   Alcoholics and Alcoholism • Brothers and Sisters • Child Abuse • Male/Female Relationships • North Carolina • Poverty • Suicide

Now try   Grimsley also wrote *The Winter Birds* and *Dream Boy*, his debut novel about young homosexual love and child abuse. Alice Walker's *The Color Purple* demonstrates the effects of abuse and neglect on the life of a woman.

Gu Hua

Virgin Widows
University of Hawaii Press. 1996. 165 pp.

In the face of oppression, two very different women in rural China—born 100 years apart—give their prescribed roles individual meaning and validity. Translated from the Chinese by Howard Goldblatt.

2d Appeal   Setting
Book Groups 📖

Subjects   China • Chinese Authors • Novels in Translation • Women's Lives

Now try   Margaret Atwood's *The Handmaid's Tale*, Ernest Gaines's *The Autobiography of Miss Jane Pittman*, and Kate Chopin's *The Awakening* all portray women having difficulty fitting their lives into the roles expected of them.

Gummerman, Jay
Chez Chance
Pantheon Books. 1995. 211 pp.

Recently paralyzed and knowing he will be in a wheelchair the rest of his life, Frank Eastman returns to Los Angeles for a trip to Disneyland and encounters a strange group of people who cross and recross his path in the run-down motel where he is living.

Subjects   Disneyland • First Novels • Los Angeles • Male/Female Relationships • Paraplegics • Physical Disabilities

Now try   Gummerman's *We Find Ourselves in Moontown* is a collection of stories. Other novels that describe contemporary southern California include Karen Karbo's *The Diamond Lane* and Sandra Tsing Loh's *If You Lived Here, You'd Be Home by Now*.

Gurganus, Allan
Plays Well with Others
Alfred A. Knopf. 1997. 337 pp.

Writer Hartley Mims, painter Alabama Byrnes, and composer Robert Gustafson, who have all come to New York in the 1970s to make their fortunes, find friendship, sexual freedom, and sorrow, as they navigate their way through a Manhattan that is ravaged by the AIDS epidemic.

2d Appeal   Story   Book Groups 📖

Subjects   1970s • 1980s • AIDS • Art and Artists • Friendship • Gay Men • Music and Musicians • New York • Writers and Writing

Now try   Gurganus also wrote a collection of short stories, *White People*, and a novel, *Oldest Living Confederate Widow Tells All*. Dale Peck's *Martin and John* and Paul Monette's *Afterlife* are both novels about gay men living during the same time period as those in Gurganus's novel. The discovery and spread of AIDS is the subject of Randy Shilts's *And the Band Played On*.

Hagedorn, Jessica
Dogeaters
Pantheon. 1990. 251 pp.

A disparate group of characters—drug addicts, school girls, and the richest man in town—have their secrets slowly revealed in the turmoil of 1950s Manila.

Subjects   1850s • Filipino American Authors • First Novels • Manila • Philippines

Now try   Hagedorn also wrote *The Gangster of Love*. Another novel set against a city in chaos is Bapsi Sidhwa's *Cracking India*.

Hale, Janet Campbell
The Jailing of Cecelia Capture
Random House. 1985. 201 pp.

In a Berkeley, California, jail for drunken driving, Cecelia Capture, 30 years old and part American Indian, finds a sustaining purpose in her pursuit of a law degree as she reflects on the circumstances that have too narrowly defined her life: prejudice, unhappy family relationships, teenage motherhood, a failing marriage, and the memory of her son's dead father.

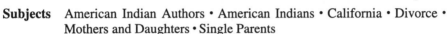

Book Groups 📖

Subjects	American Indian Authors • American Indians • California • Divorce • Mothers and Daughters • Single Parents
Now try	Hale has published a young adult novel, short stories, and poetry, but this is her first novel for adults. In ***Bloodline: Odyssey of a Native Daughter***, Hale tells her own story, which is filled with details closely related to this novel. In Jim Harrison's ***Dalva***, the main character (who is also part American Indian) tries to understand her past and present.

Hall, Brian
The Saskiad
Houghton Mifflin. 1997. 380 pp.

When 12-year-old Saskia White leaves the run-down commune where she lives with her mother to spend time in Norway with the father she never knew, Saskia discovers that the reality of her father is far different from how she's imagined him.

2d Appeal	Language	Book Groups 📖

Subjects	Coming-of-Age • Fathers and Daughters • Hippies • Sexual Abuse • Single Parents • Teenage Girls
Now try	Hall's other books include ***Dreamers***, ***Madeleine's World: A Child's Journey from Birth to Age Three***, and ***The Impossible Country: A Journey Through the Last Days of Yugoslavia***. Both Martha McPhee's ***Bright Angel Time*** and ***Little Miss Strange*** by Joanna Rose are novels about the children of aging hippies. Lisa Michaels's ***Split: A Counterculture Childhood*** is a memoir of growing up as the daughter of hippie parents. Jonathan Lethem's ***Girl in Landscape*** is also about a strong and interesting adolescent girl.

Hall, Rodney
Just Relations
Viking Press. 1983. 502 pp.

The eccentric and inbred residents of the mining village of Whitey's Falls, New South Wales, Australia, put their differences aside when the village is faced with progress in the form of a visiting government agent.

Subjects	ALA Notable Books • Australia • Australian Authors • Eccentrics and Eccentricities • First Novels • Small-Town Life
Now try	Among Hall's other novels are ***The Grisly Wife*** and ***The Second Bridegroom***. Another small town coping with the unwelcome intrusions of government representatives is found in Michael Malone's ***Dingley Falls***. ***Just Relations*** won the Miles Franklin Award.

Hamill, Pete
Loving Women: A Novel of the Fifties
Random House. 1989. 414 pp.

When 50-year-old Michael Devlin divorces his third wife and returns to Florida, where he was stationed while in the Navy 33 years before, he realizes that Eden Santana is his one true love.

2d Appeal Settings   Book Groups 📖

Subjects 1950s • ALA Notable Books • Coming-of-Age • Love Stories • Male/Female Relationships • Middle-Aged Men • Midlife Crisis • Older Women/Younger Men

Now try Hamill also wrote *A Drinking Life: A Memoir* and *Snow in August*. Although *Straight Man* by Richard Russo is much more humorous than this novel, it is also about a man turning 50 and the emotional upheaval it causes in his life.

Hamilton, Jane
The Book of Ruth
Ticknor & Fields. 1988. 328 pp.

After growing up with an abusive mother, Ruth Dahl's life does not improve when she marries a man with a violent temper. An Oprah selection.

2d Appeal Story   Book Groups 📖

Subjects Abusive Relationships • Domestic Violence • Family Relationships • First Novels • Murder • Single Parents • Small-Town Life

Now try Dorothy Allison's *Bastard Out of Carolina*, Bruce Arnold's *Running to Paradise*, and Elizabeth Jordan Moore's *Cold Times* all describe families marked by child abuse.

Hamilton-Paterson, James
Gerontius
Soho. 1991. 264 pp.

In 1923, Sir Edward Elgar, widowed, restless, and creatively stymied by his own formidable reputation, escapes on a cruise to Brazil, only to meet the one elusive figure from his past who knows him better than anyone else.

2d Appeal Language

Subjects 1920s • British Authors • Elgar, Edward • First Novels • Music and Musicians

Now try Hamilton-Paterson has also written nonfiction, poetry, and short stories. His short story collection, *The Music*, is a dark view of the creative process. Other biographical novels include Gore Vidal's *Burr*, Joanna Scott's *Arrogance*, and Irving Stone's *The Agony and the Ecstasy* and *Lust for Life*. Gerontius won the Whitbread Prize for First Novels.

Hansen, Ron
Atticus
HarperCollins Publishers. 1996. 247 pp.

When 67-year-old Atticus Cody learns that his son Scott is an apparent suicide, he travels to his son's home in Mexico to try to understand the mysterious events surrounding the death.

2d Appeal Language   Book Groups 📖

Subjects Fathers and Sons • Mexico • Suicide

Now try   In *Mariette in Ecstasy*, as in *Atticus*, Hansen writes about the relationship between the profane and the sacred in the lives of his characters. The characters in Iris Murdoch's *The Sacred and Profane Love Machine* also confront this issue in their lives. Another character named Atticus who puts together the pieces of a puzzle is Atticus Finch in Harper Lee's classic *To Kill a Mockingbird*.

Hardy, Edward
Geyser Life
Bridge Works Pub. Co. 1996. 244 pp.

After the death of their older brother, Nate Scales and his sister Sarah drive across the country in search of the troubled father who deserted the family years before.

2d Appeal   Characters   Book Groups 📖

Subjects   Brothers and Sisters • Dysfunctional Families • Fathers Deserting Their Families • First Novels • Road Novels

Now try   The main characters in both Mona Simpson's *The Lost Father* and Janette Turner Hospital's *Charades* search for missing fathers. Dennis McFarland's *The Music Room* explores how the death of a brother affects the family.

Harrison, Jim
Dalva
E.P. Putnam. 1988. 324 pp.

Middle-aged Dalva yearns for the child she gave up for adoption, while her lover Michael seeks personal and professional redemption in studying the writings of her great-grandfather, who eloquently recorded his feelings of pain and helplessness as the Sioux nation was annihilated.

2d Appeal   Story   Book Groups 📖

Subjects   Adoption • Alcoholics and Alcoholism • American Indians • Family Relationships • Incest

Now try   *The Road Home* is the sequel to *Dalva*. Catherine, the heroine of Frederick Busch's *Harry and Catherine*, is a lot like Dalva in her need for independence.

Hart, Josephine
Damage
Knopf. 1991. 195 pp.

When a successful member of Parliament becomes passionately enthralled with the woman his son plans to marry, the affair the two embark on destroys both his career and his marriage.

Subjects   Adultery • British Authors • Fathers and Sons • First Novels • Obsessive Love • Older Men/Younger Women

Now try   Hart's other novels—also about obsessive love—include *Sin* and *The Stillest Day*. Another example of obsessive love can be found in Iris Murdoch's *The Sea, The Sea*.

Haruf, Kent
The Tie That Binds
Holt, Rinehart, and Winston. 1984. 246 pp.

After giving up her life and the man she loves to care for her crippled, abusive father and mentally ill brother on the family's homestead in eastern Colorado, Edith Goodnough finds the strength to free herself.

Subjects　Abusive Relationships • ALA Notable Books • Brothers and Sisters • Colorado • Family Relationships • Fathers and Daughters • First Novels • Mental Illness

Now try　Haruf also wrote *Where You Once Belonged*. The main character in Susan M. Dodd's *No Earthly Notion* is another woman who sacrificed her own life to take care of others.

Hedges, Peter
An Ocean in Iowa
Hyperion Press. 1998. 247 pp.

The year Scotty Ocean turns seven is the year his mother leaves him, his sisters, and their father.

2d Appeal　Setting　　　　　　　　　　　　　　　　　　　　Book Groups 📖

Subjects　1960s • Brothers and Sisters • Iowa • Mothers Deserting Their Families

Now try　Hedges's first novel was *What's Eating Gilbert Grape?* Other novels in which brothers and sisters console one another during difficult times are *My Father's Geisha* by James Gordon Bennett and Annie Waters's *Glimmer*. Ardashir Vakil's novel *Beach Boy* offers another view of the world through the eyes of a young boy.

Hendrie, Laura
Stygo
MacMurray & Beck. 1994. 225 pp.

In the hardscrabble town of Stygo, Colorado, a group of frustrated and often lonely residents feed their dreams at the Rockeroy Bar while waiting for something—anything—to happen.

Book Groups 📖

Subjects　Alcoholics and Alcoholism • Cafés and Restaurants • Colorado • Family Relationships • First Novels • Mental Illness • Poverty • Small-Town Life

Now try　*Winterkill* by Craig Lesley also evokes a difficult life in the western United States. Sandra Benitez's *A Place Where the Sea Remembers* is filled with people on the margins of society.

Henkin, Joshua
Swimming Across the Hudson
G.P. Putnam's Sons. 1997. 230 pp.

Although he's always known that he was adopted, when Ben Suskind receives a letter from his birth mother asking to meet him, he is forced to examine difficult questions about family and religion.

2d Appeal　Story　　　　　　　　　　　　　　　　　　　　Book Groups 📖

Subjects　Adoption • Brothers • Family Relationships • First Novels • Jews and Judaism

Now try　*A Man and His Mother: An Adopted Son's Search* by Tim Green is a nonfiction account of Green's attempt to find his birth mother. Jeannette Haien's *Matters of Chance* and Steve Tesich's *Karoo* are both about the tragic outcome of a father searching for information about his adopted children. Both Mary Tannen's

Loving Edith and Elinor Lipman's *Then She Found Me* are about the relationship between mothers and the children they gave up for adoption years before.

Herrick, Amy
At the Sign of the Naked Waiter
HarperCollins. 1992. 246 pp.

Sarah grows up in a world filled with mystery—flying blue sponges, an enchanted frog—and the ordinary—first love, best friends, and an eccentric brother.

2d Appeal   Language

Subjects   Brothers and Sisters • Coming-of-Age • Eccentrics and Eccentricities • Family Relationships • First Novels • Magic Realism • Women's Friendships

Now try   The mixture of the mythic with the mundane is also a central part of Nancy Willard's *Things Invisible to See*.

Highbridge, Dianne
A Much Younger Man
Soho Press. 1998. 214 pp.

Divorced English teacher Aly and her 15-year-old lover, Tom, must deal with the repercussions from family, colleagues, and friends when their affair is discovered.

Subjects   Australian Authors • First Novels • Love Affairs • Older Women/Younger Men

Now try   Antonya Nelson's *Nobody's Girl* and Colleen McCullough's *Tim* both describe love affairs between older women and much younger men.

Hijuelos, Oscar
The Mambo Kings Play Songs of Love
Farrar, Straus Giroux. 1989. 407 pp.

Impoverished, aging, and in ill health, Cesar Castillo recalls the sexual exploits and family feuds of his younger years when he worked as a musician in New York during the 1950s.

2d Appeal   Setting

Subjects   1950s • Aging • Family Relationships • Men's Lives • Music and Musicians • New York • Pulitzer Prize Winners

Now try   Hijuelos also wrote *Mr. Ives' Christmas* and *Our House in the Last World*. Philip Roth's *Sabbath's Theater* and Mark Helprin's *Memoir from Antproof Case* are both about elderly men recalling their lives. Other novels about the immigrant experience include Julia Alvarez's *How the Garcia Girls Lost Their Accents* and Isabel Allende's *The Infinite Plan*. The full-bodied characters in this novel are similar to those found in Gabriel Garcia Marquez's *Love in the Time of Cholera*.

Hill, Rebecca
Blue Rise
Morrow. 1983. 296 pp.

During a crisis in her marriage, Jeannine Hinton goes home to her mother and discovers that the easiest way to live in the present is often to rewrite the past.

Subjects   Cousins • Family Relationships • First Novels • Mothers and Daughters • Southern Authors

Now try   Hill's other books include *Among Birches* and *Killing Time in St. Cloud*, which she wrote with Judith Guest. Jill McCorkle's *Tending to Virginia* also describes a nice relationship between cousins.

Hoffman, Alice
The Drowning Season
Dutton. 1979. 212 pp.

Unable to understand her suicidal son, Esther the White, a Russian émigré, strikes out at her 18-year-old granddaughter, Esther the Black, who dreams of breaking free from her angry and dysfunctional family.

2d Appeal   Language   Book Groups 📖

Subjects   ALA Notable Books • Dysfunctional Families • Family Relationships • Grandparents • Immigrants and Refugees • Suicide

Now try   Hoffman's first novel, *Property of*, has an entirely different setting but also focuses on the life of a teenage girl. Other novels of redemption include John Cheever's *Falconer*, *Joe* by Larry Brown, George Eliot's *Silas Marner*, *The Sweet Hereafter* by Russell Banks, and Reynolds Price's *Blue Calhoun*.

Hoffman, Alice
Illumination Night
Putnam. 1987. 224 pp.

Andre and Vonny's marriage is threatened by a lack of money and their teenage neighbor's obsession with Andre.

2d Appeal   Language   Book Groups 📖

Subjects   ALA Notable Books • Magic Realism • Marriage • Martha's Vineyard, Massachusetts • Massachusetts • Obsessive Love • Teenage Girls

Now try   Ann Patchett's novels, *Taft*, *The Patron Saint of Liars*, and *The Magician's Assistant*, are similar in tone to Hoffman's books. Other novels set on Martha's Vineyard include Anne Rivers Siddons's *Up Island* and Dorothy West's *The Wedding*.

Hoffman, Alice
Seventh Heaven
G.P. Putnam's. 1990. 256 pp.

When Nora Silk moves into a house on Hemlock Street in suburban Long Island, New York, her arrival triggers changes in the lives of many of her neighbors.

2d Appeal   Language   Book Groups 📖

Subjects   1950s • ALA Notable Books • Long Island, New York • Male/Female Relationships • New York • Older Women/Younger Men • Single Parents • Suburbia

Now try   Hoffman also wrote ***Practical Magic***. Nora Silk is similar to the main character, Justine, in Anne Tyler's ***Searching for Caleb***. Other novels that describe a relationship between an older woman and a younger man are Colleen McCullough's ***Tim***, Dianne Highbridge's ***A Much Younger Man***, and David Martin's ***The Crying Heart Tattoo***.

Hoffman, Alice
Turtle Moon
G.P. Putnam's Sons. 1992. 255 pp.

In Verity, Florida, where anything can happen during the month of May, single mother Lucy Rossen and policeman Julian Nash revisit their shattered pasts as they attempt to solve a murder involving a troubled adolescent.

2d Appeal   Language

Subjects   ALA Notable Books • Divorce • Florida • Juvenile Delinquents • Love Stories • Magic Realism • Single Parents • Teenage Boys

Now try   Another portrait of a troubled adolescent can be found in Jo-Ann Mapson's ***Blue Rodeo***. ***Boy's Life*** by Robert McCammon also combines a murder mystery with magic realism.

Hoffman, Alice
White Horses
Putnam. 1982. 254 pp.

Growing up with an unhappy mother who told her tales of the Arias, handsome men on white horses who sweep women off their feet, Theresa Connors struggles to free herself of the myth and face reality.

2d Appeal   Language

Subjects   ALA Notable Books • Brothers and Sisters • Drugs and Drug Abuse • Dysfunctional Families • Incest

Now try   Like Nancy Willard in ***Things Invisible to See***, Hoffman combines everyday experiences with a hint of magic realism. In Laura Esquivel's ***Like Water for Chocolate***, a bandito rides off with the heroine's sister, an event that Theresa, the main character in ***White Horses***, expected (and hoped) would also happen to her.

Hornby, Nick
High Fidelity
Riverhead Books 1995. 323 pp.

Rob, a 30-something record store owner in London in the early 1990s, approaches his place in life, his failed relationships, and his strange employees with a wry sense of humor.

Subjects   1990s • British Authors • Business and Businessmen • First Novels • London • Male/Female Relationships • Music and Musicians

Now try   Hornby also wrote ***About a Boy***. The main character in Alan Brown's ***Audrey Hepburn's Neck*** also struggles with his interpersonal relationships.

Horowitz, Eve
Plain Jane
Random House. 1992. 261 pp.

Jane Singer's life is in turmoil: her bohemian sister is marrying an Orthodox Jew, her parents' marriage is dissolving under the weight of Jane's father's criticisms of her mother, and Jane herself is clearly not living up to her own potential.

Subjects Coming-of-Age • First Novels • Humorous Fiction • Jews and Judaism • Sisters

Now try The wisecracking narrator of this novel is similar to the narrator of Jen Banbury's thriller, *Like a Hole in the Head*. Allegra Goodman's *The Family Markowitz* has a chapter about a young woman who marries an Orthodox Jew, much to the consternation of her less religiously observant family.

Howatch, Susan
Absolute Truths
Knopf. 1995. 559 pp.

Even the bishop of the largest cathedral in England can have his faith tested mightily, and the death of Charles Ashworth's beloved wife is only the first of many crises he must resolve as he struggles, all too humanly, to find his way back to God.

2d Appeal Story   Book Groups 📖

Subjects 1960s • British Authors • Death of a Spouse • Family Relationships • Ministers, Priests, and Rabbis • Religion

Now try This is Howatch's sixth book covering several decades and perspectives on the Church of England. The first book in the series is *Glittering Images*. Howatch's very early books, such as *Penmarric*, published in 1971, were romantic suspense novels similar to those written by Victoria Holt (*The India Fan* and *Snare of Serpents*). Father Emilio Sandoz, the main character in Mary Doria Russell's *The Sparrow*, also faces a crisis of faith.

Humphreys, Josephine
Dreams of Sleep
Viking Press. 1984. 232 pp.

After 10 years of marriage, Alice Reese finds herself emotionally paralyzed, as her husband, once obsessed with his medical practice, is now totally focused on his mistress.

2d Appeal Language   Book Groups 📖

Subjects Adultery • First Novels • Marriage • Midlife Crisis • South Carolina • Southern Authors

Now try Humphreys's other novels include *The Fireman's Fair* and *Rich in Love*. Humphreys's characters, like Walker Percy's in *The Moviegoer* and Julie Hecht's in *Do the Windows Open?*, have trouble adjusting to their lives.

Huston, Nancy
Instruments of Darkness
Little, Brown and Co. 1997. 317 pp.

In researching the story of an eighteenth-century servant who was executed, Nadia, a divorced American writer, exorcises her personal demons and brings her own history into harmony.

Book Groups 📖

Subjects Alcoholics and Alcoholism • Canadian Authors • Family Relationships • French authors • Research Novels

Now try   Huston's other books include *Slow Emergencies* and *Plainsong*. *Instruments of Darkness* won Canada's Governor General's Award in 1996. Other research novels include A. S. Byatt's *Possession* and Cathleen Schine's *Rameau's Niece*.

Iida, Deborah
Middle Son
Algonquin Books of Chapel Hill. 1996. 228 pp.

His mother's approaching death forces Spencer to recall the accidental drowning of his older brother Taizo at age 12 and the effect the tragedy had on the entire Fujii family.

2d Appeal   Story

Subjects   ALA Notable Books • Brothers • Death of a Child • First Novels • Hawaii • Japan • Japanese Americans

Now try   Graham Salisbury's *Blue Skin of the Sea* is another novel about how tragedy shaped a family's life. Growing up on Hawaii's plantations is the subject of Lois-Ann Yamanaka's *Wild Meat and Bully Burgers*.

Irving, John
The Cider House Rules
Morrow. 1985. 560 pp.

Orphan Homer Wells grows up as an apprentice to an abortionist.

2d Appeal   Story   Book Groups 📖

Subjects   Abortion • Coming-of-Age • Humorous Fiction • Orphans

Now try   Irving's other books include *A Son of the Circus* and *Trying to Save Pinky Sneed*. Irving portrays both sides of the abortion issue and encourages his readers to draw their own conclusions. Lewis Nordan is another novelist who examines complex moral issues in an often humorous manner in *The Sharpshooter Blues* and *Wolf Whistle*.

Irving, John
A Prayer for Owen Meany
Morrow. 1989. 543 pp.

John Wheelright's religious faith stems from a lifelong friendship with Owen Meany, the boy who accidentally killed John's mother during a baseball game.

2d Appeal   Story   Book Groups 📖

Subjects   ALA Notable Books • Death of a Parent • Dwarfs • Humorous Fiction • Men's Friendships

Now try   Among Irving's other novels are *A Widow for One Year* and *Setting Free the Bears*. Robertson Davies's novel, *Fifth Business*, is about an accident that changes the life of the main character. The complex and detailed plots devised by Irving are similar to the plots found in the novels of Charles Dickens (*The Old Curiosity Shop*), Mark Helprin (*Memoir from Antproof Case*), and Charles Palliser (*The Quincunx*).

Irwin, Robert

Exquisite Corpse
Pantheon Books. 1995. 235 pp.

Caspar, an English Surrealist painter, reflects on his art, his experiences as a member of the Serapion brotherhood, and his obsessive love for the elusive Catherine.

Book Groups 📖

Subjects   1930s • Art and Artists • British Authors • Male/Female Relationships • Obsessive Love

Now try   Among Irwin's other books are *The Arabian Nightmare* and *The Limits of Vision*. Irwin includes many real people in this novel, such as Andre Breton, Salvador Dali, Dylan Thomas, Aleister Crowley, and Orson Welles. Two biographical novels about art and artists are Irving Stone's *The Agony and the Ecstasy*, about the Renaissance artist Michelangelo, and Lust for Life, about the painter Vincent Van Gogh. Jane Urquhart's *The Underpainter* is also about an artist recalling the events of his life.

James, Clive

The Man from Japan
Random House. 1993. 173 pp.

Suzuki, a young intellectual and would-be diplomat, is sent to London to acquire "cosmopolitan ease," but his ill-chosen love affairs result in a tabloid headline: "Jap Rambo Goes Bananas," much to the embarrassment of the Japanese embassy.

2d Appeal   Story

Subjects   British Authors • Culture Clash • Humorous Fiction • Love Affairs • Single Men

Now try   James's other books include *Unreliable Memoirs* and *Falling Towards England*. Both Ishmael Reed in *Japanese by Spring* and Ruth Ozeki in *My Year of Meats* write humorously about the relationship between the Japanese and Americans.

Japrisot, Sebastien

A Very Long Engagement
Farrar, Straus Giroux. 1993. 327 pp.

Although confined to a wheelchair, 17-year-old Mathilde Donnay attempts to uncover the truth about her beloved fiancé who, along with four other wounded French soldiers, was bound and left to die in the no-man's land between the French and German armies during World War I. Translated from the French by Linda Coverdale.

Book Groups 📖

Subjects   France • Love Stories • Novels in Translation • Paraplegics • World War I

Now try   Japrisot's other books, including *The Sleeping Car Murders* and *One Deadly Summer*, are superior psychological suspense novels. Erich Maria Remarque's *All Quiet on the Western Front*, Richard Marius's *After the War*, and Mark Helprin's *A Soldier of the Great War* are all novels centered on World War I. *The Old Gringo* by Carlos Fuentes and *Inagehi* by Jack Cady both deal with exploring the mystery surrounding the death of a loved one.

Jen, Gish
Mona in the Promised Land
Knopf. 1996. 304 pp.

Chinese American Mona Chang, after moving with her family to Scarsdale, New York, decides to convert to Judaism.

2d Appeal   Story

Subjects   Chinese American Authors • Chinese Americans • Coming-of-Age • Jews and Judaism • Satirical Fiction • Suburbia • Teenage Girls

Now try   Jen's first novel, *Typical American*, is about Mona's parents' experiences in the United States after emigrating from China. (It's not necessary to read it before *Mona in the Promised Land*.) The Chinese American teenage girl in Elizabeth Tallent's *Museum Pieces* is also struggling with questions of ethnic identity.

Jhabvala, Ruth Prawer
Shards of Memory
Doubleday. 1995. 221 pp.

Four generations of an Anglo Indian family, hovering between East and West, living in London and New York, are influenced by a spiritual movement and its charismatic founder, known as The Master.

Subjects   Anglo Indians • Indian Authors • London • Male/Female Relationships • Multigenerational Novels • New York

Now try   Jhabvala is the author of 17 books, including *Heat and Dust*, which won the 1975 Booker Prize. *The Moor's Last Sigh* by Salman Rushdie is another story of several generations of an Indian family full of unusual characters. In Carolyn See's *Golden Days*, a group of people also come under the influence of a charismatic man.

Johnson, Diane
Le Divorce
Dutton. 1997. 309 pp.

Californian Isabel Walker goes to Paris to help her pregnant, divorcing sister and ends up getting a short course in love, life, and French culture by a much older French diplomat.

2d Appeal   Story

Subjects   Adultery • Culture Clash • Divorce • Family Relationships • France • Love Affairs • Male/Female Relationships • Older Men/Younger Women • Single Women • Sisters

Now try   Johnson's other novels include *Fair Game* and *Burning*. Henry James's heroines, Isabel Archer (*Portrait of a Lady*) and Daisy Miller (*Daisy Miller*), both find their American ways challenged by their experiences in Europe. *Objects in Mirror Are Closer Than They Appear* by Katherine Weber offers a similar contrast between American naïveté and European cynicism.

Johnson, Diane
Lying Low
Knopf. 1978. 278 pp.

Four days in the life of an elderly photographer and her sister, who rent rooms in their boarding house to two very different young women, both of whom are trying to escape the law.

2d Appeal   Language   Book Groups 📖

Subjects   ALA Notable Books • Elderly Women • Fugitives • Photography and Photographers • Sisters • Violence

Now try   Diane Johnson's other novels include *The Shadow Knows* and *Persian Nights*. Another novel with a similar plot—a young woman on the lam from the law—is Marge Piercy's *Vida*.

Just, Ward
The American Ambassador
Houghton Mifflin. 1987. 326 pp.

Foreign Service officer William North's seemingly idyllic life is shattered when he learns that his son Bill has joined a group of German terrorists.

Book Groups 📖

Subjects   Family Relationships • Fathers and Sons • Murder • Terrorists and Terrorism • Violence

Now try   Just, a former reporter for the *Washington Post*, often sets tales of family relationships against political events, as can be seen in his novels, *Jack Gance*, *In the City of Fear*, and *Stringer*. Andre Brink's *An Act of Treason*, set in South Africa, is also about a father whose son becomes involved with a group of terrorists. The novels of John le Carre, especially *The Little Drummer Girl*, are about the moral issues that surround pragmatic political choices. Roberta Silman's *Beginning the World Again* is another novel about a father and son at odds over political choices.

Kalpakian, Laura
Graced Land
Grove Weidenfeld. 1992. 264 pp.

The memory of Elvis allows Joyce Jackson to survive her fundamentalist father's physical abuse, her husband's betrayal, and her life on welfare, all with her spirit intact and love of humanity unshaken.

Book Groups 📖

Subjects   Abusive Relationships • Child Abuse • Fathers and Daughters • Marriage • Presley, Elvis • Religion • Single Parents

Now try   Kalpakian's other books include *Crescendo* and *Caveat*. Kalpakian's bemused attitude toward her characters is reminiscent of the way Elinor Lipman (*The Way Men Act* and others), Stephen McCauley (*The Easy Way Out* and others), and Connie Willis (*Bellwether*) all regard their creations. Two other novels in which Elvis plays a role are *Tender* by Mark Childress and *Biggest Elvis* by P. F. Kluge.

Kaplan, James
Pearl's Progress
Knopf. 1989. 303 pp.

New Yorker Philip Pearl takes a teaching job as assistant professor of English at Mississippi's Picket State University, where he finds a group of weird co-workers, a variety of students and townspeople, and love.

2d Appeal   Story

   Subjects   Academia • College Professors • Culture Clash • First Novels • Humorous Fiction • Mississippi • Single Men

   Now try   Kaplan also wrote *Two Guys from Verona*. David Lodge (*Small World: An Academic Romance*), Malcolm Bradbury (*The History Man*), Randall Jarrell (*Pictures from an Institution*), and Jane Smiley (*Moo*) have all written satirical novels about life in academia.

Karbo, Karen
The Diamond Lane
Putnam. 1991. 316 pp.

When Mouse Fitzhenry returns to Los Angeles after spending 16 years in Africa as a film maker, she finds her life complicated by her mother's insistence that she and Tony, her long-time boyfriend, get married; her attraction to her old flame Ivan; and the films that both Tony and Ivan intend to make about her life.

2d Appeal   Story

   Subjects   Humorous Fiction • Los Angeles • Los Angeles • Male/Female Relationships • Sisters

   Now try   Karbo also wrote *Trespassers Welcome Here*. Other novels that explore the culture of Hollywood include Nathanael West's *The Day of the Locust*, Michael Tolkin's *The Player*, Budd Schulberg's *What Makes Sammy Run?* and Steve Tesich's *Karoo*. Other novels set in a well-described Southern California include Alison Lurie's *The Nowhere City*, Sandra Tsing Loh's *If You Lived Here, You'd Be Home by Now*, and Jay Gummerman's *Chez Chance*.

Katz, Steve
Florry of Washington Heights
Sun & Moon. 1987. 206 pp.

As war wages in Korea, peace-loving, 15-year-old William "Swanny" Swanson and his fellow gang members fight smaller battles on the streets, basketball courts, and baseball diamonds of the Washington Heights neighborhood of Manhattan.

Book Groups 📖

   Subjects   Coming-of-Age • Gangs and Gangsters • Jews and Judaism • New York • Teenage Boys

   Now try   Katz is also the author of *Saw* and *Moving Parts*. S. E. Hinton's young-adult novel, *The Outsiders*, and *Billy Bathgate* by E. L. Doctorow both deal with the themes of gangs and loyalty.

Kauffman, Janet
Collaborators
Knopf. 1986. 129 pp.

On a Mennonite farm in Pennsylvania, life changes dramatically for 12-year-old Dovie, who must come to terms with the stroke that has nearly incapacitated her mother.

2d Appeal Language   Book Groups 📖

    Subjects Coming-of-Age • Farms and Farm Life • First Novels • Mennonites • Mothers and Daughters • Pennsylvania • Stroke Patients

    Now try Kauffman is also the author of a collection of short stories, ***Places in the World a Woman Could Walk***. Another portrait of a young girl's love for her mother is found in Ursula Hegi's ***Floating in My Mother's Palm***. A memoir written by a stroke victim is Robert McCrum's ***My Year Off: Recovering Life After a Stroke***.

Keller, Nora Okja
Comfort Woman
Viking. 1997. 213 pp.

When Beccah, a young Korean American girl growing up in Hawaii after World War II, discovers that her mother had been sold by her mother's family to the Japanese invaders to be a comfort woman during the war to raise money for the family, she finally understands her mother's often bizarre behavior.

2d Appeal Language   Book Groups 📖

    Subjects First Novels • Hawaii • Korean-Japanese Relations • Mental Illness • Mothers and Daughters • World War II

    Now try Other novels in which a child tries to understand a mother's strange behavior are Susanna Moore's ***My Old Sweetheart*** (also set in Hawaii) and ***Audrey Hepburn's Neck*** by Alan Brown. Kiana Davenport's ***Shark Dialogues*** and Norman Katkov's mystery ***Blood and Orchids*** are both set in Hawaii.

Keneally, Thomas
Passenger
Harcourt Brace Jovanovich. 1979. 241 pp.

From within the womb, Sal and Brian's unborn child relates his experiences: multiple threats to his existence, including the apparent end of his parents' marriage and his father's desire to have him aborted.

2d Appeal Language

    Subjects Adultery • ALA Notable Books • Australian Authors • Fathers and Sons • Marriage • Mothers and Sons • Sex and Sexuality

    Now try Among Keneally's many other works of fiction are ***Victim of the Aurora***, ***Dutiful Daughter***, and ***Flying Hero Class***. Another novel that begins when the narrator is in the womb is Kate Atkinson's ***Behind the Scenes at the Museum***.

Kernan, Michael
The Lost Diaries of Frans Hals
St. Martin's Press. 1994. 316 pp.

Graduate student Peter Van Overloop's aimless life gains direction when he is asked to translate a set of possibly bogus diaries written by the Dutch painter, Frans Hals.

Book Groups 📖

    Subjects Art and Artists • College Students • First Novels • Hals, Frans • Research Novels

Now try   Another fictional diary purportedly written by a real person is Jamie Fuller's *The Diary of Emily Dickinson*. Ruth Prawer Jhabvala's *Heat and Dust*, *Rameau's Niece* by Cathleen Schine, and A. S. Byatt's *Possession* are all novels that interweave the past and present.

Kingsolver, Barbara
Animal Dreams
HarperCollins. 1990. 342 pp.

Cosima Noline returns to her hometown of Grace, Arizona, to teach biology at the local high school and learns her own lessons about love, family, and the past.

2d Appeal   Story   Book Groups 📖

Subjects   ALA Notable Books • Alzheimer's Disease • Arizona • Ecofiction • Family Secrets • Fathers and Daughters • Love Stories • Sisters • Small-Town Life

Now try   Among Kingsolver's other books are *The Poisonwood Bible* and *Pigs in Heaven*. The deep love of the Southwestern setting of this novel is also seen in *Going Back to Bisbee* by Richard Shelton, as he describes a trip he takes through Arizona's desert.

Kingsolver, Barbara
The Bean Trees
Harper & Row. 1988. 232 pp.

Taylor Greer heads West from Kentucky to escape small-town life and finds an abandoned and abused Cherokee child left in her car.

2d Appeal   Story   Book Groups 📖

Subjects   Abandoned Children • Adoption • American Indians • Cherokees • First Novels • Orphans

Now try   Kingsolver also wrote *High Tide in Tucson: Essays from Now or Never*. Henry Denker's *Payment in Full* is also about interracial adoption.

Kiraly, Sherwood
Big Babies
Berkley Books. 1996. 248 pp.

When Adlai accompanies his older brother Sterling to a Public Setback Support group meeting, the lives of both change dramatically: Sterling overcomes the disaster of a flubbed line on live television and Adlai realizes he is not the complete loser he always thought he was.

2d Appeal   Story

Subjects   Actors and Acting • Adoption • Brothers • Humorous Fiction

Now try   Kiraly's other novels include *Diminished Capacity* and *California Rush*. *Bachelor Brothers' Bed & Breakfast* by Bill Richardson and *Sam and His Brother Len* by John Manderino are other humorous novels about brothers. Another novel about adopted brothers is Joshua Henkin's *Swimming Across the Hudson*. The tie between brothers is also examined (with no humor at all) in Pete Dexter's *The Paperboy* and Russell Banks's *Affliction*.

Kirn, Walter
She Needed Me
Pocket Books. 1992. 227 pp.

While stretched prone in protest in front of an abortion clinic, born-again Weaver Walquist meets Kim, the pregnant designer of X-rated greeting cards, on her way inside to have an abortion.

2d Appeal Story   Book Groups 📖

    Subjects Abortion • First Novels • Love Stories • Mothers and Sons • Satirical Fiction

    Now try Kirn is also the author of *My Hard Bargain*, a collection of short stories. Abortion issues are part of the plots of Abby Frucht's *Are You Mine?* and John Irving's *The Cider House Rules*.

Klima, Ivan
Judge on Trial
Alfred A. Knopf. 1993. 549 pp.

In 1968, Adam Kindl is designated as the judge in a murder trial in Prague, but as the trial progresses he begins to realize the government has actually put him on trial as a test of his loyalty to the Communist Party. Translated from the Czech by A.G. Brian.

2d Appeal Language

    Subjects ALA Notable Books • Communism • Concentration Camps • Czechoslovakia • Czechoslovakian Authors • Novels in Translation • Political Fiction

    Now try Klima is also the author of *Love and Garbage* and *My Golden Trades*. Milan Kundera's *The Book of Laughter and Forgetting* combines the personal with the political.

Knowles, John
The Private Life of Axie Reed
E.P. Dutton. 1986. 214 pp.

While recovering from a nearly fatal accident, Axie looks back over her life as an actress, wife, and friend, as she decides whether she wants to live or die.

Book Groups 📖

    Subjects Actors and Acting • Death and Dying • Male/Female Relationships

    Now try Other novels by Knowles include *A Separate Peace*, *Peace Breaks Out*, and *A Vein of Riches*. Other novels in which the main characters examine their lives are William Golding's *Pincher Martin* and Wallace Stegner's *Angle of Repose*.

Kogawa, Joy
Obasan
D.R. Godine. 1982. 250 pp.

As her Japanese Canadian family gathers together for a funeral, Naomi recalls the racial hatred she and her family experienced during World War II, which culminated in being interned in a relocation camp.

2d Appeal Language   Book Groups 📖

    Subjects ALA Notable Books • First Novels • Internment Camps • Japanese Canadian Authors • Japanese Canadians • Mothers and Daughters • Racism • World War II

    Now try Kogawa explored the same themes as *Obasan* in her novel *Itsuka*. Gretel Ehrlich's *Heart Mountain* is another novel about Japanese citizens interned during World War II.

Kosinski, Jerzy
Pinball
Bantam Books. 1982. 287 pp.

In return for sexual favors, Damustroy, an ex-composer of classical music, helps Andrea, a beautiful drama student, in her search for the reclusive rock star, Goodard.

Book Groups 📖

Subjects   1970s • Music and Musicians • New York • Older Men/Younger Women • Sex and Sexuality

Now try   Kosinski's other novels include *Blind Date*, *Cockpit*, and *Being There*. Patricia Duncker's *Hallucinating Foucault* is also about the search for a reclusive artist.

Kramer, Kathryn
Rattlesnake Farming
Knopf. 1992. 545 pp.

Zoe Carver—unable to speak for the 10 years since her high school boyfriend was incarcerated because he insisted he had deliberately caused his father's death—spends an eventful Christmas with her mother, her beloved older brother and his wife, and her current boyfriend.

2d Appeal   Story

Subjects   Brothers and Sisters • Family Relationships • Family Secrets • Mental Illness • Snakes

Now try   Kramer also wrote *A Handbook for Visitors from Outer Space* and *Sweet Water*. Snakes play an important part in Mary Lee Settle's *Celebration* and Tim McLaurin's *The Last Great Snake Show*.

Kuban, Karla
Marchlands
Scribner. 1998. 270 pp.

Fifteen-year-old Sophie's life on a Wyoming sheep ranch is defined by her desire to understand the past and her search for answers to present problems, including her missing father, her pregnancy, and her mother's fervor for both alcohol and religion.

2d Appeal   Setting

Book Groups 📖

Subjects   Alcoholics and Alcoholism • Coming-of-Age • Cowboys • Family Secrets • Fathers Deserting Their Families • Mothers and Daughters • Religious Extremism • Teenage Pregnancy • Wyoming

Now try   Kuban's writing style is similar to that found in Pam Houston's short story collection, *Cowboys Are My Weakness*. Sophie's voice in *Marchlands* is reminiscent of Sam Hughes's voice in Bobbie Ann Mason's *In Country*.

Kureishi, Hanif
The Buddha of Suburbia
Viking. 1990. 284 pp.

Teenage bisexual Karim Amir must decide if he should regard his home-wrecking father as a wise man or simply another eccentric suburbanite.

Subjects   1970s • Bi-sexuals • British Authors • Culture Clash • First Novels • Immigrants and Refugees • Racism • Sex and Sexuality

Now try   Kureishi's novel *My Beautiful Laundrette* deals with the same issues of British attitudes toward Indian and Pakistani immigrants. Timothy Mo's *Sour Sweet* is also about a man moving to England from a former British colony. *The Buddha of Suburbia* won the Whitbread Award.

L'Heureux, John
The Handmaid of Desire
Soho. 1996. 264 pp.

When mysterious Olga Kominska arrives at an unnamed California university to take a teaching position in the English department, she begins to change the lives of all her colleagues.

2d Appeal   Language   Book Groups 📖

Subjects   Academia • Satirical Fiction • Single Women • Writers and Writing

Now try   Other novels by L'Heureux include *The Shrine at Altamira* and *Comedians*. *Moo* by Jane Smiley, *Pictures from an Institution* by Randall Jarrell, *Changing Places* and *Small World* by David Lodge, *Japanese by Spring* by Ishmael Reed, Alison Lurie's *The War Between the Tates*, James Kaplan's *Pearl's Progress*, and *Straight Man* by Richard Russo are all satirical novels (ranging in tone from the benign to the malicious) about life, love, and campus politics in a college town.

Lamb, Wally
She's Come Undone
Pocket Books. 1992. 465 pp.

While people and events in her life may try to undo her, Dolores Price never comes totally undone, but instead survives each obstacle with perseverance and wit. An Oprah selection.

2d Appeal   Story   Book Groups 📖

Subjects   Coming-of-Age • First Novels • Sexual Abuse

Now try   Lamb is also the author of *I Know This Much Is True*. Dorothy Allison's *Bastard Out of Carolina* has a heroine who has suffered from both abuse and her mother's poor choices in men; she is also, like Dolores Price, someone a reader can care about.

Lattany, Kristin Hunter
Kinfolks
Ballantine Books. 1996. 276 pp.

Now middle aged, two African American mothers examine their uproarious and militant lives during the 1960s, the growth of their children, and a secret about both their pasts.

2d Appeal   Setting

Subjects   1960s • African American Authors • African Americans • Family Relationships • Single Parents • Women's Friendships

Now try   Henry Louis Gates's *Colored People*, an affectionate look at his home town and the people living there, has a similar sense of warmth as Lattany's novel. *Talk Before Sleep* by Elizabeth Berg describes how close friends can help one another through difficult times.

Lawrence, Karen
Springs of Living Water

Villard Books. 1990. 273 pp.

Years after fleeing her small Canadian hometown, Miranda McCune returns to her childhood home to care for her dying father and learns the redemptive quality of love.

Book Groups

Subjects   Canadian Authors • Death and Dying • Family Relationships • Fathers and Daughters • Sisters • Small-Town Life

Now try   Lawrence is also the author of ***The Life of Helen Alone***. David James Duncan's ***The Brothers K*** and Margaret Atwood's ***Surfacing*** both deal with the themes of family, childhood memories, and reconciliation.

Leavitt, Caroline
Living Other Lives

Warner Books. 1995. 327 pp.

When Matt—son, fiancé, and father—dies suddenly, the three women left behind unwillingly discover ways to help one another overcome their grief and rebuild their lives.

Subjects   Death of a Parent • Death of a Spouse • Grief • Road Novels • Stepfamilies

Now try   Leavitt also wrote ***Meeting Rozzy Halfway*** and ***Lifelines***. Lilly, Matt's fiancée, is a fortune-teller; other fortune-telling characters can be found in Anne Tyler's ***Searching for Caleb*** and Marian Thurm's ***The Clairvoyant***. Paul Estaver's ***His Third, Her Second*** is about the problems of blended families.

Lee, Chang-Rae
Native Speaker

Riverhead Books. 1995. 324 pp.

Korean American Henry Park is hired to spy on politician John Kwang at the same time that he is trying to recover from the death of his son and his wife's decision to leave him.

2d Appeal   Language   Book Groups

Subjects   ALA Notable Books • Death of a Child • Fathers and Sons • First Novels • Korean Americans

Now try   Like Lee's novel, both David Mamet's play, "Oleanna," and Eva Hoffman's memoir, ***Lost in Translation***, describe how language shapes our thoughts and behavior. David Carkeet's ***Double Negative*** is a much less serious look at the same topic.

Lee, Gus
China Boy

Dutton. 1991. 322 pp.

In 1950s San Francisco, seven-year-old Kai Ting, only American-born child of a wealthy Shanghai family, finds refuge at the YMCA from various street bullies and his insensitive stepmother as he comes to understand the world clashing around him.

Book Groups

Subjects   1950s • Boxing • California • Chinese American Authors • Chinese Americans • Coming-of-Age • Culture Clash • First Novels • San Francisco

Now try   Lee also wrote *Honor & Duty* and *Tiger's Tail*. The novels of Shawn Wong (*American Knees*) and Gish Jen (*Typical American*) both explore issues of culture, assimilation, and living a hyphenated life. Boxing is a saving grace to the young man who is the main character of Bryce Courtenay's *The Power of One*.

Lee, Helen Elaine
The Serpent's Gift
Atheneum. 1994. 374 pp.

Different ways of coping with life's troubles and appreciating its joys are described in the ways members of the intertwined Small and Staples families respond to events over the course of the twentieth century.

Book Groups 📖

Subjects   African American Authors • African Americans • Family Relationships • First Novels • Multigenerational Novels

Now try   Marita Golden's *Long Distance Life*, Linda Beatrice Brown's *Crossing Over Jordan*, and Calvin Baker's *Naming the New World* are all African American family chronicles. *Serpent's Gift* won the American Library Association Black Caucus's First Novelist award.

Lee, Sky
Disappearing Moon Café
Seal Press. 1991. 237 pp.

After giving birth to her first child, Kae Ying Woo tries to find her own place among four generations of women whose courage and determination help an immigrant Chinese family find a home in Vancouver, Canada.

2d Appeal   Language
Book Groups 📖

Subjects   Canadian Authors • Chinese Canadians • Family Relationships • First Novels • Immigrants and Refugees • Vancouver, Canada

Now try   Wayson Choy's *The Jade Peony* is about the immigrant experience as seen through the eyes of three children growing up in Vancouver's Chinatown. The main character in *The Picture Bride* by Yoshiko Uchida comes to California from Japan to marry a man who has chosen her from her photograph and discovers that her expectations are far different from the reality. Denise Chong's *The Concubine's Children* is a memoir about her mother's difficult role as second wife in Canada, while her father's first wife remained in China.

Leffland, Ella
Rumors of Peace
Harper & Row. 1979. 389 pp.

Suse Hansen comes of age in the years between the bombings of Pearl Harbor and Hiroshima, as she learns to rely on her own judgments about right and wrong.

2d Appeal   Language
Book Groups 📖

Subjects   California • Coming-of-Age • Racism • Teenage Girls • World War II

Now try   Leffland is also the author of *The Knight, Death, and the Devil* and *Mrs. Munck*. Another novel about a girl coming-of-age is Jane Gardam's *Bilgewater*. Cynthia Rylant's poignant novel, *I Had Seen Castles*, is about the coming of age of a teenage boy during World War II.

Lemann, Nancy
The Lives of the Saints
A.A. Knopf. 1985. 143 pp.

Louise's love for Claude Collier is only part of her fascination with his aristocratic and doomed New Orleans family.

2d Appeal   Setting

Subjects   Alcoholics and Alcoholism • Death of a Child • First Novels • Louisiana • Love Stories • New Orleans

Now try   Lemann also wrote *The Fiery Pantheon*. Claude Collier has the sort of anomie that's seen in Binx Bolling in Walker Percy's *The Moviegoer*. Another doomed New Orleans family can be found in *Almost Innocent* by Sheila Bosworth.

Lesley, Craig
Winterkill
Houghton Mifflin. 1984. 306 pp.

Nez Perce cowhand and rodeo rider Danny Kachiah raises his teenage son alone and teaches him native ways while both learn to cope with the vicissitudes of modern life.

2d Appeal   Setting   Book Groups 📖

Subjects   American Indians • Cowboys • Fathers and Sons • First Novels • Nez Perces • Pacific Northwest • Rodeos • Single Parents

Now try   The sequel to *Winterkill* is *Riversong*. Ken Kesey's *Sometimes a Great Notion*, Annie Dillard's *The Living*, and Ivan Doig's *Ride With Me, Mariah Montana* all offer a sense of the character of the Pacific Northwest.

Lessing, Doris
The Fifth Child
Knopf. 1988. 133 pp.

A middle-class English couple find themselves torn between their beliefs about being good parents and their aversion to their frightening, unlovable fifth child.

Book Groups 📖

Subjects   ALA Notable Books • British Authors • Family Relationships • Fathers and Sons • Juvenile Delinquents • Mothers and Sons

Now try   *The Fifth Child* combines themes that Lessing explored in her earlier novels, including *Martha Quest* and *The Golden Notebook*. The parents in *We Were the Mulvaneys* by Joyce Carol Oates have the same sense of smugness about their comfortable and successful life as Lessing's characters do, and tragedy strikes them, too.

Lipman, Elinor
The Way Men Act
Pocket Books. 1992. 305 pp.

Returning to the New England college town where she grew up, Melinda LeBlanc works as a floral arranger, takes up old friendships, and falls in love with a man apparently uninterested in her, all the while trying to live down a high school reputation of being wild and fast.

2d Appeal   Story

Subjects   Friendship • Interracial Relationships • Love Stories • Male/Female Relationships • Small-Town Life • Women's Friendships

Now try   Lipman also wrote *The Inn at Lake Devine* and *Isabel's Bed*. Other novels about the ups and downs of relationships include Ann Hood's *Ruby*, Caroline Preston's *Jackie by Josie* and Susan Trott's *Crane Spreads Wings: A Bigamist's Story*.

Lipsky, David
The Art Fair
Doubleday. 1996. 271 pp.

From adolescence to young manhood, Richard Freeley watches helplessly while his mother's promising painting career comes to a sad end, as she falls out of favor with art dealers and connoisseurs.

Subjects   Art and Artists • First Novels • Mothers and Sons • New York

Now try   Lipsky's first book was *Three Thousand Dollars*, a collection of stories about the 1980s. He also wrote a work of nonfiction, *Late Bloomers—The Coming of Age in America: The Right Place at the Wrong Time*, which focuses on the experiences of 20-somethings at the end of the twentieth century. Another view of the New York art world can be found in Fernanda Eberstadt's *When the Sons of Heaven Meet the Daughters of the Earth*.

Lodge, David
Therapy
Viking. 1995. 320 pp.

As he faces both the breakup of his marriage and growing old, British television sitcom writer Lawrence (Tubby) Passmore becomes increasingly obsessed with the philosopher Kierkegaard and the various therapies with which he has involved himself.

2d Appeal   Story

Subjects   Aging • British Authors • Middle-Aged Men • Midlife Crisis • Writers and Writing

Now try   Lodge enjoys dissecting the absurd in academia (*Small World: An Academic Romance* and *Nice Work*) and in tourism (*Paradise News*). Another man facing a midlife crisis is the protragonist of Piers Paul Read's *A Married Man*.

Lofton, Ramona (Sapphire)
Push
Alfred A. Knopf. 1996. 141 pp.

Claireece Precious Jones, a young illiterate black girl growing up in Harlem, struggles heroically to stay in school, where her teacher, Ms. Rain, helps her find words to express herself and overcome her harsh childhood of poverty and sexual abuse.

2d Appeal   Language   Book Groups 📖

Subjects   African American Authors • African Americans • Coming-of-Age • First Novels • Ghetto Life • Poverty • Sexual Abuse

Now try   Toni Morrison's *The Bluest Eye* is another novel about an African American girl growing up. Susan Sheehan's *Life for Me Ain't Been No Crystal Stair* and Alex Kotlowitz's *There Are No Children Here* are both nonfiction books exploring life in the ghettos of America.

Loh, Sandra Tsing
If You Lived Here, You'd Be Home by Now
Riverhead Books 1997. 231 pp.

For the six years they've been together, 30-somethings Bronwyn Peters and Paul Hoffstead have happily lived a bohemian lifestyle in their dreary house in a dreary and far-distant Los Angeles suburb, until Bronwyn starts yearning for a new kitchen, a new car, and a more upscale life.

2d Appeal   Setting

Subjects   California • First Novels • Humorous Fiction • Los Angeles • Male/Female Relationships • Writers and Writing

Now try   Loh has also written a collection of essays about Los Angeles, *Depth Takes a Holiday*. Two other satirical novels about the wackiness of Los Angeles are Alison Lurie's *The Nowhere City* and Karen Karbo's *The Diamond Lane*.

Lopate, Phillip
The Rug Merchant
Viking. 1987. 218 pp.

Despite a series of momentous events in his life, Cyrus Irani cannot bring himself to tear down the wall of comfortable detachment he has built around himself.

Subjects   ALA Notable Books • Iranian Americans • Middle-Aged Men

Now try   Lopate has written other works of fiction, including *In Coyoacan* and *Confessions of Summer*, but he is also recognized for his essays, including *Bachelorhood: Tales of the Metropolis* and *Portrait of My Body*. Another man who lived a momentous life is the hero of Mark Helprin's *Memoir from Antproof Case*.

Lott, Bret
Jewel
Pocket Books. 1991. 358 pp.

It takes Brenda Kay's mother, Jewel Hilburn, several years after Brenda Kay's birth before she finally understands that there is something wrong with her daughter; when she does, she decides to uproot her family from their rural Mississippi home to move to California so Brenda Kay can attend a school for retarded children. An Oprah selection.

2d Appeal   Language   Book Groups 📖

Subjects   California • Down's Syndrome • Family Relationships • Mental Retardation • Mississippi • Mothers and Daughters

Now try   Lott's other works of fiction include *The Man Who Owned Vermont* and *A Stranger's House*. Susan Straight's *I Been in Sorrow's Kitchen, and Licked out All the Pots* offers another portrait of a strong woman struggling against a world that is largely unsympathetic to her needs.

Lurie, Alison
Foreign Affairs
Random House. 1984. 291 pp.

When spinsterish college professor Vinnie Miner and her colleague, Fred Turner, arrive in London for study and research, they both become involved in foreign affairs that will change their lives.

2d Appeal   Language   Book Groups 📖

Subjects	Adultery • ALA Notable Books • College Professors • Love Affairs • Pulitzer Prize Winners • Single Women
Now try	Lurie's witty and intelligent style can be appreciated in all of her novels, including *The War Between the Tates*, *The Nowhere City*, and *Love and Friendship*. Diane Johnson's *Le Divorce* is another novel about a woman who finds her life changed by her experiences in a foreign country. Some of the same characters who appear in *Foreign Affairs* reappear in Lurie's *The Last Resort*.

MacLaverty, Bernard
Cal
G. Braziller. 1983. 170 pp.

Cal, a Catholic outsider in Protestant Ulster, finds himself falling in love with the widow of the man whom he helped to murder as he tries to break the cycle of violence in Northern Ireland.

2d Appeal	Language
Subjects	ALA Notable Books • Ireland • Male/Female Relationships • Scottish authors • Violence
Now try	MacLaverty's first novel was *Lamb*. Other novels about the partisan violence in Ireland include Tom Phelan's *In the Season of Daisies*, and Deirdre Madden's *One by One in the Darkness*.

Mailer, Norman
The Executioner's Song
Little, Brown. 1979. 1056 pp.

Over the course of nine months, Gary Gilmore kills two men, is convicted of murder, and is sent before the firing squad at a Utah prison in this fictional re-creation of actual events that occurred in the late 1970s.

Subjects	1970s • ALA Notable Books • Crime • Murder • Pulitzer Prize Winners • Utah • Violence
Now try	Among Mailer's other books are *The Naked and the Dead*, *Ancient Evenings*, and *Harlot's Ghost*. *Zombie* by Joyce Carol Oates is another novel that meticulously details the experiences of a killer. Truman Capote's *In Cold Blood* also recounts a gruesome crime. Gary Gilmore's younger brother Mikal wrote *Shot in the Heart*, a memoir of his family, which addresses the possible motivations for his brother's crimes.

Malone, Michael
Foolscap
Little, Brown. 1991. 392 pp.

Theo Ryan, a professor of theater studies, finds his life in turmoil when he becomes the biographer of a hard-living, hard-loving, hard-drinking playwright.

Subjects	Academia • ALA Notable Books • Alcoholics and Alcoholism • College Professors • Humorous Fiction • Male/Female Relationships • North Carolina • Research Novels • Writers and Writing
Now try	Malone's other novels include two character-driven mysteries, *Time's Witness* and *Uncivil Seasons*. His novel *Dingley Falls* is far darker than any of his others. Richard Russo's *Straight Man* shares some of the same exhilarating writing that is found in Malone's novels.

Malone, Michael
Handling Sin
Little, Brown. 1986. 544 pp.

While hurtling down the highway after his eccentric and elderly father, Raleigh Whittier Hayes escapes a motorcycle gang with the help of nuns, outsmarts the Ku Klux Klan, aids an escaped convict, and digs for buried treasure only to discover the riches he's had all along.

Subjects ALA Notable Books • Eccentrics and Eccentricities • Fathers and Sons • Humorous Fiction • Middle-Aged Men • Road Novels • Southern Authors

Now try J. P. Donleavy's *The Ginger Man*, Michael Chabon's *Wonder Boys*, and John Kennedy Toole's *A Confederacy of Dunces* are all fast-moving and humorous novels.

Maraire, J. Nozipo
Zenzele: A Letter to My Daughter
Crown Publishers. 1996. 194 pp.

Through letters to Zenzele, away at school in the United States, a mother in Zimbabwe tries to remind her daughter of the cultural heritage and political struggle that shaped her family's life.

Book Groups 📖

Subjects African Authors • Colonialism • Culture Clash • Epistolary Novels • First Novels • Mothers and Daughters • Zimbabwe • Zimbabwean Authors

Now try Although it is set in South Africa rather than Zimbabwe, J. M. Coetzee's *Life & Times of Michael K* reflects some of the same experiences Zenzele's mother describes.

Marius, Richard
After the War
Knopf. 1992. 621 pp.

Trying to escape the unhappy memories of his World War I experiences, Paul Alexander leaves Europe for Bourbonville, Tennessee, and finds himself enmeshed in the daily lives and passions of the town's diverse inhabitants.

2d Appeal Setting   Book Groups 📖

Subjects Immigrants and Refugees • Race Relations • Small-Town Life • Tennessee • World War I

Now try Marius also wrote *The Coming of Rain*. Other books that effectively convey the horrors of (any) war are Kazuo Ishiguro's *An Artist of the Floating World*, Nora Okja Keller's *Comfort Woman*, and Susan Choi's *The Foreign Student*.

Mark, Jan
Zeno Was Here
Farrar, Straus & Giroux. 1987. 327 pp.

When English teacher John McEvoy receives a novel written by an ex-lover containing a barely disguised and very unflattering portrait of himself, he turns for consolation to Ruth Prochak, an intense and impatient poet.

2d Appeal Language   Book Groups 📖

Subjects Academia • Adultery • College Professors • First Novels • Love Affairs • Writers and Writing

Now try   Mark is also the author of a novel for children, ***Thunder and Lightnings***. Alison Lurie's ***Foreign Affairs*** is a tale of lovers found and lost. Philip Roth's ***My Life as a Man*** and John L'Heureux's ***The Handmaid of Desire*** are both novels about writing novels.

Marshall, Alexandra
Gus in Bronze
Knopf. 1977. 242 pp.

As Augusta fights against the cancer that's taking over her body, her husband, teenage daughters, and baby son all try in their own ways to come to terms with her impending death.

2d Appeal   Story   Book Groups 📖

Subjects   Cancer • Death and Dying • Husbands and Wives • Marriage • Mothers and Daughters

Now try   Marshall's other novels include ***Tender Offer***, ***The Brass Bed***, and ***Something Borrowed***. Women dying of cancer can be found in many novels, including Jessamyn West's ***A Matter of Time*** and ***Open Water*** by Maria Flook. Alice Adams's ***Medicine Men*** is about a woman suffering from cancer and her problems with the medical community.

Marshall, Paule
Daughters
Atheneum. 1991. 408 pp.

Ursa McKenzie, daughter of an American-born mother and a father who is a crusading politician on a fictional Caribbean Island, gains strength from the women in her past and present as she attempts to make a life for herself as a well-educated, good-hearted career woman in New York.

Book Groups 📖

Subjects   African Americans • Career Women • Caribbean • Caribbean Authors • Family Relationships • Fathers and Daughters • Racism • Women's Friendships

Now try   Paule Marshall's other books include ***Brown Girl, Brownstones*** and ***Praisesong for the Widow***. Other novels set in the Caribbean include Jean Buffong's ***Snowflakes in the Sun***, Dionne Brand's ***In Another Place, Not Here***, and Edwidge Danticat's ***The Farming of Bones***.

Martin, Valerie
The Great Divorce
N.A. Talese. 1994. 340 pp.

As zoo veterinarian Ellen tries to figure out the causes of an outbreak of illness among the animals, she must also deal with the fact that her husband has fallen in love with a younger woman.

Subjects   Adultery • Animals • New Orleans • Older Men/Younger Women • Veterinarians • Women's Friendships • Zoos

Now try   Martin's other novels include ***Mary Reilly***, the story of Dr. Jekyll's servant. Another novel with a zoo background is Russell Hoban's ***Turtle Diary***.

Mason, Bobbie Ann
In Country
Harper & Row. 1985. 247 pp.

Seventeen-year-old Sam Hughes spends her days in rural Kentucky trying to understand her father's death in Vietnam and worrying about her uncle, a Vietnam veteran who may be suffering from the effects of Agent Orange.

2d Appeal Language   Book Groups 📖

Subjects Coming-of-Age • First Novels • Kentucky • Southern Authors • Teenage Girls • Vietnam Memorial • Vietnam War

Now try Mason's other books include *Shiloh and Other Stories* and *Spence + Lila*. The emotional and physical devastation caused by the Vietnam War is described in Stewart O'Nan's *The Names of the Dead*. Other novels told from the point of view of an adolescent girl include Jane Austen's *Emma*, *The Death of the Heart* by Elizabeth Bowen, and *A Tree Grows in Brooklyn* by Betty Smith.

Matthiessen, Peter
Killing Mister Watson
Random House. 1990. 372 pp.

Edgar J. Watson moves to the Florida Everglades, where his attempts to become a plantation farmer and family man are overshadowed by rumours of his past and the people he allegedly killed, including Belle Starr, the famed lady outlaw.

Subjects Florida • Murder • Violence

Now try *Lost Man's River* is a sequel to *Killing Mr. Watson*. Matthiessen is a prolific author of both fiction and nonfiction works about the Amazon, the Caribbean, and even Siberia. Other novels filled with violence that are set in Florida include Russell Banks's *Continental Drift* and Pete Dexter's *The Paperboy*.

Maupin, Armistead
Tales of the City
Harper & Row. 1978. 240 pp.

When Mary Ann moves to San Francisco, she becomes immersed in the complicated lives of her new friends, including a marijuana-growing landlady and gay neighbors, as well as in the intrigues at the advertising agency where she works.

Subjects 1970s • Adultery • California • First Novels • Gay Men • Male/Female Relationships • San Francisco • Suicide

Now try This is the first volume in the "Tales of the City" series, followed by *More Tales of the City*, *Further Tales of the City*, *Babycakes*, *Significant Others*, and *Sure of You*. *The Golden Gate: A Novel in Verse* by Vikram Seth also describes the lives of a group of friends living in San Francisco.

Mawer, Simon
Mendel's Dwarf
Harmony Books. 1998. 293 pp.

Dr. Benedict Lambert, a geneticist and a dwarf (as well as a distant relative of Gregor Mendel), finds that his love affair with a shy librarian wreaks disaster in both their lives.

Subjects Adultery • British Authors • Dwarfs • First Novels • Librarians • Love Affairs • Science and Scientists

> **Now try**   The sense of doom that is implicit from the opening pages of this novel is similar to that found in Ian McEwan's *Enduring Love*.

McCall, Dan
Bluebird Canyon
Congdon & Weed. 1983. 373 pp.

Police officer Oliver "Triphammer" Bodley watches with dismay as his old friend Rex Hooker—star of America's most popular soap opera, father of an enchanting little boy, lover of two very different women—self-destructs.

> **Subjects**   Adultery • California • Male/Female Relationships • Men's Friendships
>
> **Now try**   *Beecher* and *Messenger Bird* are two of McCall's other novels. Triphammer and Rex's friendship is similar to the friendship between the main characters in Michael Malone's *Time's Witness* and *Uncivil Seasons*.

McCauley, Stephen
The Easy Way Out
Simon & Schuster. 1992. 298 pp.

Patrick O'Neil's life is madly complicated because his aging parents are driving him crazy, both his brothers are having love problems, his job at Only Connect, a travel agency, is no longer appealing, and he can't quite commit to Arthur, his lover of the past six years.

> **Subjects**   1980s • Aging • Brothers • Family Relationships • Gay Men
>
> **Now try**   McCauley is also the author of *The Man of the House*. Elinor Lipman's *The Inn at Lake Devine* and Mark O'Donnell's *Getting Over Homer* are also novels filled with interesting characters and written in a sprightly style.

McCauley, Stephen
The Object of My Affection
Simon and Schuster. 1987. 316 pp.

The bittersweet relationship between George, a gay kindergarten teacher, and Nina, his pregnant roommate, demonstrates that sometimes love defies categorization.

> **Subjects**   1980s • First Novels • Gay Men • Male/Female Relationships • New York • Single Parents • Teachers
>
> **Now try**   Another novel about a young man taking on the role of father to a baby not his own is Walter Kirn's *She Needed Me*.

McCorkle, Jill
Tending to Virginia
Algonquin Books of Chapel Hill. 1987. 312 pp.

When Virginia Ballard's closest female relations—mother, grandmother, great aunts, and cousin—gather together to help her get through the last weeks of a difficult pregnancy, Virginia uses the time to explore her family's history and bring long-hidden secrets to light.

Book Groups 📖

> **Subjects**   Cousins • Family Relationships • Family Secrets • Marriage • Pregnancy • Southern Authors • Women's Friendships
>
> **Now try**   McCorkle also wrote *The Cheerleader* and *Crash Diet*, a collection of stories. *Charms for the Easy Life* by Kaye Gibbons is also about intergenerational relationships.

McCracken, Elizabeth
The Giant's House

Dial Press. 1996. 259 pp.

Spinster and Cape Cod librarian Peggy Cort finds companionship and love with James Sweatt, a teenage boy who suffers from a growth disorder that eventually makes him the tallest man in the world.

Subjects   Cape Cod, Massachusetts • First Novels • Librarians • Massachusetts • Older Women/Younger Men • Single Women

Now try   McCracken's collection of short stories, *Here's Your Hat, What's Your Hurry* was an ALA Notable Book. *Mrs. Caliban* by Rachel Ingalls is another novel about an unusual relationship. Dianne Highbridge's *A Much Younger Man* is also about the relationship between a young man and an older woman. In 1996, McCracken was also named one of *Granta Magazine's* "20 Best Young American Novelists."

McGahern, John
Amongst Women

Viking. 1990. 184 pp.

The story of two decades in the life of the Moran family, headed by Michael, an angry and aging former IRA officer, whose children alternately fear and love him.

Book Groups

Subjects   Family Relationships • Fathers and Daughters • Fathers and Sons • Ireland • Irish Authors

Now try   Among McGahern's other books are *The Dark*, *Collected Stories*, and *The Leavetaking*. James Hynes's *The Wild Colonial Boy*, Brian Moore's *Lies of Silence*, and *The Promise of Light* by Paul Watkins are also about violence in Ireland.

McGuane, Thomas
Nothing But Blue Skies

Houghton Mifflin. 1992. 349 pp.

Aging hippie Frank Copenhaver discovers that the success of his business empire rests on the foundation of his wife Gracie's love only when her desertion leaves him floundering in a sea of mounting debt, bitter feelings, and senseless affairs.

2d Appeal   Setting

Subjects   Business and Businessmen • Divorce • Male/Female Relationships • Middle-Aged Men

Now try   Most of McGuane's work takes on similar themes of men seeking love, meaning, and redemption in the modern West, as in *The Bushwhacked Piano* and *Nobody's Angel*. Other authors writing about similar subjects include Jim Harrison in *A Good Day to Die*, or any of the books that make up Cormac McCarthy's "Border Trilogy" (*All the Pretty Horses*, *The Crossing*, and *Cities of the Plain*). Another novel with a similar sense of irony and richly evoked setting is Jamie Harrison's *The Edge of the Crazies*, a mystery about a young sheriff in a small Montana town.

McKinney-Whetstone, Diane
Tumbling
W. Morrow. 1996. 340 pp.

Part of a close-knit church community in Philadelphia in the late 1940s, Herbie and Noon succeed in creating a family in spite of their unconsummated marriage.

2d Appeal   Setting   Book Groups 📖

Subjects   1940s • African American Authors • African Americans • Family Relationships • First Novels • Male/Female Relationships • Marriage

Now try   McKinney-Whetstone also wrote *Tempest Rising: A Novel*. A nonfiction account of a contemporary African American church is Samuel G. Freedman's *Upon This Rock: The Miracles of a Black Church*.

McLaurin, Tim
The Last Great Snake Show
G.P. Putnam's Sons. 1997. 224 pp.

An unlikely quartet—Vietnam veteran Clinton Cappy Tucker, snake handler Jubal Lee, exotic dancer Gloria Peacock, and wealthy runaway Kitty Buckstar—escort the dying Miss Darlene from their North Carolina coastal home all the way to Oregon, and along the way, the members of the group face down the missteps of the past that have stunted their lives.

Subjects   Eccentrics and Eccentricities • Friendship • Love Stories • Male/Female Relationships • Racism • Road Novels • Snakes • Southern Authors • Vietnam Veterans

Now try   McLaurin's other novels include *Cured by Fire* and *The Acorn Plan*. He also wrote a memoir, *Keeper of the Moon: A Southern Boyhood*. A nonfiction account of snake-handling in the South is *Salvation on Sand Mountain*, by Dennis Covington. Snakes play a large role in Kathryn Kramer's *Rattlesnake Farming*.

McMillan, Terry
Waiting to Exhale
Viking. 1992. 409 pp.

Close friends Savannah, Robin, Gloria, and Bernadine support and encourage one another as they grapple with their relationships with men, their families, and their identities as African American women.

Book Groups 📖

Subjects   African American Authors • African Americans • Interracial Relationships • Male/Female Relationships • Women's Friendships

Now try   McMillan also wrote *How Stella Got Her Groove Back* and *Disappearing Acts*. Other novels about the dynamics between black men and women includes Omar Tyree's *Single Mom*, Gloria Naylor's *The Women of Brewster Place*, and Ntozake Shange's *For Colored Girls Who've Considered Suicide When the Rainbow Is Enuf*.

McNeal, Tom
Goodnight, Nebraska
Random House. 1998. 314 pp.

After a series of unfortunate events land teenage delinquent Randall Hunsucker in Goodnight, Nebraska, he attempts to pull his life together, with mixed results.

2d Appeal   Story

Subjects   First Novels • Husbands and Wives • Juvenile Delinquents • Nebraska • Small-Town Life • Teenage Love • Teenagers

Now try   Other novels set in small Nebraska towns include *Strange Angels* by Jonis Agee, Jim Harrison's *Dalva*, Willa Cather's *My Antonia*, and Susan Chehak Taylor's *The Story of Annie D*.

Melville, Pauline
The Ventriloquist's Tale
Bloomsbury. 1997. 357 pp.

During the 1919 solar eclipse in Guyana, siblings Beatrice and Danny McKinnon find themselves involved in a passionate affair, an event that will have repercussions in later generations.

Book Groups 📖

Subjects   Brothers and Sisters • Colonialism • Culture Clash • First Novels • Guyana • Incest • Interracial Relationships

Now try   *The Shadow Bride* by Roy Heath is set in Guyana during the same time period as Melville's novel and deals with many of the same issues of colonialism and women's roles. Melville's novel won Britain's Whitbread Prize for First Novels.

Miller, Sue
Family Pictures
Harper & Row. 1990. 389 pp.

With the birth of their third child, an autistic boy, Lainie and David's marriage slowly and inexorably falls apart.

Book Groups 📖

Subjects   ALA Notable Books • Autism • Brothers and Sisters • Dysfunctional Families • Marriage • Mothers and Sons

Now try   Miller's other books include *The Distinguished Guest*, *The Good Mother*, and *For Love*. *Saving St. Germ* by Carol Muske-Dukes is also about the fraying of a marriage because of a child's disability.

Miller, Sue
The Good Mother
Harper & Row. 1986. 310 pp.

Anna's custody of her daughter Molly is threatened when her ex-husband accuses Anna's new lover of sexually abusing the four-year-old.

2d Appeal   Story   Book Groups 📖

Subjects   Child Abuse • Custody Battles • Divorce • Family Relationships • First Novels • Male/Female Relationships • Mothers and Daughters • Sexual Abuse

Now try   *Babel Tower* by A. S. Byatt and *Losing Isaiah* by Seth Margolis are both about bitter custody battles.

Minot, Susan
Monkeys
Dutton. 1986. 159 pp.

The seven Vincent children attempt to understand the intricacies of the adult world as they cope with their depressed and alcoholic father and loving but flighty mother.

2d Appeal   Language   Book Groups 📖

  Subjects   Alcoholics and Alcoholism • Brothers and Sisters • Death of a Parent • Dysfunctional Families • First Novels

  Now try   Among Minot's other books are ***Evening*** and ***Folly***. Another novel with a flighty mother as a central character is Susanna Moore's ***My Old Sweetheart***.

Mitchard, Jacquelyn
The Deep End of the Ocean
Viking. 1996. 434 pp.

When three-year-old Ben disappears, the nine years that pass before the Cappadoras learn what happened take their toll on everyone in Ben's family, including his parents, grandparents, his older brother Vincent (who always blamed himself for Ben's disappearance), and baby sister Kerry, who was too young to remember Ben but knows that the most important family member is missing. An Oprah selection.

2d Appeal   Story   Book Groups 📖

  Subjects   Brothers and Sisters • Family Relationships • First Novels • Kidnapping • Loss of a Child

  Now try   Mitchard's other books include a memoir (***Mother Less Child: The Love Story of a Family***) and a collection of essays (***The Rest of Us***), as well as a novel (***The Most Wanted***). Other novels about the disappearance of a child are Beth Gutcheon's ***Still Missing*** and ***The Odd Sea*** by Frederick Reiken.

Momaday, N. Scott
The Ancient Child
Doubleday. 1989. 313 pp.

Painter Locke Setman returns to his tribal lands for his grandmother's funeral and finds his world changed by Grey, a beautiful medicine woman.

2d Appeal   Language   Book Groups 📖

  Subjects   American Indian Authors • American Indians • Art and Artists • Billy the Kid • Folktales

  Now try   The author won the Pulitzer Prize in 1969 for ***House Made of Dawn***. Other books based on folktales include Vikram Chandra's ***Red Earth and Pouring Rain*** and Diana Darling's ***The Painted Alphabet***.

Monette, Paul
Afterlife
Crown Publishers. 1990. 278 pp.

After a year of mourning the loss of their partners to AIDS, Del, Sonny, and Steven are ready to move forward, each choosing a different path of denial, anger, or hope.

Book Groups 📖

  Subjects   1980s • AIDS • Death and Dying • Family Relationships • Gay Men • Los Angeles

  Now try   Monette's other novels include ***Taking Care of Mrs. Carroll*** and ***Halfway Home***. Nonfiction by Monette includes ***Borrowed Time: An AIDS Memoir*** and ***Becoming***

a Man: Half a Life Story, both of which discuss his life as a gay man and the loss of his partner. Vance Bourjaily's *Old Soldier* explores the relationship between brothers, one of whom is dying from AIDS.

Moore, Susanna
My Old Sweetheart   Houghton Mifflin. 1982. 211 pp.

Lily's childhood in Hawaii is dominated by her mother's mental illness and her father's indifference to his wife and three children.

2d Appeal   Language   Book Groups 📖

   Subjects   Adultery • Fathers and Daughters • First Novels • Hawaii • Mental Illness • Mothers and Daughters

   Now try   Moore followed this novel with *Sleeping Beauty*, *The Whiteness of Bones*, and *In the Cut*. Another daughter taking care of her mentally unstable mother is the main character in Nora Okja Keller's *Comfort Woman*.

Morris, Mary
A Mother's Love   N.A. Talese. 1993. 287 pp.

As she struggles—financially and emotionally—to raise her son Bobby, Ivy lives with the memory of her mother, who left home for good when Ivy was seven, taking Ivy's younger sister with her.

2d Appeal   Language   Book Groups 📖

   Subjects   Mothers and Sons • Mothers Deserting Their Families • Single Parents • Sisters

   Now try   This was reprinted in 1997 under the title *The Night Sky*. Julie Schumacher's novel, *The Body Is Water*, and Gail Godwin's *Father Melancholy's Daughter* both explore the scars left when a mother deserts her children. *Caucasia* by Danzy Senna describes the emotional scarring that occurs when a family breaks up, with the father taking one daughter and leaving the mother with the other daughter.

Morris, Mary McGarry
A Dangerous Woman   Viking. 1991. 358 pp.

A long-time social outcast, novelist-vagabond Martha Horgan finds that her relationship with Colin Mackey confuses and hurts her, but eventually drives her to attempt to take control of her life.

                                                  Book Groups 📖

   Subjects   ALA Notable Books • Sexual Abuse • Small-Town Life • Vermont • Writers and Writing

   Now try   Morris's first novel, *Vanished*, was nominated for the National Book Award and the PEN/Faulkner Award. Like *A Dangerous Woman*, *Vanished* portrays three characters cut off from society whose lives have spiraled out of control. Morris's subsequent novel, *Songs in Ordinary Time*, is about a vulnerable female protagonist who is taken advantage of by an unscrupulous man. *Suspicious River* by Laura Kasischke also details the life of a woman on the fringes of life. Dorothy Allison's *Cavedweller* is the story of an outsider who returns to her hometown and tries to make a place for herself.

Morris, Wright
Plains Song, for Female Voices
Harper & Row. 1980. 229 pp.

On a Nebraska farm, matriarch Lora Atkins presides over a growing family and watches as their meager joys and painful relationships are shaped by her quiet will.

2d Appeal   Setting

Subjects   ALA Notable Books • Family Relationships • Farms and Farm Life • Nebraska • National Book Award Winner

Now try   Morris's other books include *Field of Vision* and *Ceremony in Lone Tree*, as well as *Collected Stories, 1948–1986*. Another novel in which landscape shapes character is James Galvin's *The Meadow*. There is also a resolute farm matriarch in Joan Chase's *During the Reign of the Queen of Persia*. Willa Cather's *My Antonia* is also set in Nebraska.

Mortimer, John
Paradise Postponed
Viking Penguin. 1985. 373 pp.

A surprising bequest in his father's will sends Fred Simcox hunting through his family's past to discover reasons for the Reverend Simcox's odd behavior.

2d Appeal   Story   Book Groups 📖

Subjects   British Authors • Brothers • Death of a Parent • Family Relationships • Family Secrets • Fathers and Sons • Ministers, Priests, and Rabbis

Now try   Among Mortimer's other novels are *Summer's Lease*, *Titmuss Regained* (a sequel to *Paradise Postponed*), and the very funny "Rumpole of the Bailey" series. The exploration of character that is typical of Iris Murdoch's novels (*Under the Net* and *An Accidental Man*, among others) is similar to that found in *Paradise Postponed*. James Agee's *A Death in the Family* is also about a father's death.

Morton, Brian
The Dylanist
HarperCollins. 1991. 312 pp.

Sally Burke is a dylanist—one who puts feelings first—who drifts through high school, college, and most of her 20s, while she searches for what she believes in and most values.

2d Appeal   Story

Subjects   Coming-of-Age • Family Relationships • First Novels • Liberal Politics • Love Stories

Now try   Morton also wrote *Starting Out in the Evening*. *The Saskiad* by Brian Hall is another novel about the coming-of-age of a young woman. Nora Johnson's *A Step Beyond Innocence* is also about a young woman searching for happiness.

Mosby, Katherine
Private Altars
Random House. 1995. 322 pp.

During the 1920s, educated and urbane Vienna Daniels struggles unsuccessfully to become the kind of wife and mother that both her husband and the citizens of Winsville, West Virginia, expect.

Book Groups 📖

Subjects   1920s • First Novels • Husbands and Wives • Small-Town Life • Southern Authors • West Virginia

Now try   Mosby also wrote *The Book of Uncommon Prayer*, a collection of poetry. Anne Michaels (*Fugitive Pieces*) is another poet with a beautifully written novel. Another novel about a woman's struggle to be herself is Kate Chopin's *The Awakening*.

Mosher, Howard Frank
Northern Borders
Doubleday. 1994. 291 pp.

In 1948, six-year-old Austen Kittredge spends the summer on his grandparents' farm near the Vermont-Canada border; over the next 12 years, he soaks up the ongoing history of family and friends.

2d Appeal   Setting

Subjects   Coming-of-Age • Family Relationships • Grandparents • Marriage • Small-Town Life • Vermont

Now try   Mosher's other works of fiction include *A Stranger in the Kingdom* and *Where the Rivers Flow North*. The love of the land that is so clear in Mosher's novel can also be seen in Chris Bohjalian's *Water Witches* and John Thorndike's *The Potato Baron*. Austen's grandparents' marriage is known locally as the "40 years' war"; similar marriages can be found in Walter Sullivan's *A Time to Dance* and Lawrence Naumoff's *The Night of the Weeping Women*.

Muller, Herta
The Land of Green Plums
Metropolitan Books. 1996. 242 pp.

During Ceausescu's terrorist regime in Romania, a young unnamed narrator tries to survive with her ideals intact in the face of betrayal, lies, and constant fear. Translated from the Romanian by Michael Hofmann.

2d Appeal   Setting   Book Groups 📖

Subjects   Communism • Friendship • Novels in Translation • Political Fiction • Romania

Now try   Norman Manea's *The Black Envelope*, *The Year of the Frog* by Martin Simecka, and *Under the Frog* by Tibor Fischer are all political novels set in Eastern Europe. Human rights abuses are chillingly related in Omar Rivabella's *Requiem for a Woman's Soul*, set not in Eastern Europe, but in Latin America. Muller's novel won the IMPAC/Dublin award in 1998.

Muske-Dukes, Carol
Saving St. Germ
Viking. 1993. 292 pp.

The disagreement biochemist Esme Charbonneau has with her husband Jay over Olivia, their possibly autistic, possibly brilliant preschool-age daughter, leads to a bitter custody fight and, for Esme, a reassessment of her own past.

2d Appeal   Story   Book Groups 📖

Subjects   Autism • Custody Battles • First Novels • Gifted Children • Mothers and Daughters • Science and Scientists • Women Scientists

Now try   Carol-Muske Dukes is also a poet, writing under the name Carol Muske. *Family Pictures* by Sue Miller shows how an autistic child can affect family relationships. Bitter custody battles are the basis of Sue Miller's *The Good Mother* and Seth Margolis's *Losing Isaiah*. Another emotionally disturbed child is the main character in Elizabeth Shepard's *H*.

Naylor, Gloria
Bailey's Café
Harcourt Brace Jovanovich. 1992. 229 pp.

A small restaurant caters to a varied group of outcasts, misfits, and the walking wounded, each with a different and difficult story to tell.

2d Appeal   Language   Book Groups 📖

Subjects   1940s • African American Authors • African Americans • ALA Notable Books • Cafes and Restaurants • Magic Realism

Now try   Naylor also wrote *The Men of Brewster Place* and *Linden Hills*. Gita Mehta's *A River Sutra* also uses the technique of having many characters tell their individual stories. Alice Hoffman's *Turtle Moon* has a hint of magic realism. Other novels in which a café functions as part of the plot include Carson McCullers's *The Ballad of the Sad Café*, Fannie Flagg's *Fried Green Tomatoes at the Whistle-Stop Café*, *Midnight Sandwiches at the Mariposa Express* by Beatriz Rivera, and *Buster Midnight's Café* by Sandra Dallas. *The Serpent's Gift* by Helen Elaine Lee and *Tumbling* by Diane McKinney-Whetstone are other portraits of African American community life.

Naylor, Gloria
Mama Day
Ticknor & Fields. 1988. 312 pp.

Mama Day, the matriarch of an African American family long resident on Willow Springs, an island off the Georgia/South Carolina coasts, calls on all her powers of traditional healing to save her great-niece Cocoa, now married to George, an outsider from the North.

2d Appeal   Setting   Book Groups 📖

Subjects   African American Authors • ALA Notable Books • Family Relationships • Georgia • Husbands and Wives • Small-Town Life • Voodoo

Now try   Another novel set in the same locale as *Mama Day* is Pat Conroy's *The Prince of Tides*. Kaye Gibbons, in her novel *Charms for the Easy Life*, has created a strong woman character who is as eager as Mama Day to help one of her young relatives. Alice Hoffman's *Practical Magic* is about two aunts who teach their nieces how to use magic in their lives.

Ng, Fae Myenne
Bone
Hyperion. 1993. 193 pp.

Weaving through time and memory, Leila tries to make sense of her sister's suicide, the history of her family in San Francisco's Chinatown, and her own heart.

2d Appeal   Language   Book Groups 📖

Subjects   California • Chinese American Authors • Chinese Americans • Family Relationships • First Novels • San Francisco • Sisters • Suicide

Now try   Wayson Choy in *The Jade Peony* and Amy Tan in *The Joy Luck Club* write about growing up in Chinese communities in Canada and the United States, respectively. In *The Virgin Suicides* by Jeffrey Eugenides, a group of middle-aged men look back on, and try to comprehend, the reasons for the suicides of a group of sisters. In 1996, *Granta Magazine* named Ng one of the "20 Best Young American Novelists."

Nichols, John
A Ghost in the Music
Holt, Rinehart and Winston. 1979. 230 pp.

Marcel Thompson meets (as if for the first time) his hedonistic, risk-greedy father—a Harvard-educated Hollywood stuntman—who is scheduled to make a suicidal leap for his latest movie.

2d Appeal   Characters   Book Groups

Subjects Fathers and Sons • Hollywood • Motion Picture Industry

Now try Nichols's other novels include *The Sterile Cuckoo* and *The Wizard of Loneliness*. Michael Malone's *Handling Sin* and Richard Russo's *The Risk Pool* both describe relationships between fathers and sons. Other novels about the motion picture industry include Steve Tesich's *Karoo*, Budd Schulberg's *What Makes Sammy Run*, and Michael Tolkin's *The Player*.

Nicholson, Joy
The Tribes of Palos Verdes
St. Martin's Press. 1997. 218 pp.

As her parents' marriage dissolves in bitterness and anger and her twin brother starts using drugs on a regular basis, Medina learns to surf in the Pacific Ocean; her growing ability to conquer the waves contrasts sharply with her inability to put her life and family back together.

Subjects Brothers and Sisters • California • Dysfunctional Families • Family Relationships • First Novels • Suicide • Surfing • Teenage Boys • Teenage Girls • Twins

Now try Another close relationship between a mother and a son is described in Howard Norman's *The Bird Artist*. Kem Nunn's *Tapping the Source* and Daniel Duane's *Looking for Mo* are both novels about surfing. *I Know This Much Is True* by Wally Lamb and Nora Johnson's *The Two of Us* are both about sets of twins.

Nordan, Lewis
The Sharpshooter Blues
Algonquin Books of Chapel Hill. 1995. 291 pp.

When the two lovely children who try to rob the William Tell Grocery in the Mississippi delta town of Arrow Catcher get shot and killed in the process, sweet and simple Hydro Raney decides to remove himself from the pain of it all.

2d Appeal   Language   Book Groups

Subjects ALA Notable Books • Black Humor • Fathers and Sons • Mississippi • Murder • Southern Authors • Violence

Now try Nordan's other books include *Lightning Song* and *Wolf Whistle*. Other novelists who mix tragic and comic elements in their novels include Pat Conroy in *The Prince of Tides* and Steve Tesich in *Karoo*.

Oates, Joyce Carol
Unholy Loves
Vanguard Press. 1979. 335 pp.

During an academic year marked by the arrival of a doddering but distinguished poet as a visiting faculty member, the novelist and college teacher Brigit Stott has a final passionate and sobering affair with a fellow professor.

Book Groups 📖

Subjects   Academia • ALA Notable Books • College Professors • Love Affairs • Music and Musicians • Satirical Fiction • Writers and Writing

Now try   Among Oates's many other works of fiction are *them* (an ALA Notable Book), *Wonderland, Do With Me What You Will, The Assassins: A Book of Hours*, and *Son of the Morning*. Another novel about a visiting professor who shakes up an English department is John L'Heureux's *The Handmaid of Desire*.

O'Donnell, Mark
Getting Over Homer
Knopf. 1996. 193 pp.

Gay New York transplant Blue Monahan valiantly tries to chart the stormy seas of family ties and the definition of masculinity as he recovers from two confusing love affairs.

Subjects   Coming-of-Age • First Novels • Gay Men • Humorous Fiction • Love Affairs

Now try   O'Donnell has also written two collections of short stories, *Vertigo Park* and *Elementary Education*, and a novel, *Let Nothing You Dismay*. O'Donnell shares with Stephen McCauley's *The Easy Way Out* both mismatched (male) lovers and a humorously poignant writing style.

O'Hehir, Diana
I Wish This War Were Over
Atheneum. 1984. 278 pp.

While on a cross-country train trip during World War II to visit her mother, 19-year-old Helen Reynolds falls in love with Lt. John O'Connell, her mother's former lover.

2d Appeal   Story

Subjects   1940s • Alcoholics and Alcoholism • First Novels • Love Stories • Mothers and Daughters • Older Men/Younger Women

Now try   O'Hehir also wrote the novel *The Bride Who Ran Away*, as well as collections of poetry (*The Power to Change Geography* and *Home Free*). Other daughters who feel responsible for their mothers can be found in Mona Simpson's *Anywhere But Here*, Kaye Starbird's *The Lion in the Lei Shop*, and Susanna Moore's *My Old Sweetheart*.

O'Nan, Stewart
Snow Angels
Doubleday. 1994. 305 pp.

In 1974, in western Pennsylvania, 15-year-old Arthur Parkinson faces two tragedies: the end of his parents' marriage and the murder of his beloved childhood babysitter.

2d Appeal   Story

Book Groups 📖

Subjects   ALA Notable Books • Coming-of-Age • Divorce • First Novels • Murder • Pennsylvania • Teenage Boys

Now try   *Hotel Paradise* by Martha Grimes is another novel in which a crime pro-
pels the coming-of-age of the main character. In William Maxwell's *So
Long, See You Tomorrow*, a young man tries to understand the deaths of
three people close to him. In 1996, *Granta Magazine* named O'Nan one
of the "20 Best Young American Novelists."

Otto, Whitney
How to Make an American Quilt
Villard Books. 1991. 179 pp.

As eight women get together in a small California town to create an intricate
quilt, they also bring together the experiences that have wounded and healed them.

2d Appeal   Language   Book Groups 📖

Subjects   California • First Novels • Interracial Relationships • Quilting • Sisters •
Small-Town Life • Women's Friendships

Now try   Otto's other books include *The Passion Dream Book* and *Now You See
Her*. Other novels about quilting include Carol Shields's *Happenstance*
and Sandra Dallas's *The Persian Pickle Club*.

Oz, Amos
Black Box
Harcourt Brace Jovanovich. 1988. 259 pp.

The letters between an Israeli housewife and her ex-husband (now living in the
United States) begin by focusing on their troubled son, but quickly move into an exploration of why their relationship failed a decade before. Translated from the Hebrew
by Nicholas de Lange.

Book Groups 📖

Subjects   Adultery • Arab-Israeli Conflicts • Epistolary Novels • Israeli Authors •
Male/Female Relationships • Marriage • Novels in Translation

Now try   Oz's other novels include *Don't Call It Night*, *Fima*, and *Panther in the
Basement*. Hanan al-Shayk's *Beirut Blues* offers an Arab view of the
conflict between the Arabs and Israelis.

Pall, Ellen
Among the Ginzburgs
Zoland Books. 1996. 245 pp.

Thirty years after deserting his wife and five children, Meyer Ginzburg returns
to the family home to die, and his presence brings up issues of the past that have long
been suppressed.

Subjects   Brothers and Sisters • Death of a Parent • Family Relationships • First
Novels

Now try   Pall's first novel was *Back East*. The return of another wandering father
and its effect on his children can also be found in Judith Rossner's *Nine
Months in the Life of an Old Maid*. In some respects—their snappy dialogue, the interwined relationships—the Ginzburg children resemble the
Glass family in J. D. Salinger's *Raise High the Roof Beam, Carpenters*
and *Seymour: An Introduction*.

Parker, Michael
Hello Down There
Scribner. 1993. 273 pp.

When aristocratic Edwin Keane meets Eureka Speight, he believes his love for her can overcome both their difference in class and his inability to conquer his addiction to morphine.

2d Appeal Language

Subjects Drugs and Drug Abuse • Family Relationships • First Novels • Love Stories • Male/Female Relationships • Small-Town Life • Southern Authors

Now try Nancy Lemann's *The Lives of the Saints* is another exploration of the importance of class distinctions in Southern culture.

Parks, Tim
Goodness
Grove Weidenfeld. 1991. 185 pp.

Son of a murdered missionary and a mother who is an incurable optimist, George's attempt to escape his family and live a good life is challenged by his wife's unhappiness, which is exacerbated by the birth of their profoundly deformed and retarded daughter.

Book Groups 📖

Subjects Adultery • ALA Notable Books • Black Humor • British Authors • Husbands and Wives • Mental Retardation • Physical Disabilities

Now try Parks's other novels include *Tongues of Flame* (about the difficult life of an Anglican vicar), *Family Planning* (about a group of family members overly preoccupied with their own problems), and *Loving Roger* (about love and murder). In *Lucky Jim*, Kingsley Amis shares Parks's world view.

Patchett, Ann
The Magician's Assistant
Harcourt Brace. 1997. 359 pp.

When her magician husband dies unexpectedly of an aneurism, 41-year-old Sabine discovers he had a family and a tumultuous past that he never shared with her.

Book Groups 📖

Subjects Death of a Spouse • Family Relationships • Wives of Gay Men

Now try Another of Patchett's novels is *Taft*. Like Patchett's novel, *If Morning Ever Comes* by Anne Tyler and Alice Hoffman's *Fortune's Daughter* also have interesting plots and a fine use of language. Paul Theroux's *Millroy the Magician* shares Patchett's subject matter.

Patchett, Ann
The Patron Saint of Liars
Houghton Mifflin. 1992. 336 pp.

Rose embarks on a life filled with lies after she deserts her husband and ends up in a home for unwed mothers.

2d Appeal Story   Book Groups 📖

Subjects ALA Notable Books • First Novels • Kentucky • Male/Female Relationships • Nuns • Single Parents

Now try *The Sweetheart Season* by Karen Joy Fowler is another novel that raises the question of whether the narrator is reliable in the story she tells. Susan Pope's *Catching the Light* is also about a single mother keeping her baby.

Pears, Tim

In the Place of Fallen Leaves

D.I. Fine. 1995. 310 pp.

During one hot, dry summer in Devonshire, England, 13-year-old Alison Freemantle listens to the stories her grandmother tells about relatives and neighbors and explores a friendship with a local boy.

2d Appeal   Setting   Book Groups 📖

   Subjects   British Authors • Coming-of-Age • Devonshire, England • England • Family Relationships • First Novels • Grandparents

   Now try   Pears is also the author of ***In the Land of Plenty***. Alison's grandmother in this novel displays the same strength of character as the grandmother in Kaye Gibbons's ***Charms for the Easy Life***. D. E. Stevenson's novel, ***Music in the Hills***, is also about sheep farming in Britain.

Peck, Dale

The Law of Enclosures

Farrar, Straus, Giroux. 1996. 306 pp.

The 40 years of Beatrice and Henry's difficult relationship, from the time they meet, through their marriage and beyond to old age, are seen through different viewpoints offering differing versions of the same events.

   Subjects   Dysfunctional Families • Marriage • Postmodern Fiction

   Now try   Peck's other novels include ***Martin and John*** (about the lives of gay men during the AIDS epidemic) and ***Now It's Time to Say Goodbye*** (about two New Yorkers who arrive in Galatea, Kansas, and discover its violence and bigotry). Another portrait of a difficult marriage is found in Lawrence Naumoff's ***The Night of the Weeping Women***.

Peery, Janet

The River Beyond the World

Picador. 1996. 286 pp.

Over the years, family, losses, and mutual misunderstanding bind together two very different women—Eddie, a bitter and unhappy farmer's wife, and Luisa, her Mexican immigrant maid—in a Texas bordertown.

2d Appeal   Language   Book Groups 📖

   Subjects   Family Relationships • First Novels • Male/Female Relationships • Race Relations • Small-Town Life • Texas • Women's Friendships

   Now try   This book was a finalist for the National Book Award. Peery also wrote a collection of short stories, ***Alligator Dance***. Other books with a southwest setting include Barbara Kingsolver's ***Pigs in Heaven***, Linda Hogan's ***Solar Storms***, and Demetria Martinez's ***Mother Tongue***. Ellen Douglas's ***Can't Quit You, Baby*** both concerns the relationship between a white woman and her black servant.

Pei, Lowry
Family Resemblances
Random House. 1986. 264 pp.

Trying to separate 15-year-old Karen from her boyfriend, her parents send Karen to spend the summer with an eccentric aunt; there, ironically, Karen discovers driving, drinking, sex, and the disillusionments of growing up.

2d Appeal Story
Book Groups 📖

Subjects Adultery • Coming-of-Age • Eccentrics and Eccentricities • Family Relationships • First Novels • Teenage Girls • Teenage Love

Now try Herman Raucher's *Summer of '42* and Alice McDermott's *That Night* share themes with Pei's novel. Mary Rockcastle's *Rainy Lake* and Ellen Akins's *Home Movie* are two other novels about teenagers coming of age. In Marilynne Robinson's *Housekeeping* an eccentric aunt takes on the job of rearing her nieces.

Pelletier, Cathie
The Funeral Makers
Macmillan. 1986. 247 pp.

The isolated hamlet of Mattagash, Maine, forms the backdrop for this hilarious, yet heartbreaking, tale of the McKinnons, eccentric descendants of the town's founders.

2d Appeal Setting

Subjects Eccentrics and Eccentricities • Family Relationships • First Novels • Humorous Fiction • Maine • Small-Town Life

Now try Pelletier wrote several books about Mattagash, Maine, including the sequels to this novel: *Once Upon a Time on the Banks* and *The Weight of Winter*. Other books with a fine sense of place are Howard Norman's *The Bird Artist*, E. Annie Proulx's *The Shipping News*, Carolyn Chute's *The Beans of Egypt*, *Maine*, and Erskine Caldwell's *God's Little Acre* and *Tobacco Road*. Michael Malone's *Handling Sin* and Mark Childress's *Crazy in Alabama* both display the wacky humor found in Pelletier's novel.

Percy, Walker
The Second Coming
Farrar, Straus, Giroux. 1980. 360 pp.

Millionaire Will Barrett, despondent following the death of his philanthropic wife, finds himself embracing life for a second try after he encounters a confused young woman who has just escaped from a local sanitarium.

2d Appeal Language
Book Groups 📖

Subjects ALA Notable Books • Death and Dying • Death of a Spouse • Mental Illness • Older Men/Younger Women • Religion • Southern Authors • Suicide

Now try Percy won the National Book Award for his first novel, *The Moviegoer*. He introduced Will Barrett in *The Last Gentleman*. Percy's novels *Lancelot* and *Love in the Ruins* were both ALA Notable Books. *Hello Down There* by Michael Parker exhibits the same smooth writing style as do Percy's books.

Perrotta, Tom
The Wishbones 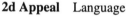 G.P. Putnam's Sons. 1997. 290 pp.

When 31-year-old guitar-playing, wedding band member Dave Raymond pops the question to the woman he's been dating—on and off—for the the last 15 years, he discovers just how ambivalent about marriage he is.

2d Appeal Story

Subjects 1990s • ALA Notable Books • First Novels • Humorous Fiction • Love Stories • Male/Female Relationships • Music and Musicians

Now try Perrotta's other books are a collection of short stories, ***Bad Haircut: Stories of the 70s***, and ***Election: A Novel***. Richard Russo's ***Straight Man*** has the same laugh-out-loud quality as this novel. ***Jack Frusciante Has Left the Band*** by Enrico Brizzi and ***The Commitments*** by Roddy Doyle are both entertaining novels about love and rock and roll.

Pesetsky, Bette
Author from a Savage People  Knopf. 1983. 197 pp.

May Alto, beset by aging parents, life as a single mother, and the difficulty of eking out a living as a ghostwriter in New York, reaches a breaking point when she learns that one of her clients has won the Nobel Prize for a book actually written by May.

2d Appeal Language

Subjects First Novels • Humorous Fiction • New York • Single Parents • Writers and Writing

Now try Among Pesetsky's other novels are ***Midnight Sweets*** and ***Cast a Spell***. Grace Paley's ***Collected Stories*** are written in a similar elliptical style and are also set in New York. Muriel Spark's ***A Far Cry from Kensington*** has a main character somewhat similar to May Alto (although she's British and lives several decades before May does).

Phillips, Jayne Anne
Machine Dreams Dutton. 1984. 331 pp.

Wars, family problems, work, and love shape the Hampsons into strong, independent people who face life with courage and humor.

2d Appeal Language Book Groups 📖

Subjects ALA Notable Books • Brothers and Sisters • Family Relationships • First Novels • Male/Female Relationships • Vietnam War • World War II

Now try Among Phillips's other books are ***Shelter*** and ***Black Tickets***. Other books about the Vietnam War's effect on families include David James Duncan's ***The Brothers K*** and Bobbie Ann Mason's ***In Country***. Phillips's spare use of language is similar to Ann Beattie's novel ***Chilly Scenes of Winter***.

Phillips, Jayne Anne
Shelter
Houghton Mifflin. 1994. 279 pp.

In a West Virginia girls' camp in 1963, sisters Lenny and Alma become aware of the plight of their new friend Buddy, the abused son of the camp cook.

2d Appeal   Language   Book Groups 📖

Subjects   1960s • Appalachia • Child Abuse • Coming-of-Age • Good vs. Evil • Sisters • West Virginia

Now try   Jayne Anne Phillips is also the author of ***Machine Dreams***. The sense of evil in ***Shelter***—of adults menacing children—can also be found in Robert McCammon's ***Boy's Life***.

Phillips, Kate
White Rabbit
Houghton Mifflin Co. 1996. 212 pp.

Indomitable even at 88 years of age, Ruth Hubble spends what will be the last day of her life reconsidering her two marriages and the man she loved.

Book Groups 📖

Subjects   Death and Dying • Elderly Women • First Novels • Male/Female Relationships • Marriage

Now try   Cees Nooteboom's ***The Following Story*** is about the last two seconds of a man's life. James Joyce's ***Ulysses*** is probably the best known novel that takes place over the course of one day. Elizabeth Taylor's ***Mrs. Palfrey at the Claremont*** is another moving novel about aging.

Pinckney, Darryl
High Cotton
Farrar Straus Giroux. 1992. 309 pp.

From his childhood in Indianapolis to college in New York and life as an expatriate in Paris, the African American protagonist tries to understand the nature of being black in the 1960s.

2d Appeal   Language   Book Groups 📖

Subjects   1960s • African American Authors • African Americans • First Novels • France • New York • Upper Classes • Writers and Writing

Now try   Like the protagonist of ***High Cotton***, James Baldwin (***Go Tell It on the Mountain***) moved to Paris and continued writing his novels there. The hero's family in ***High Cotton*** are members of the black upper class, much like the characters in Dorothy West's ***The Wedding***.

Pineda, Cecile
Face
Viking. 1985. 194 pp.

After he is disfigured in a fall from a cliff, Helio Cara must find a way to rebuild both his life and his face.

Book Groups 📖

Subjects   Disfigurement • First Novels • Male/Female Relationships • Physical Disabilities

Now try   Pineda's other works of fiction include ***The Love Queen of the Amazon*** and ***Frieze***. Other books about physical disabilities include Jon Cohen's ***The Man in the Window***, Sara Maitland's ***Ancestral Truths***, and Isabelle Holland's ***The Man Without a Face***.

Plante, David
The Country
Atheneum. 1981. 159 pp.

Returning to his family home, Daniel finds that he and his brothers must contend with their aging parents and the eventual death of their father.

2d Appeal Characters   Book Groups 📖

   Subjects Aging • ALA Notable Books • British Authors • Brothers • Death of a Parent • Family Relationships • Fathers and Sons

   Now try This is the middle novel in a trilogy called "The Francoeur Novels," preceded by *The Family* and followed by *The Woods*. Plante also wrote *Difficult Women: A Memoir of Three* about his friendships with Jean Rhys, Germaine Greer, and Sonia Orwell. Other difficult relationships among brothers are described in David James Duncan's *The Brothers K*, Donald Antrim's *The Hundred Brothers*, Martin Amis's *Success*, and Jonis Agee's *Strange Angels*.

Plesko, Les
The Last Bongo Sunset
Simon & Schuster. 1995. 269 pp.

College leaves his middle-class existence in Boston for Venice, California, where he meets Gary and Cassandra, who sell sex to support their drug habit; not until College befriends homeless 13-year-old Maria is he able to put his life back together.

   Subjects 1970s • California • Death of a Parent • Drugs and Drug Abuse • First Novels • Homelessness • Hungarian Revolution • Venice, California

   Now try James Fogle's *Drugstore Cowboy* also graphically describes the effects of drug addiction. Nelson Algren's *The Man with the Golden Arm* is a National Book Award-winning novel about drug addicts.

Porter, Connie
All-Bright Court
Houghton Mifflin. 1991. 224 pp.

The harsh realities of life—over two decades—confront the Taylor family after the promise of jobs and opportunity has drawn them from Mississippi north to a housing development adjacent to the mills outside Buffalo, New York.

2d Appeal Setting   Book Groups 📖

   Subjects African American Authors • African Americans • ALA Notable Books • Buffalo, New York • Family Relationships • First Novels • Housing Projects

   Now try The attitudes of Porter's black characters to whites is similar to the attitudes seen in Toni Morrison's characters in *Paradise*. Morrison's *Jazz* is also about African Americans who migrated north for a better life.

Potok, Chaim
Davita's Harp
Knopf. 1985. 371 pp.

As Davita leaves her childhood behind, she must reconcile her growing attraction to Orthodox Judaism with the Marxism of her parents.

Book Groups 📖

   Subjects 1930s • Coming-of-Age • Communism • Jews and Judaism

Now try   Potok's *My Name Is Asher Lev* and *The Promise* are about young men whose lives inevitably (and with much conflict) take them away from their ultra-religious Jewish roots. *Hilda and Pearl* by Alice Mattison is a novel about American communists told from the point of view of Frances, Hilda's pre-adolescent daughter. Pearl Abraham's *The Romance Reader* is about a young woman chafing against her Orthodox Jewish upbringing.

Poverman, C. E.
Solomon's Daughter
Viking Press. 1981. 268 pp.

After Rose Solomon almost loses her life in a car accident and ends up immobile in the hospital, her parents and brother find their memories of Rose's troubled adolescence and the deep strains her behavior put on the family flooding back.

Subjects   Car Accidents • Emotional Disability • Family Relationships • Fathers and Daughters • Mothers and Daughters

Now try   Poverman's other books include a collection of stories, *The Black Velvet Girl*, and a novel, *Susan*. Russell Banks (*The Sweet Hereafter*) and Rosellen Brown (*Tender Mercies*) both explore the effect a serious accident has on family dynamics. Joanne Greenberg's novel, *I Never Promised You a Rose Garden*, describes how an emotionally disturbed teenager can strain family relationships. Life with a mentally ill sibling is graphically described in Laurie Fox's first novel, *My Sister from the Black Lagoon*.

Powell, Padgett
Edisto
Farrar, Straus, Giroux. 1983. 183 pp.

Growing up in an unorthodox South Carolina family, teenager Simons Everson Manigault learns from his friend and babysitter, Taurus, how to fully observe life without any limiting expectations.

Subjects   ALA Notable Books • Coming-of-Age • First Novels • Friendship • South Carolina • Southern Authors • Teenage Boys

Now try   Powell's other books include *A Woman Named Drown*, *Aliens of Affection: Stories*, and *Edisto Revisited*, the sequel to *Edisto*. Other coming-of-age novels include Eli Gottlieb's *The Boy Who Went Away* and Jane Gardam's *A Long Way from Verona*, about a young woman whose greatest desire is to grow up to be a writer.

Price, Reynolds
Kate Vaiden
Atheneum. 1986. 306 pp.

Kate Vaiden narrates the story of her own life, proud that she has survived the difficulties that threatened to destroy her.

Book Groups 📖

Subjects   ALA Notable Books • Elderly Women • National Book Critics Circle Award Winners • Southern Authors • Women's Lives

Now try   Price's other books include *Roxanna Slade* (also told in the voice of an elderly woman), *Blue Calhoun*, *A Long and Happy Life* (also an ALA Notable Book), and *The, Promise, of, Rest*. Price's *A Whole New Life*, also an ALA Notable Book, relates his struggle with cancer of the spine. Other novels exploring the relationship between mothers and sons are Rachel Billington's *The Garish Day* and *Elvis Presley Calls His Mother After the Ed Sullivan Show* by Samuel Charters. Carol Shields's *The Stone Diaries* and Mary Lee Settle's *Celebration* both explore women's lives.

Price, Richard
Clockers
Houghton Mifflin. 1992. 599 pp.

The lives of charismatic Strike, a weak-willed crack cocaine dealer, and Rocco, an alcoholic homicide detective, collide in a decayed inner-city housing project.

2d Appeal   Setting   Book Groups 📖

Subjects   Alcoholics and Alcoholism • Drugs and Drug Abuse • Housing Projects • Policemen • Violence

Now try   Among Price's other novels are *Freedomland* (about what follows when a white woman tells police that a black man hijacked her car with her young child in the back seat) and *The Wanderers* (about a 1960s teenage gang in the Bronx). The characters found in Katherine Dunn's *Geek Love* are also isolated from mainstream life, although for very different reasons. Price's gritty realism is also found in Theodore Weesner's *The True Detective*.

Prose, Francine
Hunters and Gatherers
Farrar, Straus, and Giroux. 1995. 247 pp.

After she loses her job as a magazine fact checker, Martha rescues Isis Moonwagon from drowning and joins Isis's group of goddess worshippers as they travel from New York to Arizona.

2d Appeal   Language, Story

Subjects   Arizona • Goddess Worship • Satirical Fiction • Single Women • Women's Friendships

Now try   Prose is also the author of *Bigfoot Dreams*, a satirical look at tabloid journalism, and *Guided Tours of Hell*. Prose's satirical take on feminism and feminists is similar to Blanche McCrary Boyd's *Terminal Velocity*. Norman Rush's *Mating* is also a satirical look at a matriarchal society. The theme of goddess worship (in this case, a pre-Columbian statue of a woman) is found in Peter Gadol's *Mystery Roast*.

Pym, Barbara
The Sweet Dove Died
Dutton. 1979. 208 pp.

When wealthy, middle-aged spinster Leonore Eyre becomes acquainted with an antique dealer and his nephew at a book auction in London, she ignores the uncle's growing affection for her and instead attaches herself to the young man.

Subjects   British Authors • Gay Men • Male/Female Relationships • Older Women/Younger Men • Single Women

Now try   Pym's other novels include *Less Than Angels*, *No Fond Return of Love*, and *Some Tame Gazelle*. Her novel *Quartet in Autumn* won the Booker Prize. Another, much tarter look at the English can be found in Nancy Mitford's *Don't Tell Alfred* and *Love in a Cold Climate*.

Quindlen, Anna
Object Lessons
Random House. 1991. 262 pp.

In 1960s Westchester County, New York, 13-year-old Maggie Scanlan chooses her future after her large Irish Catholic family is buffeted by a series of tragedies.

2d Appeal Story   Book Groups 📖

Subjects 1960s • Coming-of-Age • Family Relationships • First Novels • New York • Suburbia • Teenage Girls

Now try Quindlen's other novels include *Black and Blue*, *One True Thing*, and *Living Out Loud*, a collection of her syndicated newspaper columns. Carol Ascher's *The Flood*, Elizabeth Benedict's *The Beginner's Book of Dreams*, and Colette's *Claudine and Annie* are all about the coming-of-age of young girls.

Raymo, Chet
The Dork of Cork
Warner Books. 1993. 354 pp.

Frank Bois, 43 inches tall and 43 years old, finds his life changed forever when he writes an unexpected best-selling book about the night sky.

2d Appeal Language   Book Groups 📖

Subjects Dwarfs • Loneliness • Love Stories • Middle-Aged Men • Mothers and Sons

Now try Other novels with dwarfs include Ursula Hegi's *Stones from the River*, Armistead Maupin's *Maybe the Moon*, *Mendel's Dwarf* by Simon Mawer, and *The Tin Drum* by Gunter Grass. Other novels as sweet as *The Dork of Cork* are Jon Cohen's *The Man in the Window* and Joe Coomer's *The Loop*. Herman Wouk's *Youngblood Hawke* also relates the life of a young writer after he becomes a best-selling novelist.

Reiken, Frederick
The Odd Sea
Harcourt Brace. 1998. 201 pp.

Philip Shumway relates how each member of his family reacted to the unaccountable disappearance of his older brother, who walked out of the house when he was 15 and never returned.

Book Groups 📖

Subjects Brothers • Coming-of-Age • Family Relationships • First Novels • Loss of a Child

Now try Other novels in which the unthinkable occurs include Kevin O'Brien's *Only Son* and John Burnham Schwartz's *Reservation Road*. Novels in which the ending is somewhat ambiguous include Jon Cohen's *The Man in the Window* and Tim O'Brien's *In the Lake of the Woods*.

Reuss, Frederick
Horace Afoot
MacMurray & Beck. 1997. 278 pp.

Quintus Horatius Flaccus, known as Horace, moves to the town of Oblivion and tries to escape life through Socratic dialogues with strangers and wandering the streets at all hours (occasionally unclothed), but when he befriends a dying librarian, rescues a rape victim, and becomes the target of an angry teenager, he realizes that he can't shut out the real world.

2d Appeal Language

Subjects Death and Dying • Eccentrics and Eccentricities • First Novels • Librarians • Small-Town Life

Now try   Another eccentric character can be found in William Kotzwinkle's *Fan Man*. The hero of John Dufresne's *Love Warps the Mind a Little* is also struggling with life's ironies.

Reynolds, Sheri

The Rapture of Canaan   G.P. Putnam's Sons. 1995. 320 pp.

Despite her strict religious upbringing, 14-year-old Ninah finds herself pregnant and insists she is carrying God's child, to the disbelief of her family and the entire church community. An Oprah selection.

2d Appeal   Setting   Book Groups 📖

Subjects   Coming-of-Age • Family Relationships • Religion • Religious Extremism • Southern Authors • Teenage Girls • Teenage Pregnancy

Now try   Reynolds's other novels include *Bitterroot Landing* and *A Gracious Plenty*. Two other coming-of-age novels set in the South with young women as protagonists are Zora Neale Hurston's *Their Eyes Were Watching God* and Toni Morrison's *Sula*. Jeanette Winterson's *Oranges Are Not the Only Fruit* is another novel in which the heroine, a young girl, comes of age in an evangelical household.

Rock, Peter

This Is the Place   Anchor Books. 1997. 245 pp.

Pyro, a blackjack dealer, justifies the crime he commits by blaming it on his love for Charlotte, a woman young enough to be his granddaughter.

Subjects   First Novels • Gambling • Loneliness • Mormons and Mormonism • Nevada • Older Men/Younger Women • Utah

Now try   Rock's second novel was *Carnival Wolves*. Andre Dubus's collection of short stories, *Dancing After Hours*, deals with many of the same themes found in Rock's book: loneliness, desire, and sadness.

Ronyoung, Kim

Clay Walls   University of Washington Press. 1990. 301 pp.

Korean immigrants Haesu and Chun and their American-born children learn to adjust to life in pre-World War II Los Angeles.

Book Groups 📖

Subjects   California • Family Relationships • First Novels • Immigrants and Refugees • Korean Americans • Korean Authors • Korean-Japanese Relations • Los Angeles

Now try   Mira Stout's novel *One Thousand Chestnut Trees* is about life in Korea under the Japanese occupation. Chang-Rae Lee's *Native Speaker* is about a Korean father and his Americanized son trying to adjust to each other's world view.

Rosen, Jonathan
Eve's Apple
Random House. 1997. 309 pp.

Recent college graduates Joseph Zimmerman and Ruth Simon's relationship is threatened by Joseph's obsessive need to both understand and save Ruth from her self-destructive cycles of anorexia nervosa and bulimia.

Book Groups 📖

Subjects Eating Disorders • First Novels • Male/Female Relationships • Suicide

Now try Other novels about young women with anorexia include Steven Levenkron's *The Best Little Girl in the World* and *Early Disorder* by Rebecca Josephs. Nonfiction about the subject of eating disorders include *Wasted: A Memoir of Anorexia and Bulimia* by Marya Hornbacher and *The Art of Starvation: A Story of Anorexia and Survival* by Sheila MacLeod.

Rouaud, Jean
Fields of Glory
Arcade Pub. 1992. 154 pp.

During the 1950s in the Loire Valley, a young boy comes to love and understand his grandparents and his crazy Aunt Marie, whose memories of World War I have profoundly affected their lives. Translated from the French by Ralph Manheim.

Book Groups 📖

Subjects 1950s • Family Relationships • France • French Authors • Grandparents • Novels in Translation • Small-Town Life • World War I

Now try This is the first of a trilogy that includes *Of Illustrious Men*, a novel about Roaud's father's experiences during World War II, and *The World More or Less*, Roaud's own post-war coming-of-age story. Marcel Pagnol's series about growing up in Marseille (*My Father's Glory* and *My Mother's Castle*) is another reminiscence of the era, with the same sentiment and innocent perception of character. *Fields of Glory* won the Prix Goncourt.

Rudnick, Paul
I'll Take It
Knopf. 1989. 291 pp.

Yale graduate Joe Reckler accompanies his mother and her two sisters on a shopping tour of New England outlet stores, where they accumulate items to their hearts' content, all without paying for a thing.

Subjects Crime • Eccentrics and Eccentricities • Humorous Fiction • Mothers and Sons • New England • Shoplifting • Sisters

Now try Rudnick also wrote *Social Disease*. Another eccentric relative can be found in Patrick Dennis's *Auntie Mame*.

Russo, Richard
Nobody's Fool
Random House. 1993. 549 pp.

Sully, a sometime construction worker in a small town in upstate New York who is down on his luck, still manages to keep from going completely under by helping out, or hindering when it's called for, the people who make up his community.

2d Appeal Story

Book Groups 📖

Subjects   ALA Notable Books • Family Relationships • Humorous Fiction • Men's Friendships • New York • Single Men • Small-Town Life

Now try   Other books by Russo include *Straight Man*, *The Risk Pool*, and *Mohawk*. Other books about men dealing with life in their own unique way include Carol Shields's *Larry's Party*, the husband's half of the tale in Shields's *Happenstance*, and *Love Warps the Mind a Little* by John Dufresne.

Russo, Richard
Straight Man
Random House. 1997. 391 pp.

Hank Devereaux's inability to take anything too seriously wreaks havoc in his relationship with his family and friends, as well as in his job as acting head of an English department in a third-rate college.

2d Appeal   Story

Subjects   Academia • College Professors • Fathers and Sons • Humorous Fiction • Husbands and Wives • Marriage • Midlife Crisis • Mothers and Sons

Now try   Similar shenanigans to those in Russo's novels are also found in Michael Malone's *Handling Sin*. Michael Chabon's *Wonder Boys* has a character bedeviled by his inability to write. James Hynes's *Publish and Perish* is filled with much darker humor than *Straight Man*. *False Years* by Josefina Vicens is another novel about a character who measures his worth against his father.

Sanders, Dori
Her Own Place
Algonquin Books of Chapel Hill. 1993. 243 pp.

Mae Lee Barnes faces her changed world—children grown and white women coming to her house for tea—with strength and humor.

Book Groups 📖

Subjects   African American Authors • African Americans • Family Relationships • Race Relations • Southern Authors

Now try   Sanders's first novel, *Clover*, also looks at race relations in the American South. Kristin Hunter Lattany's *Kinfolks*, describes the lives of two single African American mothers raising their families in the 1970s. Although considered a young adult novel, *Toning the Sweep* by Angela Johnson offers a moving portrayal of intergenerational life in an African American family.

Sandlin, Tim
Social Blunders
H. Holt. 1995. 281 pp.

Sam Callahan, attempting to get over abandonment by his second wife, Wanda (who has absconded with his Datsun 240Z and his baseball card collection), decides to find his long-lost father, only to open a Pandora's box of sexual escapades and mistaken identity involving five different families.

Subjects   Family Relationships • Fathers and Daughters • Fathers and Sons • Humorous Fiction • Male/Female Relationships

> **Now try**   *Skipped Parts* and *Sorrow Floats* precede *Social Blunders* in Sandlin's "Gro-Vont" trilogy. Sons tracking down their fathers can be found in Michael Malone's *Handling Sin* and *The Dork of Cork* by Chet Raymo.

Sarton, May
A Reckoning
Norton. 1978. 254 pp.

Newly diagnosed with inoperable cancer, Laura, a widow and now a successful editor for a major publisher, determines to spend her remaining time and energy on only the most important connections as she embarks on the great adventure of dying.

Book Groups ☐

> **Subjects**   ALA Notable Books • Cancer • Career Women • Death and Dying • Family Relationships • Mothers and Daughters • Women's Friendships
>
> **Now try**   Sarton wrote several other novels (including *Mrs. Stevens Hears the Mermaids Singing*) and memoirs (including *At Seventy*, *Endgame*, and *Encore*). All her writings have a dual focus on the world of the senses and the interior emotional life of her characters. Gail Godwin's *The Good Husband* is another portrait of a woman facing death determined to live what's left of her life to the fullest extent possible.

Sayer, Paul
The Comforts of Madness
Doubleday. 1990. 120 pp.

His body frozen and immobile, Peter reflects on the traditional and experimental treatments that have failed to cure his willed catatonic condition and remembers his past, which has brought him to find a retreat and prison inside his motionless limbs.

> **2d Appeal**   Language
>
> Book Groups ☐
>
> **Subjects**   British Authors • First Novels • Neglect • Physical Disabilities
>
> **Now try**   Another character who must cope with paralysis is found in Rosellen Brown's *Tender Mercies*. Memoirs by people who are paraplegics include John Hockenberry's *Moving Violations: War Zones, Wheelchairs, and Declarations of Independence* and John Callahan's *Don't Worry, He Won't Get Far on Foot*. *The Comforts of Madness* won the Whitbread Award.

Sayers, Valerie
Brain Fever
Doubleday. 1996. 308 pp.

Timothy Rooney, an unemployed philosophy professor, goes rapidly crazy as he gives up his medications and leaves his fiancée and her son in Due East, South Carolina, to find his ex-wife Bernadette.

> **Subjects**   College Professors • Male/Female Relationships • Mental Illness • Road Novels • Small-Town Life • South Carolina • Southern Authors
>
> **Now try**   Sayers's other novels, some of which are set in the same locale, include *Due East*, *How I Got Him Back, or, Under the Cold Moon's Shine*, and *Who Do You Love*. Mary Faith Rapple (Timothy's fiancee) is the main character in *Due East*. Sarah Gilbert's *Hairdo* is another novel set in a small South Carolina town.

Schaeffer, Susan Fromberg

Buffalo Afternoon
Knopf. 1989. 535 pp.

Pete Bravado, grandson of Italian immigrants, finds it nearly impossible to adjust to civilian life after the horrors he witnessed during his tour of duty in Vietnam.

2d Appeal Story — Book Groups 📖

Subjects ALA Notable Books • Family Relationships • Italian Americans • Male/Female Relationships • Vietnam Veterans • Vietnam War

Now try Schaeffer's other books include two novels, *Mainland* and *Time in Its Flight*, and a collection of poetry, *Granite Lady*. Stewart O'Nan's *The Names of the Dead* and Tim O'Brien's *In the Lake of the Woods* are other novels that describe how difficult returning to civilian life was for Vietnam veterans.

Schlink, Bernhard

The Reader
Pantheon Books. 1997. 218 pp.

Michael Berg's passionate and illicit affair with an emotionally remote older woman when he was a teenager reverberates years later when he encounters her as a defendant in a war crimes trial. Translated from the German by Carol Brown Janeway. An Oprah selection.

Book Groups 📖

Subjects Coming-of-Age • German Authors • Holocaust • Love Affairs • Novels in Translation • Older Women/Younger Men • Women in Prison • World War II

Now try Jonathan Dee's *The Liberty Campaign* also deals with what it means to care for someone who has committed unspeakable crimes. Schlink's spare prose style is similar to *Night Over Day Over Night* by Paul Watkins. *The Reader* won the Boston Book Review's Fisk Prize.

Schoemperlen, Diane

In the Language of Love
Viking. 1996. 358 pp.

Joanna's search for happiness is complicated by growing up with an angry mother and by an affair with a married man, but she finally achieves a satisfying marriage and a wonderful relationship with her son.

2d Appeal Language — Book Groups 📖

Subjects Canadian Authors • Dysfunctional Families • Family Relationships • Fathers and Daughters • First Novels • Marriage • Mothers and Sons

Now try Schoemperlen used 100 stimulus words from the Standard Word Association Test as the framework for this novel. *The Man of My Dreams*, a collection of Schoemperlen's short stories, was nominated for Canada's Governor General's Award. Several of Margaret Atwood's novels share Schoemperlen's themes, particularly *Bodily Harm* and *Life Before Man*.

Schumacher, Julie
The Body Is Water
Soho Press. 1995. 262 pp.

Pregnant, unmarried, and wondering what to do with her life, Jane Haus returns to her father's run-down house on the New Jersey shore and realizes that she needs to understand the past before she can deal with the future.

2d Appeal   Language   Book Groups 📖

Subjects   ALA Notable Books • Fathers and Daughters • First Novels • Mothers Deserting Their Families • New Jersey • Single Women • Sisters

Now try   Schumacher is also the author of *An Explanation for Chaos*, a collection of short stories. The complicated relationship between Jane and her sister Bea is similar to the relationship of the sisters in Gail Godwin's *A Mother and Two Daughters*.

Schwartz, John Burnham
Reservation Road
Alfred A. Knopf. 1998. 292 pp.

Two men—Dwight Arno and Ethan Learner—are forever linked when Dwight, driving recklessly, kills 10-year-old Josh Learner and then flees the scene of the accident.

2d Appeal   Story   Book Groups 📖

Subjects   Car Accidents • Death of a Child • Grief • Husbands and Wives • Marriage • Midlife Crisis

Now try   Schwartz is also the author of *Bicycle Days*. Other novels about families whose lives are changed by a death include Jodi Picoult's *The Pact* and Rosellen Brown's *Before and After*.

Schwartz, Lynne Sharon
Disturbances in the Field
Harper & Row. 1983. 371 pp.

The consolation of philosophy fails Lydia Rowe, who, after college, marriage, and a family tragedy, is forced to question her life's choices.

2d Appeal   Story   Book Groups 📖

Subjects   Death of a Child • Grief • Husbands and Wives • Marriage • Midlife Crisis • Philosophical Novels • Women's Friendships

Now try   Among Schwartz's other novels are *The Fatigue Artist* and *Rough Strife*. Frederick Busch's *Girls* is another novel about a husband and wife torn apart by grief. Leonard Michaels's *The Men's Club* describes other characters who spend a lot of time analyzing life and its mysteries. Rebecca Goldstein's *The Late-Summer Passion of a Woman of Mind* is also a novel about professors of philosophy.

Schweighardt, Joan
Homebodies
Permanent Press. 1994. 205 pp.

The Arroways find their family relationships stretched to the breaking point by real and imagined memories of the past and events of the present.

Book Groups 📖

Subjects   Death of a Child • Family Relationships • Family Secrets • Fathers and Sons • Husbands and Wives • Mental Illness • Sisters

Now try Schweighardt's first novel was *Island*, published in 1992. Jacquelyn Mitchard's *The Deep End of the Ocean* also describes the guilt a young boy feels about the terrible events surrounding a sibling's disappearance.

Scofield, Sandra
A Chance to See Egypt
HarperCollins. 1996. 252 pp.

Following the death of his wife Eva, a grieving Tom Riley goes to the small Mexican village where they had honeymooned and, to his surprise, finds love and happiness.

2d Appeal Setting

Subjects Art and Artists • Death of a Spouse • Male/Female Relationships • Mexico • Small-Town Life

Now try Scofield is also the author of *Opal on Dry Ground*, *Beyond Deserving*, and *Walking Dunes*. Harriet Doerr's *Stones for Ibarra* is another novel, set in Mexico, about the death of a spouse.

Scott, Joanna
Arrogance
Linden Press. 1990. 283 pp.

Before his death at age 28 from the Spanish flu, Austrian Egon Schiele spent his days seducing young girls, scandalizing rural villagers, hobnobbing in Viennese art circles, and becoming one of the most controversial and respected expressionist painters of the twentieth century.

2d Appeal Language   Book Groups 📖

Subjects Art and Artists • Austria • Brothers and Sisters • Male/Female Relationships • Schiele, Egon

Now try Other novels by Scott include *Fading*, *My Parmacheene Belle*, and *The Manikin*. Other examples of fictionalized biography include Irving Stone's *The Agony and the Ecstacy*, E. L. Doctorow's *Ragtime*, and Margaret Atwood's *Alias Grace*.

Segal, Lore
Her First American
Knopf. 1985. 287 pp.

Coming to America after World War II—her father dead and her mother missing in Hitler's cauldron of hate—Ilka's first American friend and lover is Carter Bayoux, a black intellectual, prodigious drinker, and teller of tales.

2d Appeal Language   Book Groups 📖

Subjects African Americans • Alcoholics and Alcoholism • Immigrants and Refugees • Interracial Relationships • Love Stories

Now try Segal's other books include several for children, as well as *Lucinella: A Novel*. Ilka's problems learning to speak English—recounted in a humorous yet compassionate way—bring to mind Leo Rosten's novels about immigrants learning their new language (*The Education of H*Y*M*A*N* K*A*P*L*A*N* and others). The trickiness of English words that have different meanings in different contexts is also a theme of David Carkeet's novels, especially *Double Negative*.

Selvadurai, Shyam
Funny Boy
Wm. Morrow and Co. 1996. 310 pp.

As the Sinhalese and Tamil forces clash violently in Sri Lanka in the 1970s and 1980s, a young and sensitive Tamil boy struggles with his emerging homosexuality and the impact it has both on himself and his family.

2d Appeal   Setting   Book Groups 📖

Subjects   1970s • 1980s • ALA Notable Books • Coming-of-Age • First Novels • Gay Teenagers • Indian Authors • Sri Lanka • Violence

Now try   Other books about race relations in the Indian subcontinent following the establishment of India and Pakistan include Rohinton Mistry's *Such a Long Journey* and *A Fine Balance*.

Settle, Mary Lee
Celebration
Farrar, Straus & Giroux. 1986. 355 pp.

In 1960s London (with stops in Turkey, Hong Kong, and Africa), a widowed American anthropologist and a convalescing Scottish geologist become the center of a star-crossed group of faithful friends.

2d Appeal   Story   Book Groups 📖

Subjects   1960s • Death of a Spouse • Friendship • Gay Men • Hong Kong • London • Male/Female Relationships • Turkey

Now try   Other novels by Settle include *Prisons*, *O Beulah Land*, *The Killing Ground*, *Know Nothing*, and *The Scapegoat*, all set in West Virginia. Settle's interest in Turkey is reflected in her novel *Blood Tie* (which won the National Book Award) and in *Turkish Reflections*, a nonfiction account of her visits to Turkey. Other books set in Turkey include *Tales from the Garbage Hills* by Berji Kristin and *The Sultan's Daughter* by Ann Chamberlin.

Sexton, Linda Gray
Points of Light
Little, Brown. 1988. 308 pp.

When her secure world of home and family is rocked by the tragic death of one of her children, artist Allie Yates refuses to accept reality and instead loses herself in her painting and in her vivid dreams.

2d Appeal   Story   Book Groups 📖

Subjects   ALA Notable Books • Art and Artists • Death of a Child • Family Relationships • Male/Female Relationships

Now try   Sexton's other novels include *Private Acts* and *Mirror Images*. She also wrote a memoir about her relationship with her mother, poet Anne Sexton, called *Searching for Mercy Street*. Other works of fiction dealing with the death of a child include Alice Hoffman's *At Risk*, Judith Guest's *Ordinary People*, and Doris Betts's *Souls Raised from the Dead*.

Shacochis, Bob
Swimming in the Volcano
Scribner's Sons. 1993. 519 pp.

Naïve American economist Mitchell Wilson realizes too late how deadly life can become on a seemingly carefree Caribbean island.

2d Appeal   Language

Subjects   1970s • Caribbean • Expatriates • First Novels • Interracial Relationships • Male/Female Relationships

Now try   This book was a finalist for the 1993 National Book Award. Susan Sontag also brewed a mixture of sexual relationships, revolutionary politics, and volcanoes in her novel ***The Volcano Lover***. The life of expatriates is described in Francesca Marciano's ***Rules of the Wild*** and Mark Jacobs's ***Stone Cowboy***.

Shapiro, Jane
After Moondog
Harcourt Brace Jovanovich. 1992. 323 pp.

Twenty-five years in the life of Joanne and Willie Green, who deal with child rearing, aging parents, careers, adultery, and ultimately divorce.

Book Groups 📖

Subjects   Divorce • Family Relationships • First Novels • Marriage

Now try   Cathie Pelletier's ***A Marriage Made at Woodstock*** and John Updike's collection of linked short stories, ***Too Far to Go***, both examine the unraveling of a marriage.

Shea, Lisa
Hula
Norton. 1994. 155 pp.

A young girl on the verge of adolescence starkly details her life in a family wounded by abuse and neglect, where her only comfort comes from a tough older sister and the family's pet dog.

Book Groups 📖

Subjects   Abusive Relationships • Coming-of-Age • Dogs • Family Relationships • First Novels • Sisters

Now try   Elizabeth Berg's ***Durable Goods*** also deals with sisters trying to survive in an abusive family situation. Roddy Doyle's ***Paddy Clarke Ha Ha Ha*** is told from the perspective of a young boy watching his parents' marriage fall apart. Other nice sister relationships can be found in John Welter's ***I Want to Buy a Vowel*** and Dodie Smith's ***I Capture the Castle***.

Shearer, Cynthia
The Wonder Book of the Air
Pantheon Books. 1996. 305 pp.

Three generations (wives, children, grandchildren) and an Army friend alternate telling of the life and loves of Harrison Durrance, child of the Depression, who came of age during World War II.

2d Appeal   Story

Subjects   Coming-of-Age • Divorce • Family Relationships • First Novels • Marriage • Multigenerational Novels • World War II

Now try   Another multigenerational novel is Mary Gordon's *The Other Side*. In their memoirs, both James Salter (***Burning the Days: Recollections***) and Paul Fussell (***Doing Battle: The Making of a Skeptic***) describe their own coming-of-age in World War II.

Shepard, Elizabeth
H   Viking. 1995. 160 pp.

The experiences, told entirely in letters, of Benjamin Sherman, an autistic and deeply depressed 12-year-old boy, whose best friend is a stuffed letter "H" named Elliott.

Book Groups 📖

Subjects   Autism • Coming-of-Age • Epistolary Novels • First Novels • Mothers and Sons

Now try   *Saving St. Germ* by Carol Muske-Dukes is also about a different child. Other epistolary novels include Elizabeth Forsythe Hailey's *A Woman of Independent Means* and Amos Oz's *Black Box*. Another novel in which the main character's grasp of reality is frighteningly weak is William Trevor's *Children of Dynmouth*.

Shields, Carol
Happenstance   McGraw-Hill Ryerson. 1980. 216 pp.

When Brenda Bowman goes off to a week-long quilting convention, the time apart, as seen through the eyes of both Brenda and her husband Jack, gives both halves of a mostly happy marriage the chance to learn more about themselves and each other.

2d Appeal   Story   Book Groups 📖

Subjects   Husbands and Wives • Marriage • Middle-Aged Men • Middle-Aged Women • Midlife Crisis • Quilting

Now try   Shields also wrote *The Orange Fish*, *The Box Garden*, and *Small Ceremonies*. Evan Connell's two novels, *Mr. Bridge* and *Mrs. Bridge*, and David Gates's *Preston Falls* all present both sides of a marriage.

Shields, Carol
The Republic of Love   Viking. 1992. 366 pp.

Fortyish Tom Avery, a three-times-married late-night-radio talk show host, and never-married Fay McLeod, 35, a researcher of mermaids, alternate telling the story of the complications attendant on falling in love.

2d Appeal   Story

Subjects   Male/Female Relationships • Middle-Aged Men • Middle-Aged Women • Radio • Single Men • Single Women

Now try   Another example of a much-married man is found in Paul Estaver's *His Third, Her Second*.

Shields, Carol

Swann
Viking. 1989. 313 pp.

Feminist scholar Sarah Maloney may have discerned the enigmatic poet Mary Swann, but she is only one of many so-called experts who pompously interpret (and re-create as needed) the deceased poet's work.

Book Groups

Subjects   Academia • Male/Female Relationships • Satirical Fiction • Small-Town Life • Writers and Writing

Now try   Shields makes readers aware of the different ways people interpret the same event, or the same life, as does Robertson Davies in *Fifth Business*. Brian Morton's *Starting Out in the Evening* is about a young woman who wants to write the biography of a writer she admires and comes up against the differences between the way she sees the writer and the way the writer perceives himself.

Shields, David

Dead Languages
Knopf. 1989. 245 pp.

In a family that loves to talk, Jeremy Zorn's speech from the age of four is marked by his stuttering until, in college, a speech therapist helps him put his disability in perspective.

2d Appeal   Language
Book Groups

Subjects   1960s • Brothers and Sisters • Coming-of-Age • Family Relationships • Stuttering

Now try   Shields has written short stories and nonfiction, including *Remote*, a look at modern culture and its passion for celebrity. The eponymous heroine of *Icy Sparks*, by Gwyn Hyman Rubio, also has a condition that sets her apart from her contemporaries. *Stuttering: A Life Bound Up in Words* is Marty Jezer's nonfiction account of his experiences in a lifetime of stuttering.

Silko, Leslie Marmon

Almanac of the Dead
Simon & Schuster. 1991. 763 pp.

On a smuggler's ranch in the desert outside Tucson, six people live and work, offering stories from their pasts, which range from the tragic, to the humorous, to the mystical.

2d Appeal   Setting
Book Groups

Subjects   American Indian Authors • Apocalyptic Fiction • Arizona • Ecofiction • Homelessness • Spirituality

Now try   Among Silko's other books are *Yellow Woman and a Beauty of the Spirit: Essays on Native American Life Today* and the novel *Ceremony*. Another novel that unfolds gradually is Susan Power's *The Grass Dancer*.

Simons, Paullina
Tully
St. Martin's Press. 1994. 594 pp.

Tully's horrific adolescence (rape by an uncle, a physically abusive and mentally ill mother, the suicide of her best friend) leads her to make unfortunate choices in the men she loves.

2d Appeal Story

Subjects 1970s • Child Abuse • Coming-of-Age • Dysfunctional Families • First Novels • Friendship • Male/Female Relationships • Sexual Abuse • Suicide

Now try Simons's other books include ***Red Leaves*** and ***Eleven Hours***. Mary Hood's ***Familiar Heat***, like Simon's novel ***Tully***, is filled with enough incidents to keep a soap opera running for years.

Simpson, Mona
Anywhere But Here
Knopf. 1987. 406 pp.

Divorced mother Adele August and her teenage daughter, Anne, leave a Midwestern factory town and head for California, where Adele hopes to make Anne a movie star.

2d Appeal Language   Book Groups 📖

Subjects ALA Notable Books • California • Dysfunctional Families • Mothers and Daughters • Road Novels • Single Parents

Now try ***The Lost Father*** is the sequel to ***Anywhere But Here***. ***Was*** by Geoff Ryman imagines the story of Judy Garland's mother's push to make her a movie star and its effect on the entire Garland family. Jill Ciment's ***Law of Falling Bodies*** is another exploration of mother/daughter relationships. In 1996, *Granta Magazine* named Simpson one of the "20 Best Young American Novelists."

Small, David
The River in Winter
Norton. 1987. 320 pp.

Violence is never far from 17-year-old Joe Weatherfield's life as he becomes involved in a kidnapping, witnesses a murder, and learns the hard way about love and loss, responsibility and redemption.

2d Appeal Language

Subjects Elderly Men • First Novels • Juvenile Delinquents • Love Stories • Maine • Murder • Small-Town Life • Teenage Boys • Teenagers • Violence

Now try Small also wrote ***Almost Famous***, a novel about a failed baseball player, and Alone, about a middle-aged man who learns the meaning of solitude. ***Goodnight, Nebraska*** by Tom McNeal is another love story set against an atmosphere of teenage violence and its repercussions.

Smith, Charlie
Cheap Ticket to Heaven
Henry Holt. 1996. 286 pp.

Jack and Clare, bank robbers, killers, husband and wife, define themselves by the crimes they commit and the violent deaths they know await them.

2d Appeal Story

Subjects Fugitives • Husbands and Wives • Murder • Violence

Now try   Among Smith's other novels are ***Chimney Rock***, ***Red Roads***, and ***Shine Hawk***. The grimness found in this novel can also be found in the novels of Pete Dexter (***The Paperboy*** and others). ***Paradise Junction*** by Phillip Finch is another novel about a married couple with criminal tendencies.

Smith, Dinitia
The Illusionist
Scribner. 1997. 253 pp.

As the residents of Sparta, New York, discover Dean Lily's secrets, they respond with mistrust, anger, and finally violence.

2d Appeal   Story   Book Groups 📖

Subjects   First Novels • Gender Roles • Male/Female Relationships • Murder • New York • Sexual Identity • Small-Town Life • Violence

Now try   Rose Tremain's ***Sacred Country*** and Virginia Woolf's ***Orlando*** are both about issues of sexual identity.

Smith, Lee
Family Linen
Putnam's. 1985. 272 pp.

A Virginia woman's childhood memory (recovered through hypnosis), the funeral that reunites her family, and the digging of a swimming pool all lead to the unearthing of a long-kept family secret.

2d Appeal   Language   Book Groups 📖

Subjects   Family Relationships • Family Secrets • Small-Town Life • Southern Authors • Virginia

Now try   Bobbie Ann Mason (***Shiloh and Other Stories***, ***Spence + Lila***, and others) also reflects her southern heritage in her fiction. Carol Dawson's ***Body of Knowledge*** is another novel with a long-buried family mystery.

Solomon, Andrew
A Stone Boat
Faber & Faber. 1994. 241 pp.

The two years his mother spends fighting the cancer that will eventually kill her lead her son Harry to reflect on the nature of love: for his parents, for his lover Bernard, and for his close friend Helen.

Book Groups 📖

Subjects   Cancer • Death of a Parent • First Novels • Gay Men • Mothers and Sons • Music and Musicians • Single Men

Now try   Solomon is also the author of ***The Ivory Tower: Soviet Artists in a Time of Glasnost***. The complicated relationship between an adult son and his mother is described in Michael Ignatieff's ***Scar Tissue***. Karin Cook's ***What Girls Learn*** and Alexandra Marshall's ***Gus in Bronze*** both describe the wrenching death of a mother from cancer, as seen through the eyes of their children.

Spanbauer, Tom
The Man Who Fell in Love with the Moon
Atlantic Monthly Press. 1991. 355 pp.

Shed, a half-breed American Indian, leaves the whorehouse in which he has grown up to begin a search for self, which leads him to truths about his parents, his sexuality, and the stories people create about their lives.

Subjects   American Indians • Coming-of-Age • Sexual Identity

Now try   Spanbauer also wrote the novel *Faraway Places*. Leslie Marmon Silko, in *Storyteller*, explores more deeply the stories people create for and about themselves. Pam Houston offers a similarly frank voice in her short story collection, *Cowboys Are My Weakness*.

Spanidou, Irini
God's Snake
Norton. 1986. 252 pp.

As she emerges from adolescence during the 1950s, Anna Karystinou, the daughter of a Greek military officer, struggles to live with her father's brutal domination.

2d Appeal   Setting

Subjects   1950s • Coming-of-Age • Fathers and Daughters • First Novels • Greece

Now try   Spanidou's second novel is *Fear*, the sequel to *God's Snake*. Catherine Temma Davidson's *The Priest Fainted* covers some of the same time period in Greece. Stratis Haviaras's *The Heroic Age* is also about growing up in Greece immediately following World War II. Another good novel about a dominating father in the military is Pat Conroy's *The Great Santini*.

Spencer, Brent
The Lost Son
Arcade Pub. 1995. 225 pp.

Now in his 40s, Redmond confronts issues of abuse from his own childhood as he attempts to develop a relationship with an alcoholic woman and her son.

Book Groups 📖

Subjects   Alcoholics and Alcoholism • Child Abuse • Dysfunctional Families • Fathers and Sons • First Novels • Male/Female Relationships

Now try   Spencer also wrote *Are We Not Men: Stories*. The protagonists in David Gates's *Jernigan* are a man and a woman who are drawn together by their dysfunctional personalities. Life with an alcoholic parent is described in Timothy Findley's *You Went Away*.

Spencer, Scott
Men in Black
A.A. Knopf. 1995. 321 pp.

Unable to make a living writing the sort of literary fiction he wants, Sam Holland unhappily churns out a variety of shlock, so when his newest potboiler, *Visitors from Above*, hits the bestseller list, Sam is unprepared for the hoopla that follows.

2d Appeal   Story

Subjects   Adultery • Book Publishing • Husbands and Wives • Writers and Writing

Now try   Among Spencer's other novels are *Preservation Hall* and *Last Night at the Brain Thieves Ball*. Other novels with wonderful accounts of authors and their book tours include William Kotzwinkle's *The Bear Went Over the Mountain* and Michael Chabon's *Wonder Boys*.

Spencer, William Browning
Maybe I'll Call Anna

Permanent Press. 1990. 275 pp.

Blonde and beautiful Anna Shockley has a succession of abusive relationships that serve only to compound her emotional instability.

Book Groups 📖

Subjects   1960s • Domestic Violence • Drugs and Drug Abuse • Male/Female Relationships • Sex and Sexuality • Small-Town Life • Southern Authors

Now try   Spencer also wrote the novel *Resume with Monsters*. Another example of a woman who stays in an abusive relationship can be found in Roddy Doyle's *The Woman Who Walked into Doors*.

Stegner, Wallace
Crossing to Safety

Random House. 1987. 277 pp.

Two young couples—one with no prospects, the other with wealth and connections—form a painfully close and lifelong friendship that sustains them through successes, defeats, and illness.

2d Appeal   Language   Book Groups 📖

Subjects   Aging • ALA Notable Books • Friendship • Marriage • Polio

Now try   Stegner won the 1971 Pulitzer Prize for his novel *Angle of Repose*. Among his other novels are *The Big Rock Candy Mountain*, *All the Little Live Things*, and *The Spectator Bird*, as well as a collection of essays, *Where the Bluebird Sings to the Lemonade Springs: Living and Writing in the West*. In their journals, both Doris Grumbach (*Fifty Days of Solitude*, *Extra Innings: A Memoir*, and others) and May Sarton (*Endgame: A Journal of the Seventy-Ninth Year*, *Encore: A Journal of the Eightieth Year*, and others) record their feelings about growing old, long-time friendships, and the prospect of death. Walter Sullivan's *A Time to Dance* is also about the effects of illness on a marriage.

Stevens, April
Angel Angel

Viking. 1995. 211 pp.

When Gordie Iris walks out on his family, his wife Augusta falls into a deep depression; Mathew and Henry try unsuccessfully to help their mother and themselves, but the situation begins to improve only when Henry brings home his banana-flavored-gum-chewing, chain-smoking girlfriend.

2d Appeal   Story

Subjects   Art and Artists • Brothers • First Novels • Mental Illness • Mothers and Sons

Now try   Another novel in which two brothers compete for the same woman (also someone who has come into the family's house to help out) is Anne Tyler's *The Clock Winder*.

Stollman, Aryeh
The Far Euphrates
Riverhead Books. 1997. 206 pp.

Alexander, a rabbi's son growing up in Windsor, Ontario, during the 1950s and 1960s, is deeply affected by secrets having their origin in Hitler's concentration camps.

2d Appeal Language   Book Groups 📖

Subjects 1950s • 1960s • ALA Notable Books • Canada • Coming-of-Age • Concentration Camps • Family Secrets • First Novels • Jews and Judaism • Ministers, Priests, and Rabbis • Ontario, Canada • World War II

Now try The moral questions raised by this novel are the same sort that Chaim Potok explores in *The Chosen* and *The Promise*. *The Sparrow* by Mary Doria Russell is also concerned with questions of faith, forgiveness, and belief. Mordecai Richler's *Joshua Then and Now* is another novel about a young man coming-of-age in Canada. Another novel set in Ontario, Canada, is Kerri Sakamoto's *The Electrical Field*.

Stone, Robert
Children of Light
Knopf. 1986. 258 pp.

After his wife leaves him, drug-juggling actor and screenwriter Gordon Walker heads for a Mexican movie location to see his old flame, Lee Verger.

2d Appeal Language

Subjects Adultery • ALA Notable Books • Drugs and Drug Abuse • Hollywood • Male/Female Relationships • Mental Illness • Mexico • Motion Picture Industry

Now try Stone's other novels include *Dog Soldiers*, *Outerbridge Reach*, and *Damascus Gate*. Other novels about Hollywood and the motion picture industry include Michael Tolkin's *The Player*, Muriel Spark's *Reality and Dreams*, Bruce Wagner's *I'm Losing You*, Steve Tesich's *Karoo*, and *The Last Tycoon*, F. Scott Fitzgerald's last, unfinished novel. Drugs and their illicit pleasures are also described in Jay McInerney's *Bright Lights*, *Big City*.

Stowe, Rebecca
The Shadow of Desire
Pantheon Books. 1996. 228 pp.

During her annual—and much dreaded—Christmas visit home, 38-year-old Virginia Moore realizes that her career researching and writing biographies of women who never lived up to their early promise is actually an attempt to understand her mother and herself.

2d Appeal Language   Book Groups 📖

Subjects Alcoholics and Alcoholism • Dysfunctional Families • Family Relationships • Male/Female Relationships • Mothers and Daughters • Single Women • Writers and Writing

Now try Stowe's first novel was *Not the End of the World*. Other difficult mother/daughter relationships are found in Rebecca Wells's *Divine Secrets of the Ya-Ya Sisterhood* and Dani Shapiro's *Fugitive Blue*. *Starting Out in the Evening* by Brian Morton and Carol Shields's *Swann* are both about the art of writing biography.

Stracher, Cameron
The Laws of Return
W. Morrow and Co. 1996. 245 pp.

Brought up as a non-observant Jew, Colin Stone searches for his religious roots as he attends Harvard Law School and goes to work for a high-powered New York law firm, where he is forced to face the anti-Semitism of his colleagues.

2d Appeal   Story

Subjects   Anti-Semitism • Coming-of-Age • First Novels • Humorous Fiction • Jews and Judaism • Law and Lawyers • New York

Now try   Anti-semitism is the theme of Laura Hobson's novel, ***Gentleman's Agreement***. Joshua Henkin's ***Swimming Across the Hudson*** is another first novel dealing with the question of what it means to be Jewish in today's secular world.

Straight, Susan
I Been in Sorrow's Kitchen and Licked Out All the Pots
Hyperion. 1992. 355 pp.

Marietta Cook sees football as her twin sons' ticket out of the Gullah-speaking low country of South Carolina.

2d Appeal   Language   Book Groups 📖

Subjects   African Americans • First Novels • Football • Mothers and Sons • Single Parents • South Carolina • Twins

Now try   Straight also wrote ***Blacker Than a Thousand Midnights*** and ***The Gettin Place***. Another strong woman who struggles to make a good life for herself and her family can be found in Bret Lott's ***Jewel***.

Strong, Albertine
Deluge
Harmony Books. 1997. 277 pp.

Aja, the granddaughter of Peke (an Ojibwe Indian) and Isabel (the daughter of Swedish immigrants), tries to find a balance between her Indian heritage and the life she desires away from the reservation, her family, and its history.

2d Appeal   Language   Book Groups 📖

Subjects   American Indian Authors • American Indians • Family Relationships • First Novels • Magic Realism • Minnesota • Ojibwas

Now try   The main character, Aja, is herself similar to Cecelia Capture, the American Indian protagonist in Janet Campbell Hale's ***The Jailing of Cecelia Capture***.

Sullivan, Walter
A Time to Dance
Louisiana State University Press. 1995. 195 pp.

After almost 60 years of a sometimes difficult marriage, life changes radically for the Howards, when Bunnie (now 86) has a stroke and Max (now 90) tries to care for her with the help of their nephew, Justin.

Subjects   Aging • Alzheimer's Disease • Elderly Men • Elderly Women • First Novels • Marriage • Stroke Patients

Now try   Angela Carter's ***Wise Children*** also deals with the subject of growing (very) old. Wallace Stegner's ***Crossing to Safety*** is about the effects of illness on a marriage. Michael Ignatieff's ***Scar Tissue*** is a son's view of an Alzheimer's patient, while Sullivan's novel offers the view of the patient himself.

Svendsen, Linda
Marine Life
Farrar, Straus, and Giroux. 1992. 165 pp.

Adele analyzes the effect of her mother's three marriages on the lives of herself and her siblings: self-doubts and mistrust of intimacy color all their relationships

Book Groups 📖

Subjects   Brothers and Sisters • Canadian Authors • Family Relationships • First Novels • Marriage • Mothers and Daughters

Now try   *Intimacy* by Susan Chace also portrays the effect of parental relationships on the emotional well-being of their children. Other books with characters who have been married many times include Paul Estaver's *His Third, Her Second* and Carol Shields's *The Republic of Love*.

Swift, Graham
Last Orders
A.A. Knopf. 1996. 294 pp.

Driving from London to scatter their friend Jack's ashes along the English coast, Vic, Ray, Lenny, and Jack's son Vince look back on their intertwined lives with humor and emotion.

2d Appeal   Language   Book Groups 📖

Subjects   ALA Notable Books • Booker Prize Winners • British Authors • England • Men's Friendships • World War II

Now try   Swift also wrote *Learning to Swim and Other Stories*. Another novel about a group of old friends traveling together is Bob Greene's *All Summer Long*. *Last Orders* also won the James Tait Black Award.

Syal, Meera
Anita and Me
The New Press. 1996. 328 pp.

Ten-year-old Meena Kumar, the only Punjabi girl in her working-class British neighborhood, fights both prejudice and her parents' high expectations as she tries to win the friendship of Anita Rutter, the toughest girl in town.

Book Groups 📖

Subjects   1970s • Coming-of-Age • Culture Clash • England • First Novels • Indian Authors • Working Classes

Now try   Henry Denker's *Horowitz and Mrs. Washington* and Lynda Barry's *The Good Times Are Killing Me* are also about friendship that transcends racial boundaries. *Anita and Me* won the Betty Trask Award.

Tan, Amy
The Joy Luck Club
Putnam's. 1989. 288 pp.

Four immigrant Chinese women and their American-born daughters portray the complexities of combining a Chinese heritage with American culture.

Book Groups 📖

Subjects   ALA Notable Books • Chinese American Authors • Chinese Americans • First Novels • Immigrants and Refugees • Mothers and Daughters

Now try   Although set in an earlier era than Tan's novel, Ruthanne Lum McCunn's *Wooden Fish Songs* is also about Chinese immigrants. Karen Joy Fowler's *Sarah*

Canary begins in a railroad camp filled with Chinese immigrant men. Anchee Min's novel *Katherine* and her nonfiction *Red Azalea* both offer interesting views of China and Chinese Americans.

Tannen, Mary
After Roy
Knopf. 1989. 243 pp.

When a series of coincidences reunites Maggie, Sparks, and Yolanda at a remote West African chimpanzee research station, the three, who nearly a decade before orbited around rock superstar Roy, must re-evaluate their ties to the past and plans for the future.

Book Groups 📖

> **Subjects**   Africa • Chimpanzees • Friendship • Male/Female Relationships • Music and Musicians • West Africa
>
> **Now try**   Tannen's other novels include *Easy Keeper* and *Loving Edith*. William Boyd's *Brazzaville Beach* is also about the relationship a young woman develops with the animals she is studying. Peter Dickinson's *The Poison Oracle* is a mystery featuring a primate.

Taylor-Hall, Mary Ann
Come and Go, Molly Snow
Norton. 1995. 269 pp.

Bluegrass fiddler Carrie Marie Mullins attempts to control her guilt and grief after her five-year-old daughter dies in a senseless accident

Book Groups 📖

> **Subjects**   Death of a Child • First Novels • Grief • Loss of a Child • Male/Female Relationships • Music and Musicians
>
> **Now try**   Anne Tyler's *The Tin Can Tree* and Linda Gray Sexton's *Points of Light* both explore the repercussions from the unexpected death of a child. Laura Watt's *Carry Me Back* and Reed Arvin's *The Wind in the Wheat* are also about country music.

Tesich, Steve
Karoo
Harcourt Brace & Co. 1998. 406 pp.

Script doctor Saul Karoo learns to his sorrow that it is not possible to rewrite a life the way a good writer can improve a movie.

> **2d Appeal**   Story
>
> **Subjects**   Adoption • Fathers and Sons • Hollywood • Love Affairs • Motion Picture Industry • Writers and Writing
>
> **Now try**   Tesich's first novel was *Summer Crossing*. Another novel with a distinct narrative voice is Merle Miller's *A Gay and Melancholy Sound*.

Theroux, Paul
The Mosquito Coast
Houghton Mifflin. 1982. 374 pp.

Determined to make his family self-sufficient, dangerously eccentric inventor Allie Fox relocates them to the primitive coast of Honduras.

2d Appeal Setting   Book Groups 📖

Subjects Central America • Eccentrics and Eccentricities • Family Relationships • Fathers and Sons • Honduras

Now try Theroux is also well known for his armchair travel books, including *The Great Railway Bazaar* and *The Happy Isles of Oceania*. Pat Conroy's *The Great Santini* is another novel about a difficult relationship between a father and his son. William Golding's *Lord of the Flies* and Alex Garland's *The Beach* both parallel Theroux's theme of supposedly civilized people going mad in the wilderness. *The Mosquito Coast* won the James Tait Black Award.

Thurm, Marian
Walking Distance
Random House. 1987. 279 pp.

Laura believes herself to be perfectly happy as Zachary's wife and Mia's mother until David, a man dying of cancer, declares his love for her.

2d Appeal Story   Book Groups 📖

Subjects Adultery • Cancer • Death and Dying • First Novels • Male/Female Relationships • Marriage

Now try Thurm's other books include *Henry in Love*, *The Way We Live Now*, and *The Clairvoyant*. Marti Leimbach's *Dying Young* is another view of the relationship between a healthy woman and a dying man. Laurie Colwin's novel, *Family Happiness*, questions whether a happy marriage can be compatible with adultery.

Tilghman, Christopher
Mason's Retreat
Random House. 1996. 290 pp.

An American family seals its tragic fate by leaving England in the late 1930s to begin a new life at their ancestral estate in Maryland.

2d Appeal Setting   Book Groups 📖

Subjects Adultery • Death of a Child • Family Relationships • Fathers and Sons • First Novels • Maryland

Now try Tilghman also wrote a collection of short stories, *In a Father's Place*. Other novels relating the history of a family include Reynolds Price's trilogy, *The Surface of Earth*, *The Source of Light*, and *The Promise of Rest*, and Martin Boyd's "The Langton Quartet" (*The Cardboard Crown*, *Outbreak of Love*, *A Difficult Young Man*, and *When Blackbirds Sing*). John Barth's *Tidewater Tales* is also about family relationships in the Chesapeake Bay area of Maryland. The dissolution of a once grand family is the theme of Carol Dawson's *Body of Knowledge*.

Toibin, Colm

The Story of the Night
Henry Holt and Co. 1997. 324 pp.

As Argentina limps through the Falklands War and turns towards democracy and privatization, Richard Garay emerges from the shelter of his mother's apartment to find love in the gay underworld of Buenos Aires and make his fortune under the wing of his new American friends, diplomats Susan and Donald Ford.

2d Appeal Setting   Book Groups 📖

  Subjects AIDS • Argentina • Friendship • Gay Men • Irish Authors

  Now try Another novel by Toibin is ***The Heather Blazing***. In Toibin's novel, political repression and torture in Argentina are merely dark undercurrents, while ***Imagining Argentina*** by Lawrence Thornton and ***Kiss of the Spider Woman*** by Manuel Puig bring these issues to the fore. E. M. Forster's ***Maurice*** also deals with British views of class and love affairs between men.

Toole, John Kennedy

A Confederacy of Dunces
Louisiana State University Press. 1980. 338 pp.

Obese, gaseous, unemployed social critic Ignatius J. Reilly transforms a succession of employment opportunities into full-blown comical disasters as a result of an ongoing revolt against his devoted and mildly alcoholic mother, his beatnik girlfriend, and the entire modern world.

2d Appeal Language   Book Groups 📖

  Subjects ALA Notable Books • First Novels • Humorous Fiction • Mothers and Sons • New Orleans • Pulitzer Prize Winners

  Now try This novel's publishing history demonstrates how much mother love can accomplish. Unable to get his book published, Toole, in despair, committed suicide. His mother, determined to see the book in print, got Pulitzer Prize-winning novelist Walker Percy to look at the manuscript. Percy submitted it to LSU Press, and the rest is history. Katherine Dunn's ***Geek Love*** is another book filled with bizarre characters. Jerry Strahan's ***Managing Ignatius: The Lunacy of Lucky Dogs and Life in the Quarter*** is the real story of Ignatius J. Reilly.

Trollope, Joanna

The Men and the Girls
Random House. 1992. 248 pp.

James and Hugh, lifelong friends now in their 60s (and both married to women 25 years younger), find the generation gap unbridgeable as their wives insist on lifestyle changes and careers of their own.

2d Appeal Story

  Subjects Adultery • British Authors • Marriage • Older Men/Younger Women • Oxford University

  Now try Trollope's other novels include ***A Spanish Lover***, ***The Rector's Wife***, and ***A Passionate Man***. Trollope has a gently acerbic sense of humor, less harsh than Angela Carter's (***Saints and Strangers*** and others) and A. N. Wilson's (***Wise Virgin, Incline Our Hearts***, and others).

Trott, Susan
Crane Spreads Wings: A Bigamist's Story   Doubleday. 1998. 222 pp.

Convinced that her husband of a month has lied to her—he told her that he had nearly finished writing a novel when he had barely begun it—Jane Croy decides to leave him for a new life as a nanny, only to complicate her life when she falls in love with her employer.

2d Appeal   Story

Subjects   Adultery • Bigamists and Bigamy • Birds • Humorous Fiction • Small-Town Life • T'ai Chi • Triangles

Now try   Trott's other novels include *Divorcing Daddy* and *Pursued by the Crooked Man*. The novels of Elinor Lipman (*The Inn at Lake Devine* and others) and Christina Bartolomeo's *Cupid & Diana* have similar high-spirited main characters.

Troy, Judy
West of Venus   Random House. 1997. 237 pp.

Holly's less-than-positive relationships with men—her married boss at the restaurant where she works, the veterinarian next door—change when state trooper Gene Rollison starts showing up just when Holly needs him most.

2d Appeal   Story

Subjects   Adultery • First Novels • Love Stories • Policemen • Small-Town Life • Veterinarians

Now try   Troy is also the author of *Mourning Doves*, a collection of stories. Tom Drury's *The End of Vandalism* displays an affection for life in a small town and its people that is similar to Troy's. Jonis Agee's *Sweet Eyes* shares some plot elements with Troy's novel.

Tyler, Anne
The Accidental Tourist   Knopf. 1985. 355 pp.

Travel writer Macon, numbed by his young son's death and wife's abandonment, slowly emerges from his self-imposed cocoon after meeting Muriel, an eccentric dog walker.

2d Appeal   Language   Book Groups 📖

Subjects   ALA Notable Books • Death of a Child • Divorce • Dogs • Eccentrics and Eccentricities • Grief • Loss of a Child • Male/Female Relationships • Marriage • National Book Critics Circle Award Winners

Now try   Among Anne Tyler's other novels are *The Clock Winder*, *Celestial Navigation*, *Morgan's Passing*, and *Earthly Possessions*. Frederick Busch's *Girls* also describes the ways grief can manhandle a marriage. The sudden death of a son and its effect on both family members and the man who killed him, is sensitively explored in John Burnham Schwartz's *Reservation Road*.

Tyler, Anne
Breathing Lessons   Knopf. 1988. 327 pp.

During their long marriage, Ira and Maggie Moran have grown used to each other's eccentricities and annoying habits but discover, at the end of a trip to a funeral, there are still things to learn about one another.

2d Appeal   Language   Book Groups 📖

Subjects   ALA Notable Books • Husbands and Wives • Marriage • Pulitzer Prize Winners • Road Novels

Now try   Among Tyler's other novels are *The Accidental Tourist*, *The Tin Can Tree*, *If Morning Ever Comes*, and *A Patchwork Planet*. Walter Sullivan's *A Time to Dance* is another novel about a married couple who have more or less learned to live with each other's foibles.

Tyler, Anne
Dinner at the Homesick Restaurant
Knopf. 1982. 303 pp.

As Pearl Tull lies dying, her three children—bully Cody, nurturer Jenny, and Ezra, who dreams of owning a cozy and comforting restaurant—each offers a version of the dreadful childhood they shared after their father deserted the family.

2d Appeal   Language   Book Groups 📖

Subjects   ALA Notable Books • Baltimore • Brothers and Sisters • Cafés and Restaurants • Death and Dying • Dysfunctional Families • Family Relationships • Mothers and Daughters • Mothers and Sons

Now try   All of Tyler's works have intriguing, somewhat eccentric characters. *Searching for Caleb*, for example, is about elderly Daniel Peck, who, with the help of his fortune-telling granddaughter, searches for his dreamy, musical brother who disappeared without a trace 60 years before. The three children of Pearl Tull are similar to the three siblings found in Deirdre McNamer's *One Sweet Quarrel*.

Unger, Douglas
Leaving the Land
Harper & Row. 1984. 277 pp.

Marge Hogan's attachment to her South Dakota farm is threatened by the end of the agricultural boom following World War II and her son's indifference to his inheritance.

2d Appeal   Setting   Book Groups 📖

Subjects   ALA Notable Books • Farms and Farm Life • First Novels • Mothers and Sons • South Dakota

Now try   Unger's other novels include *The Turkey War* and *Voices from Silence*. John Edgar Wideman's *Sent for You Yesterday* also describes the ways that communities—both rural and urban—struggle to survive. John Thorndike's *The Potato Baron* depicts another character's strong attachment to the land.

Unsworth, Barry
The Rage of the Vulture
Houghton Mifflin Co. 1983. 443 pp.

As the Ottoman Empire comes to a bloody end during World War I, Captain Robert Markham returns to Constantinople and wreaks his own havoc in an ultimately impossible effort to redeem himself.

2d Appeal   Setting   Book Groups 📖

Subjects   Constantinople • Ethnic Wars • Genocide • Guilt • Turkey

Now try Other novels by Unsworth include his Booker Prize-winning *Sacred Hunger*, *Morality Play*, and *The Rage of the Vulture*. Another complex novel set in an interesting locale is *Corelli's Mandolin* by Louis de Bernieres, which also creates a powerful sense of place and deals with war, ethnicity, and family relations.

Updike, John
Bech Is Back
Knopf. 1982. 195 pp.

Turning 50, Bech finds his life changing with a new wife, a new family, and a new book, but his wry, biting humor keeps him rolling with the punches.

2d Appeal Language   Book Groups 📖

Subjects ALA Notable Books • Humorous Fiction • Jews and Judaism • Male/Female Relationships • Middle-Aged Men • Writers and Writing

Now try Other books in the Bech saga include *Bech: A Book* and *Bech at Bay: A Quasi Novel*. Among Updike's other novels are *Memories of the Ford Administration* and *Toward the End of Time*. John Cheever (*The Stories of John Cheever* and others) and J. P. Marquand (*Wickford Point*, *The Late George Apley*, and others) both set their books among the upper classes in the Eastern United States.

Vakil, Ardashir
Beach Boy
Scribner. 1998. 239 pp.

In Bombay, India, Cyrus Readymoney (a movie-mad, sex-crazed, ever-hungry eight year old) attempts to hold on to his world as his parents' marriage comes to an end.

2d Appeal Setting   Book Groups 📖

Subjects ALA Notable Books • Bombay • Coming-of-Age • Divorce • First Novels • India • Indian Authors • Zoroastrians

Now try Other novels that look at the world through the eyes of a young boy include Peter Hedges's *An Ocean in Iowa*, Steven Millhauser's *Edwin Mullhouse: The Life and Death of an American Writer, 1943–54*, and Roddy Doyle's *Paddy Clarke Ha Ha Ha*. *Beach Boy* won the Betty Trask Award.

Vargas Llosa, Mario
Aunt Julia and the Scriptwriter
Farrar Straus Giroux. 1982. 374 pp.

When glamorous and sexy Julia divorces her husband in Bolivia and returns home to Peru, she and her much younger nephew fall in love, to the consternation of the rest of the family; meanwhile a series of soap operas are keeping all Peru glued to their radios. Translated from the Spanish by Helen R. Lane.

2d Appeal Language

Subjects ALA Notable Books • Humorous Fiction • Middle-Aged Men • Novels in Translation • Older Women/Younger Men • Peru • Peruvian Authors • Radio • South America • South American Authors • Writers and Writing

Now try Other novels by Vargas Llosa include the humorous *Captain Pantoja and the Special Service*, *The Notebooks of Don Rigoberto*, *In Praise of the Stepmother*, *The Storyteller*, and *The Real Life of Alejandro Mayta*. Garrison Keillor's *WLT: A Radio Romance* is another novel in which radio plays an important part.

Verdelle, A. J.

The Good Negress   Algonquin Books of Chapel Hill. 1995. 298 pp.

When Denise Palms leaves her grandmother's home in rural Virginia to move north to Detroit in 1963, she is torn between her desire for an education and her family's belief that she will cook, clean, and take care of the new baby her mother and stepfather are expecting.

Book Groups 📖

Subjects   1960s • African American Authors • African Americans • Coming-of-Age • Detroit, Michigan • Family Relationships • First Novels • Teenage Girls

Now try   Denise is about the same age as the main character in Thulani Davis's *1959*, whose life changes dramatically. Susan Straight's *I Been in Sorrow's Kitchen and Licked Out All the Pots* is another novel written in dialect that is still quite easy to read.

Vicens, Josefina

False Years   Latin American Literary Review Press. 1989. 94 pp.

Everyone wants Luis Alfonso to be like his popular, though deceased father—so much so that Luis soon feels he himself has died while his father lives on. Translated from the Spanish by Peter Earle.

Book Groups 📖

Subjects   Fathers and Sons • Mexican Authors • Mexico • Novels in Translation

Now try   Vicens's first novel was *The Empty Book*, which scrutinized the writing process itself. The protagonist in Richard Russo's *Straight Man* is also frequently compared—to his detriment—to his father.

Von Herzen, Lane

The Unfastened Heart   Dutton. 1994. 241 pp.

Unforeseen complications arise when a group of well-meaning, lovelorn women concoct a scheme to make their beloved friend Anna fall in love with the widower next door.

2d Appeal   Language

Subjects   Adoption • Grief • Mothers and Daughters • Women's Friendships

Now try   Von Herzen's first novel was *Copper Crown*. The course of true love also runs less than smoothly in Anne Tyler's *The Clock Winder*. The lyrical writing in Von Herzen's novel can also be found in Sara Maitland's *Ancestral Truths* and Mary Karr's memoir, *The Liar's Club*.

Walker, Alice

The Color Purple   Harcourt Brace Jovanovich. 1982. 245 pp.

In the deep South during the 1930s, an alternately abused and neglected Celie writes letters to God as she struggles to take charge of her life and heal her damaged spirit.

2d Appeal   Language   Book Groups 📖

Subjects   1930s • Abusive Relationships • African American Authors • African Americans • National Book Award Winners • Pulitzer Prize Winners

Now try   Walker's other books include *Possessing the Secret of Joy* and *The Temple of My Familiar*. Women responding to abusive relationships are also part of the plots of Dorothy Allison's *Bastard Out of Carolina*, Toni Morrison's *The Bluest Eye*, and Jane Smiley's *A Thousand Acres*.

Wang, Anyi
Baotown
Norton. 1989. 144 pp.

The residents of a remote, poverty-stricken village in the Anhui province of China cope with famine, flood, and family relationships. Translated from the Chinese by Martha Avery.

Book Groups 📖

Subjects   China • Chinese Authors • Family Relationships • First Novels • Poverty • Small-Town Life

Now try   Wang is also the author of *Love in a Small Town*, *Love on a Barren Mountain*, and *Lapse of Time*. Other stories of life in contemporary rural China are *The Garlic Ballads* by Yan Mo, *The Chinese Western: Short Fiction from Today's China*, translated by Zhu Hong, *In the Pond* by Ha Jin, and *South of the Clouds: Tales from Yunnan*, edited by Lucien Miller. Other works that portray community life include *The Growth of the Soil* by Knut Hamsun, *Chronicle of a Death Foretold* by Gabriel Garcia Marquez, *Winesburg, Ohio* by Sherwood Anderson, and *Under Milkwood* by Dylan Thomas.

Wassmo, Herbjorg
The House with the Blind Glass Windows
Seal Press. 1987. 227 pp.

In post-war Norway, 12-year-old Tora tries to cope with the knowledge of her parents' sympathy for the Nazis and her sexually abusive stepfather. Translated from the Norwegian by Roseann Lloyd and Allen Simpson.

Book Groups 📖

Subjects   Abusive Relationships • Coming-of-Age • Holocaust • Norway • Norwegian Authors • Novels in Translation • Sexual Abuse

Now try   This novel shares several themes with Ursula Hegi's *Stones from the River*.

Waters, Annie
Glimmer
Putnam. 1997. 207 pp.

Only the loving support of her older brothers and sisters and the reintroduction into her life of the father she never knew save Sage from a suicide attempt after her mother's death, a tumultuous first year of college, and her confusion over her bi-racial heritage.

2d Appeal   Story

Book Groups 📖

Subjects   Bi-racial Characters • Brothers and Sisters • Fathers and Daughters • First Novels • Suicide

Now try   The ever-changing relationships among the various siblings in *Glimmer* is similar to the family described in Judith Rossner's *Nine Months in the Life of an Old Maid*. A suicide attempt plays an important part in Sylvia Plath's autobiographical novel, *The Bell Jar*, just as it did in Plath's real life. The main characters in Danzy Senna's *Caucasia* are also bi-racial.

Weber, Katherine
Objects in Mirror Are Closer Than They Appear   Crown Publishers. 1995. 262 pp.

In Geneva, Switzerland, 26-year-old photographer Harriet Rose finds herself confronting old wounds and losses as she struggles with the quandary of whether to rescue her friend Anne from a disastrous affair with an older man.

2d Appeal	Story
Subjects	Dysfunctional Families • First Novels • Older Men/Younger Women • Photography and Photographers • Switzerland • Women's Friendships
Now try	Weber is also the author of *The Music Lesson*. The contrast between American naïveté and European cynicism can also be found in Diane Johnson's *Le Divorce*, as well as in Henry James's *The Wings of the Dove*.

Weesner, Theodore
The True Detective   Summit Books. 1987. 383 pp.

In a distorted bid for love, a desperate and confused college student abducts and rapes a young boy, changing forever the lives of those involved.

2d Appeal	Story Book Groups 📖
Subjects	ALA Notable Books • College Students • Family Relationships • Mothers and Sons • Pedophilia • Rape • Violence
Now try	William Trevor's *Felicia's Journey* offers a similarly grim view of humanity. Richard Price's *Clockers* and *Freedomland* have some of the same grittiness of place and character as Weesner's novel.

Weldon, Fay
Life Force   Viking. 1992. 222 pp.

Four ex-lovers of Leslie Beck reconnect after the death of his second wife, inspiring one of them to record a history of their entanglements.

2d Appeal	Language Book Groups 📖
Subjects	Adultery • British Authors • Male/Female Relationships • Women's Friendships
Now try	Among Weldon's other books are *The Cloning of Joanna May*, *Trouble*, and *The Life and Loves of a She-Devil*. Her witty, satirical tone brings to mind Evelyn Waugh's *Men at Arms* and *Officers and Gentlemen*. Weldon's jaundiced view of male/female relationships is similar to that of Carol Clewlow (*A Woman's Guide to Adultery*), Martin Amis (*The Rachel Papers*), and Kingsley Amis (*Stanley and the Women*).

Wells, Rebecca
Divine Secrets of the Ya-Ya Sisterhood   HarperCollins Publishers. 1996. 356 pp.

After struggling with painful childhood memories, Sidda Lee Walker grows to understand and accept her colorful and troubled mother Vivi through appreciating her mother's lifelong friendships with the three other women who belonged to the Ya-Ya Sisterhood.

2d Appeal	Story Book Groups 📖

Subjects   Dysfunctional Families • Male/Female Relationships • Mothers and Daughters • Southern Authors • Women's Friendships

Now try   This is the sequel to *Little Altars Everywhere*, which is an account of Vivi's childhood. The friendship among the four women is similar to the relationships described in Fannie Flagg's *Fried Green Tomatoes at the Whistle Stop Café*. Sheila Bosworth's novel *Almost Innocent* is another view of the steamy South and a dysfunctional family.

Welter, John
I Want to Buy a Vowel
Algonquin Books. 1996. 314 pp.

In a small Texas town, 11-year-old Eva and her younger sister Ava try to help illegal alien Alfredo Santayana (whose minimal English skills come from watching television), with hilarious and bittersweet results.

Subjects   Humorous Fiction • Immigrants and Refugees • Sisters • Small-Town Life • Texas

Now try   Welter's first novel was *Night of the Avenging Blowfish: A Novel of Covert Operations, Love, and Luncheon Meat*. A far darker look at the problem of undocumented workers in the United States is T. Coraghessan Boyle's *The Tortilla Curtain*.

Wesley, Mary
Jumping the Queue
Pengion Books. 1988. 217 pp.

Weary British widow Matilda Poliport has decided to end it all, but finds a reason to live after persuading a young man on the run from the police not to take his own life.

Subjects   British Authors • Incest • Suicide • Widows

Now try   Wesley's *An Imaginative Experience* is another novel that hinges on an impulsive, yet kindly act. Fay Weldon (*Life Force*) and Angela Carter (*Wise Children*) are other British writers whose subjects, style, and use of black humor are similar to Wesley's.

White, Bailey
Quite a Year for Plums
Knopf. 1998. 220 pp.

Everyone in his small Georgia hometown is interested in finding peanut pathologist and banjo player Roger Meadows the perfect wife, but they doubt it's Della, a painter of chickens.

Subjects   First Novels • Georgia • Humorous Fiction • Science and Scientists • Small-Town Life • Southern Authors

Now try   White's nonfiction books include *Mama Makes Up Her Mind: And Other Dangers of Southern Living* and *Sleeping at the Starlite Motel: And Other Adventures on the Way Back Home*. The southern charm of White's novel is also found in Olive Ann Burns's *Cold Sassy Tree* and Fannie Flagg's *Fried Green Tomatoes at the Whistle-Stop Café*.

White, Edmund
A Boy's Own Story
Dutton. 1982. 217 pp.

A boy growing up in the Midwest during the 1950s finds his attempts to reconcile his relationships with his parents and prepare for adulthood complicated by his homosexuality.

2d Appeal Characters Language   Book Groups 📖

  Subjects 1950s • Coming-of-Age • Fathers and Sons • Gay Teenagers

  Now try This story is continued in *The Beautiful Room Is Empty* and *The Farewell Symphony*. Martin Schecter's *Two Halves of New Haven* and Robert Rodi's *Closet Case* are other novels that deal with the same topic.

Wideman, John Edgar
Sent for You Yesterday
Avon Books. 1983. 208 pp.

In 1930s Homewood, a black community of Pittsburgh, the lives of three generations are bound together by the music of Albert Wilkes.

2d Appeal Setting   Book Groups 📖

  Subjects 1930s • African American Authors • African Americans • ALA Notable Books • Multigenerational Novels • Music and Musicians • Pittsburgh

  Now try This series of interconnected short stories follows *Damballah* and *The Hiding Place* to form a trilogy. *The Serpent's Gift* by Helen Elaine Lee and Connie Porter's *All-Bright Court* are both set in African American communities. Wideman's memoir about his brother, *Brothers and Keepers*, was also an ALA Notable Book. African American life in Pittsburgh in the 1950s is the subject of Albert French's *I Can't Wait on God*. *Sent for You Yesterday* won a PEN/Faulkner Award.

Willard, Nancy
Things Invisible to See
Knopf. 1984. 263 pp.

Baseball, a good twin and a bad one, and a crippled young woman are woven together in this novel of life in Ann Arbor, Michigan, during World War II.

2d Appeal Language   Book Groups 📖

  Subjects Baseball • Brothers • First Novels • Love Stories • Magic Realism • Michigan • Twins • World War II

  Now try Willard's other books include the novel, *Sister Water*, and several books for children, as well as collections of poetry and short stories. Robertson Davies's *Fifth Business* and John Irving's *A Prayer for Owen Meany* are other novels in which an accident changes the lives of the people involved. Lawrence Thornton's *Imagining Argentina* is another example of magic realism in an American novel.

Williams, Niall
Four Letters of Love
Farrar, Straus and Giroux. 1997. 257 pp.

The lives of Nicholas and Isabel and their troubled Irish families intertwine as they struggle to understand the magic and mysteries of love.

Book Groups 📖

Subjects Family Relationships • First Novels • Ireland • Love Stories • Male/Female Relationships

Now try Niall Williams and his wife Christine Breen have written a series of books about their life in Ireland (where they moved to escape the rat race of New York City), including *O Come Ye Back to Ireland: Our First Year in County Clare*. The magical quality and lyrical language of this novel can also be found in Lane Von Herzen's *The Unfastened Heart*.

Willis, Connie
Bellwether
Bantam Books. 1996. 247 pp.

In the huge and impersonal corporation where both are employed, it takes a misdelivered package to bring together Sandra Foster (who studies fads) and Bennett O'Reilly (who studies chaos theory).

2d Appeal Story

Subjects Business and Businessmen • Humorous Fiction • Male/Female Relationships • Science and Scientists

Now try Willis is an award-winning science fiction writer. Another of her novels is *To Say Nothing of the Dog*. The sweet relationship between Sandra and Bennett is similar to the relationship between the two main characters in Carol Shields's *The Republic of Love*.

Wilson, Robert McLiam
Ripley Bogle
Deutsch. 1989. 273 pp.

Born of an Irish mother and Welsh father, Ripley Bogle slogs his way through life, beginning as a child genius, progressing to cynical college student, and finally to bemused bum, living on the streets of London, always viewing life through a slightly skewed lens.

Subjects British Authors • First Novels • Gifted Children • Homelessness • London

Now try Wilson's other books include *Eureka Street: A Novel of Ireland Like No Other*. Another novel about homelessness is Marge Piercy's *The Longings of Women*. Geoff Nicholson's *Bleeding London* is another novel set in London. *Ripley Bogle* won the Betty Trask Award.

Wing, Avra
Angie, I Says
Warner Books. 1991. 214 pp.

When Brooklyn-born Tina, half-Italian and half-Jewish, discovers that she is pregnant, she has to decide whether to marry the baby's father (her long-time boyfriend Vinnie), or skip the marriage, have the baby, and pursue an affair with a wealthy and handsome lawyer she meets at a museum.

2d Appeal Story

Subjects   Birth Defects • First Novels • Male/Female Relationships • Pregnancy • Single Parents • Women's Friendships

Now try   Angie's bluntness and bravado are reminiscent of Holden Caulfield's language in J. D. Salinger's *The Catcher in the Rye*.

Winterson, Jeanette

Oranges Are Not the Only Fruit
Atlantic Monthly. 1987. 176 pp.

The adopted daughter of eccentric evangelical parents struggles to assert her growing homosexual identity in the face of her tyrannical mother and the fanatic religiosity of the pastor and congregation of their church.

2d Appeal   Language   Book Groups 📖

Subjects   Adoption • British Authors • Eccentrics and Eccentricities • First Novels • Lesbians • Mothers and Daughters • Religious Extremism

Now try   Winterson's other books include *The Passion*, *Sexing the Cherry*, and *Written on the Body*. Another look at growing up in a repressive religious society is Sheri Reynolds's *The Rapture of Canaan*. A memoir that explores the same topic is *In the Wilderness: Coming of Age in Unknown Country* by Kim Barnes. Another wry British novel about a quirky family and written in a wry tone is Angela Carter's *Wise Children*. *Oranges Are Not the Only Fruit* won the Whitbread Prize for First Novels.

Winton, Tim

Cloudstreet
Penguin Books. 1991. 426 pp.

Two neighboring families—the Pickles and the Lambs—are brought together at first by the hard times following World War II and at last by a marriage.

2d Appeal   Language   Book Groups 📖

Subjects   Australia • Australian Authors • Eccentrics and Eccentricities • Family Relationships • Magic Realism

Now try   Among Winton's other books are *Shallows*, *The Riders*, and *That Eye, That Sky*. Winton shares with his fellow Australian, Peter Carey (*Oscar and Lucinda* and others), a love of language, the ability to create fascinating characters, and writing of incredible vigor. *Cloudstreet* won the Miles Franklin Award.

Wolff, Tobias

The Barracks Thief
Ecco Press. 1984. 101 pp.

While guarding an ammunition dump threatened by a nearby fire, three men find their friendship challenged when a "barracks thief" infiltrates their ranks.

Subjects   First Novels • Men's Friendships • Military Life • Vietnam War

Now try   Among Wolff's other books are two memoirs: *This Boy's Life* and *In Pharaoh's Army: Memories of the Lost War*, which was an ALA Notable Book. Another novel about parachute troops in the Vietnam War is Joseph Ferrandino's *Firefight*. *The Barracks Thief* won a PEN/Faulkner Award.

Wong, Shawn
American Knees
Simon & Schuster. 1995. 240 pp.

Race, culture, and identity issues all surface when Chinese American Raymond Ding falls in love with Irish-Japanese Aurora Crane and the two discover that falling out of love is not as easy as it seems.

2d Appeal   Story

Subjects   Chinese American Authors • Chinese Americans • Humorous Fiction • Interracial Relationships • Japanese Americans • Male/Female Relationships

Now try   Wong's first novel, *Homebase*, is a coming-of-age story whose protagonist is a young, fourth-generation Chinese American. Sections of *American Knees* appeared in the anthology, *Charlie Chan Is Dead: An Anthology of Contemporary Asian-American Literature*, edited by Jessica Hagedorn. This unsentimental look at the life of a hyphenated American is similar to the presentation by Chang-Rae Lee in his novel *Native Speaker*.

Wood, Clement Biddle
Ocean Vu, Jog to Beach
St. Martin's Press. 1988. 308 pp.

A group of summer renters on Long Island, New York, includes two yuppies, a writer whose book is due to the publisher in September, her gambling sportswriter boyfriend, two brothers who sell real estate, and a Russian émigré poet who observes their lives and loves with a sociological detachment, complete with footnotes.

2d Appeal   Story

Subjects   Humorous Fiction • Long Island, New York • Male/Female Relationships • New York • Writers and Writing

Now try   Wood's first novel was *Welcome to the Club*. The character of the Russian poet brings to mind two books by Vladimir Nabokov: *Pnin*, the adventures of a bewildered Russian immigrant to the United States, and *Pale Fire*, another novel replete with scholarly paraphernalia.

Wright, Stephen
Meditations in Green
C. Scribner's Sons. 1983. 342 pp.

Through a series of flashbacks and meditations, Specialist 4 James Griffin details his physical and mental deterioration during the Vietnam War, as well as his re-entry into civilian life accompanied by madness and drug addiction.

2d Appeal   Language   Book Groups 📖

Subjects   ALA Notable Books • Drugs and Drug Abuse • First Novels • Vietnam Veterans • Vietnam War

Now try   Wright is also the author of *Going Native: A Novel* and *M31: A Family Romance*. Two other gritty works of fiction about Vietnam are Robert Flynn's *The Last Klick* and Rick Christman's *Falling in Love at the End of the World*. Larry Heinemann's *Paco's Story* is also about a Vietnam veteran trying to exist in the civilian world.

Yamanaka, Lois-Ann
Blu's Hanging
Farrar, Straus and Giroux. 1997. 261 pp.

Three young Japanese children deal with the grief of losing their mother while learning how to cope with the perverse adult world of their impoverished community on a Hawaiian island.

2d Appeal Language   Book Groups 📖

Subjects ALA Notable Books • Brothers and Sisters • Death of a Parent • Hawaii • Japanese American Authors • Orphans

Now try Yamanaka's first novel was *Wild Meat and Bully Burgers*. *Comfort Woman* by Nora Okja Keller and *My Old Sweetheart* by Susanna Moore are both novels about girls growing up in Hawaii with emotionally ill mothers.

Yehoshua, A. B.
Five Seasons
Doubleday. 1989. 359 pp.

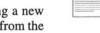

Newly widowed, Molkho seeks to put his life back together by finding a new wife for himself while remaining faithful to his deceased partner. Translated from the Hebrew by Hillel Halkin.

2d Appeal Characters   Book Groups 📖

Subjects ALA Notable Books • Cancer • Death of a Spouse • Israel • Israeli Authors • Jews and Judaism • Male/Female Relationships • Middle-Aged Men • Novels in Translation

Now try Yehoshua also wrote *Mr. Mani*. Life following the death of a spouse is also the topic of Hilma Wolitzer's *Silver*.

Yehoshua, A. B.
A Late Divorce
Doubleday. 1984. 354 pp.

During Passover, Kaminka returns to Israel from America to divorce his wife of many years, an event that brings about a family crisis. Translated from the Hebrew by Hillel Halkin.

Book Groups 📖

Subjects ALA Notable Books • Divorce • Family Relationships • Israel • Israeli Authors • Jews and Judaism • Novels in Translation

Now try Yehoshua's other works of fiction include *The Open Heart*. The stream-of-consciousness writing style of *A Late Divorce* is reminiscent of James Joyce's *Ulysses*. Like *A Late Divorce*, Susan Howatch's *The Wonder Worker* is told from the viewpoint of different characters.

Zuravleff, Mary Kay

The Frequency of Souls
Farrar, Straus Giroux. 1996. 244 pp.

George Mahoney's staid life as a designer of refrigerators gets a jump start when he becomes attracted to his co-worker, Niagra Spense, a six-foot, nearsighted, deaf genius.

2d Appeal Story

Subjects Adultery • Fathers and Sons • First Novels • Midlife Crisis • Science and Scientists

Now try Connie Willis's *Bellwether* is another novel about co-workers falling in love. Zuravleff's affection for George and Niagra is similar to the affection Stephen McCauley (*The Object of My Affection*) and Elinor Lipman (*The Way Men Act*) show to their characters.

Chapter 4

Language

Adler, Renata
Pitch Dark
Knopf. 1983. 144 pp.

Three loosely interwoven stories of the travels, reminiscences, and ruminations of Kate Ennis, a woman involved with a married man.

2d Appeal   Characters

   Subjects   Adultery • Male/Female Relationships • Middle-Aged Women • Single Women

   Now try   Adler is also the author of the novel ***Speedboat*** and several works of nonfiction, including a collection of film criticism, ***A Year in the Dark: Journal of a Film Critic, 1968–69***. The novels of Joan Didion (***Run River*** and others), Francine du Plessix Gray (***Lovers and Tyrants***), Lily Tuck's ***The Woman Who Walked on Water***, and Merle Miller's ***A Gay and Melancholy Sound*** are written in a style similar to Adler's.

Allende, Isabel
Eva Luna
Knopf. 1988. 271 pp.

In the course of her life Eva Luna encounters wealthy eccentrics, drag queens, guerrilla leaders, and gutter waifs and weaves their stories with her own. Translated from the Spanish by Margaret Sayers Peden.

2d Appeal   Characters

   Subjects   ALA Notable Books • Chilean Authors • Magic Realism • Novels in Translation • South American Authors

   Now try   The novels of Gabriel Garcia Marquez share with Allende's books lyrical language and richly evoked settings. Eva Luna, like the heroine of Laura Esquivel's ***Like Water for Chocolate***, is a woman with whom readers can easily fall in love.

Allende, Isabel
The House of the Spirits
A.A. Knopf. 1985. 368 pp.

During political unrest in an unnamed South American country, the men and women of the Trueba clan struggle to uphold their traditions, their connections with the spirit world, and their family. Translated from the Spanish by Magda Bogin.

2d Appeal   Characters   Book Groups 📖

Subjects   ALA Notable Books • Chilean Authors • Family Relationships • First Novels • Magic Realism • Male/Female Relationships • Multigenerational Novels • Novels in Translation • Political Unrest • South American Authors

Now try   Among Allende's other books are a novel, *Of Love and Shadows*, and a memoir about the death of her daughter, *Paula.* The magnificent sweep and magic realism of this novel can also be found in Gabriel Garcia Marquez's *Love in the Time of Cholera* and other novels. The political terror and torture that feature so prominently in this novel is the subject of Lawrence Thornton's *Imagining Argentina*.

Allison, Dorothy
Bastard Out of Carolina
Dutton. 1992. 309 pp.

Bone, growing up in the proud, independent Boatwright clan in South Carolina, struggles to overcome neglect and physical abuse as she matures.

2d Appeal   Characters   Book Groups 📖

Subjects   Alcoholics and Alcoholism • Coming-of-Age • Family Relationships • First Novels • Poverty • Sexual Abuse • South Carolina

Now try   Allison also published a collection of short stories, *Trash*, and a second novel, *Cavedweller*. Wally Lamb's *She's Come Undone* shares some themes with Allison's novel. Lisa Reardon's *Billy Dead* and Carolyn Chute's *The Beans of Egypt, Maine* are other novels that explore bleak and troubled lives. *My Drowning* by Jim Grimsley shows the effects of abuse and neglect on a woman's life, as does *The Color Purple* by Alice Walker

Anshaw, Carol
Seven Moves
Houghton Mifflin. 1996. 220 pp.

When her lover Taylor disappears after a minor argument, Chris Snow is at first angry and then worried, emotions that lead her on a voyage of discovery.

2d Appeal   Characters

Subjects   Lesbians • Morocco • Psychiatrists, Psychoanalysts, Psychotherapists • Women's Friendships

Now try   Anshaw's first novel was *Aquamarine*. Other novels about people who disappear and the effect that has on those left behind include Scott Spencer's *Waking the Dead*, Tim O'Brien's *In the Lake of the Woods*, Jacquelyn Mitchard's *The Deep End of the Ocean*, and Beth Gutcheon's *Still Missing*.

Antunes, Antonio Lobo
Act of the Damned
Grove Press. 1995. 246 pp.

As the dictatorial patriarch of a once wealthy Portuguese family lies dying, his immoral son-in-law schemes to grab for himself whatever is left of the estate. Translated from the Portuguese by Richard Zenith.

2d Appeal   Setting

Subjects   Aging • Dysfunctional Families • Novels in Translation • Portugal • Portuguese Authors

Now try   This novel won the Portuguese Writers' Association Grand Prize for Fiction. Other novels by Antunes include *South of Nowhere* and *An Explanation of the Birds*. *The Grab* by Maria Katzenbach has a similar theme.

Aslam, Nadeem
Season of the Rainbirds
Andre Deutsch. 1993. 196 pp.

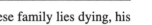

A sack of letters missing for two decades suddenly reappears, setting a quiet Pakistani villlage abuzz, adding to the turmoil already mounting due to politics, local crime, and an illicit love affair.

2d Appeal   Setting   Book Groups 📖

Subjects   First Novels • Pakistan • Pakistani Authors • Small-Town Life

Now try   Three novels from India that share the beautiful writing of Aslam's book are *The Book of Secrets* by M. G. Vassanji, *The God of Small Things* by Arundhati Roy, and Salman Rushdie's *Midnight's Children.* Letters play an important part in the plots of *The Love Letter* by Cathleen Schine and Louis Buss's *The Luxury of Exile*. Other novels that depict the effects of political change on Muslim culture at the family level are Naguib Mahfouz's *Palace Walk*, set in Egypt, and Abdal Rahman Munif's "Cities of Salt" trilogy, set in an unnamed country on the Persian Gulf. *Season of the Rainbirds* won a Betty Trask Award.

Atxaga, Bernardo
Obabakoak
Pantheon Books. 1992. 326 pp.

Tales of the people and events of the Basque village of Obaba are interwoven in a series of interlocking episodes. Translated from the Basque by Margaret Jull Costa.

2d Appeal   Setting

Subjects   First Novels • Novels in Translation • Small-Town Life • Spain • Spanish Authors

Now try   Atxaga's novel won Spain's National Prize for Literature. He also wrote *The Lone Man*, a novel set in Barcelona. Other tales that involve the Basque region of Spain include Leif Davidson's *The Sardine Deception*, *Child of the Holy Ghost* by Robert Laxalt, and Samuel Edwards's *The Caves of Guernica*. Another novel that consists of interlocking episodes is Gita Mehta's *The River Sutra*.

Auster, Paul
Leviathan
Viking. 1992. 275 pp.

Novelist Peter Aaron races to record the life of his recently deceased friend Sachs—a writer turned political terrorist—before the FBI and the press can misrepresent his friend's career and intentions.

2d Appeal	Characters	Book Groups 📖

Subjects   ALA Notable Books • Men's Friendships • Moral/Ethical Dilemmas • Terrorists and Terrorism • Writers and Writing

Now try   Auster's other works of fiction include *Mr. Vertigo*. The novels of Don DeLillo (*The Names* and others), like those of Auster, encourage readers to look at the world in different ways. The title of this novel comes from Thomas Hobbes's *Leviathan*, which would be worth reading just to see what light it sheds (or doesn't shed) on this novel. The novels of Siri Hustvedt (*The Enchantment of Lily Dahl* and *The Blindfold*) also describe a slightly off-key world.

Banks, Russell
The Sweet Hereafter
HarperCollins Publishers. 1991. 257 pp.

After a tragic school bus accident, the residents of a small town in upstate New York react in different ways to their loss and to the attorney who encourages them to channel their rage in a lawsuit.

2d Appeal	Characters	Book Groups 📖

Subjects   ALA Notable Books • Death of a Child • Family Relationships • Fathers and Daughters • Grief • New York • Sexual Abuse • Small-Town Life

Now try   Banks's other works of fiction include *Hamilton Stark* and *Family Life*. Other novels that dwell on the effects a tragedy has on a family are Rosellen Brown's *Before and After*, John Burnham Schwartz's *Reservation Road*, and Chris Bohjalian's *Past the Bleachers*. The setting of this novel—New York State in the winter—is similar to the setting of Frederick Busch's *Girls*.

Barker, Pat
The Ghost Road
Dutton. 1996. 277 pp.

As the first World War draws to a close, pioneering psychologist William Rivers falls ill with Spanish influenza and broods on his experiences with the headhunters of Melanesia, while the blue-collar officer he was treating for shell shock, Lieutenant Billy Prior, confronts moral and sexual issues in his life.

2d Appeal	Characters	Book Groups 📖

Subjects   Bi-sexuals • Booker Prize Winners • British Authors • Psychiatrists, Psychoanalysts, Psychotherapists • Working Classes • World War I

Now try   This is the final novel in Barker's World War I trilogy, which includes *Regeneration* and *The Eye in the Door*. She is also the author of *Blow the House Down*, another bleak portrait of life in England. Other World War I novels include James Carroll's *Supply of Heroes*, Ford Madox Ford's *Parades End*, and Patricia Anthony's *Flanders*.

Barker, Pat
Regeneration
Dutton. 1992. 251 pp.

During World War I, psychiatrist William Rivers, after attempting to cure the very sane poet Siegfried Sassoon, begins to doubt the rationality of restoring young shell-shocked soldiers to service.

2d Appeal   Language   Book Groups 📖

    Subjects   British Authors • Gay Men • Mental Illness • Political Fiction • World War I • Writers and Writing

    Now try   This is the first in a trilogy that includes *The Eye in the Door* and *The Ghost Road*. Other World War I novels include Elizabeth Bowen's beautifully written *The Heat of the Day*, Erich Maria Remarque's *All Quiet on the Western Front*, and Liam O'Flaherty's autobiographical novel, *Return of the Brute*. Paul Fussell in *The Great War and Modern Memory* discusses the literature of World War I, including the poetry of Siegfried Sassoon, Rupert Brooke, and Wilfred Owen.

Barnes, Julian
Talking It Over
Knopf. 1991. 275 pp.

When Stuart and Gillian marry, they are unprepared when Oliver, Stuart's best friend since childhood, almost immediately falls in love with Gillian.

2d Appeal   Language   Book Groups 📖

    Subjects   British Authors • Humorous Fiction • Male/Female Relationships • Men's Friendships • Triangles

    Now try   Barnes explored the subjectiveness of memory, a basic theme of this novel, in *Flaubert's Parrot* as well. Among Barnes's other books are *Porcupine*, *Cross Channel*, and *Metroland*. As in William Faulkner's *As I Lay Dying*, the characters in this novel address the reader directly, explaining their own points of view. In *Love in the Time of Cholera*, Gabriel Garcia Marquez explores how memory can alter the past. In chapters of May Sarton's *Crucial Conversations* the same conversation is repeated from different viewpoints.

Begley, Louis
The Man Who Was Late
Knopf. 1993. 243 pp.

Jack pieces together the last two years in the life of his best friend Ben, a Jewish refugee and Harvard-trained financier, whose essential loneliness is not assuaged by success or love.

2d Appeal   Characters   Book Groups 📖

    Subjects   Adultery • Jews and Judaism • Men's Friendships • Suicide • Upper Classes

    Now try   Begley's other novels include *As Max Saw It* and *Mistler's Exit.* His use of language will remind readers of the novels of Anita Brookner (*Fraud* and others). Begley's upper-class settings are similar to the settings used by Louis Auchincloss (*The Great World and Timothy Colt* and others) and J. P. Marquand (*B. F.'s Daughter* and others). Laurie Colwin in *Family Happiness* gives her characters worldly success but shows that it doesn't necessarily ensure happiness.

Ben Jelloun, Tahar
The Sand Child
Harcourt Brace Jovanovich. 1987. 165 pp.

Tragic events are set in motion when Hajji Ahmed's eighth female child is born and he decides his daughter should be a boy, his heir, regardless of her actual sex, an act that appears to doom her to a life of deception and isolation. Translated from the French by Alan Sheridan.

Subjects France • French Authors • Gender Roles • Middle East • Novels in Translation • Sexual Identity

Now try The story of Mohammed Ahmed is continued in *The Sacred Night*, in which she tries to make herself back into a woman. *The Oblivion Seekers* looks at life in Muslim North Africa in the late nineteenth century through the diaries of Isabelle Eberhardt, a European woman who, for many years, lived and traveled through Algeria dressed as a man. Other books touching on ambiguities of gender include *Orlando* by Virginia Woolf and *The Illusionist* by Dinitia Smith.

Betts, Doris
Souls Raised from the Dead
Knopf. 1994. 339 pp.

When their 10-year-old daughter is diagnosed with kidney disease, her estranged parents must come to terms with their impending loss.

2d Appeal Characters

Subjects ALA Notable Books • Death of a Child • Divorce • Fathers and Daughters • Illness • Male/Female Relationships • North Carolina • Southern Authors • Terminal Illness

Now try Betts's other works of fiction include *The Sharp Teeth of Love* and *Heading West*, as well as collections of short stories. Other novels about the loss of children include Lorene Cary's *The Price of a Child*, Russell Banks's *The Sweet Hereafter*, Jo-Ann Mapson's *Shadow Ranch*, *Points of Light* by Linda Gray Sexton, *The Tin Can Tree* by Anne Tyler, *Girls* by Frederick Busch, and *At Risk* by Alice Hoffman.

Boyle, T. Coraghessan
The Tortilla Curtain
Viking. 1995. 355 pp.

When the lives of young Southern California professionals Delaney and Kyle Mossbacher intersect with illegal Mexican immigrants, Candido and America Rincon, the result is tragic for both couples.

2d Appeal Story   Book Groups 📖

Subjects California • Culture Clash • Immigrants and Refugees • Southern California

Now try Boyle's collection of stories *If the River Were Whiskey* was an ALA Notable Book. *The Tortilla Curtain* is a much darker view of the immigrant experience than is found in John Welter's *I Want to Buy a Vowel*. This novel is told in shifting viewpoints, like Russell Banks's *The Sweet Hereafter*, Lorna Landvik's *Your Oasis on Flame Lake*, and *A Late Divorce* by A. B. Yehoshua. *Macho!* by Victor Villasenor is another portrait of illegal immigrants from Mexico.

Brookner, Anita
Hotel du Lac

Pantheon Books. 1984. 184 pp.

Romance novelist Edith Hope finds herself preoccupied with her fellow guests at the Swiss hotel where she's gone to recover from an embarrassing love affair.

2d Appeal   Characters   Book Groups

Subjects   Booker Prize Winners • British Authors • Single Women • Switzerland • Writers and Writing

Now try   All of Brookner's novels feature men and women living repressed and solitary lives. Her first novel, *The Debut*, begins with a line to treasure: Dr. Weiss, at 40, knew that her life had been ruined by literature. Writers whose style and use of language resemble Brookner's include Louis Begley (*As Max Saw It* and others) and Barbara Pym (*Some Tame Gazelle*, among others).

Brown, Larry
Joe

Algonquin Books of Chapel Hill. 1991. 345 pp.

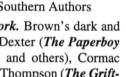

Deep in the back woods of Mississippi, 15-year-old migrant Gary Jones strikes up an unlikely friendship with hard-drinking, hard-living Joe Ransom.

2d Appeal   Characters   Book Groups

Subjects   ALA Notable Books • Alcoholics and Alcoholism • Dysfunctional Families • Men's Friendships • Mississippi • Poverty • Southern Authors

Now try   Brown also wrote *Father and Son* and *Dirty Work*. Brown's dark and gritty novel is reminiscent of the novels of Pete Dexter (*The Paperboy* and others), Harry Crews (*A Feast of Snakes* and others), Cormac McCarthy (*Blood Meridian* and others), and Jim Thompson (*The Grifters* and others).

Burgess, Anthony
Any Old Iron

Random House. 1989. 360 pp.

From the sinking of the Titanic through World War II, two families—one Welsh-Russian, one Jewish-French—find themselves bound together by an unusual marriage, an unrequited love, a strange but enduring friendship, and a mysterious sword.

2d Appeal   Characters   Book Groups

Subjects   ALA Notable Books • British Authors • Family Relationships • Friendship • World War II

Now try   Tim Winton's novel *Cloudstreet* is also about the intertwined relationship of two families. The fiction of Angela Carter, including *Nights at the Circus* and *Saints and Strangers*, shares with Burgess's novels a vitality and energy that comes when an author is really enjoying what he's writing. *Any Old Iron* is loosely based on the legend of King Arthur. Other historical novels about King Arthur include Rosemary Sutcliff's *Sword at Sunset*, Mary Stewart's *The Crystal Cave* and others in her "Merlin" trilogy, and T. H. White's *The Once and Future King*.

Byatt, A. S.

Possession
Random House. 1990. 555 pp.

In the process of studying the lives of two Victorian poets, post-doctoral student Roland Mitchell and Dr. Maud Bailey meet and fall in love.

2d Appeal   Characters
Book Groups 📖

Subjects   Academia • ALA Notable Books • Booker Prize Winners • British Authors • College Professors • College Students • Research Novels • Writers and Writing

Now try   Byatt's other novels include *The Virgin in the Garden*, *Still Life*, and *Babel Tower*. John Fowles (*The Magus* and others), Margaret Drabble (Byatt's sister and the author of *The Needle's Eye* and others), and Iris Murdoch (*The Italian Girl* and others), are all formidably intelligent writers who can also tell a good story. (Byatt has also written extensively about Murdoch's novels.) Other novels about literary scholars include Cathleen Schine's *Rameau's Niece*, *Hallucinating Foucault* by Patricia Duncker, Lindsay Clarke's *The Chymical Wedding*, and Jane Urquhart's *Changing Heaven*. Valerie Townsend Bayer's *City of Childhood* is another novel within a novel.

Carr, J. L.

A Month in the Country
St. Martin's Press. 1980. 111 pp.

Two World War I survivors meet in a small English town while one is restoring a painting in a church and the other is searching for a lost grave.

2d Appeal   Characters
Book Groups 📖

Subjects   British Authors • England • Men's Friendships • Small-Toen Life • World War I

Now try   The effect of war on its survivors is vividly described in Pat Barker's *Regeneration* and the two subsequent novels that make up her World War I trilogy. A remarkable nonfiction book about World War I is Paul Fussell's *The Great War and Modern Memory*. *A Month in the Country* won the Guardian Fiction Prize.

Casey, John

Spartina
Knopf. 1989. 375 pp.

As fisherman Dick Pierce builds his boat, Spartina, he feels at sea amidst the buffeting waves of his life, financial, environmental, and personal.

2d Appeal   Characters
Book Groups 📖

Subjects   Adultery • ALA Notable Books • Boats and Boating • Ecofiction • Middle-Aged Men • Midlife Crisis • National Book Award Winners

Now try   Casey also wrote *The Half-Life of Happiness*. Another novel combining the themes of a midlife crisis and boats is Robert Stone's *Outerbridge Reach*. A nonfiction book that uses a real event to portray man's struggle against the elements is Sebastian Junger's *The Perfect Storm*.

Chamoiseau, Patrick

Texaco
Pantheon Books. 1997. 401 pp.

Marie-Sophie Laborieux recounts her family's struggles from slavery to the founding and final recognition of a shantytown called Texaco, on the island of Martinique. Translated from the French and Creole by Rose-Myriam Rejouis and Val Vinokurov.

2d Appeal Setting Book Groups 📖

  Subjects Colonialism • Creole Culture • Magic Realism • Martinique • Multigenerational Novels • Novels in Translation

  Now try Chamoiseau won the Prix Goncourt for this novel. He also wrote *Solibo Magnificent* and *School Days*. Another look at Creole culture can be found in Kate Chopin's *The Awakening*.

Choi, Susan

The Foreign Student
Harper Flamingo. 1998. 325 pp.

Two loners—Chang Ahn, escaping war-torn Korea for an education in Sewanee, Tennessee, and Katherine Monroe, long involved in a hopeless love affair with a charismatic English professor at the college in Sewanee—gradually, and almost unwillingly, fall in love.

2d Appeal Characters Book Groups 📖

  Subjects 1950s • Acculturation • Coming-of-Age • First Novels • Interracial Relationships • Korea • Korean War • Love Affairs • Tennessee

  Now try Two other novels in which two lonely people fall in love are Jon Cohen's *The Man in the Window* and Joe Coomer's *The Loop*. The Korean War provides background for Martin Quigley's novel *Winners and Losers*.

Clark, Robert

In the Deep Midwinter
Picador USA. 1997. 278 pp.

Two events work together to change Richard McEwan's life: He discovers a letter among his dead brother's papers that implies an affair between his wife Sarah and his brother, and his daughter falls in love with the wrong man.

2d Appeal Story

  Subjects 1940s • Abortion • Adultery • Family Relationships • First Novels • Upper Classes

  Now try Clark is the author of the novel *Mr. White's Confession*, as well as *Rivers of the West; Stories from the Columbia* and *The Solace of Food: The Life of James Beard*. Clark's book shares both a writing style and subject matter—upper-class characters and their country club lives—with John O'Hara's novels, including *A Rage to Live*, *From the Terrace*, and others. Jeanette Haien's *Matters of Chance* also illuminates the moral complexities of her characters' lives.

Clarke, Lindsay
The Chymical Wedding
Knopf. 1989. 536 pp.

Alex Darken, a young Englishman, falls into a romantic triangle with a beautiful psychic and an elderly alcoholic poet as they all explore their shared obsession: Louisa Agnew, the brilliant daughter of the alchemist, Sir Henry Agnew.

Subjects   Alchemy • British Authors • Mysticism • Research Novels • Triangles

Now try   Graham Swift's *Waterland* is set in the same area of England as *The Chymical Wedding*. A. S. Byatt's *Possession* is another exploration of the lives of people living in the nineteenth century. Like Clarke's novel, Kathleen Cambor's *Book of Mercy*, Umberto Eco's *The Name of the Rose*, and Iain Pears's *An Instance of the Fingerpost*, are all moody and mysterious novels. Clarke won the Whitbread Prize for this novel.

Coetzee, J. M.
Age of Iron
Random House. 1990. 198 pp.

As Mrs. Curren, a retired white classics professor, lies dying of cancer, she writes to her daughter in the United States about her illness and the sickness in South Africa's political system of apartheid.

2d Appeal   Characters   Book Groups 📖

Subjects   ALA Notable Books • Apartheid • Cancer • College Professors • Death and Dying • Epistolary Novels • Mothers and Daughters • South Africa • South African Authors

Now try   Included among Coetzee's other novels are *Waiting for the Barbarians* and *In the Heart of the Country*. His spare writing style is similar to that of Aharon Appelfeld's novels *Badenheim, 1939* and *Unto the Soul*. Andre Brink's *Imaginings of Sand* is about a dying, elderly white South African woman trying to understand her own and her country's past.

Coetzee, J. M.
Life & Times of Michael K.
Viking Press. 1984. 184 pp.

In the civil war zone of South Africa, Michael K, pushing his dying mother in a wheelbarrow back to her childhood home, begins his search for a life outside of internment camps and beyond the war.

2d Appeal   Characters   Book Groups 📖

Subjects   ALA Notable Books • Apartheid • Booker Prize Winners • Homelessness • Mothers and Sons • Racism • South Africa • South African Authors

Now try   Coetzee's other books include *The Master of Petersburg*, a novel, and *Boyhood: Scenes from Provincial Life*, a memoir of his life in South Africa. *Housekeeping* by Marilynne Robinson is another slim book without a wasted word. Nadine Gordimer (*Burger's Daughter* and other novels and short stories) and Andre Brink (*Rumours of Rain* and other works) are both South Africans who write about their native land. "The Road to Mecca" by South African playwright Athol Fugard depicts life during the civil war in South Africa.

Conroy, Pat
The Prince of Tides
Houghton Mifflin. 1986. 567 pp.

After Savannah Wingo's third suicide attempt, her twin brother works with her psychiatrist to uncover their family's troubled past.

2d Appeal   Characters   Book Groups 📖

Subjects   Adultery • Brothers and Sisters • Child Abuse • Coming-of-Age • Dysfunctional Families • Fathers and Sons • Mothers and Sons • Psychiatrists, Psychoanalysts, Psychotherapists • Southern Authors • Twins

Now try   Conroy's first book, *The Water Is Wide* (made into the movie *Conrack*) is a nonfiction account of his experiences teaching on Ocracoke, an island off the coast of North Carolina. Conroy explored other aspects of his family's life in his novels *The Great Santini*, *The Lords of Discipline*, and *Beach Music*. Conroy's influence on young Southern writers can be seen in David Payne's *Ruin Creek*. Other novels that draw their readers deep into the lives of their characters are Michael Malone's *Dingley Falls* and David James Duncan's *The Brothers K*.

Cooley, Martha
The Archivist
Little, Brown. 1998. 328 pp.

Literary archivist Matthias Lane, guardian of T. S. Eliot's love letters to Emily Hale, finds himself painfully reliving his past when a young poet, who reminds him of his dead wife, seeks access to the letters.

2d Appeal   Characters   Book Groups 📖

Subjects   Eliot, T. S. • First Novels • Jews and Judaism • Writers and Writing

Now try   Other novels that center on a poet are Judith Farr's *I Never Came to You in White* (about Emily Dickinson) and Peter Ackroyd's *Chatterton*, about the eighteenth-century poet Thomas Chatterton.

Crace, Jim
Arcadia
Atheneum. 1991. 311 pp.

Victor, a wealthy English businessman turning 80, makes plans to level and then rebuild an inner-city farmer's market, the scene of his destitute beginnings.

Subjects   Business and Businessmen • Elderly Men • England • Poverty • Upper Classes • Urban Development

Now try   Among Crace's other novels are *Continent*, *Quarantine*, and *Signals of Distress*. Anne Michaels's *Fugitive Pieces* and Michael Ondaatje's *The English Patient* both have the same vivid poetic imagery as the writing in *Arcadia*.

Cunningham, Michael
A Home at the End of the World
Farrar, Straus Giroux. 1990. 342 pp.

Jonathan Glover, who is gay, and Bobby Morrow have been best friends since childhood, so when Jonathan's roomate Clare becomes pregnant with Bobby's baby, the three decide to raise the child as theirs.

2d Appeal   Characters   Book Groups 📖

Subjects   1970s • Gay Men • Gay Teenagers • Men's Friendships • Triangles

Now try   Cunningham also wrote *Flesh and Blood*, *Golden States*, and *The Hours*. Stephen McCauley's *The Object of My Affection* and Jonathan Dee's *The Lover of History* are both also about the intricate relationship of two men and a woman.

Danticat, Edwidge
Breath, Eyes, Memory
Soho. 1994. 234 pp.

A Haitian immigrant mother and her illegitimate daughter share a horrific bond as they attempt to overcome the sexual traumas that have shaped their lives. An Oprah selection.

2d Appeal   Characters   Book Groups ▢

Subjects   Caribbean Authors • Coming-of-Age • First Novels • Haiti • Haitian Authors • Mothers and Daughters • Rape • Sexual Abuse

Now try   Danticat also wrote *Krik? Krak!*, a collection of short stories about life in Haiti and *The Farming of Bones: A Novel*. Jamaica Kincaid's *Annie John* is another view of a young Caribbean girl coming of age. In 1996, *Granta Magazine* named Danticat one of the "20 Best Young American Novelists."

Davies, Robertson
What's Bred in the Bone
Viking. 1985. 436 pp.

Two angels discuss the varied aspects of the life of philanthropic art collector Francis Cornish, who was at one time an extremely talented art forger.

2d Appeal   Characters   Book Groups ▢

Subjects   Art and Artists • Canadian Authors

Now try   This novel is the second book in "The Cornish Trilogy," which includes *The Rebel Angels* and *The Lyre of Orpheus*. His other books (all characterized by Davies's witty, intelligent prose, and inventive plots) include *Fifth Business* and *The Manticore*. Louis Buss's *The Luxury of Exile* also concerns art forgeries. Norman Rush's *Mating* is another novel with rich, complex language and psychological insights into the characters.

De Bernieres, Louis
Corelli's Mandolin
Pantheon Books. 1994. 437 pp.

Widowed Dr. Iannis and his daughter Pelagia suffer during the Italian and German occupation of the Greek island of Cephallonia, but find their faith and love restored by a charming, humane Army officer, Captain Antonio Corelli.

2d Appeal   Characters   Book Groups ▢

Subjects   Fathers and Daughters • Greece • Love Stories • Widowers • World War II

Now try   The novel *Zorba the Greek* by Nikos Kazantzakis, like De Bernieres's novel, is a tragic-comic masterpiece about Greece. Three other beautifully crafted novels with a World War II setting are Anne Michaels's *Fugitive Pieces*, Ursula Hegi's *Stones from the River*, and Michael Ondaatje's *The English Patient*. De Bernieres's unique writing style is also seen in his other novels, especially *The War of Don Emmanuel's Nether Parts*. Nicholas Flokos's *Nike* is also set on a Greek island.

De Botton, Alain
On Love
Atlantic Monthly Press. 1993. 231 pp.

An anonymous narrator analyzes his relationship with Chloe, step by step, from their first sight of one another to their eventual parting.

2d Appeal   Characters

Subjects   British Authors • Humorous Fiction • Love Stories • Male/Female Relationships • Postmodern Fiction • Psychological Fiction

Now try   De Botton's other books, ***The Romantic Movement*** and ***How Proust Can Change Your Life: Not a Novel***, are also good examples of postmodern fiction. Jeanette Winterson's ***Written on the Body*** is a novel in which the passion is in the body rather than the mind, as in De Botton's book, but both describe the effects of postmodernism on relationships.

Deane, Seamus
Reading in the Dark
Knopf. 1997. 245 pp.

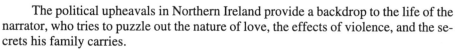

The political upheavals in Northern Ireland provide a backdrop to the life of the narrator, who tries to puzzle out the nature of love, the effects of violence, and the secrets his family carries.

2d Appeal   Setting   Book Groups 📖

Subjects   ALA Notable Books • Coming-of-Age • Family Relationships • Family Secrets • First Novels • Ireland • Irish Authors • Northern Ireland

Now try   The writings of Isaac Babel (***Collected Stories***), although set in a different time and place, offer the same sense of how history can affect family relationships. Another good evocation of childhood can be found in Tim Pears's ***In the Place of Fallen Leaves***. Deane's novel was a finalist for the 1996 Booker Prize and won the Guardian Prize for fiction.

DeLillo, Don
Libra
Viking. 1988. 456 pp.

Embarrassed by the failed Bay of Pigs invasion, CIA agents plot the assasination of President John F. Kennedy, intending to pin the deed on Lee Harvey Oswald, a supposed supporter of Cuba's president, Fidel Castro.

2d Appeal   Story   Book Groups 📖

Subjects   1960s • ALA Notable Books • Kennedy, John F. • Murder • Political Fiction

Now try   DeLillo's other novels include ***Running Dog***, ***Americana***, and ***Great Jones Street***. Other novels about the assassination include ***Flying in to Love*** by D. M. Thomas, Marly Swick's ***Paper Wings***, Charles McCarry's ***The Tears of Autumn***, and Jack Gerson's ***The Back of the Tiger***.

DeLillo, Don
The Names
Knopf. 1982. 339 pp.

Risk analyst James Axton decides to track down a strange ritual murder cult, known as the Names, and follows their trail throughout the world.

Subjects   ALA Notable Books • Cults • Postmodern Fiction

Now try DeLillo's other novels include *Ratner's Star* and *End Zone*. In *A Flag for Sunrise* and *Damascus Gate*, Robert Stone combines political and personal issues.

DeLillo, Don
White Noise
Viking. 1985. 326 pp.

College professor and Hitler expert Jack Gladney and his plump fifth wife, Babette, energetically maintain a household of wise stepchildren while actively ignoring a society that makes less sense all the time.

Book Groups 📖

Subjects ALA Notable Books • College Professors • Ecofiction • Family Relationships • National Book Award Winners • Satirical Fiction • Stepfamilies

Now try DeLillo is also the author of *Underworld*. His major preoccupation, as seen in all his novels, is the foibles of contemporary society. Joseph Heller's *Catch 22* shares a satirical tone with DeLillo's novel.

Dexter, Pete
The Paperboy
Random House. 1995. 307 pp.

Jack James looks back on his brother Ward's fall from fame with sorrow and regret.

2d Appeal Characters

Book Groups 📖

Subjects ALA Notable Books • Brothers • Fathers and Sons • Florida • Violence • Writers and Writing

Now try Dexter's other books include *Brotherly Love*, *God's Pocket*, and *Deadwood*. Interesting relationships between brothers are found in Adrian Louis's *Skins* and Russell Banks's *Affliction*.

Dexter, Pete
Paris Trout
Random House. 1988. 306 pp.

A white shopkeeper senselessly murders a young black woman and lurches into insanity.

2d Appeal Characters

Book Groups 📖

Subjects ALA Notable Books • Georgia • Marriage • Murder • National Book Award Winners • Race Relations • Racism

Now try All of Dexter's novels are bleak, grim, and extremely well written. In these respects, they are similar to the novels of Russell Banks (*Continental Drift*, *Rule of the Bone*, and others). Charlie Smith's *Cheap Ticket to Heaven* is another gritty novel about people on the fringes of society.

Doctorow, E. L.
Billy Bathgate
Random House. 1989. 323 pp.

Teenage Billy Bathgate learns about life, death, and love when he is taken under the wing of notorious gangland leader Dutch Schultz in the 1930s in the Bronx, New York.

2d Appeal Characters

Book Groups 📖

Subjects 1930s • ALA Notable Books • Coming-of-Age • Gangs and Gangsters • Jews and Judaism • National Book Critics Circle Award Winners • New York • Teenage Boys

Now try Among Doctorow's other novels are *Welcome to Hard Times*, *Loon Lake*, and *Ragtime.* Other classic coming-of-age stories include Mark Twain's *Huckleberry Finn* and J. D. Salinger's *The Catcher in the Rye*. Mordecai Richler's *Solomon Gursky Was Here* is another novel with characters both real and imagined. *Billy Bathgate* won a PEN/Faulkner Award.

Doctorow, E. L.
World's Fair
Random House. 1985. 288 pp.

1930s New York is seen through the eyes of an impressionable young boy whose greatest desire is to go the World's Fair in Flushing Meadows, New York.

2d Appeal Characters   Book Groups 📖

Subjects 1930s • ALA Notable Books • Bronx, New York • Jews and Judaism • National Book Award Winners • New York

Now try *Beach Boy* by Ardashir Vakil, Peter Hedges's *An Ocean in Iowa*, and Nicholson Baker's *The Everlasting Story of Nory* all evoke the mysterious world of childhood.

Doerr, Harriet
Stones for Ibarra
Viking. 1984. 214 pp.

Sara and Richard Everton move to Ibarra, Mexico, to reopen the mine once owned by Richard's grandfather, and in the process discover much about life, love, and the relentlessness of fate.

2d Appeal Characters   Book Groups 📖

Subjects Culture Clash • Death of a Spouse • First Novels • Mexico • Small-Town Life

Now try Doerr was 73 when she published *Stones for Ibarra.* Her novel *Consider This, Senora* is also set in Mexico. *The Good Husband* by Gail Godwin and *Gus in Bronze* by Alexandra Marshall both deal with the death of a spouse. Mining plays an important part in Wallace Stegner's *Angle of Repose*. Another wonderful evocation of Mexican village life is found in Sandra Benitez's *A Place Where the Sea Remembers*.

Duras, Marguerite
The Lover
Pantheon Books. 1985. 117 pp.

In the sultry heat of Indochina, a 15-year-old and her wealthy older Chinese lover revert to miserable self-absorption as the circumstances of family and their situation drive them apart. Translated from the French by Barbara Bray.

Subjects ALA Notable Books • Erotica • French Authors • Indochina • Love Affairs • Novels in Translation • Older Men/Younger Women

Now try Other novels by Duras include *North China Lover* and *Emily L*. As in Albert Camus's novel *The Stranger*, the description of heat in *The Lover* is central to the story. Vladimir Nabokov's *Lolita* has a similar plot: an older man bewitched by a young woman. *The Lover* won the Prix Goncourt.

Elkin, Stanley
Mrs. Ted Bliss
Hyperion. 1995. 291 pp.

After a life of sheltered tidiness, newly widowed septuagenarian Dorothy Bliss comes of age, confronting the poignancies and piquancies of her existence in a 1980s Miami populated with drug lords and people with questionable morals.

2d Appeal   Characters   Book Groups 📖

Subjects   Coming-of-Age • Elderly Women • Florida • Miami • National Book Critics Circle Award Winners • Widows

Now try   Elkin's other books include *Van Gogh's Room at Arles: Three Novellas*. In *Mrs. Bridge*, Evan Connell treats his subject with a bemused compassion and fine detail akin to Elkin's. John Gardner shares Elkin's concerns and sensibilities in his offbeat novel of later life, *October Light*. Jessica Anderson's *Tirra Lirra by the River* is another novel about an older woman trying to cope with a change in her life.

Eugenides, Jeffrey
The Virgin Suicides
Farrar, Straus Giroux. 1993. 249 pp.

The narrators, a group of men who write in one voice, try to make sense of the defining event of their adolescence: the deaths by suicide of their friends, the five Lisbon sisters.

2d Appeal   Characters   Book Groups 📖

Subjects   ALA Notable Books • First Novels • Men's Friendships • Suicide • Teenage Boys • Teenage Girls • Teenagers

Now try   *That Night* by Alice McDermott also describes a neighborhood watching events play out. Suicide and its effects on the people left behind is the subject of Yukio Mishima's *Spring Snow*, Kate Chopin's *The Awakening*, and William Faulkner's *The Sound and the Fury*. In 1996, *Granta Magazine* named Eugenides one of the "20 Best Young American Novelists."

Fink, Ida
The Journey
Farrar, Straus Giroux. 1992. 249 pp.

After fleeing the Polish ghetto disguised as peasants, two Jewish sisters survive World War II by obtaining false identity papers and working as hired laborers in wartime Germany. Translated from the Polish by Joanna Weschler and Francine Prose.

2d Appeal   Story   Book Groups 📖

Subjects   First Novels • Germany • Novels in Translation • Poland • Sisters • World War II

Now try   Fink's two collections of short stories, *A Scrap of Time and Other Stories* and *Traces*, are both about the Holocaust in Poland, as is Andrzej Szczypiorski's *The Beautiful Mrs. Seidenman*.

Fischer, Tibor
Under the Frog: A Black Comedy
New Press. 1992. 250 pp.

Just before the failed Hungarian Revolution in 1956, Gyuri and his fellow members of a traveling basketball team work equally hard at undermining the existing Communist government and looking for sex.

2d Appeal   Setting   Book Groups 📖

Subjects   1950s • Basketball • Black Humor • British Authors • Communism • First Novels • Hungary • Love Stories • Men's Friendships • Political Fiction • World War II

Now try   Fischer also wrote *The Thought Gang*, a novel about a dysfunctional duo in France, and *The Collector Collector: A Novel*. Fischer's brand of black humor resembles Martin Amis's in *Dead Babies* and *The Rachel Papers*. George Konrad's *A Feast in the Garden* is also set against events in Hungary's history. *Under the Frog* won the Betty Trask Award.

Fitzgerald, Penelope
Offshore
H. Holt. 1987. 141 pp.

Neena and her daughters, as well as an odd assortment of men and women also living on barges in London's Battersea Reach, move uneasily in a world neither at sea nor ashore.

2d Appeal   Characters   Book Groups 📖

Subjects   1960s • Boats and Boating • Booker Prize Winners • British Authors • England • Male/Female Relationships • Mothers and Daughters

Now try   Among Fitzgerald's other novels are *The Blue Flower*. Other British novelists whose books share Fitzgerald's ability to capture odd lives in clear and precise prose are Barbara Pym (*Jane and Prudence*) and Anita Brookner (*The Debut*).

Ford, Richard
Independence Day
A.A. Knopf. 1995. 451 pp.

New Jersey real estate agent Frank Bascombe's plans for a trip to the Basketball Hall of Fame with his troubled teenage son go awry.

2d Appeal   Characters

Subjects   Business and Businessmen • Fathers and Sons • Middle-Aged Men • Midlife Crisis • Pulitzer Prize Winners • Teenage Boys

Now try   In addition to *The Sportswriter*, in which Frank Bascombe is introduced, Ford's other books include *Women with Men: Three Long Short Stories* and *Wildfire*. Like Ford, John Updike, in his series of books about Rabbit Angstrom (*Rabbit, Run* and others), evokes the angst of growing older in the United States during the 1980s. Bascombe's ennui and depression are similar to Binx Bolling's in Walker Percy's *The Moviegoer*. *Independence Day* won a PEN/Faulkner Award as well as the Pulitzer Prize.

Fowler, Connie May
River of Hidden Dreams
Putnam's. 1994. 318 pp.

Thoroughly Americanized Sadie, in whose veins run African, Hispanic, and American Indian blood, tells the stories of her mother, a hard-drinking mulatto, and her grandmother, a Plains Indian raised as a white child in St. Augustine, Florida, and herself: three women who cast a skeptical eye on love.

2d Appeal   Characters   Book Groups 📖

Subjects	American Indians • Florida • Magic Realism • Mothers and Daughters • Multigenerational Novels
Now try	***Sugar Cage***, Fowler's first novel, is also beautifully written and set in Florida. Kaye Gibbons's ***Charms for the Easy Life*** and Joan Barfoot's ***Duet for Three*** are both about three generations of women in one family. ***Fortune's Daughter*** and other novels by Alice Hoffman share Fowler's lyrical writing style.

Gaddis, William
A Frolic of His Own

Poseidon Press. 1994. 586 pp.

A series of lawsuits, including Oscar Crease's suit against a Hollywood director for plagiarism; Oscar himself being sued for plagiarizing from Eugene O'Neill's "Mourning Becomes Electra"; Oscar's attempts to decide whom to sue in order to recover damages for injuries suffered when his car ran over his foot while he was trying to hot-wire it; and a dog's death in an outdoor sculpture all provide much work for the legal profession.

Subjects	Humorous Fiction • Law and Lawyers • National Book Award Winners • Postmodern Fiction • Satirical Fiction
Now try	Gaddis's first novel was ***The Recognitions***, followed by ***JR*** and ***Carpenter's Gothic***. Another darkly humorous look at the legal profession and an endless lawsuit can be found in Charles Dickens's ***Bleak House.*** Gaddis and his contemporary, Thomas Pynchon (***Gravity's Rainbow*** and others), are both leading innovators in the world of twentieth-century American fiction, and both owe a debt of gratitude to James Joyce (***Ulysses*** and others).

Gaines, Ernest
A Lesson Before Dying

A.A. Knopf. 1993. 256 pp.

University-educated, agnostic, African American Grant Wiggins is coerced by an overbearing aunt to impart pride, knowledge, and religion to her best friend's godson, an innocent young man condemned to die. An Oprah selection.

2d Appeal	Characters	Book Groups 📖
Subjects	1940s • African American Authors • African Americans • ALA Notable Books • Friendship • Mississippi • National Book Critics Circle Award Winners • Racism	
Now try	Gaines's other books include ***The Autobiography of Miss Jane Pittman*** and ***A Gathering of Old Men.*** The poignancy of the diary Jefferson keeps while he is in prison is also found in the diary described in Daniel Keyes's ***Flowers for Algernon***.	

Garcia, Cristina
The Aguero Sisters

Knopf. 1997. 299 pp.

Half-sisters Reina and Constancia, whose lives diverged when one remained in Havana as a master electrician and the other moved to America and went into the cosmetics business, find when they meet after 30 years that their memories of their parents' marriage and the death of their mother are quite different.

2d Appeal	Characters	Book Groups 📖
Subjects	ALA Notable Books • Cuba • Cuban Authors • Death of a Parent • Magic Realism • Sisters	

Now try Garcia also wrote ***Dreaming in Cuban***, which was nominated for a National Book Award. Herbert Gold's fictional history of his parents (***Fathers and Family***) describes the experiences of another ethnic group becoming Americanized. Garcia makes use of magic realism in the same way that Alice Hoffman does in ***Turtle Moon*** and her other novels.

Garcia Marquez, Gabriel
Chronicle of a Death Foretold
Knopf. 1983. 120 pp.

Six hours after marrying Angela Vicario, Bayardo San Roman returns her to her family, touching off a chain of events that ends in tragedy. Translated from the Spanish by Gregory Rabassa.

2d Appeal Characters

Subjects ALA Notable Books • Colombian Authors • Magic Realism • Murder • Novels in Translation • South American Authors • Weddings

Now try Among Garcia Marquez's other works are ***Autumn of the Patriarch***, ***One Hundred Years of Solitude***, and ***Innocent Erendira, and Other Stories***. Garcia Marquez's circuitous manner of storytelling is similar to Julio Cortazar's novel ***Hopscotch***, in which Cortazar advises his readers that his novel can be read from chapter one on, or can be read in another order, skipping from chapter to chapter in an alternate order that he provides at the beginning of the book.

Garcia Marquez, Gabriel
Love in the Time of Cholera
Alfred A. Knopf. 1988. 348 pp.

Florentino has loved Jermina since they were teenagers, and now that she is a widow, he thinks (even after 50 years) he can reclaim her elderly heart and hand. Translated from the Spanish by Edith Grossman.

2d Appeal Characters   Book Groups 📖

Subjects ALA Notable Books • Colombian Authors • Love Stories • Magic Realism • Novels in Translation • South American Authors • Widows

Now try Another of Garcia Marquez's books is ***Strange Pilgrims***. Other examples of relationships between older couples can be found in Lane Von Herzen's ***The Unfastened Heart*** and Jo-Ann Mapson's ***Shadow Ranch***. Other novelists whose use of language is as rich as Garcia Marquez's include Jose Saramago (***Blindness***) and Amitav Ghosh (***The Circle of Reason***). Marcel Proust (***Remembrance of Things Past***) and Julian Barnes (***Talking It Over***) share with Garcia Marquez an interest in exploring how memory frequently alters the past.

Gardner, John
Mickelsson's Ghosts
Knopf. 1982. 590 pp.

Having lost control of his life (despite his genius), college professor Peter Mickelsson buys an old farmhouse and during its renovation uncovers ghosts and murder.

2d Appeal Characters   Book Groups 📖

Subjects Academia • College Professors • Ghosts • Murder

Now try Gardner's *On Moral Fiction* is a thought-provoking and influential book on contemporary writing. Both Richard Russo's *Straight Man* and Jane Smiley's *Moo* are humorous depictions of academia. No ghosts in either book, though.

Gordimer, Nadine

July's People
Viking Press. 1981. 160 pp.

When the white South African government topples, the Smales family flee from their suburban home to the bush, where they become utterly dependent upon the hospitality and protection of their house servant July and his unreceptive and impoverished family.

2d Appeal Setting
Book Groups 📖

Subjects ALA Notable Books • Apartheid • Friendship • Poverty • Race Relations • South Africa • South African Authors

Now try Other books by Gordimer include *Burger's Daughter* and *None to Accompany Me*. The stream-of-consciousness writing style of *July's People* is similar to the technique used by Virginia Woolf in *Mrs. Dalloway*. Rohinton Mistry's *A Fine Balance* is about the attempt to survive during a political state of emergency in India. Gordimer won the Nobel Prize in 1991.

Graham, Philip

How to Read an Unwritten Language
Scribner. 1995. 254 pp.

Michael Kirby's harrowing childhood sets the pattern for his life as a collector of various objects and his desire to heal the emotionally stunted lives of his family and lovers.

2d Appeal Characters

Subjects Brothers and Sisters • Dysfunctional Families • Family Relationships • Fathers and Sons • First Novels • Mothers and Sons

Now try Graham also published *The Art of the Knock*, a collection of short stories. *My Drowning* by Jim Grimsley is another account of an unhappy childhood.

Gustafsson, Lars

A Tiler's Afternoon
New Pub. Corp. 1993. 117 pp.

A single day in the life of aging and lonely Torsten Bergman, including his work, his memories, and the real and imagined people he meets. Translated from the Swedish by Tom Geddes.

Subjects Elderly Men • Loneliness • Men's Lives • Novels in Translation

Now try Kazuo Ishiguro's *The Unconsoled* conveys the same sense of uneasiness of not being quite sure what's real and what's imagined in a man's life. Kate Phillips's *White Rabbit* is about the last day in the life of an elderly woman.

Harrison, Kathryn

Exposure  Random House. 1993. 218 pp.

Videographer Ann Rogers, now in her 20s, struggles with issues of sexual abuse and self-worth as she is faced with the opening of a retrospective exhibit of her famous father's photographs of Ann as a child. An Oprah selection.

Book Groups 📖

Subjects Child Abuse • Diabetes • Fathers and Daughters • Incest • Photography and Photographers • Sex and Sexuality • Sexual Abuse

Now try Four years after the publication of this novel, Harrison wrote *The Kiss*, a memoir about her complicated relationship with her father. The main character in *Going to the Sun* by James McManus also has diabetes. The protagonists in Ann Beattie's *Picturing Will* and Anne Tyler's *Earthly Possessions* are photographers. Robert Olen Butler's *They Whisper* is another intensely written sexual fiction.

Hazzard, Shirley

The Transit of Venus Viking Press. 1980. 337 pp.

Two orphaned sisters travel from their native Australia to England to create new lives for themselves; in the process, they experience love, hopefulness, passion, disappointments, and betrayals.

2d Appeal Characters Book Groups 📖

Subjects Australia • Australian Authors • England • Love Stories • Male/Female Relationships • National Book Critics Circle Award Winners • Orphans • Sisters

Now try Among Hazzard's other books is *The Evening of the Holiday*. E. M. Forster's *Howards End* is also about relationships and connections that last a lifetime. *The Death of the Heart* by Elizabeth Bowen is another strong character-driven novel. Laura Kalpakian's *Fair Augusto and Other Stories* features strong women and the sometimes heartbreaking relationships between them and the men in their lives.

Hegi, Ursula

Stones from the River Poseidon Press. 1994. 507 pp.

As she grows up in a small German town during Hitler's rise to power, Trudi Montag, a dwarf, uses her storytelling ability to avenge herself on those who hurt her, to chronicle the painful realities of the war years, and finally to find peace within herself.

2d Appeal Characters Book Groups 📖

Subjects Dwarfs • Fathers and Daughters • Germany • Small-Town Life • World War II

Now try Hegi also wrote *Floating in My Mother's Palm*, which shares some characters with *Stones from the River*. Another beautifully written account of a Holocaust survivor is *For Every Sin* by Aharon Appelfeld. The plot of *Stones from the River* is reminiscent of Gunter Grass's *The Tin Drum*.

Heinemann, Larry

Paco's Story
Farrar, Straus Giroux. 1986. 209 pp.

The sole survivor of a devastating Viet Cong attack, infantry man Paco Sullivan takes a job washing dishes at the Texas Lunch, a small-town greasy spoon, to try to keep his physical and mental scars from destroying him.

2d Appeal   Characters   Book Groups 📖

Subjects   Cafes and Restaurants • National Book Award Winners • Small-Town Life • Vietnam Veterans • Vietnam War

Now try   Heinemann's first novel was *Close Quarters*, also about the Vietnam War experience. Other novels of the Vietnam War and its aftermath are *Zombie Jamboree* by Robert Merkin, Ninh Bao's *The Sorrow of War*, Stephen Wright's *Meditations in Green*, Nicholas Proffitt's *Gardens of Stone*, *Dispatches* by Michael Herr, and Stewart O'Nan's *The Names of the Dead*.

Helprin, Mark

Memoir from Antproof Case
Harcourt Brace & Co. 1995. 514 pp.

Eighty-year-old Oscar, coming to the end of a full life that has been dominated by his hatred of coffee, recounts the adventures that brought him to where he is, including his experiences as a fighter pilot in World War II, a bank robber and murderer, his stay in an exclusive Swiss insane asylum, and years spent as a successful businessman.

2d Appeal   Story   Book Groups 📖

Subjects   Business and Businessmen • Death of a Parent • Elderly Men • Men's Lives • Mental Illness • Murder • Psychiatric Hospitals

Now try   Helprin's other novels include *A Soldier of the Great War* and *A City in Winter*. Like Salman Rushdie in *The Moor's Last Sigh*, Helprin comes up with such bizarre plots that it is impossible to believe that anyone could imagine them. Another novel in which coffee plays an important part is Peter Gadol's *Mystery Roast*.

Hewat, Alan V.

Lady's Time
Harper & Row. 1985. 338 pp.

Lady Winslow has created a respectable life for herself and her son in a small New England town, but she is always haunted by the ragtime music and voodoo magic of her Creole roots in New Orleans.

2d Appeal   Setting

Subjects   ALA Notable Books • First Novels • Jazz • Magic Realism • Mothers and Sons • Music and Musicians • New England • New Orleans • Race Relations

Now try   Robert Girardi's *Madeleine's Ghost* shares the setting as well as elements of magical realism of Hewat's novel. E. L. Doctorow's *Ragtime* is another novel incorporating the history of jazz in its plot.

Hogan, Linda
Solar Storms

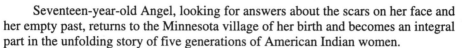

Scribner. 1995. 351 pp.

Seventeen-year-old Angel, looking for answers about the scars on her face and her empty past, returns to the Minnesota village of her birth and becomes an integral part in the unfolding story of five generations of American Indian women.

2d Appeal   Characters   Book Groups 📖

   Subjects   American Indian Authors • Coming-of-Age • Family Relationships • Minnesota • Multigenerational Novels • Women's Friendships

   Now try   Linda Hogan's first novel, ***Mean Spirit***, is also about American Indian culture. She has written both nonfiction and poetry, including ***Book of Medicines: Poems***. The connections Hogan makes between women and nature are similar to the connections made in Terry Tempest Williams's memoir, ***Refuge: An Unnatural History of Family and Place***. Susan Power's ***The Grass Dancer*** is another novel about American Indians written with a similar lyrical use of language.

Hope, Christopher
Darkest England
W.W. Norton. 1996. 283 pp.

African bushman David Mungo Booi, on behalf of the Society for Promoting the Discovery of the Interior of England, travels to England to remind Queen Elizabeth II of the promises her predecessor, Queen Victoria, made to the Africans a century before.

2d Appeal   Story

   Subjects   Africa • British Authors • Colonialism • England • Humorous Fiction • Racism • Satirical Fiction

   Now try   Hope's other books include ***Black Swan*** and ***Serenity House***. ***White Man's Grave*** by Richard Dooling is another satirical novel set in Africa.

Hospital, Janette Turner
Charades
Bantam. 1989. 291 pp.

Charade learns about the fickleness of memory and the elusiveness of the past as she searches for the truth about the father she never knew and the three very different women who loved him.

2d Appeal   Characters

   Subjects   Australian Authors • Love Stories • Male/Female Relationships • Mothers and Daughters

   Now try   Hospital has written novels set in India (***The Tiger in the Tiger Pit***) and Australia (***Oyster***). Joseph Monninger's ***New Jersey*** and Edward Hardy's ***Geyser Life*** are both about children who search for a father.

Hulme, Keri

The Bone People
Louisiana State University Press. 1985. 450 pp.

In the South Islands of New Zealand, a Maori artist of mixed ancestry living in self-exile is called from her isolation by a young, mute boy and his abusive but loving foster father; together this trio of outcasts struggles to heal themselves and one another through love, myth, and ritual.

2d Appeal   Characters   Book Groups 📖

Subjects   Alcoholics and Alcoholism • Art and Artists • Booker Prize Winners • Child Abuse • Fathers and Sons • Male/Female Relationships • Maoris • New Zealand • New Zealand Authors

Now try   Hulme's other books include *Strands*, a collection of poetry, and *The Windeater*, a book of short stories. Other books about Maori life include Alan Duff's *Once Were Warriors* and *One Night Out Stealing*.

Hustvedt, Siri

The Blindfold
Poseidon Press. 1992. 221 pp.

Iris Vegan, a graduate student at Columbia University, gains a semblance of self-knowledge through her interactions with four unnerving people: a blind man, a photographer, an older woman Iris meets during her stay in a hospital, and the professor (her lover) with whom she translates a book.

2d Appeal   Characters

Subjects   College Students • First Novels • Male/Female Relationships • Postmodern Fiction

Now try   Hustvedt also wrote *The Enchantment of Lily Dahl.* Paul Auster (*City of Glass*, *In the Country of Last Things*) shares many of Hustvedt's novelistic concerns with identity, the difficulty of distinguishing between fact and fiction, and other existential questions.

Ignatieff, Michael

Scar Tissue
Farrar, Straus Giroux. 1994. 199 pp.

A professor of philosophy mourns the slow and terrible descent of his mother into senility as a result of Alzheimer's disease and discovers that modern medicine is as powerless as philosophy to help him comprehend what is happening.

2d Appeal   Story   Book Groups 📖

Subjects   ALA Notable Books • Alzheimer's Disease • Brothers • College Professors • Death of a Parent • Mothers and Sons

Now try   Among Ignatieff's other books are *The Russian Album* and *Asya: A Novel.* Beverly Coyle's *In Troubled Waters* includes a character suffering from Alzheimer's disease. *A Time to Dance* by Walter Sullivan shows the effects of Alzheimer's disease from inside the mind of the person suffering from it. Andrew Solomon's *A Stone Boat* also deals with the close relationship between a son and his dying mother. The lack of consolation that philosophy offers in a time of tragedy is also revealed in Lynne Sharon Schwartz's *Disturbances in the Field*.

Ishiguro, Kazuo
An Artist of the Floating World
Putnam's. 1986. 206 pp.

In post-World War II Japan, a retired painter, Masuji Ono, looks back over the choices he made, including his support of Japan's imperialist leanings.

2d Appeal   Setting

Subjects   ALA Notable Books • Art and Artists • British Authors • Japan • Japanese Authors • World War II

Now try   The main character in Jane Urquhart's *The Underpainter* also reflects on the moral and emotional choices he made in his life. Franz Kafka ("The Hunger Artist," in *The Complete Stories*) also writes about art in the service of the state. *An Artist of the Floating World* won the Whitbread Prize.

Ishiguro, Kazuo
A Pale View of the Hills
Putnam. 1982. 183 pp.

The bombing of Nagasaki becomes a metaphor for the misplaced and disjointed lives of two Japanese widows now living in England and their troubled relationships with their daughters.

2d Appeal   Characters   Book Groups 📖

Subjects   ALA Notable Books • Atomic Bomb • British Authors • Elderly Women • England • First Novels • Japan • Japanese Authors • Mothers and Daughters • Nagasaki • Widows

Now try   Another author who writes of a disaster only elliptically is Aharon Appelfeld (*The Retreat*, *The Age of Wonders*, and others); his books are about the Holocaust but never deal directly with it.

Ishiguro, Kazuo
The Remains of the Day
Knopf. 1989. 245 pp.

Stevens, an impeccable English butler from the last days of the great country houses, philosophizes about his profession, post-war British culture, class differences, and the personal choices that have shaped his life.

2d Appeal   Setting

Subjects   Aging • ALA Notable Books • Booker Prize Winners • British Authors • Elderly Men • England • Japanese Authors • Loneliness • Single Men

Now try   The protagonist of Jessica Anderson's *Tirra Lirra by the River* is another elderly character who looks back on how seemingly small decisions changed the course of her life. Life in the great country houses during the 1930s and 1940s is described in Evelyn Waugh's *Brideshead Revisited*. Penelope Fitzgerald's *The Bookshop* presents another view of class consciousness in England.

Ishiguro, Kazuo
The Unconsoled
A.A. Knopf. 1995. 535 pp.

Arriving in an unnamed and imaginary European city, presumably to give a piano recital, Ryder constantly confronts the uneasy feelings that he should know more than he does and that people expect more of him than he can give.

2d Appeal	Characters	Book Groups 📖

Subjects   ALA Notable Books • British Authors • Japanese Authors • Male/Female Relationships • Music and Musicians

Now try   This, Ishiguro's fourth novel, is suffused with an uncomfortable, dream-like quality that is strongly reminiscent of the works of Franz Kafka (*The Trial*). Although Ryder is unfamiliar with the variety of people he meets, they all seem to know him, much like the situation Alice finds herself in, in Lewis Carroll's *Alice in Wonderland*.

Johnson, Denis
Already Dead
HarperCollins. 1997. 435 pp.

Teetering on the edge of America's Northwest coast, the lives of a drug-addled giant, a suicide wannabe, a paranoid pot grower, and a displaced cop intertwine amongst murder, misadventure, and madness.

2d Appeal	Characters	Book Groups 📖

Subjects   California • Counterculture • Drugs and Drug Abuse • Male/Female Relationships • Policemen • Suicide • Violence

Now try   Thomas Pynchon's *Vineland* is another novel involving drugs and the people who use them. Bob Shacochis's *Swimming in the Volcano* and the works of Robert Stone (*A Flag for Sunrise* and *Children of Light*) are filled with characters who seem to be on the brink of disaster as they invite violence into their lives.

Kelman, James
How Late It Was, How Late
Norton. 1995. 373 pp.

Awakening from a two-day drinking binge, ex-con Sammy stumbles home, only to find his girlfriend missing and more trouble around the corner.

2d Appeal	Characters	Book Groups 📖

Subjects   Alcoholics and Alcoholism • Booker Prize Winners • Glasgow, Scotland • Scotland • Scottish Authors • Working Classes

Now try   Kelman's other works of fiction include *Busted Scotch: Selected Stories*, *A Chancer*, and *A Disaffection*. *How Late It Was, How Late* is written in Glaswegian, a dialect particular to Glasgow. Irvine Welsh's *Trainspotting* and *The Acid House*, Duncan McLean's *Bunker Man*, and Alan Warner's *These Demented Lands* are all novels firmly set in their authors' homeland, Scotland.

Kennedy, William
Ironweed
Viking Press. 1983. 227 pp.

Francis Phelan's guilt over the accidental death of his son drives him to the streets of Albany, New York, in the 1930s.

2d Appeal   Setting   Book Groups 📖

   Subjects   1930s • ALA Notable Books • Albany, New York • Death of a Child • Family Relationships • Homelessness • Husbands and Wives • National Book Award Winners • National Book Critics Circle Award Winners • New York • Poverty

   Now try   Kennedy's first novel was *The Ink Truck* (the first in his "Albany Cycle"), followed by *Legs*, *Billy Phelan's Greatest Game*, and *Very Old Bones*. Marge Piercy's *The Longings of Women* and Elizabeth Forsythe Hailey's *Home Free* are both about homelessness.

Kundera, Milan
The Unbearable Lightness of Being
Harper & Row. 1984. 314 pp.

The lives of two men and two women—Tomas, a womanizer; Tereza, the woman who tries to capture his heart; Sabina, an artist and one of Tomas's lovers; and Franz, Sabina's married lover—affect and are affected by each other and the world around them. Translated from the Czech by Michael Henry Heim.

2d Appeal   Setting   Book Groups 📖

   Subjects   Adultery • Art and Artists • Czechoslovakia • Czechoslovakian Authors • Love Stories • Male/Female Relationships • Novels in Translation • Political Fiction

   Now try   Other examples of the way Kundera combines politics and personal relationships include his novels *Immortality* and *The Book of Laughter and Forgetting*. Ward Just (*Echo House* and others) and Robert Stone (*Damascus Gate* and others) are also novelists who combine political and social themes in their books.

Langley, Lee
Persistent Rumours
Milkweed Editions 1994. 294 pp.

Parallel stories of two troubled marriages, that of Elizabeth to Henry Oakley, the superintendent of a new prison in the Andaman Islands off the coast of India, and, nearly a century later, that of their son James and his wife Daisy, whose relationship is compromised by the continuing mystery surrounding James's mother's disappearance.

2d Appeal   Characters   Book Groups 📖

   Subjects   Culture Clash • Death of a Parent • Husbands and Wives • India • Marriage • Mothers and Sons

   Now try   Langley also wrote *The Dying Art. Heat and Dust* by Ruth Prawer Jhabvala is a novel about parallel experiences—a generation apart—in India. Using a similarly restrained tone in his novel *Acts of Fear*, Francis King describes how the mysterious death of a young man's mother haunts his adult life.

Leavitt, David
The Lost Language of Cranes
Knopf. 1986. 319 pp.

When Philip falls in love with Eliot and finally tells his parents that he is homosexual, it forces his father Owen to face his own issues of sexual identity.

2d Appeal　Story

Book Groups 📖

Subjects　Fathers and Sons • First Novels • Gay Men • Wives of Gay Men

Now try　Leavitt's other books include *Arkansas: Three Novellas*, *The Page Turner*, and *Equal Affections*. Another novel about a young man coming out to his family is Brian Bouldrey's *The Genius of Desire*.

Leithauser, Brad
The Friends of Freeland
A.A. Knopf. 1997. 508 pp.

On the imaginary island of Freeland, Hannibal Hannibalsson is running for yet another term as president—this will be his fifth—and his oldest friend, Eggert Oddason, decides they need to call in advisers from the United States to help determine campaign strategy.

2d Appeal　Characters

Subjects　Men's Friendships • Political Fiction • Satirical Fiction

Now try　Leithauser also wrote *Equal Distance* and *Seaward*. This exuberantly poetic novel demands close attention, much the way Kazuo Ishiguro's *The Unconsoled* and Jose Saramago's *The History of the Siege of Lisbon* do. Another good election parody is *Primary Colors* by Joe Klein.

Lester, Julius
Do Lord Remember Me
Holt, Rinehart, and Winston . 1985. 210 pp.

Reverend Joshua Smith remembers growing up poor and black in Ouichitta, Mississippi, and how his family story reflects the changing African American experience from slavery through the Civil Rights movement.

Book Groups 📖

Subjects　African American Authors • African Americans • ALA Notable Books • Civil Rights Movement • Family Relationships • First Novels • Ministers, Priests, Rabbis • Mississippi • Race Relations • Slavery

Now try　Lester, a well-known writer of books for children, is also the author of *And All Our Wounds Forgiven*. Toni Morrison's *Song of Solomon* and Ernest Gaines's *The Autobiography of Miss Jane Pittman* both trace the colorful, sometimes tragic, history of an African American family. Maya Angelou's memoir *I Know Why the Caged Bird Sings* is also about growing up poor and black.

Lightman, Alan
Einstein's Dreams
Pantheon Books. 1993. 179 pp.

Time in its many personas is the real protagonist of this novel and Albert Einstein merely an interlude.

Book Groups 📖

Subjects　First Novels • Physics • Postmodern Fiction • Science and Scientists

Now try   Lightman's subject matter, time, is also the subject of Michael Ende's novel *Momo*. Cees Nooteboom's *The Following Story* is a surrealistic look at the last few minutes in a man's life. Another novel with Einstein as a subject is Anna McGrail's *Mrs. Einstein*.

Lively, Penelope
Moon Tiger
Grove Press. 1987. 207 pp.

As Claudia Hampton lies dying in a London hospital, she recalls her life as a World War II newspaper correspondent, mother, novelist, and lover to a British tank commander who died in the North African campaign.

2d Appeal   Characters   Book Groups 📖

Subjects   Booker Prize Winners • British Authors • Death and Dying • Elderly Women • England • Grief • Journalists • Love Affairs • North Africa • World War II • Writers and Writing

Now try   Penelope Lively's other books, including the novels, *Treasures of Time*, *Next to Nature*, *Art*, and *According to Mark*, all display her beautiful and subdued writing style. Her memoir, *Oleander, Jacaranda: A Childhood Perceived*, is about her childhood growing up in Egypt. Michael Ondaatje's *The English Patient* is also set in North Africa. Alison Lurie's *Foreign Affairs* and Hilary Mantel's *A Change of Climate* both explore different ways of coping with grief.

Lively, Penelope
Passing On
Grove Weidenfeld. 1990. 210 pp.

Even after her death, Dorothy Glover manages to manipulate the lives of her three middle-aged children in a small English town in the Cotswolds.

2d Appeal   Characters   Book Groups 📖

Subjects   ALA Notable Books • British Authors • Brothers and Sisters • England • Family Relationships • Gay Men • Male/Female Relationships • Mothers and Daughters • Mothers and Sons

Now try   Jessica Anderson's *Tirra Lirra by the River* is another novel about a woman and her difficult relationship with her father. Lively's use of language is similar to Hilary Mantel's in *A Change of Climate*.

Livesey, Margot
Criminals
Alfred A. Knopf. 1996. 271 pp.

On his way to visit his distraught sister in Scotland, Ewan, a staid London banker, discovers an abandoned baby on the floor of the bus station men's room and decides, almost without thinking, to take the baby to his sister.

2d Appeal   Characters   Book Groups 📖

Subjects   Abandoned Babies • British Authors • Brothers and Sisters • Kidnapping • Loss of a Child • Mental Illness • Scotland

Now try   Livesey's first novel was *Homework.* Ian McEwan's *Enduring Love* is another novel with the combination of violence, love, and the workings out of fate that Livesey's book encompasses. There's also an abandoned baby in Tom Drury's *The End of Vandalism*.

Lodge, David
Small World: An Academic Romance
Macmillan Pub. Co. 1984. 338 pp.

As they travel around the world from one academic conference to another, various college professors vie for the coveted UNESCO Chair of Literary Criticism, a sinecure where the salary is immense and the duties nonexistent.

2d Appeal   Characters   Book Groups 📖

Subjects   Academia • British Authors • College Professors • Humorous Fiction • Satirical Fiction

Now try   Characters in *Small World* also appeared in Lodge's earlier novel, *Changing Places*. Michael Malone's *Foolscap*, Richard Russo's *Straight Man*, Malcolm Bradbury's *The History Man*, and Randall Jarrell's *Pictures from an Institution* are other satires set in the world of academia.

Loewinsohn, Ron
Magnetic Field(s)
Knopf. 1983. 181 pp.

A burglar, a composer, and the composer's best friend find their lives intersecting within the same magnetic field of existence.

Subjects   ALA Notable Books • First Novels • Friendship • Marriage • Music and Musicians

Now try   Loewinsohn is also the author of the novel *Where All the Ladders Start*. John Guare's play "Six Degrees of Separation" and Douglas Cooper's *Amnesia* are both about the strange interweaving of lives.

Long, David
The Falling Boy
Scribner. 1997. 287 pp.

At 22, when Mark marries Olivia, the third of the four Stavros sisters, he doesn't expect to fall in love with her older sister Linny, but when he's 30, he does.

2d Appeal   Characters   Book Groups 📖

Subjects   Adultery • Fathers and Daughters • First Novels • Marriage • Montana • Sisters

Now try   Long's first book was *Blue Spruce*, a collection of short stories. Long's writing style is similar to that of both Larry Watson (*Montana 1948*) and Deirdre McNamer (*One Sweet Quarrel*), whose books are also set in Montana. Colin Harrison's *Break and Enter* and John Updike's *Marry Me* are both about marital infidelity. Laurie Colwin's *Shine On, Bright and Dangerous Object* is about a man falling in love with his brother's widow.

Mackay, Shena
The Orchard on Fire
Moyer Bell. 1996. 214 pp.

In a small English town in the 1950s, 8-year-old April Harlency must cope with the unwanted sexual advances of a lonely neighbor and the knowledge of her best friend's life with an abusive family.

2d Appeal   Setting   Book Groups 📖

Subjects   1950s • Child Abuse • Coming-of-Age • England • Scottish Authors • Sexual Abuse • Small-Town Life

Now try   Other books by Mackay include *The Advent Calendar* and *Dreams of Dead Women's Handbags: Collected Stories*. Graham Swift's *Waterland*, Howard Norman's *The Bird Artist*, and E. Annie Proulx's *The Shipping News* are, like Mackay's novel, superb evocations of place.

Mahfouz, Naguib

Palace Walk
Doubleday. 1990. 498 pp.

A cloistered wife, her adolescent children, and her tyrannical husband hold fast to their Islamic faith amidst domestic scandals and violent uprisings against British occupation. Translated from the Egyptian by W. M. Hutchins and O. E. Kenny.

2d Appeal Setting **Book Groups** 📖

Subjects ALA Notable Books • Egypt • Egyptian Authors • Family Relationships • Marriage • Novels in Translation • Oppression of Women • World War I

Now try This is the first volume of the author's "Cairo Trilogy," followed by *Palace of Desire* and *Sugar Street*. Mahfouz won the Nobel Prize for Literature in 1989. While Mahfouz's novel has a slower moving plot and less endearing characters than Rohinton Mistry's *A Fine Balance*, both works share political instability as a backdrop for family affairs, and both authors explore the sanctioned oppression of women in their respective cultures.

Maitland, Sara

Ancestral Truths
H. Holt. 1994. 295 pp.

Clare is unable to remember what happened when she and her abusive lover were mountain climbing in Zimbabwe, but she knows that David is missing and that her right hand has been amputated.

2d Appeal Characters **Book Groups** 📖

Subjects Abusive Relationships • ALA Notable Books • Amnesia • British Authors • Brothers and Sisters • Deafness • Family Relationships • Middle-Aged Women • Physical Disabilities • Zimbabwe

Now try Maitland's other novels include *Daughter of Jerusalem* and *Three Times Table*, about a day in the life of three generations of women living in a house in London. Cees Nooteboom's *The Following Story* also deals with amnesia. Marianne Wiggins's novel *Almost Heaven* is also about a woman who is unable to remember the events surrounding a terrible accident.

Makine, Andrei

Dreams of My Russian Summers
Arcade Publishing. 1997. 241 pp.

Every summer Andrei and his sister travel from their city home in the Soviet Union to visit their grandmother, Charlotte Lemonnier, who, though born in France, has spent her adult life in Siberia; with Charlotte, they learn not only about turn-of-the-century Paris, but also of her experiences during all the Russian upheavals in the 20th century. Translated from the French by Geoffrey Strachan.

2d Appeal Characters **Book Groups** 📖

Subjects Elderly Women • France • Grandparents • Novels in Translation • Russia

Now try Makine is also the author of *Once Upon the River Love*. Marcel Proust's *Remembrance of Things Past* is a natural follow-up to Makine's novel, because it, too, is concerned with memory. This novel won the Prix Goncourt.

Malamud, Bernard
Dubin's Lives
Farrar, Straus Grioux. 1979. 362 pp.

Frustrated by writer's block, turning 60, and caught in a loveless marriage, biographer William Dubin pursues a relationship with 23-year-old Fanny.

2d Appeal Characters

Subjects Adultery • Aging • ALA Notable Books • Family Relationships • Marriage • Midlife Crisis • Older Men/Younger Women • Writers and Writing

Now try Other works of fiction by Malamud include the novels *The Fixer* and *God's Grace* and *Rembrandt's Hat*, a collection of stories. Other explorations of men and aging are found in Saul Bellow's *Henderson the Rain King* and Richard Russo's *Straight Man*.

Malouf, David
The Great World
Pantheon Books. 1990. 330 pp.

During World War II, Vic Curran and Digger Keen meet as Australian prisoners of war in Thailand and find their lives uneasily but irrevocably connected following the war.

2d Appeal Characters   Book Groups 📖

Subjects Australia • Australian Authors • Men's Friendships • Prisoners of War • Southeast Asia • Thailand • World War II

Now try Other novels by Malouf include *Remembering Babylon* (which won the first IMPAC/Dublin Award in 1996) and *The Conversations at Curlew Creek*. Nevil Shute's *A Town Like Alice* is a good story also set in Southeast Asia, in which an Australian POW plays an important part.

Manea, Norman
The Black Envelope
Farrar, Straus and Giroux. 1995. 329 pp.

In Bucharest during the 1980s, Tolea searches for answers about the mysterious death of his father 40 years before. Translated from the Romanian by Patrick Camiller.

2d Appeal Setting

Subjects 1980s • Bucharest • Death of a Parent • Fathers and Sons • Novels in Translation • Romania • Romanian Authors

Now try Manea is also the author of *Compulsory Happiness: Four Novellas*, also set in Romania. Other novels about the hellish quality of life during the Ceausescu regime in Romania include Marianne Wiggins's *Eveless Eden* and *The Land of Green Plums* by Herta Muller.

Mantel, Hilary
An Experiment in Love
H. Holt and Co. 1996. 250 pp.

During Carmel McBain's journey from growing up with her angry mother and defeated father in a British mill town, to her poverty-stricken life at college in London, she is accompanied by her friend and nemesis, Karina, whose stoicism contrasts with the ups and downs of Carmel's life.

2d Appeal Characters   Book Groups 📖

Subjects 1970s • British Authors • College Students • Eating Disorders • Family Relationships • Women's Friendships • Working Classes

Now try Mantel's other novels include *A Change of Climate* and *Eight Months on Ghazzah Street*. Mantel's descriptions of women living together are as acute as Mary McCarthy's in *The Group* and Muriel Spark's *The Girls of Slender Means* and *The Prime of Miss Jean Brodie*. Carmel's descent into anorexia is reminiscent of Margaret Atwood's heroine in *The Edible Woman*.

Marciano, Francesca
Rules of the Wild
Pantheon Books. 1998. 293 pp.

Esme leaves her native Italy for life among the white expatriates in Nairobi, Kenya, and falls into relationships with two very different men: Adam, a second-generation Kenyan who runs luxury tours for American tourists, and Hunter, an American journalist addicted to a life of danger.

2d Appeal Setting

Subjects Colonialism • Expatriates • First Novels • Journalists • Kenya • Love Affairs • Male/Female Relationships • Nairobi • Women's Friendships

Now try Marciano's novel is almost an updating of Isak Dinesen's tales of life in Kenya in the 1930s, *Out of Africa*. Barbara Kingsolver's *The Poisonwood Bible* also depicts the life of expatriates in Africa. Marciano's spare and direct writing is similar to that of Renata Adler (*Pitch Dark*) and Jean Rhys (*Quartet*).

Marias, Javier
All Souls
Harvill. 1992. 210 pp.

A Spanish visiting lecturer at Oxford falls in love with Clare Bayes, a young tutor whose husband is unaware of the affair. Translated from the Spanish by Margaret Jull Costa.

2d Appeal Characters

Subjects Academia • Adultery • College Professors • Male/Female Relationships • Novels in Translation • Oxford University • Satirical Fiction

Now try *All Souls* won the Cuidad de Barcelona Prize in 1990 and was voted by the critics of El Pais one of the two best Spanish novels published since 1975. Marias's *A Heart So White* won the IMPAC/Dublin Literary Prize in 1997. The satire found in *All Souls* is similar to the satire in David Lodge's novels, including *Changing Places*. Marias's writing style is reminiscent of Eric Linklater's *Poet's Pub*.

Maso, Carole
Ghost Dance
North Point Press. 1986. 275 pp.

Vanessa struggles to understand her mother's life and death and, in the process, comes to terms with those parts of her mother that both kept them together and drove them apart.

2d Appeal Characters   Book Groups 📖

Subjects Art and Artists • Death of a Parent • First Novels • Mental Illness • Mothers and Daughters

Now try   Maso is also the author of *Ava*, *The Art Lover*, and *Defiance*. *Two Girls*, *Fat and Thin* by Mary Gaitskill explores the way family relationships shape children. *Written on the Body* by Jeanette Winterson, about two women struggling to define love within a relationship and to understand and contain its excesses, is written in the same disconnected and poetic style as *Ghost Dance*.

Maxwell, William
So Long, See You Tomorrow   Knopf. 1980. 135 pp.

Three deaths scar the life of a teenager growing up in a small Illinois town in the 1920s.

2d Appeal   Setting   Book Groups 📖

Subjects   1920s • Adultery • Coming-of-Age • Illinois • Small-Town Life • Teenage Boys

Now try   Among Maxwell's many other works of fiction are *They Came Like Swallows* and *Time Will Darken It*. Maxwell's collection of short stories, *All the Days and Nights*, was an ALA Notable Book. Larry Watson's *Montana 1948* uses the same simple and direct language that Maxwell employs.

McCarthy, Cormac
All the Pretty Horses   Knopf. 1992. 301 pp.

In the 1930s, two teenage boys go south to Mexico for an adventure, but their experiences turn them into men.

2d Appeal   Setting   Book Groups 📖

Subjects   1930s • ALA Notable Books • Coming-of-Age • Mexico • National Book Award Winners • National Book Critics Circle Award Winners • Teenage Boys

Now try   This is the first book in "The Border Trilogy," followed by *The Crossing* and *Cities of the Plain*. Other books by McCarthy include *Blood Meridian*. The violence found in all of McCarthy's novels is also a characteristic of the novels of Ian McEwan (*The Cement Garden* and *Amsterdam*).

McDermott, Alice
That Night   Farrar, Straus and Giroux. 1987. 183 pp.

When Sheryl discovers that she's pregnant by her high school boyfriend Rick, her mother forbids the lovers to meet, a decision that leads to violence.

2d Appeal   Setting

Subjects   1960s • Mothers and Daughters • Teenage Boys • Teenage Girls • Teenage Love • Teenage Pregnancy • Teenagers • Violence

Now try   McDermott's other novels, including *The Bigamist's Daughter*, *At Weddings and Wakes*, and *Charming Billy*, share the deliberate writing style used so well here. Other novels in which a child observes the behavior of the adults in his life include Douglas Bauer's *The Book of Famous Iowans* and Stewart O'Nan's *Snow Angels*. The sense of a neighborhood watching events play out can be found in *The Virgin Suicides* by Jeffrey Eugenides.

McEwan, Ian

Black Dogs
Nan A. Talese. 1992. 149 pp.

June and Bernard Tremaine's stormy marriage begins during their honeymoon, when June is nearly attacked by two large and vicious black dogs.

2d Appeal   Characters   Book Groups 📖

Subjects   British Authors • Marriage • Philosophical Novels • Political Fiction • Psychological Fiction

Now try   A prolific novelist, short story writer, and playwright, McEwan's other works include *Enduring Love*, *The Cement Garden*, *Amsterdam*, and *The Comfort of Strangers*. In *Family Pictures* Sue Miller also creates a wrenching portrait of a stormy and steadily failing marriage.

McFarland, Dennis

The Music Room
Houghton Mifflin. 1990. 275 pp.

His brother's unexpected and unexplained suicide leads Martin Lambert on a search for causes and answers in his family's relationships to one another and themselves.

2d Appeal   Characters   Book Groups 📖

Subjects   Alcoholics and Alcoholism • Brothers • Death and Dying • First Novels • Music and Musicians • Suicide

Now try   McFarland's other novels include *A Face at the Window* and *School for the Blind.* Other novels about alcoholics include Peter Benchley's *Rummies*, Thomas Berger's *Robert Crews*, and Thomas Cobb's *Crazy Heart*. *Geyser Life* by Edward Hardy is another novel about how the unexpected death of a sibling causes a family to reassess the past. Frank Conroy's *Body and Soul* and Mark Salzman's *The Soloist* are both novels about music and musicians.

McPherson, William

Testing the Current
Simon and Schuster. 1984. 348 pp.

Tommy McAllister's ninth year—1939—is marked not only by the ordinary events and holidays, but by his growing realization of the lies and deceptions by which his parents, their friends, and neighbors live their lives.

2d Appeal   Story

Subjects   1930s • Adultery • Coming-of-Age • Family Relationships • First Novels • Marriage

Now try   In *Testing the Current*, the reader knows much more than the characters do, which adds an interesting layer of irony to the reading of the novel. *Los Alamos* by Joseph Kanon offers readers the same sense of irony. Other novels about boys growing up are Frank Conroy's *Stop-Time* and Peter Hedges's *An Ocean in Iowa*.

Michaels, Anne
Fugitive Pieces
A.A. Knopf. 1997. 294 pp.

Despite being rescued and adopted by a kindly Greek geologist during World War II, Jacob Beer forever carries the trauma and grief of witnessing the slaughter of his Polish family.

2d Appeal   Characters   Book Groups 📖

Subjects   Canadian Authors • First Novels • Greece • Grief • Holocaust • Poland • World War II

Now try   *Corelli's Mandolin* by Louis de Bernieres is also set during World War II. Marisa Kantor Stark's *Bring Us the Old People* is also about a young person whose parents perish during the war. Andrzej Szczypiorski's *The Shadow Catcher* is a coming-of-age novel set in Warsaw, Poland during the rise of Hitler. *Fugitive Pieces* won both the Guardian Fiction Prize and the Orange Prize.

Mistry, Rohinton
A Fine Balance
Knopf. 1996. 603 pp.

Two lower-caste tailors, an upper-caste widow, and a student all form an unlikely alliance while sharing a cramped apartment during a state of emergency in India in 1975.

2d Appeal   Setting   Book Groups 📖

Subjects   1970s • ALA Notable Books • Family Relationships • Friendship • India • Indian Authors • Violence

Now try   Mistry's novel *Such a Long Journey* is about a bank clerk who becomes involved in a political plot, with terrible results. Mistry's epic tales are not unlike those of Leo Tolstoy (*Anna Karenina* and *War and Peace*) in their scope and vision. Caste plays an important part in Arundhati Roy's novel, *The God of Small Things*. Mistry's harrowing novel has unexpected touches of humor, much like the fiction of Lewis Nordan (*Wolf Whistle* and *The Sharpshooter Blues*, among others). *A Fine Balance* won both the Giller Prize and a Governor General's Literary Award.

Morrison, Toni
Jazz
Knopf. 1992. 229 pp.

The rhythms of 1920s Harlem punctuate this non-linear novel of the urban black experience and a marriage gone bad.

2d Appeal   Setting   Book Groups 📖

Subjects   1920s • Adultery • African American Authors • African Americans • ALA Notable Books • Jazz • Male/Female Relationships • Marriage • New York

Now try   Among Morrison's other novels are *Sula, Paradise, Beloved*, and *The Bluest Eye*. *Jonah's Gourd Vine* by Zora Neale Hurston is another view of the black experience. Both David Lewis's *When Harlem Was in Vogue* and Ann Douglas's *Terrible Honesty: Mongrel Manhattan in the 1920s* are about the New York world where Morrison's characters live. Connie Porter's *All-Bright Court* is another novel about African Americans who migrated to the North in search of a better life.

Mulisch, Harry

The Assault
Pantheon Books. 1985. 185 pp.

As an adult, Anton Steewijk unravels the mystery of the 1945 murder of a Nazi collaborator, the brutal retaliation on his own family, and the interlocking stories of the four households on his childhood street in Holland. Translated from the Dutch by Claire Nicolas White.

2d Appeal Story Book Groups 📖

Subjects Coming-of-Age • Dutch Authors • Family Relationships • Holland • Murder • Nazis • Netherlands • Novels in Translation • World War II

Now try Mulisch is also the author of *The Discovery of Heaven*, about two very different characters who discover they were conceived on the same day in 1933. Other novels that evoke the same depth of feelings as *The Assault* include Rink van der Velde's *The Trap*, Marisa Kantor Stark's *Bring Us the Old People*, and Ursula Hegi's *Stones from the River*.

Murakami, Haruki

A Wild Sheep Chase
Kodansha International. 1989. 299 pp.

A search for an overly ambitious sheep leads the unnamed narrator from Tokyo to Hokkaido and into the lives of, among others, a young woman with beautiful ears, a brilliant but despondent professor, and a war criminal. Translated from the Japanese by Alfred Birnbaum.

2d Appeal Characters

Subjects Eccentrics and Eccentricities • Humorous Fiction • Japan • Japanese Authors • Magic Realism • Novels in Translation

Now try Murakami's other works of fiction include *Dance Dance Dance* and *The Elephant Vanishes: Stories*. Murakami's writing style is reminiscent of the hard-boiled detective novels of Raymond Chandler (*The Big Sleep* and others) and Ross Macdonald (*The Galton Case* and others). *Bellwether* by Connie Willis is also about sheep.

Murakami, Haruki

The Wind-Up Bird Chronicle
Alfred A. Knopf. 1997. 613 pp.

When his wife mysteriously disappears, Toru Okada sets out to search for her, encountering along the way a variety of bizarre people and events, all linked by the remembrance of a massacre in 1939 of Japanese troops by the Soviet army at Nomonhan, on the Manchurian border. Translated from the Japanese by Jay Rubin.

2d Appeal Characters

Subjects ALA Notable Books • Eccentrics and Eccentricities • Husbands and Wives • Japan • Japanese Authors • Novels in Translation • Political Fiction • World War II

Now try Murakami is also the author of *South of the Border, West of the Sun*, *Hard-boiled Wonderland*, and *The End of the World*. The main character in Kazuo Ishiguro's *The Unconsoled* also drifts through events that may be real or may be simply hallucinations.

Murdoch, Iris
The Good Apprentice
Viking. 1986. 522 pp.

Edward Baltram feeds his friend Mark a drugged sandwich, and Mark, on a trip, jumps out a window and dies; Edward faces an agonizing but nonetheless adventurous quest for absolution and the meaning of his life.

2d Appeal   Characters   Book Groups 📖

Subjects   Adultery • Art and Artists • British Authors • Grief • Men's Friendships • Psychiatrists, Psychoanalysts, Psychotherapists

Now try   Murdoch is more hopeful and less harsh and enigmatic than Isak Dinesen is in *Winter Tales*, but she raises some similar religious and moral questions. Many of Iris Murdoch's other novels were ALA Notable Books, including *Bruno's Dream*. Donna Tartt's *The Secret History* is another novel about guilt and redemption.

Murdoch, Iris
The Philosopher's Pupil
Viking Press. 1983. 576 pp.

In the spa town of Ennistone, a bitter George McCaffrey, hoping to be reconciled with his former tutor, Professor John Rozanov, becomes hopelessly embroiled in the philosopher's plans for his orphaned grandaughter.

2d Appeal   Characters   Book Groups 📖

Subjects   ALA Notable Books • British Authors • College Professors • Male/Female Relationships • Orphans • Philosophical Novels

Now try   Among Murdoch's other novels are *The Italian Girl*, *The Black Prince*, and *The Sacred and Profane Love Machine.* In their complexity, intelligence, and wit, Murdoch's novels resemble the novels of Margaret Drabble (*The Needle's Eye*) and A. S. Byatt (*The Virgin in the Garden*).

Murdoch, Iris
The Sea, The Sea
Viking Press. 1978. 502 pp.

Charles Arrowby, a retired actor and director, moves to an isolated house on the English seaside to write his memoirs, but when his long-lost love unexpectedly appears on the scene, he decides to rescue her from her boorish husband.

2d Appeal   Characters   Book Groups 📖

Subjects   Actors and Acting • ALA Notable Books • Booker Prize Winners • British Authors • Male/Female Relationships • Men's Lives • Obsessive Love • Philosophical Novels

Now try   Among Murdoch's many other novels are *The Message to the Planet*, *The Red and the Green*, and *Jackson's Dilemma*. Like John Fowles (*The Magus*) and Vladimir Nabokov (*Ada*), Murdoch writes intensely philosophical novels. Ever present in this novel is the sea itself, and William Shakespeare's "The Tempest," a favorite of Arrowby's, is also centered on the sea and its power. Nadine Gordimer's *The Conservationist* is also about an elderly man who reflects on the events of his life.

Nordan, Lewis

Wolf Whistle
Algonquin Books of Chapel Hill. 1993. 290 pp.

In this tragicomic version of the real-life 1955 murder of a black teenager who had dared to whistle at a white woman, the lost souls of Arrow Catcher, Mississippi, grapple with their differing levels of complicity in the crime as well as the true meaning of evil.

2d Appeal Characters

Subjects ALA Notable Books • Black Humor • Magic Realism • Mississippi • Murder • Racism

Now try Some of the same characters from *Wolf Whistle* also appear in Nordan's *Music of the Swamp*. Nordan's Southern blend of humor and pathos can be found in William Baldwin's *The Hard to Catch Mercy*.

Oates, Joyce Carol

What I Lived For
Dutton. 1994. 608 pp.

At the age of 11, Corky witnessed the murder of his father; as an adult, small-town politician Corky Corcoran tries to understand the suicide of a young black woman.

2d Appeal Characters   Book Groups 📖

Subjects African Americans • Death of a Parent • Middle-Aged Men • Midlife Crisis • Murder • Politics • Psychological Fiction • Small-Town Life • Stepfamilies • Suicide

Now try This novel, Oates's twenty-fourth, is told in the form of Corky's interior monologue. Stanley Elkin's *The MacGuffin* also deals with the subject of local politics. In its attitude toward middle age, this novel resembles Richard Ford's *Independence Day*.

O'Brien, Edna

Down by the River
Farrar, Straus & Giroux. 1997. 265 pp.

Pregnant with her father's child, 13-year-old Mary's attempt to have an abortion creates a religious furor all over Ireland.

2d Appeal Setting   Book Groups 📖

Subjects Abortion • Catholics and Catholicism • Child Abuse • Incest • Ireland • Irish Authors • Sexual Abuse • Teenage Pregnancy

Now try Other books by O'Brien include a trilogy, comprising *The Country Girl*, *The Lonely Girl*, and *Girls in Their Married Bliss*. Doris Grumbach's *Book of Knowledge* and Georgia Savage's *The House Tibet* both describe incestuous relationships.

O'Brien, Tim

Going After Cacciato
Delacorte. 1978. 301 pp.

Private Cacciato decides he is no longer going to participate in the war in the jungles of Vietnam and sets off to walk from Indochina to Paris.

2d Appeal Setting   Book Groups 📖

Subjects ALA Notable Books • Magic Realism • National Book Award Winners • Vietnam War

Now try   Among O'Brien's other books are ***The Things They Carried*** and ***The Nuclear Age.*** The same intensity found in O'Brien's writing about the Vietnam War can also be found in Larry Heinemann's ***Paco's Story. Buffalo Afternoon*** by Susan Fromberg Schaeffer is about the difficulties Vietnam veterans faced after they returned home.

O'Brien, Tim
In the Lake of the Woods
Houghton Mifflin. 1994. 306 pp.

When leaked information about his past in Vietnam scuttles John Wade's political career, he and his wife Kathy reassess their lives at a cottage in a small Minnesota town until Kathy disappears.

2d Appeal   Characters   Book Groups 📖

Subjects   ALA Notable Books • Marriage • Midlife Crisis • Minnesota • Vietnam Veterans • Vietnam War

Now try   ***Seven Moves*** by Carol Anshaw is another novel about a disappearance and how it affects those left behind. James McManus's ***Going to the Sun*** and Jon Cohen's ***The Man in the Window*** also have ambiguous endings.

Oe, Kenzaburo
An Echo of Heaven
Kodansha International. 1996. 204 pp.

A Japanese woman, mother, and scholar, Marie Kuraki takes up the role of enigmatic saint at a commune in the Mexican desert after her personal life is devastated by the tragic double suicide of her two young sons. Translated from the Japanese by Margaret Mitsutani.

2d Appeal   Characters   Book Groups 📖

Subjects   Death of a Child • Japanese Authors • Mental Illness • Mexico • Novels in Translation • Physical Disabilities • Single Parents • Spirituality • Suicide • Writers and Writing

Now try   Oe is credited with being a revitalizing force in Japanese literature after World War II. His novels include ***A Personal Matter***, ***The Silent City***, and ***The Pinch Runner Memorandum.*** Other Japanese writers working in a similar fatalistic tone include Kobo Abe (***The Woman in the Dunes***) and Yoshikichi Furui (***Child of Darkness: Yoko and Other Stories***).

O'Faolain, Julia
No Country for Young Men
Carroll & Graf Publishers. 1986. 368 pp.

When American James Duffy tries to solve the murder of Sparky Driscoll, more than half a century in the past, he discovers that Sister Judith Clancy's history of mental illness and shock treatments have left her unable to answer his questions.

2d Appeal   Characters

Subjects   Irish Authors • Mental Illness • Murder • Nuns

Now try   O'Faolain's other novels include ***Three Lovers*** and ***The Obedient Wife***. Seamus Deane's ***Reading in the Dark*** is another view of the complexity of Irish politics. Geoffrey Ryman's ***Was*** is another novel in which a character's mental illness interferes with his ability to uncover the truth about the past.

Okri, Ben
The Famished Road
N.A. Talese. 1992. 500 pp.

The child Azaro leads a double life, enduring the poverty and political upheaval of modern Nigeria while experiencing the wonders and terrors of a spirit world that only he can see.

2d Appeal   Setting   Book Groups 📖

Subjects   Africa • African Authors • Booker Prize Winners • Magic Realism • Nigeria • Nigerian Authors • Poverty

Now try   Okri's other novels include *Flowers and Shadows* and *Songs of Enchantment.* Other works of fiction that bring Africa to life are *Things Fall Apart* by Nigerian exile Chinua Achebe, activist Ken Saro-Wiwa's *Adaku & Other Stories*, and Alan Paton's *Cry, the Beloved Country.* Buchi Emecheta's *Second-Class Citizen* and *The Slave Girl* address poverty in Nigeria from a woman's viewpoint.

Ondaatje, Michael
The English Patient
Knopf. 1992. 307 pp.

As World War II draws to a close, a young nurse in a bomb-damaged villa near Florence, Italy, devotedly tends a mysterious English patient, a nameless burn victim haunted by his own memories of passion, betrayal, and rescue.

2d Appeal   Characters   Book Groups 📖

Subjects   ALA Notable Books • Booker Prize Winners • Canadian Authors • Italy • Male/Female Relationships • North Africa • World War II

Now try   Ondaatje also wrote a memoir, *Running in the Family* (an ALA Notable Book), and three books of poetry that echo the themes of this novel. The elegant language that characterizes Ondaatje's novel can also be found in Anne Michaels's *Fugitive Pieces* and *Corelli's Mandolin* by Louis de Bernieres. Penelope Lively's *Moon Tiger* shares the North African setting with Ondaatje's novel. J. L. Carr's *A Month in the Country* is another novel that describes the effects of war on its survivors. Jim Crace's *Arcadia* is also written in vividly poetic prose. *The English Patient* won a Governor General's Literary Award.

Ozick, Cynthia
The Cannibal Galaxy
Knopf. 1983. 161 pp.

A survivor of Nazi-occupied France, Joseph Brill comes to America to set up a school that fuses traditional Jewish and contemporary European cultures; his search for genius among his students is deflected when his love for brilliant Hester causes him to overlook the true prodigy, her daughter Beulah.

2d Appeal   Characters   Book Groups 📖

Subjects   Jews and Judaism • Male/Female Relationships • Midlife Crisis • Mothers and Daughters • Teachers • World War II

Now try   Ozick's *The Shawl*, a collection of two novellas, was an ALA Notable Book. Ozick's genius can be fully appreciated in her collections of essays, including *Art and Ardor* and *Fame and Folly.* Anne Michaels's *Fugitive Pieces*, Aharon Appelfeld's *For Every Sin*, Stanislaw Benski's *Missing Pieces*, and *The Court Jesters* by Avigdor Dagan are also about the experiences of survivors of the Holocaust.

Phillips, Max
Snakebite Sonnet
Little, Brown and Co. 1997. 307 pp.

Nicky Wertheim's life from age 10 to his early 30s is measured by the joy and pain he endures during an on-again off-again love affair with an older woman.

2d Appeal   Characters

Subjects   Adultery • First Novels • Love Stories • Obsessive Love • Older Women/Younger Men

Now try   This novel is somewhat of a mirror image of Herman Wouk's *Marjorie Morningstar*, in which Marjorie's life is defined by her love for Noel, an older man. *Aunt Julia and the Scriptwriter* by Mario Vargas Llosa is also the story of a young man's love for an older woman. Of course, in neither of these books do the couples meet when one of them is 10 years old!

Powers, Charles T.
In the Memory of the Forest
Scribner. 1997. 384 pp.

After the fall of Communism, the residents of a small Polish village try to come to terms with their pasts and make sense of a local murder and some mysterious acts of vandalism.

2d Appeal   Characters   Book Groups 📖

Subjects   Communism • First Novels • Murder • Poland • Small-Town Life

Now try   David Guterson's *Snow Falling on Cedars* also combines a mystery with a story about the lives of ordinary people. Fyodor Dostoyevsky's *Crime and Punishment* shares the dark ambiance of Powers's novel.

Powers, J. F.
Wheat That Springeth Green
A.A. Knopf. 1988. 335 pp.

Father Joe Hackett's years as a curate and then serving a Midwestern parish reveal him to be not a saint (to which he always aspired) but a human being with attendant flaws and much heart.

2d Appeal   Characters   Book Groups 📖

Subjects   ALA Notable Books • Catholics and Catholicism • Coming-of-Age • Humorous Fiction • Ministers, Priests, Rabbis • Minnesota • Religion

Now try   Powers's other books include the story collections *Look How the Fish Live*, *The Presence of Grace*, and *Prince of Darkness and Other Stories*, as well as the novel *Morte D'Urban*. Other portraits of priests who face crises of confidence can be found in Mary Doria Russell's *The Sparrow* and Carlo Coccioli's *Heaven and Earth*.

Powers, Richard
Galatea 2.2
Farrar, Straus Giroux. 1995. 329 pp.

An English professor uses his literary knowledge to help a cognitive neurologist create a thinking machine that can pass a comprehensive master's exam for a degree in English; in the process, he discovers that Helen has developed a mind of her own.

2d Appeal   Setting

Subjects   College Professors • Computers

Now try   Among Powers's other novels—all extremely intelligent and thought provoking—are ***Three Farmers on Their Way to a Dance***, ***Prisoner's Dilemma***, ***The Gold Bug Variations***, ***Gain***, and ***Operation Wandering Soul.*** A human's attraction to a non-living object can also be found in Jonathan Lethem's *As She Climbed Across the Table*.

Puig, Manuel
Kiss of the Spider Woman
 Knopf. 1978. 281 pp.

In an Argentine prison, fiercely dogmatic political prisoner Valentin and Molina, a self-centered, gay window dresser, are gradually transformed by their growing friendship and the fantastical world created by Molina as he retells the plots of old movies. Translated from the Spanish by Thomas Colchie.

2d Appeal   Characters   Book Groups

Subjects   ALA Notable Books • Argentina • Argentinian Authors • Gay Men • Men's Friendship • Novels in Translation • Political Fiction • Political Prisoners • South America • South American Authors

Now try   Other books by Puig include ***Betrayed by Rita Hayworth***, ***Blood of Requited Love***, and ***Heartbreak Tango.*** Puig's ***Eternal Curse on the Reader of These Pages***, like *Kiss of the Spider Woman*, is written mostly in dialogue form. Another novel about gay men in Argentina is Colm Toibin's *The Story of the Night*.

Pynchon, Thomas
Vineland
Little, Brown. 1990. 385 pp.

The lives of Zoyd Wheeler, his ex-wife Frenesi Gates, and their daughter Prairie, plus scores of their friends and neighbors, are thrown into turmoil when Frenesi's former lover, Federal Prosecutor Brock Vond, storms into Vineland on a personal vendetta, backed up by troops from the government's war on drugs.

Subjects   Counterculture • Drugs and Drug Abuse • Northern California

Now try   The poetic waves of words and ever-digressing stories in this novel can also be found in Pynchon's ***Mason and Dixon*** and ***Gravity's Rainbow***. Another novel with a continually expanding plot is Tom Drury's ***The Black Brook.*** The precursor of Pynchon's writing style is James Joyce (***Ulysses***), and following the tradition in the next generation of writers is David Foster Wallace in ***Infinite Jest***.

Reed, Ishmael
Japanese by Spring
Atheneum. 1993. 225 pp.

Benjamin "Chappie" Puttbutt, a junior professor lusting after tenure and revenge, finds himself head of the English department after his Japanese tutor becomes president of the college.

2d Appeal   Story

Subjects   Academia • African American Authors • College Professors • Culture Clash • Humorous Fiction • Racism • Satirical Fiction

Now try   Among Reed's many other books of both fiction and nonfiction are *Mumbo Jumbo* and *The Terrible Twos.* The hero of Richard Russo's *Straight Man* also becomes the head of an English Department through a variety of zany incidents. *The Man from Japan* by Clive James is another humorous tale of Japanese and English interactions.

Robinson, Marilynne
Housekeeping
Farrar, Straus Giroux. 1980. 219 pp.

After their mother's suicide, sisters Ruth and Lucille go to live with an eccentric aunt in eastern Washington.

2d Appeal   Characters   Book Groups 📖

Subjects   ALA Notable Books • Death of a Parent • First Novels • Mental Illness • Sisters • Small-Town Life • Suicide • Washington

Now try   Lowry Pei's *Family Resemblances* is another book with an eccentric aunt. The sisters in Karin Cook's *What Girls Learn* must also learn to cope with the death of their mother. Joan Chase's *During the Reign of the Queen of Persia* is another novel with meticulously described characters. Another beautifully written novel is Charles Frazier's *Cold Mountain*.

Roth, Philip
American Pastoral
Houghton Mifflin. 1997. 423 pp.

Seymour Swede Levov, hero-worshipped by everyone growing up in his Jewish neighborhood in Newark, New Jersey, finds his golden youth is no protection against suffering when, during the height of the Vietnam War protests, his beloved daughter Merry detonates a bomb in a suburban post office.

2d Appeal   Setting   Book Groups 📖

Subjects   Fathers and Daughters • Jews and Judaism • New Jersey • Pulitzer Prize Winners • Vietnam War • Violence

Now try   Among Roth's many other books are *My Life as a Man* and *Goodbye, Columbus, and Five Short Stories*. The narrator of this novel, Nathan Zuckerman, appears in other novels by Roth, including *The Ghost Writer*, *Zuckerman Unbound*, and *The Anatomy Lesson.* Another novel involving the consequences of violence as a protest against the Vietnam War is Marge Piercy's *Vida*.

Roth, Philip
The Counterlife
Farrar Straus Giroux. 1986. 324 pp.

Roth creates a series of alternate universes in which novelist Nathan Zuckerman and his brother Henry each suffer the results of impotence and an operation to cure the condition, or perhaps neither does.

2d Appeal   Characters   Book Groups 📖

Subjects   ALA Notable Books • Brothers • Jews and Judaism • Male/Female Relationships • Men's Lives • National Book Critics Circle Award Winners • Writers and Writing

Now try   The character of Nathan Zuckerman also appeared in *The Prague Orgy*. Roth continues to experiment and stretch the limits of the novelistic form, just as he did in his early novel, *My Life as a Man*.

Roth, Philip
The Ghost Writer   Farrar, Straus Giroux. 1979. 179 pp.

Now middle-aged, Nathan Zuckerman looks back on his 23rd year and a visit to the New England home of E. I. Lonoff, his literary idol, where he encounters Lonoff's disintegrating marriage and meets a young woman who may or may not be Anne Frank.

2d Appeal   Characters   Book Groups 📖

Subjects   1950s • ALA Notable Books • Frank, Anne • Jews and Judaism • Male/Female Relationships • Marriage • Writers and Writing

Now try   Another novel in which a meeting with a literary idol changes the protagonist's life is Brian Morton's *Starting Out in the Evening*. Saul Bellow's *Humboldt's Gift* is another novel about the relationship between a mentor and his student. *The Moviegoer* by Walker Percy also depicts a somewhat self-centered young man who is trying to understand who he really is.

Roth, Philip
Sabbath's Theater   Houghton Mifflin. 1995. 451 pp.

The death of 64-year-old bad boy Mickey Sabbath's long-time lover brings him face to face with his own mortality and memories of a life defined by angry outbursts and sexual exploits.

Subjects   Male/Female Relationships • National Book Award Winners • Sex and Sexuality

Now try   Sabbath might be described as an older version of Alexander Portnoy, the main character in Roth's *Portnoy's Complaint* (an ALA Notable Book). Among Roth's other books is a memoir, *Patrimony: A True Story* (also an ALA Notable Book). Sabbath is a character who is difficult to like, much like the main character in David Gates's *Preston Falls*.

Roy, Arundhati
The God of Small Things   Random House. 1997. 321 pp.

In Kerala, South India, in the 1960s, the mysterious death of their half-English cousin, Sophie Mol, forever alters the lives of fraternal twins Estha and Rahel, their mother, and the family handyman.

2d Appeal   Setting   Book Groups 📖

Subjects   Booker Prize Winners • Brothers and Sisters • Death of a Child • First Novels • India • Indian Authors • Love Affairs • Political Unrest • Twins

Now try   Other novels about complex family relationships in India include Anita Desai's *Clear Light of Day* and Salman Rushdie's *The Moor's Last Sigh*. Another picture of the unhealthy closeness of fraternal twins can be found in *The Tribes of Palos Verdes* by Joy Nicholson.

Rush, Norman
Mating
A.A. Knopf. 1991. 480 pp.

The narrator, an anthropologist, pursues utopian scientist Nelson Denoon across the Kalahari to his experimental, self-sustaining, matriarchal community, where she hopes to gain acceptance and love.

2d Appeal   Characters   Book Groups 📖

Subjects   Africa • First Novels • Love Stories • Male/Female Relationships • National Book Award Winners • Science and Scientists • Utopian Novels

Now try   Rush's first book, *Whites*, a collection of short stories, was an ALA Notable Book. (The heroine of *Mating* first appeared in a short story in *Whites*.) Another novel written by a man in the voice of a strong, very smart heroine whose determination and dogged pursuit of a goal lead to precarious situations is Peter Hoeg's *Smilla's Sense of Snow*. A satirical look at a matriarchal society in action can be found in Francine Prose's *Hunters and Gatherers*.

Rushdie, Salman
Midnight's Children
Knopf. 1981. 446 pp.

Saleem Sinai, born on the stroke of midnight on August 15, 1947, the moment that India received her independence from Britain, finds his life, like the lives of the 1,001 other children born at the same time, bound up with India's fate as an independent nation.

2d Appeal   Characters   Book Groups 📖

Subjects   Booker Prize Winners • Coming-of-Age • India • Indian Authors • Magic Realism • Multigenerational Novels

Now try   Among Rushdie's other works of fiction is *Haroun and the Sea of Stories*. Rushdie's stunning use of language is similar to Gabriel Garcia Marquez in *One Hundred Years of Solitude* and his other novels, as well as Arundhati Roy's *The God of Small Things*. *Midnight's Children* won the James Tait Black Memorial Prize.

Rushdie, Salman
The Moor's Last Sigh
Pantheon Books. 1995. 435 pp.

Moraes Moor Zogoiby describes his colorful family and their spicy life in Cochin, filled with failed relationships, early deaths, betrayals, passion, a hunger for power, and the seductions of art.

2d Appeal   Story   Book Groups 📖

Subjects   Art and Artists • Family Relationships • India • Indian Authors • Men's Lives • Multigenerational Novels

Now try   Rushdie's breathtaking use of language is similar to Jose Saramago's in *The Stone Raft* and Alexander Theroux's in *D'Arconville's Cat*.

Rushdie, Salman
Shame
Knopf. 1983. 319 pp.

For three generations, the families of Raza Hyder and Iskander Harappa struggle for control of their country, while Raza's daughter, Sufiya, absorbs the shame and violence of those around her.

2d Appeal Setting   Book Groups 📖

Subjects ALA Notable Books • Family Relationships • Indian Authors • Magic Realism • Multigenerational Novels • Pakistan • Violence

Now try The characters of Hyder and Harappa are loosely based on Pakistani political leaders General Zia ul-Haq and Zulfikar Ali Bhutto, respectively. Rushdie's magical interpretation of events is reminiscent of Gabriel Garcia Marquez's writings, found in *Love in the Time of Cholera* and other novels. *Shame* was shortlisted for the Booker Prize.

Sahgal, Nayantara
Rich Like Us
Norton. 1986. 236 pp.

Two generations of entrepreneurs, including the Cockney wife of an Indian manufacturer, struggle to succeed in two very different Indian cultures: the one before independence from Britain and the one after.

2d Appeal Setting   Book Groups 📖

Subjects Business and Businessmen • Colonialism • Culture Clash • Family Relationships • India • Indian Authors • Interracial Relationships • Polygamy • Widows

Now try Among Sahgal's other books are *Plans for Departure* and *Mistaken Identity.* As a snapshot of a time and place, Sahgal's novel ranks with other outstanding novels about India, including Paul Scott's *The Jewel in the Crown* and the other three novels that make up "The Raj Quartet," Salman Rushdie's *Midnight's Children*, and Arundhati Roy's *The God of Small Things. So Long a Letter* by Mariama Ba is another novel about polygamy, related through the eyes of the first wife.

Saramago, Jose
The History of the Siege of Lisbon
Harcourt Brace. 1996. 314 pp.

Raimundo Silva, a proofreader for a Portuguese publishing house, is shocked that even after he changed the whole meaning of a paragraph in a history textbook by adding the word not to one sentence, rather than being fired, his supervisor asks him to write an alternative history. Translated from the Portuguese by Giovanni Pontiero.

Subjects History • Novels in Translation • Portugal • Portuguese Authors • Writers and Writing

Now try Saramago's other novels include *Blindness* and *The Gospel According to Jesus Christ.* Saramago's novelistic cohorts are Gabriel Garcia Marquez (*One Hundred Years of Solitude* and others) and Salman Rushdie (*The Moor's Last Sigh* and others), with whom he shares linguistic brilliance and inventiveness, intelligence, and wit. Saramago won the 1998 Nobel Prize for Literature.

Shields, Carol
The Stone Diaries
Viking. 1994. 361 pp.

The long and ordinary life of Daisy Stone Goodwill unfolds in bittersweet detail through a collage of narrative, letters, newspaper clippings, and multiple voices.

2d Appeal   Characters   Book Groups 📖

Subjects   Canada • Family Relationships • National Book Critics Circle Award Winners • Pulitzer Prize Winners • Women's Lives

Now try   Shields is also the author of *Larry's Party*, the story of a man's life. Both *Kate Vaiden* and *Roxanna Slade* by Reynolds Price are the life stories of remarkably ordinary women.

Simon, Claude
The Acacia
Pantheon Books. 1991. 289 pp.

This is a post-modern account of a French family's loves, losses, and hardship set against two centuries of wars. Translated from the French by Richard Howard.

Subjects   Family Relationships • France • Multigenerational Novels • Novels in Translation • Postmodern Fiction • World War I • World War II

Now try   Among Simon's other novels are *The Flanders Road* and *The Wind*. *India Song* by Marguerite Duras is a semi-autobiographical novel written in the same Nouveau Roman style as Simon's novel. *All Quiet on the Western Front* by Erich Maria Remarque and Sebastien Japrisot's *A Very Long Engagement* both eloquently describe the horrors of war.

Slavitt, David R.
Lives of the Saints
Atheneum. 1989. 213 pp.

A reporter for a tabloid newspaper investigates a murder case by studying the belongings of the victims, all the while reading the works of an eighteenth-century philosopher and studying the lives of the saints, hoping to find consolation for his own losses, the deaths of his wife and daughter.

2d Appeal   Story   Book Groups 📖

Subjects   Death of a Child • Death of a Spouse • Journalists • Love Stories • Murder • Philosophical Novels • Religion • Writers and Writing

Now try   Slavitt's other novels include *Alice at 80*, *Turkish Delights*, and *The Cliff*. The heroine of Francine Prose's *Bigfoot Dreams* is also a reporter for a tabloid newspaper. In Nino Ricci's *Book of Saints*, a young boy tries to console himself by studying about the saints. The intensity of Slavitt's writing style resembles the novels of Iris Murdoch (*The Sea, The Sea* and others).

Smith, Lee
Fair and Tender Ladies
Putnam. 1988. 316 pp.

Ivy Rowe's life in the hills of Virginia—from her childhood through her long life as the matriarch of a large family—is told in a series of letters to friends and relations.

2d Appeal   Characters

Subjects   ALA Notable Books • Epistolary Novels • Family Relationships • Southern Authors • Virginia • Women's Lives

Now try Among Smith's other books are ***Black Mountain Breakdown***, ***Family Linen***, and ***Oral History***. Her collection of short stories, ***Me and My Baby View the Eclipse***, was an ALA Notable Book. Gwyn Hyman Rubio's ***Icy Sparks*** is another southern novel about the life of a strong woman. Sharyn McCrumb's mystery novels (***If Ever I Return***, ***Pretty Peggy-O*** and others) are also set in Appalachia.

Spark, Muriel
A Far Cry from Kensington

Houghton Mifflin. 1988. 189 pp.

In post-war London, Mrs. Hawkins, a widowed book editor, finds her life spinning out of control after she unwittingly offends a hack writer who then seeks revenge.

2d Appeal Characters   Book Groups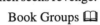

Subjects ALA Notable Books • Book Publishing • British Authors • London • Widows • Writers and Writing

Now try Spark's other novels include ***The Prime of Miss Jean Brodie*** and ***The Takeover*** (an ALA Notable Book). Her dry wit and meticulous attention to nuance of character can also be found in Angela Carter's ***Wise Children*** and Fay Weldon's ***Life Force***. (Weldon is, however, quite a bit more caustic than Spark.) Another novel about hack writers is Mary Bringle's ***Hacks at Lunch***. Cathleen Schine's ***The Love Letter*** and Diane Johnson's ***Le Divorce*** both display the dry wit found in Spark's book.

Spencer, Elizabeth
The Night Travellers   Viking. 1991. 366 pp.

Sheltered during her Southern childhood, Mary Kerr marries Jefferson Blaise; together, they get involved in protesting the Vietnam War, move to Canada, go underground, and face separation and loss.

Book Groups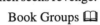

Subjects 1970s • Male/Female Relationships • Mothers and Daughters • Southern Authors • Vietnam War

Now try Among Spencer's other books are a memoir, ***Landscapes of the Heart***, and novels, ***The Salt Line*** and ***The Light in the Piazza***, as well as several collections of short stories. Marge Piercy's ***Vida*** is another example of sacrifices made in the name of political beliefs. Another book in which one of the main characters goes to Canada rather than be drafted is David James Duncan's ***The Brothers K***. ***Caucasia*** by Danzy Senna is about a family separated by their fear of government reprisal for their political beliefs.

Spencer, Scott
Endless Love   Knopf. 1979. 418 pp.

After 16-year-old Jade Butterfield's father bans 17-year-old David Axelrod from their home, David's overwhelming, endless love for Jade leads him to commit an act of violence that will alter his life.

2d Appeal Characters   Book Groups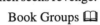

Subjects ALA Notable Books • Love Stories • Obsessive Love • Teenage Boys • Teenage Girls • Teenage Love • Teenagers • Violence

> **Now try**   Among Spencer's other novels are *Secret Anniversaries* and *Waking the Dead.* Spencer also wrote about obsessive love—the love of a son for the father who won't acknowledge him—in *The Rich Man's Table.* Another novel about the emotional volatility of teenage love is Alice McDermott's *That Night*.

Styron, William
Sophie's Choice
Random House. 1979. 515 pp.

Sophie Zawistowska, a beautiful Polish Auschwitz survivor living in Brooklyn after World War II, reveals her horrific past to two men, her schizophrenic genius lover and a young admiring Southern writer.

2d Appeal   Characters   Book Groups 📖

Subjects   Concentration Camps • Holocaust • Male/Female Relationships • Mothers and Daughters • National Book Award Winners • Poland • World War II • Writers and Writing

Now try   Styron's early novel, *The Confessions of Nat Turner*, was an ALA Notable Book. He is also the author of *Lie Down in Darkness*, *Set This House on Fire*, and *Darkness Visible: A Memoir of Madness.* Anne Michaels's *Fugitive Pieces* and Joseph Skibell's *A Blessing On the Moon* are both novels set around the Holocaust.

Taylor, Peter
A Summons to Memphis
Knopf. 1986. 209 pp.

When middle-aged bachelor Phillip Carver reluctantly agrees to return to Memphis to help his sisters prevent the remarriage of their 81-year-old father, Phillip realizes he is still mourning the family's move from Nashville when he was 13.

2d Appeal   Characters   Book Groups 📖

Subjects   ALA Notable Books • Family Relationships • Fathers and Sons • Middle-Aged Men • Pulitzer Prize Winners • Remarriage • Southern Authors • Tennessee

Now try   Among Taylor's other books of fiction are *In the Tennessee Country*, *The Old Forest and Other Stories*, and *In the Miro District and Other Stories*. A humorous exploration of a marriage late in life is *Cold Sassy Tree* by Olive Ann Burns. William Maxwell (*Time Will Darken It* and others) is another novelist with an elegant writing style.

Thornton, Lawrence
Imagining Argentina
Doubleday. 1987. 214 pp.

After his wife vanishes, Argentinian playwright Carlos Rueda finds he has the ability to know the fates of the men, women, and children who disappeared during the political repression of Buenos Aires in the 1970s.

2d Appeal   Characters   Book Groups 📖

Subjects   1970s • ALA Notable Books • Argentina • First Novels • Magic Realism • Political Fiction • PoliticalUnrest

Now try   This is the first of a trilogy that also includes *Tales from the Blue Archives* and *Naming the Spirits*. *In the Time of the Butterflies* by Julia Alvarez and *They Forged the Signature of God* by Viriato Sencion are both about political repression in the Dominican Republic.

Torrington, Jeff
Swing Hammer Swing!

Harcourt Brace. 1994. 406 pp.

A week in the life of Tom Clay, whose failure to get his novel published leads to several job applications and musings on time, death, slums, cleanliness, and the disappointments life inevitably brings.

2d Appeal Characters Book Groups 📖

Subjects 1960s • First Novels • Glasgow, Scotland • Scotland • Scottish Authors • Working Classes • Writers and Writing

Now try Writers who share with Torrington a wicked wit and a facility with language are Salman Rushdie (*Haroun and the Sea of Stories* and others) and Thomas Pynchon (*Gravity's Rainbow* and others). Alasdair Gray's *Poor Things: Episodes from the Early Life of Archibald McCandless, M.D., Scottish Public Health Officer* is another Whitbread Award winner that is set in Glasgow. *Swing Hammer Swing!* won the Whitbread Prize for First Fiction.

Tremain, Rose
Sacred Country

Atheneum. 1993. 323 pp.

Mary Ward's journey to adulthood is complicated by the fact that, ever since she was six years old, she has realized that she was supposed to be a boy.

2d Appeal Characters Book Groups 📖

Subjects British Authors • Coming-of-Age • Gender Roles • Sexual Identity

Now try Tremain also wrote *Restoration*, *The Way I Found Her*, and *The Colonel's Daughter and Other Stories*. Jan Morris's memoir, *Conundrum*, is about her growing realization that she was born the wrong sex.

Trevor, William
Felicia's Journey

Viking. 1995. 212 pp.

A pregnant young Irish girl flees a family shamed by her situation and vainly seeks her lover in England, only to fall into the path of a deceptively mild-mannered serial killer—or maybe a worse fate.

2d Appeal Characters Book Groups 📖

Subjects England • Family Relationships • Ireland • Irish Authors • Pregnancy • Sexual Abuse

Now try Trevor's other books include *The Children of Dynmouth*, *The Collected Stories*, and *Fools of Fortune*, as well as *Excursions in the Real World: Memoirs*. *Zombie* by Joyce Carol Oates is another novel about a serial killer. Roddy Doyle's *The Snapper* is a much more humorous novel about an Irish girl's unwanted pregnancy. Like Felicia in Trevor's novel, the main character in William Faulkner's *Light in August* is also searching for the father of her child. *Felicia's Journey* won the Whitbread Prize.

Tuck, Lily
The Woman Who Walked on Water
Riverhead Books. 1996. 241 pp.

As two women talk at a Caribbean resort, Adele tells the unnamed narrator why she left her Connecticut home and upper-class life to follow a guru to his ashram in India.

Subjects   Caribbean • India • Spirituality • Women's Friendships

Now try   Tuck is also the author of *Interviewing Matisse*, or *The Woman Who Died Standing Up*. Tuck's writing style resembles that of Renata Adler in *Speedboat* and *Pitch Dark*.

Updike, John
The Coup
Knopf. 1978. 298 pp.

Now in exile, Colonel Hakim Felix Ellollou recounts his overthrow of the king of Kush, his four extremely different wives, and his ongoing struggle to keep America out of his African nation.

2d Appeal   Characters   Book Groups 📖

Subjects   Africa • ALA Notable Books • Male/Female Relationships • Marriage • Political Fiction

Now try   Among Updike's many other books are *The Music School*, *In the Beauty of the Lilies*, and *Brazil*. Other novels set in Africa include Chinua Achebe's *Man of the People*, *Stool Wives: A Fiction of Africa* by William Van Wert, and Isidore Okpewho's *The Last Duty*. The history of another fictional African country is detailed in *Bound to Violence* by Yambo Ouologuem.

Updike, John
Rabbit at Rest
Knopf. 1990. 512 pp.

After suffering from a heart attack while saving his granddaughter from drowning, 55-year-old Harry (Rabbit) Angstrom struggles to find reasons to live in an America ridden with drugs, crime, and AIDs.

2d Appeal   Characters

Subjects   Drugs and Drug Abuse • Family Relationships • Grandparents • Male/Female Relationships • Middle-Aged Men • National Book Critics Circle Award Winners • Men's Lives • Pulitzer Prize Winners

Now try   Rabbit's passage through life is chronicled in Updike's *Rabbit, Run*, *Rabbit Redux*, *Rabbit Is Rich*, and now *Rabbit at Rest*. Another tale of a man's life is found in *Larry's Party* by Carol Shields.

Updike, John
Rabbit Is Rich
Knopf. 1981. 467 pp.

Complacent, middle-aged Harry (Rabbit) Angstrom sells Toyotas to fellow suburbanites while the newspaper clippings hailing him as a teenage basketball star continue to yellow in their frames on the walls of his car dealership.

2d Appeal   Characters   Book Groups 📖

Subjects   1970s • ALA Notable Books • Male/Female Relationships • Middle-Aged Men • National Book Award Winners • National Book Critics Circle Award Winners • Pulitzer Prize Winners • Suburbia

Now try   Richard Ford's *Independence Day* is another novel about a middle-aged man assessing his life. A humorous account of middle-aged angst is Richard Russo's *Straight Man*.

Urquhart, Jane

The Underpainter   Viking. 1997. 340 pp.

Seventy-five-year-old Austin Fraser reflects on his life as a painter, in which his total absorption into his art has caused him to carelessly (and cruelly) destroy the lives of his two closest friends.

2d Appeal   Characters   Book Groups ▢

Subjects   Art and Artists • Canadian Authors • Elderly Men • Men's Friendships • Men's Lives

Now try   Urquhart's other novels include *Changing Heaven* and *Away*. *What's Bred in the Bone* by Robertson Davies and Chaim Potok's *My Name Is Asher Lev* each offer a view of a painter's life. Merle Miller's *A Gay and Melancholy Sound* is another example of someone who willfully damages the lives of those who love him. *The Underpainter* won a Governor General's Award.

Van der Velde, Rink

The Trap   Permanent Press. 1997. 147 pp.

When his son is caught by the Nazis, a fisherman is brought in for questioning and must decide whether to cooperate with his interrogators in an attempt to save his son's life. Translated from the Dutch by Henry J. Baron.

Book Groups ▢

Subjects   Fathers and Sons • Netherlands • Novels in Translation • Torture • World War II

Now try   Van der Velde's novel was originally published in the Netherlands in 1966 and brought out in the United States in 1997. Harry Mulisch's *The Assault* is another powerful novel about courage in the face of certain death.

Wallace, David Foster

Infinite Jest   Little, Brown and Company. 1996. 1079 pp.

In 2014, when America is defined by commercialism and entertainment, the lives of various characters revolve around a tennis academy founded by James Incandenza and the Ennet House, a residence for recovering addicts.

2d Appeal   Characters   Book Groups ▢

Subjects   Alcoholics and Alcoholism • Brothers • Drugs and Drug Abuse • Family Relationships • Suicide • Tennis

Now try   Wallace's other books include *A Supposedly Fun Thing I'll Never Do Again*, *Girl with Curious Hair*, and *The Broom of the System*. Wallace added explanatory footnotes at the end of this gargantuan novel, just as Vladimir Nabokov did in his satirical *Pale Fire*. The Incandenzas—with their brilliance and despair—are similar to the Glass family in J. D. Salinger's *Seymour: An Introduction*, *Franny and Zooey*, and *Raise High the Roofbeams*, *Carpenters*. Jonathan Franzen (*The Twenty-Seventh City*) and Timothy Findley (*Headhunter*) both make good use of black humor in their novels about life in the late twentieth century.

Weldon, Fay

The Shrapnel Academy

Viking. 1987. 186 pp.

As a group of upper-crust military enthusiasts gathers for the Shrapnel Academy's annual Eve-of-Waterloo dinner, Third World counterparts (the servants) plot a revolution below-stairs.

2d Appeal   Story

Subjects   ALA Notable Books • British Authors • Culture Clash • Upper Classes • Working Classes

Now try   Like Erica Jong (*Fear of Flying* and others), Marilyn French (*The Women's Room* and others), and Marge Piercy (*Braided Lives* and others), Fay Weldon hits her readers over the head with her point of view.

West, Paul

Love's Mansion

Random House. 1992. 339 pp.

Novelist Clive Moxon imagines his parents' relationship following World War I, when his father Harry and his mother Hilly attempt to overcome the loss of innocence and trust that Harry's war injuries and infidelity have created.

2d Appeal   Characters   Book Groups 📖

Subjects   Adultery • British Authors • Love Stories • Marriage • World War I • Writers and Writing

Now try   Vera Brittain's autobiographies, including *Testament of Friendship*, are all about World War I and its aftermath. Pat Barker's trilogy, beginning with *Regeneration*, offers another view of young men at war. West's attention to detail is not unlike Proust's in *Remembrance of Things Past*.

Wiggins, Marianne

Eveless Eden

HarperCollins Publishers. 1995. 337 pp.

Foreign correspondent Noah John's love affair with a photojournalist is compromised and complicated by the appearance of a sinister British spy who is also an official in the Romanian government.

2d Appeal   Characters   Book Groups 📖

Subjects   ALA Notable Books • Foreign Correspondents • Journalists • Love Stories • Photography and Photographers • Romania

Now try   Among Wiggins's other novels are *John Dollar* and *Almost Heaven*. The spy novels of Len Deighton (*Berlin Game* and others) and John le Carre (*A Perfect Spy* and others) come the closest to the intensity of Wiggins's novel.

Yates, Richard

Cold Spring Harbor

Delacorte Press. 1986. 182 pp.

Charles Shepard transfers his dreams of worldy success and a better life to his son Evan, whose own life is blighted by circumstances often beyond his control.

2d Appeal   Story

Subjects   1940s • Adultery • Family Relationships • Fathers and Sons • Marriage • Middle-Aged Men

Now try   An economy of prose is also seen in Yates's *The Easter Parade* and *Young Hearts Crying*. Like Tim Winton in *Cloudstreet*, Yates shows how chance rules the lives of his characters.

Appendix: Book Awards

American Library Association Notable Books
(50 E. Huron St., Chicago, IL 60611-2765)

Selected annually by a 12-member Notable Books Council of the American Library Association. Books are chosen for their exceptional literary merit.

Betty Trask Prize/Awards
(The Society of Authors, 84 Drayton Gardens, London SW 10 9SB, England)

Begun in 1983, the prize and awards are given by the Society of Authors in the United Kingdom for best first novels by a commonwealth citizen under the age of 35.

The Booker Prize
(Book Trust (England), Book House, 5 East Hill, London SW 18 2QZ, England)

Founded in 1969 by Booker McConnell, Ltd., and administered by the National Book League in the United Kingdom. Awarded to the best novel written in English by a citizen of the United Kingdom, the Commonwealth. Eire, Pakistan, or South Africa.

The Boston Book Review/Fisk Fiction Prize
(Boston Book Review, 30 Brattle St., 4th Flr., Cambridge, MA 02138)

Established in 1994 to recognize the finest literary fiction.

The Giller Prize
(Kelly Duffin, Administrator, 21 Steepleview Crescent, Richmond Hill, ONT, Canada L4C9R1)

Established in 1994 to highlight excellence in creative writing. It is awarded to the author of a Canadian novel or short story collection published in English.

The Governor General's Literary Awards
(Canada Council, 350 Albert St., PO Box 1047, Ottawa, ONT, Canada K1P5V8)

Presented annually by the Canada Council for outstanding English and French language works of fiction.

The Guardian Fiction Prize

Sponsored by the Guardian newspaper, on the recommendation of a panel of five judges. The award winner must be a work of fiction by a British or Commonwealth writer that has been published in the United Kingdom.

The International IMPAC/Dublin Literary Award
(Cumberland House, Fenian St., Dublin 2, Ireland)

Created in 1995 as a joint initiative of the Municipal Government of Dublin, Ireland, the Dublin Corporation, and IMPAC, a productivity improvement company. It is administered by Dublin City Public Libraries.

The James Tait Black Memorial Prize
(University of Edinburgh Center, 7-11 Nicolson St., Edinburgh, Scotland EH89BE)

Presented annually to a work written in English originating with a British publisher.

The Kiriyama Pacific Rim Book Prize
(USF Center for the Pacific Rim, 2130 Fulton St., San Francisco, CA 94117-1080)

Co-sponsored by the Kiriyama Pacific Rim Foundation and the Center for the Pacific Rim at the University of San Francisco, the award is given to the book that best contributes to greater understanding among nations and peoples of the Pacific Rim.

The Miles Franklin Award
(Administered by the Permanent Trustee Co., Ltd., of Sydney, Australia)

Given annually since 1957 to an Australian novel or play of the highest literary merit that presents aspects of Australian life. It is adminsitered by the Permanent Trustee Co., Ltd., of Sydney, Australia.

The National Book Award
(260 Fifth Ave., Rm. 904, New York, NY 10001)

Given annually by the National Book Foundation to honor American books of the highest literary merit.

The National Book Critics' Circle Award
(c/o Art Winslow, The Nation, 72 Fifth Ave., New York, NY 10011)

Chosen by the National Book Critics' Circle, a group of professional book review editors and critics.

The Orange Prize
(Administered by Orange Pic)

Established in 1996, the prize is open to women writing English worldwide. It is given by Orange, Ltd.

The PEN/Faulkner Award
(Folger Shakespeare Library, 201 E. Capital St. SE, Washington, DC 20003)

Created by writers in 1980 to honor their peers. It is awarded annually by the PEN/Faulkner Foundation.

The Prix Goncourt
(Academie Goncourt, Place Gaillon, 75002 Paris, France)

Given to recognize an author for an outstanding work of French prose.

The Pulitzer Prize
(Columbia University, 702 Journalism, New York, NY 10027)

Given annually by Columbia University since 1917, on the recommendation of a Pulitzer Prize Board.

The Whitbread Award
(Booksellers Association of Great Britain & Ireland, Minister House, 272 Vauxhall Bridge Rd., London SW1V 1BA, England)

Given to a novel and a first novel; authors must have lived in Great Britain or Ireland for more than three years.

Title Index

Titles in bold italic are main entries.

Subject Index

Author Index